Reforming the Civil Service

The Fulton Committee
on the
British Home Civil Service
of 1966–1968

GEOFFREY K. FRY

EDINBURGH UNIVERSITY PRESS

TO OWEN AND SHEILA HARTLEY

© Geoffrey K. Fry, 1993
Edinburgh University Press Ltd
22 George Square, Edinburgh

Typeset in Lasercomp Times Roman
by BPCC-AUP Glasgow Ltd and
printed in Great Britain by
Page Bros Ltd, Norwich and
bound by Hunter & Foulis Ltd, Edinburgh

A CIP record for this book is
available from the British Library

ISBN 0 7486 0412 x

Contents

Abbreviations

AIT	Association of HM's Inspectors of Taxes
AOML	Association of Officers of the Ministry of Labour
CAS	Centre for Administrative Studies
CBI	Confederation of British Industry
CEI	Council of Engineering Institutions
CSC	Civil Service College
CSCA	Civil Service Clerical Association
CSD	Civil Service Department
CSO	Central Statistical Office
CSSB	Civil Service Selection Board
DEA	Department of Economic Affairs
DES	Department of Education and Science
ENA	Ecole Nationale d'Administration
FDA	First Division Association
IPA	Institute of Public Administration
IPCS	Institution of Professional Civil Servants
IRSF	Inland Revenue Staff Federation
MLSA	Ministry of Labour Staff Association
MPNI	Ministry of Pensions and National Insurance
NHS	National Health Service
PED	Public Expenditure Department
PEP	Policy and Economic Planning
PESC	Public Expenditure Survey Committee
PRO	Public Records Office
PSD	Public Service department
SCS	Society of Civil Servants
TUC	Trades Union Congress

(Where appropriate, abbreviations have been substituted in direct quotations.)

Preface

This book is about the Fulton Committee on the British Home Civil Service of 1966 to 1968. It is based on the official papers of that Committee and interviews with participants. The book places the work of the Fulton Committee in its historical context.

The support of the Economic and Social Research Council (ESRC) is gratefully acknowledged. The work was funded by ESRC Award Number R000231033.

Whatever the case in the future, at the time that access was given to the papers of the Fulton Committee they were subject to the Thirty Year Rule relating to public documents, and how access was obtained may be of interest to scholars. In a public lecture delivered in the University of London in 1984, the former Head of the Home Civil Service, Lord Bancroft, drew attention to what he believed to be the regrettable fact that relatively few academics had taken advantage of provisions originally made in 1970 for them to have access, for research purposes, to government records within the period of the Thirty Year Rule – subject, of course, to obtaining official permission. The Wilson Committee on Modern Public Records: Selection and Access (Cmnd. 8204, 1981) similarly regretted the lack of research activity and blamed this on the academics. I reviewed the Report of the Working Party on Material for Training in Government of 1967 to 1969 when it was published in 1970, and by the 1980s it seemed to me to be a creature of a different era. Nevertheless, citing Lord Bancroft's remarks, I wrote to the Keeper of Public Records about the possibility of access to the papers of the Fulton Committee, and, encouraged by him, I wrote to the then Head of the Home Civil Service to ask for permission. Such permission was granted to me by Sir Robert Armstrong as an established academic working in the relevant field of study, on condition that I undertook to submit any manuscript intended for publication, and that I would accept any amendments required in the interests of confidentiality or security. I gave these undertakings, and the research proceeded. I am grateful to Lord Armstrong of Ilminster and Sir Robin Butler for the constructive attitude that they displayed in relation to the research project and to material for publication.

The access to the official papers of the Fulton Committee enabled me to interview the members of that Committee, its Secretariat, and the Management Consultancy Group. I had the earlier advantage of discussions about the work of the Fulton Committee with one of its members, Lord Boyle of Handsworth, when he was Vice-Chancellor of the University of Leeds. To put the matter mildly, Lord Boyle was generous with his time, and this was also the case with those members of the Committee and those associated with it, and with the implementation of the Fulton programme, whom I interviewed. Not all the members of the Committee survived, of course; and, of a seminar held in 1988 by the Institute of Contemporary History to mark the twentieth anniversary of the Fulton Report, John Garrett, who had been a member of the Management Consultancy Group, remarked to me that the tone of the discussions then had 'showed again that the dead are always wrong. The people there would not have talked that way about them had Norman Hunt and Lord Fulton been there to defend themselves' (Interview, 1989). In this book I have tried to take an impartial position, which was less difficult than it could have been because I have always been mystified by the controversy that the Fulton Committee and its works attracted. Further, I have no need to go back on what I wrote at the time. As the Fulton Report appeared only a matter of months after I had completed a doctorate on the history of the Civil Service, the reader may well conclude that this was a matter of good fortune rather than good judgement.

The author was fortunate too in the access granted by Lady Crowther-Hunt and by Lady Fulton to the papers of Norman Hunt and Lord Fulton respectively, and permission to quote from them. With regard to the papers of Lord Crowther-Hunt, scholars should note that the box numbers referred to in relation to those papers are from the provisional sort and that these papers are closed for the foreseeable future. As regards Lord Fulton's papers, I record my thanks to Dr Oliver Fulton for his constructive help, and I ask scholars to note that, though it is the intention that these papers will eventually be housed in catalogued form in the University of Sussex, they were not in that form when I read them – and hence there are no box numbers shown. I thank Mrs Mary Gold for permission to have access to, and quote from, the papers of Lord Boyle, and I thank Margaret Simey for drawing attention to relevant material not conventionally boxed with the rest of Lord Simey's papers, as well as for permission to quote from those papers. I am also grateful to the Keeper of Public Records and the Controller of HM Stationery Office for permission to quote from material that is subject to Crown copyright, and to the Chairman of the Conservative Party and the General Secretary of the Fabian Society for access to archive material.

Acknowledgement is made too of the help given by various former higher civil servants and others in the form of correspondence. These include Lord Armstrong of Ilminster, R. A. Chapman, Sir Kenneth Clucas, Sir Frank Cooper, Ivor Crewe, Lord Croham, A. H. Halsey, Sir Edward Heath, Michael

Heseltine, Lord Hunt of Tanworth, Lord Jenkins of Hillhead, Dame Anne Meuller, Sir Antony Part, J. F. Pickering, Lord Rayner, John Rosselli, L. J. Sharpe, Sir Douglas Wass and Sir Leslie Williams.

As in earlier books, I am indebted to the Civil Service unions for their help. I record with thanks the aid given in particular by the Civil and Public Services Association, the National Union of Civil and Public Servants, the Institution of Professionals, Managers and Specialists, the Association of First Division Civil Servants, and the Council of Civil Service Unions. Peter Jones of the last named organisation deserves and receives special mention.

Though so much is owed to others, I take full responsibility for what is written in this book. I add that considerations of length have meant that the book largely ends with the reception accorded to the Fulton Report in 1968. Of the following twenty years down to 1988 and the Ibbs Report, only the main developments are indicated, having been written about elsewhere, and the material used tends to be that which might not otherwise be available to later scholars.

I am grateful to the editors of *Public Administration* and *Public Policy and Administration* for permission to use material published in another form in those journals.

It is the case that I could not have completed this book, or the others before it, without the facilities of, and the help of the staff employed in, the Brotherton Library of the University of Leeds, and I acknowledge the professionalism shown.

As for all I know this may be my last book, I take this opportunity to pay tribute to the many able people with whom I have worked in academic life, none more so than Owen Hartley of the University of Leeds, and it is to Owen and his wife, Sheila, that I dedicate this book.

Geoffrey K. Fry
July 1992

Chapter 1

Origins, Appointment and Membership of the Fulton Committee

Origins of the Fulton Committee

'The fact that we have in Britain what is probably the best Civil Service in the world should not prevent us from asking how it may be improved', declared a Fabian Society committee in 1947, which, like so many reformers, proceeded to show itself to be uninhibited by its professed admiration for the career Civil Service. 'It is possible to argue that the Civil Service has been saved from disaster by two wars, both of which brought in new blood in large quantities,' the Fabians said, making it clear that 'We think that there is little doubt that the time is ripe for another overhaul of the Civil Service' (Fabian Society, 1947, p.5). No such 'overhaul' took place, but, although a fairly extreme attack on dilettantism in the Treasury and in the Administrative Class of the Civil Service by the Fabian economist, Thomas Balogh, in 1959 (Balogh, 1959, pp.81–126) seemed to attract little support at that time, Britain's continuing economic difficulties, and her failure to obtain membership of the European Economic Community in 1963 – together with the evident professionalism of the French Higher Civil Service in the relevant negotiations – were factors which eventually helped to produce a climate conducive to change. 'Today there are signs that a consensus of opinion in favour of reform of the Civil Service is emerging amongst those in all parties who are concerned with the problems of modernising Britain', a Fabian group stated in a pamphlet called *The Administrators* published in 1964. With a general election bound to be held in the near future, 'No party need fear that in introducing the reforms we propose they will be attacked for acting on doctrinaire grounds for the sake of narrow party interests. Nor need they set up a Royal Commission or committee to tread the ground again. They can be sure that if they act they will be making a real contribution to the progress of Britain' (Fabian Group, 1964, p.43). By the time that the Labour Government of Harold Wilson took office in 1964, it was familiar ground for Fabians as for others to ask whether the sort of career Civil Service that Britain had was what the country needed in the era of the Keynesian Welfare State. Though the Fabians themselves had seen no need for such an investigatory body, it was in this context that the Fulton

Committee of 1966–8 conducted its review of the British Home Civil Service.

'An opportunity had been missed of reforming the Civil Service after the War,' Sir Philip Allen, a higher civil servant as well as a member of the Fulton Committee was later to observe. 'We simply went back to the old order of things. The Norman Brooks and co. were weighed down with work. The Civil Service was not in a very happy position in the post-war period until the 1962 changes at the Treasury, which meant for the first time people had spare capacity to think about these things. Norman Brook had an impossible task as Head of the Home Civil Service and Secretary of the Cabinet' (Interview, 1989). Certainly the Priestley Royal Commission on the Civil Service of 1953–5, confined by its terms of reference to making recommendations about pay and conditions of service, made no direct reforming contribution. What was clear from the evidence submitted to the Priestley Commission, though, was that the structure of the Civil Service was not only more extensive than that which, for instance, the Tomlin Royal Commission of 1929–31 had reviewed, it was also a much changed one. The status and organisation of scientists, engineers, lawyers, accountants, and other professionals had been improved following the activities of a succession of Treasury committees reporting between 1944 and 1952; and the structural relationship between the Executive and Clerical Classes had been changed too. The development of the Method II means of direct entry recruitment to the Administrative Class would seem to count as an important reform. It was not one, though, that was designed to change the character of the Administrative Class or of its heartland, the Treasury, the prime targets of the Civil Service's critics.

The reorganisation of the Treasury which took place in 1962 had followed from the recommendation of the Plowden Report on the Control of Public Expenditure. The Treasury's arrangements for its core activity of controlling public spending had been found wanting by the House of Commons Select Committee on Estimates in a highly critical report published in 1958. This had proposed that 'a small independent committee' should conduct a 'more detailed and more expert' review of the subject (HC 254–I, 1957–8, para.95). The Plowden Committee was appointed in October 1959 comprising four former Civil Service insiders, including Lord Plowden himself and six Permanent Secretaries and Deputy Secretaries from the Treasury and other government departments. Though its opaque style attracted comment when it was published in July 1961, the recommendations were clear enough and easily discussed at the time (Chester, 1963, pp.3–15; Clarke, 1963, pp.17–24; Morton, 1963, pp.25–35; Wall, 1963, pp.37–50).

Sir Richard Clarke, one the Treasury officials who was a member of the Plowden Committee, saw the 'central point' of its Report as having been that 'the forces of public opinion, political parties, Parliament, and generally speaking Ministers were increasingly committed to a rapid growth of public expenditure, and that there was now no significant body of opinion opposing this' (Clarke, 1978, p.149). The Plowden Committee believed that 'the traditional system of decision making can no longer be expected to be effective in containing the growth of expenditure within whatever limit the Government have set'. In the Committee's opinion, that system needed to be reconstructed on the basis of 'regular surveys of public expenditure as a whole [made] over a number of years ahead and in relation to prospective resources,' and 'that decisions involving substantial future expenditure should be taken in the light of these surveys' (Cmnd. 1432, 1961, p.6). The Public Expenditure Survey Committee (PESC) system for the control of public spending was developed along these lines. The Plowden Committee also said that the time had come for the Treasury and higher civil servants generally to give a higher priority than before to managerial responsibilities, given the scale of activities undertaken by modern government departments (ibid., pp.16 ff). The Treasury Centre for Administrative Studies was established in 1963, at which direct entrants to the Administrative Class received formal training primarily in economics and related subjects; and a Treasury led review to consider further expansion of provision for training was under way before the Fulton Committee was appointed.

That changes of this kind were taking place in the Civil Service made insufficient difference in the political context of the 1960s to the contemporary case against that Service which various members of the Fabian intellectual coalition had developed. The original *Fabian Essays* of 1889 had celebrated the Northcote-Trevelyan reformed Civil Service because its presumed efficiency undermined the economic liberal belief that the State was too poorly organised to run anything but the simplest activity efficiently (Shaw, 1889, pp.171–201). Ironically, in the years before the establishment of the Fulton Committee, Fabian reformers, among others, were given to portraying the Civil Service as being too much the creature of economic liberalism. The conventional wisdom of that time, as relayed in popularised radical tracts (e.g. Shonfield, 1959; Brittan, 1964), was that the Treasury was still in the grip of classical liberal orthodoxy and that if only it would embrace Keynesianism fully then Britain's relative economic decline would be arrested and then reversed. As that decline had Victorian origins, the notion that a British economic miracle could be effected by the more enlightened practice of Keynesian demand management invited as much scepticism as did the notion of comparable results following from the emerging fashion for institutional change, of which the reform of the Civil Service and the recasting of the Treasury were only a part. The arrangements comprising the PESC system did seem to have Keynesian intent, and the pushing to one side of the Gladstonian means of Treasury control of public expenditure and the abandonment of cash limits for whatever supposedly sophisticated reasons was the antithesis of economic liberalism.

Though economic liberalism still ranked with Fabianism as one of the two main traditions of outside advocacy of reform of the Civil Service, it was relatively unimportant in the immediate pre-Fulton period. After 1945, electoral considerations as well as the convictions of the leadership had led to the statist or paternalist side of Conservatism becoming dominant in the Tory party. The Keynesian Welfare State, and the Conservative involvement in its construction and commitment to its maintenance, seemed to have relegated the economic liberalism that had informed, say, the Geddes Reports of 1922 and the May Report of 1931 into an historical curiosity. Of course, the familiar economic liberal belief that 'business methods' were superior to those commonly employed in government departments, and needed to be applied to promote greater efficiency in them, still had a place in Tory rhetoric. Nevertheless, when Conservative groups published reports in 1946 and then, under the title *Change or Decay*, in 1963 making proposals for change in the Civil Service, there was none of the old distinctive confidence about business being best, and the most that was asked for was to have its ways known. Where economic liberal sentiment remained important was among the lawyers, even if the strident *Bureaucracy Triumphant* type of attack of former times on what was perceived to be excessive Civil Service power was less in evidence. The Crichel Down affair of 1954 did encourage what became a broadly based campaign among lawyers and others, urging the establishment of a British equivalent of the French *Conseil d'Etat* or of the Scandanavian Ombudsman, to provide a closer control over the behaviour of government departments and their officials than existing arrangements managed to exert.

What eventually revived economic liberalism in the Conservative Party was dismissal from office in 1964, which, despite the continuing electoral popularity of the Keynesian Welfare State, some Tories interpreted as undermining the case against market philosophy. To them there was nothing to be lost by intending to govern on the Conservatives' own terms, which were assumed to be economic liberal ones. The change to an elective leadership in 1965 translated the Conservatives into a programmatic party, but the domestic programme that Edward Heath seemed to prefer was one aimed only at making the Keynesian Welfare State more efficient. So, there was tension between the Conservative leadership and many in the party. That responsibility for the various policy groups in opposition fell to Sir Edward Boyle as Deputy Chairman of the Advisory Committee on Policy was no consolation to the economic liberals. In March 1967, Edward Heath appointed Ernest Marples to head a Public Sector Research Unit, which was to include David Howell. This Unit promoted a different line of enquiry, and its influence on Tory thinking about the machinery of government was evident when the Conservatives returned to office in 1970. The Conservative Party did not choose to give evidence to the Fulton Committee, though individual former Tory ministers did do so. As for Edward Heath's own views on the reform of the Civil Service, the Fulton Committee was forced at first to rely on a report of them contained in *The Times* for 20 January 1967, which was circulated to members at the Committee's request (PRO: BA1/29). The Chairman and some other members of the Fulton Committee met Heath informally on 19 June 1967 and at that meeting the then Leader of the Conservative Party set out his views on the Civil Service and on the machinery of government at some length (PRO: BA 1/38). While by no means hostile to the Fulton Committee, the Conservatives in preparing for Government had made themselves independent of its findings.

In the public debate about the Civil Service as it developed from Balogh's polemic in 1959 down to the appointment of the Fulton Committee in 1966, economic liberalism was relatively unimportant and Fabianism held the field as, indeed, it was to do during the period when the Committee did its work and reported. Fabianism was still the main strand in what from the 1930s onwards had tended to be perceived as 'middle opinion', embracing the output of bodies like Political and Economic Planning and 'moderate ' Conservatism too (Marwick, 1964, pp.285–98). Those Fabians interested in the reform of the Civil Service in the early 1960s seemed to be undeterred by the reality that the recommendations of the Fabian committee that had reported on the matter in 1947 had made little impact. In July 1962, what was called 'the Civil Service group' within the Fabian Society held its first meeting at the home of the Society's then General Secretary, Shirley Williams, who was to work with it. Anthony Crosland attended this opening meeting, but seemed to limit his contribution after that. The membership of the group changed over time, involving sixteen people in all at various stages, drawn mainly from academic life and the Higher Civil Service. Robert Neild, the Cambridge economist, who acted as Chairman throughout, and Thomas Balogh made no secret later of their membership of the Fabian group. Of course, Shirley Williams's involvement was obvious; but many years later others involved still wished for anonymity, including two future Permanent Secretaries, who, in fact, played little part in the group's work (Fabian Society Papers E34/1:K65–7). Though the group had considered wider issues, when its report, *The Administrators*, was published in June 1964, the reformers concentrated their fire on the Administrative Class and the Treasury. They produced a reform programme that they believed had broad support outside Fabian ranks, and which was thus ready for implementation without the need for the further consideration of an official inquiry.

Before becoming Labour Prime Minister in 1964, Harold Wilson placed more emphasis on reshaping the machinery of central government and on creating new government departments than on the reform of the Civil Service, about which contemporary public discussions of the *Whitehall and Beyond* (Grimond et al., 1964) type showed him to be cautious. At that stage, Wilson showed no sign of sharing views of the kind expressed by Thomas Balogh, who was to be Economic Adviser to the Cabinet between 1964 and 1967 and then Consultant to the Prime Minister in 1968. Balogh had written in 1959 that 'Civil Service reform [was] one of the most essential and fundamental pre-conditions [for] a successful Socialist Government' (Balogh, 1959, p.126).

Like Robert Neild, Balogh was a member of the Finance and Economic Policy Sub-Committee of the Labour Party in the years leading up to the party's return to office in 1964. The reform of the Civil Service was on the agenda, with a study group including Balogh being established in 1962. Balogh's polemical attack on the Civil Service, an extract of which was circulated to the Sub-Committee, may have helped to set the tone; but, to judge from the other papers produced by Neild and others, there was plenty of hostility to the Treasury and the Administrative Class present on the Sub-Committee and in the Party's research department anyway (*Minutes of the Finance and Economic Policy Sub-Committee of the Labour Party 1958–66*, RD202, 215, 247, 434).

'The trouble with Tommy is that he has not got enough to do' was Anthony Wedgwood Benn's explanation of how Balogh had the time to plague his 'immediate circle' with his latest notions (Benn, 1987, p.94), the flow of which did not cease with Labour's return to office, and which often seemed to be about the need to change the Civil Service. 'Tommy told me that the real curse was the civil servants', Barbara Castle recorded in her diary on 26 July 1965 (Castle, 1984, p.51). Another of the 'circle', Richard Crossman, accepted Balogh's thesis about the Civil Service totally, or at least so he maintained in his later evidence to the Fulton Committee (Crossman, II, 1976, p.200). In opposition, Wedgwood Benn, also of the 'circle', had not seemed particularly interested in Balogh's thesis; but as Postmaster General he was soon discussing the Civil Service with Balogh and others and trying to work out 'how to beat them' (Benn, 1987, p.222). By March 1965, Benn was comparing notes with Balogh about what the latter called the 'sabotage' said by him to be being practised by the Civil Service, presumably in relation to the activities of the Labour Government. Benn had found dealing with the Civil Service to be 'a nightmare' (ibid., p.226).

By late May 1963, according to Benn, Balogh had prepared, at the request of Harold Wilson,

> a major document on Civil Service reform which he claims could be started within two weeks by dividing the Treasury into two halves and giving half of it over to a Ministry of Expansion or Production. The rump of the Treasury would handle financial matters and would act as a Bureau of the Budget. The Prime Minister's Office would then be expanded to absorb the National Economic Development Council and all disputes between the Treasury and the Ministry of Production would automatically be settled by the Economic Committee of the Cabinet under the Chairmanship of the Prime Minister (ibid., p.25).

Though Balogh appeared to be among the 'favourites at the court of King Harold' (ibid., p.319) when the Labour Party attained office, the most that could be said of his structural proposals was, that he was one of the authors of the idea of establishing a separate Department of Economic Affairs. It seems doubtful if Balogh and some of those who shared his outlook initially knew a great deal about how the Civil Service worked, that is if we believe the testimony of Richard Crossman who wrote of 'the system of official committees, which neither Tommy Balogh nor I knew anything about before we got into Whitehall' (Crossman, I, 1974, p.616).

Experience, as much as the advocacy of advisers like Balogh, may well have been what persuaded Harold Wilson to give the reform of the Civil Service a higher priority. Marcia Williams, Personal and Political Secretary to Wilson as Prime Minister later recalled:

> When the Labour Government came into office in 1964 with a small majority after thirteen years of Conservative Government, we found the Civil Service to be an unhelpful vehicle when it came to governing. The Civil Service seemed to be reserving its position, waiting to see what happened to us electorally. To us it seemed then that they were much more sympathetic to the Conservative Party. After the 1966 Election when we obtained a substantial majority it was a different show altogether. When we had a small majority, we just got stonewalling. It went beyond civil servants playing their familiar role of devil's advocate. There seemed therefore to us to be a need to open up the Civil Service to promote a different attitude. This did not mean that we wanted the wholesale slaughter of the Civil Service. Harold Wilson was an admirer of the Civil Service but he thought that, like many other institutions by that time, it needed to change and he set up the Fulton Committee to bring this about (Interview, 1989).

The then Chancellor of the Exchequer, James Callaghan, was later described as playing an important part in the establishment of the Fulton Committee by two of its members, the Permanent Secretaries Sir Philip Allen and Sir James Dunnett. 'James Callaghan, no doubt after talking to Harold Wilson, came to the conclusion that it would be as well to set up some sort of inquiry – not a traditional departmental inquiry but something rather different,' Allen recalled. Sir James Dunnett, supporting this, said that 'Callaghan asked for my advice on who should be Chairman of the Committee. At that stage he was very much in control of the exercise'. Sir Philip Allen added that he discussed the membership of the Committee with the Chancellor 'and nobody else' (Hennessy et al., 1988, p.44). James Callaghan's recollection was that

> It is quite true that I was dissatisfied with the organisation of affairs in the Treasury and this led to the appointment of the Fulton Committee. At that time there was something that we called 'two sides' in the Treasury, namely: Finance and Economic Affairs, and Pay and Management. There were also two Permanent Secretaries: Sir William Armstrong who oversaw the Finance and Economic side, whilst Pay and Management was under the control of Sir Laurence Helsby. He in particular seemed to be semi-detached from the Treasury and I saw him only rarely. I thought this was by his own decision, but since I left the

Treasury I have been told that he wished to see me more frequently but could not penetrate my Private Office, basically because I was so pre-occupied with the Finance and Economic side. I also had the strong impression that there was little enthusiasm on the part of high fliers in the Treasury to serve on the Pay and Management side, and all this led to a belief on my part that it would be wise to review the organisational set up. I discussed these matters with the Prime Minister, Harold Wilson, from time to time and found he was really keen to examine the organisation of the Treasury. He was undoubtedly the moving spirit in getting the Fulton Committee established. So there was agreement between us. I signed the letters of invitation to the members of the Committee.

Callaghan added that 'although I was not aware of it at the time, I found later that William Armstrong had been in favour of splitting the Treasury and had left that impression with the Committee. Unfortunately, the new department did not obtain the stature and prestige that was necessary' (letter to author, 27.10.88).

The question of the appointment of an inquiry into the Civil Service was made a matter of more prominent public debate in August 1965 with the publication of a very critical review of the work of the Civil Service Commission which had been conducted by the House of Commons Select Committee on Estimates. Though this study was mainly concerned with direct entry recruitment to the Civil Service, inevitably broader issues were raised about the structure of that Service. The Select Committee was sceptical about the role of the Administrative Class (HC 308, 1964–5 p.xvi), and, in his evidence, Professor W. J. M. Mackenzie, an academic authority on public administration, wondered if the Service ought to remain 'a secluded career bureaucracy'. As Mackenzie observed, in its reports on the Treasury Control of Public Expenditure (HC 254-I, 1957–8) and on the Treasury Control of Establishments (HC 228, 1963–4) as in this review of Recruitment to the Civil Service, the Estimates Committee had 'performed some of the functions of a Royal Commission' (HC 308, 1964–5, Evidence, p.138). Naturally what interested the Estimates Committee was whether or not what was needed was an inquiry which would carry out all of the functions of a Royal Commission on the Civil Service. The Joint Permanent Secretaries to the Treasury, Sir William Armstrong and Sir Laurence Helsby, urged delaying the appointment of a committee of inquiry, whatever form it might take, because of the need for the Service to be given time to absorb the changes in the machinery of government which had accompanied the return of the Labour party to office in 1964 (ibid., questions 788, 790, 842). Professor Mackenzie himself thought that the arguments in favour of a Royal Commission, or presumably any other form of widely based inquiry, were no more than 'equally balanced', but that if such a Commission was appointed, 'it should be a relatively small one, of independent standing, empowered to recruit its own research staff, and not placed (as was the Priestley Commission) in a situation which demands an urgent and specific report' (ibid., p.138f). Another academic, D. N. Chester, argued for a Royal Commission not being appointed before 1967, and being preceded by a Plowden-style committee within the Treasury, but including people from outside the Service, to do the preparatory research, including studies of other Civil Services, notably that of France (ibid., p.233f).

When asked by the Estimates Committee about the respective merits of the Plowden form of committee and a Royal Commission as a means of investigating the Civil Service, Sir Laurence Helsby, who, as Head of the Home Civil Service, was well placed to give advice to the Prime Minister if asked for it, said that he had no 'strong opinion' but added that

> there is a great advantage . . . in having a review of the Service undertaken by a group of people some of whom at any rate have had direct experience of how the machine works, and what it feels like to be part of it, and that you lose if you have a Royal Commission when by tradition no civil servant will be a member of it. I suppose a retired civil servant might, but even that is, I believe, unusual. By contrast the Plowden Committee had a proportion of civil servants, and I think those others who were members of the Committee found the mixture helpful. But it could be argued that a Royal Commission has a weight which no other body is recognised as having in this country, and that only that weight would achieve the major changes that might be required at the end of the day (ibid., question 846).

The Estimates Committee, noting Helsby's views, effectively opted for Chester's two stage approach. It recommended

> that a committee of officials, aided by members from outside the Civil Service, on the lines of the Plowden Committee, be appointed to initiate research upon, to examine, and to report upon the structure, recruitment and management of the Civil Service, . . . [and] that the position be reviewed by the Government immediately upon receipt of the report; that the Government report to Parliament the action they propose to take; and that if a further enquiry by a Royal Commission be then found to be necessary, such Commission be appointed forthwith (HC 308, 1964–5, *Report*, para. 112).

At a time when a Labour Government felt that many British national institutions would be invigorated by having their activities reviewed by a committee or Royal Commission, it was not to be expected that the Civil Service would escape investigation, and so the Estimates Committee's recommendation in favour of an inquiry was always likely to be welcomed by the government. In preceding years there seemed to have been even more attacks than usual upon the Civil Service – and particularly its Administrative Class – from outsiders who, among other things, had questioned the Service's ability to conduct some of its more important functions, notably as regards advice about the management of the economy, and who had criticised the Service's structure and organisation. The Civil Service was accused of being 'amateur' when the need was for professionalism, and this was the context in which the Fulton Committee was appointed.

Appointment of the Fulton Committee

It was on 8 February 1966 that, in a statement to the House of Commons, the Prime Minister, Harold Wilson announced that, in response to the recommendation in the Report of the Select Committee on Estimates, a committee was being appointed under the chairmanship of Lord Fulton, the Vice-Chancellor of the University of Sussex, 'to examine the structure, recruitment and management, including training, of the Home Civil Service'. The Prime Minister added that:

> There have been so many changes both in the demands placed on the Civil Service and in the educational organisation of the country that the Government believe that the time has come to ensure that the Service is properly equipped for its role in the modern State. The very broad terms of reference will require a fundamental and wide-ranging inquiry in the tradition of the great inquiries of the past, such as Northcote-Trevelyan in 1853 and the Tomlin Commission in 1931. This is a strong committee, and I hope that its recommendations will enable the Civil Service to meet the country's needs for many years to come. At the outset, however, I should like to make two points about the scope of the Committee's inquiry. First, the decision to set up this committee does not mean that the Civil Service has been found lacking in any way by the Government in its current operations. On the contrary, it is the experience of Ministers . . . that the Service meets the demands put on it with flexibility and enterprise. Secondly, the Government's willingness to consider changes in the Civil Service does not imply any intention on their part to alter the basic relationship between Ministers and civil servants. Civil servants, however eminent, remain the confidential advisers of Ministers, who alone are answerable to Parliament for policy; and we do not envisage any change in this fundamental feature of our parliamentary system of democracy (724 HC Deb. 5s c.209–10).

In the exchanges that followed the Prime Minister's announcement of the appointment of the Fulton Committee, questions were asked about its remit and about the support that it would be given. Jeremy Bray, the Labour MP who had been chairman of the Estimates Committee's inquiry, asked if the Fulton Committee would have 'all the staff and research assistance' that its 'very fundamental task' required. The Prime Minister replied that 'certainly, the Committee will have all the help, statistical and otherwise, that it needs' (ibid., c.211). Edward Heath, the Conservative Leader of the Opposition asked whether or not the Committee would be able 'to examine the actual methods of work of the Civil Service'. In his reply, Harold Wilson said that it would be 'within the terms of reference and competence of the Committee to inquire into all aspects of the functioning of and recruitment for the Civil Service' (ibid., c.210).

The Leader of the Liberal party, Jo Grimond, asked why the terms of reference excluded the Foreign Service and the Commonwealth Service. In fact, these Services had been merged already to form the Diplomatic Service with effect from the beginning of 1965, and the Prime Minister said that the Committee on Representational Services Overseas of 1962–3, chaired by Lord Plowden, had 'exhaustively examined' that area, while adding that he did not exclude the possibility of another but 'more limited inquiry, perhaps on the question of recruitment, when the inquiry into the Home Civil Service has got a little further'. The Prime Minister also assured Grimond that the Fulton Committee would be enquiring into the question of 'exchanges between the Civil Service and business, and between the Civil Service and local government'. The Prime Minister was asked by the same MP about what experience the Fulton Committee possessed of the work of the Scottish Office and of Scottish conditions generally (ibid., c.211–12), and the eventual reply made on Wilson's behalf stated that the Committee's work did not need one of its members to be 'a specifically Scottish civil servant' and added that 'Lord Fulton is himself a very distinguished Scot, both by birth and education' (725 HC Deb. 5s c. 236). In the exchanges nobody asked either about the explicit exclusion of the current working of the doctrine of ministerial responsibility from the Fulton Committee's terms of reference or about the implicit exclusion of the machinery of government.

'Under the Chairmanship of Lord Fulton (the Vice-Chancellor of the University of Sussex), three dons, four very able top civil servants (at least three of them rather unconventional), two extremely intelligent MPs, two leading industrialists, and the statutory white collar trade unionist are to examine the "structure, recruitment, training and management of the Home Civil Service"' was how *The Economist* (12.2.66, p.578) greeted the appointment of the Fulton Committee. The 'three dons' were Fulton himself; Dr Norman Hunt, University Lecturer in Politics and Fellow of Exeter College, Oxford; and Lord Simey, Charles Booth Professor of Social Science at Liverpool University. The 'four very able top civil servants' were Sir Philip Allen, KCB, a Second Secretary at the Treasury; Sir William Cook, CB, FRS, Deputy Chief Scientific Adviser at the Ministry of Defence; Sir James Dunnett, KCB, Permanent Secretary of the Ministry of Labour; and Robert Neild, Economic Adviser to the Treasury. Presumably Cook, Dunnett and Neild were the officials believed to be 'unconventional', and in an obvious sense this was the case with Neild, given that he was not a career civil servant at all, but a political appointee of the Labour government. The 'two extremely intelligent MPs' were Sir Edward Boyle, Conservative MP for Birmingham Handsworth, and Mrs Shirley Williams, Labour MP for Hitchin. When Mrs Williams became Parliamentary Secretary to the Ministry of Labour on 6 April 1966, she was replaced by Robert Sheldon, Labour MP for Ashton-Under-Lyne.

The 'two leading industrialists' were Sir Norman Kipping, KBE, formerly Director General of the Federation of British Industry and at the time Senior Consultant on International Trade at the Confederation of British Industry, and John Wall, OBE, Managing Director of Electrical and Musical Industries Ltd. The 'statutory white collar trade unionist' was W. C. Anderson, the General Secretary of the National and Local Government Officers Association. The Secretary and the Assistant Secretary serving the Committee were not named in the official announcement, but it can be noted that for almost all the life of the Fulton Committee these posts were held by, respectively, Richard Wilding of the Treasury and Michael Simons of the Ministry of Labour.

'The Civil Service is now to be the subject of a close and important examination into its structure, recruitment and management, including training,' the Staff Side of the Civil Service National Whitley Council stated in response to the appointment of the Fulton Committee, adding 'It is a high powered committee and can be expected to tackle its immense task with considerable knowledge and skill'. The staff side anticipated that, in conducting the first 'far ranging inquiry' into the Civil Service for 'over thirty years', the Fulton Committee would have 'a long and difficult road to travel and an early report cannot be expected'. They observed that

> The Civil Service itself will be on trial in the kind of evidence it produces. There will be an eagerness to see whether it places progressive views before Lord Fulton and his colleagues. As for the Civil Service staff movement, this inquiry will undoubtedly be their most testing time since the Tomlin Royal Commission in 1929/31. This is a great opportunity for the staff movement to make a real contribution towards the building of a modern Civil Service. This will require a bold and imaginative approach, unrestricted by insularity. Let us hope that everyone concerned will rise to the occasion. It may well be their last chance (*Whitley Bulletin*, March 1966, pp. 37–8).

The response of the Civil Service Clerical Association was forthright and positive:

> The CSCA, representing 150,000 members in the Clerical and allied grades welcomes this inquiry. Though its members are generally engaged in the more humble, but equally essential, duties, they can make a significant contribution to overall efficiency . . . The CSCA is convinced that the present grading structure, laid down in 1920 and virtually unchanged since, is unsuitable for the totally different conditions of the Civil Service and the community it serves. Its proposals envisage greater flexibility, a wider range of responsibility, and a streamlining of procedures, which would result in increased individual output, more job satisfaction, and, eventually, a smaller overall Clerical complement (*Red Tape*, March 1966, p.165).

Leslie Williams, the General Secretary of the Society of Civil Servants, representing the Executive Class and analogous grades, welcomed the appointment of the Fulton Committee, 'a lively committee' which was 'unlikely to bless the *status quo*' (*Civil Service Opinion*, March 1966, p.69). 'There will be changes, make no mistake,' Williams told the Annual Conference, 'and it is vitally important that the Society influences those changes' (*Civil Service Opinion*, June 1966, p.170).

R. B. M. King, Chairman of the Structure Sub-Committee of the First Division Association, which primarily represented the Administrative Class, described the establishment of the Fulton Committee as presenting 'one of the greatest challenges' that the FDA had faced 'in recent years' (FDA *Monthly Notes*, July 1966, p.12). The Annual Report for 1966 of the Institution of Professional Civil Servants, which represented specialist groups in the Service, noted that 'the National Executive Committee welcomed the appointment of the Fulton Committee and recognised that its recommendations would have fundamental and long term significance for the Civil Service in general and for the Professional, Technical, and Scientific Classes in particular' (*State Service*, March 1967, p.11).

All told, Leslie Williams was right when he described the establishment of the Fulton Committee as having had less initial impact on the Civil Service than the appointment of the Priestley Commission had done (*Civil Service Opinion*, June 1966, p.170).

The appointment of the Fulton Committee was generally welcomed by those few newspapers and journals which elected to comment. 'The Civil Service is to get its first serious inspection since 1931', *The Guardian* (9.2.66) observed, seeing the Committee as being 'a small, expert, workmanlike group' whose members 'should be able to work fast and effectively. Moreover the appointment of a committee instead of a Royal Commission should allay the fears expressed last year by Sir Laurence Helsby, the Head of the Home Civil Service . . . Sir Laurence should like the Fulton Committee. Four of the twelve members are civil servants.' *The Guardian* also noted with approval that the Committee included 'a former Secretary of the Fabian Society, Mrs Williams, who sponsored some penetrating research into Civil Service problems before she entered Parliament.' *The Times* (9.2.66) thought that the establishment of the Fulton Committee was 'timely'. There was 'need for a fresh assessment of the demands' imposed upon the Civil Service by the reality that 'the tasks of government continually expand and change, and the social conditions in which public administration is carried on change even more rapidly.' *The Financial Times* (9.2.66) said that 'it is thirty-five years since a Royal Commission last reported on the organisation and recruitment policies of the Civil Service. Great changes have taken place since 1931, not only in the size of the Service and the nature of its responsibilities but in the pattern of higher education. Although the Service has responded to the changes with admirable flexibility . . . the time has come for another outside look. The Fulton Committee is well qualified for its task.' It was described as 'a powerful Committee'. *The Spectator*, (18.2.66, p.187) saw the Labour government's decision to set up the Fulton Committee as coming at 'an opportune time', not only because of the need to recast the structure of the Civil Service, but also because of the 'mounting disquiet' in Whitehall, which the journal shared, about the manner in which the machinery of government was currently working, especially as regards the relationship between ministers and civil servants. *The Spectator* particularly had in mind what it called 'the Padmore affair', seeing Barbara Castle's attempt, on becoming Minister of Transport in late 1965, to replace the Permanent Secretary, Sir Thomas Padmore, as threatening the future of the career Civil Service. That said, though, the journal added that 'the grey eminences whose role in the formulation of policy is so vital can no longer hope to remain unpersons. Their only hope is to brazen it out, and become existent participants in the public debate.' *The Spectator* had in mind the introduction of 'specialist parliamentary committees . . . in the American manner able to interrogate civil servants.'

Public discussion of the supposed policy preferences of higher civil servants had already gone too far in the opinion of Lord Bridges, who as Sir Edward Bridges had been Head of the Home Civil Service between 1945 and 1956 (*The Times*, 18.2.66). 'Of course, I entirely agree that it is appropriate that there should be an examination into the structure of the Civil Service,' Bridges wrote, 'This follows the long standing practice whereby, at intervals of about twenty years, there has been a major inquiry into Civil Service organisations.' The 'proper functioning of a Permanent Civil Service', though, Bridges emphasised, had as a requirement that 'advice given by senior civil servants to their Ministers is confidential' (*The Times*, 28.2.66). That the Prime Minister in announcing the appointment of the Fulton Committee had re-affirmed this principle of confidentiality was noted by Bridges (*The Times*, 18.2.66), and this was cited too in a supporting letter from Lord Strang, who as Sir William Strang had been Permanent Under Secretary of the Foreign Office between 1949 and 1953. 'Let those who are now calling into question the conduct of civil servants hold their fire until they can make their complaints and put their case for change to Lord Fulton and his colleagues,' Strang wrote, 'and meantime in the interest of morale and recruitment let the present system continue to work undisturbed as we understand the Government wish it to do' (*The Times*, 2.3.66). Of course, the Prime Minister's re-affirmation of the doctrine of ministerial responsibility was the opposite of an invitation to discussion, as *The Economist* (12.2.66, p.579) recognised, observing that 'this Civil Service imposed gag on the deliberations of the Fulton Committee is in fact a classic illustration of the magnitude of the problem which the Committee now has to handle.'

Membership of the Fulton Committee

'In the 1960s it was still the Committee/Commission period. If you wanted to do something about the Civil Service you set up a committee,' observed

Clive Priestley, a higher civil servant who was later to be involved with the Rayner exercises after 1979. Priestley thought that, 'in the context of the 1960s, Lord Fulton was the sort of person who should head such a inquiry. He seemed to be an exemplar of the best of the post-war developments in British society. The Fulton Committee seemed to be fairly broadly based for those times. It seemed a good Committee' (Interview, 1988). 'Fulton was not first choice' to be Chairman, 'nor the happiest choice', Sir Philip Allen, one of the members of the Committee has stated on public record, being of the belief that the Committee itself composed of insiders and outsiders was 'pretty disastrous as a combination' (Hennessy et al., 1988, p. 45). Before examining this matter further, it seems best to consider the membership of the Fulton Committee in more detail.

It was common knowledge that John Scott Fulton (1902–86), created Baron Fulton of Falmer in 1966, was a personal friend of the then Prime Minister, Harold Wilson. As Lady Fulton observed, 'the friendship was first formed at Oxford and they became close friends after working together as temporary civil servants during the war' (Interview, 1989). Lord Fulton had been a Principal and then an Assistant Secretary in the Mines Department between 1940 and 1942, and then a Principal Assistant Secretary in the Ministry of Fuel and Power between 1942 and 1944 with responsibilities relating to the coal industry. Wilson was working in the same division as an economist and statistician. Previously, Lord Fulton had been an academic, and as a Fellow of Balliol College, Oxford, he had taught philosophy and then politics. From 1947 onwards, Lord Fulton had made his career in university administration eventually becoming the first Vice-Chancellor of Sussex University, which position he held from 1959 to 1967 (*The Times* 19.3.86).

The Fulton Committee appointed Sir Norman Victor Kipping (1901–79) to be its Vice-Chairman. Kipping had been Director General of the Federation of British Industries between 1946 and 1965, relinquishing that role on the formation of the Confederation of British Industry which he had played a major part in establishing. He had begun his career as an engineer in the Post Office, but it was in the electrical engineering industry that he made his mark, becoming a works manager of Standard Telephones and Cables. In 1942 he set up and then led the regional organisation of the Ministry of Production, and ended the war as an Under Secretary at the Board of Trade. For these services he was knighted, and he then became what his biographer called an industrial stateman (Whitehorn, 1986, pp. 466–7). 'Having been in industry, I respected Norman Kipping,' a fellow member of the Fulton Committee, Robert Sheldon, observed; 'His presence on the Committee ensured that the industrialists' point of view was very well presented' (Interview, 1988). Another member, Walter Anderson, thought that Kipping 'made a good contribution as Vice-Chairman. He seemed to know a lot of civil servants and about the Civil Service' (Interview, 1988).

Some other assessments were less admiring, and Kipping himself did not seem to consider his membership of the Fulton Committee to have been of much importance, granting it only two brief mentions in his memoirs (Kipping, 1972, pp.35, 231).

Sir Philip Allen (b.1912) was a career civil servant. After success in the Administrative Class Open Competition he entered the Home Office in 1934, eventually becoming Deputy Under Secretary of State at that department between 1960 and 1962, having also served at various times in the Office of the War Cabinet, the Prison Commission, and the Ministry of Housing and Local Government. In 1963 Allen was made a Second Secretary in the Treasury. Shortly after the appointment of the Fulton Committee he was transferred to become Permanent Under Secretary of State at the Home Office, a post which he held from 1966 to 1972. He was later to observe,

> I did not have the time to make a full contribution to the work of the Fulton Committee. Indeed, I thought that I would be let off once I had moved from the Treasury to the Home Office, where the burden of work was very great, but Harold Wilson would not permit this. Shirley Williams had already had to leave the Committee, and the Prime Minister did not want any more changes of personnel. The heavy load that I had to carry at the Home Office was one reason why I was desperately anxious for the Committee to keep to its timetable (Interview, 1988).

Walter Charles Anderson (b. 1910), a solicitor, apart from war service had spent his working life in local government and then in the National Association of Local Government Officers, of which he was General Secretary between 1957 and 1973, being a member of the General Council of the TUC between 1965 and 1973. Anderson said that he 'was on the Fulton Committee as the statutory trade union man. I was suggested by Leslie Williams who was then running the Civil Service National Whitley Council Staff Side. I did not see myself as being bound by the trade union line. What I saw my role as being was to ensure that the trade union view was fairly represented.' Anderson added, 'I was an ordinary member of the Committee. I found it a disadvantage never to have been in the Civil Service or to have worked closely with civil servants. Fulton was on Christian name terms with most of them' (Interview, 1988).

Sir Edward Charles Gurney Boyle (1923–81) was Conservative MP for the Handsworth division of Birmingham between 1950 and 1970, and had been a cabinet minister in the Ministry of Education and then the Department of Education and Science in Conservative governments between 1962 and 1964. Edward Heath was later to write of him that, 'his intellectual characteristics . . . comprised a wide breadth of interest, a remarkable store of information, and a phenomenal memory for everything which he encountered, but his was not a mind full of innovative ideas or penetrating analysis. His strength lay in his deep-seated and moderate convictions which guided him all through his life' (Heath, 1990, p.50). Sir Edward always maintained that he had been right wing in early career, but his resignation from the post of Economic Secretary to the Treasury in protest against the Suez expedition in 1956 and his association with progressive ideas in educational policy certainly subsequently gave him the more familiar image of being a Tory 'moderate', and acceptability to the Labour government as the Conservative nominee on the Fulton Committee. Sir James Dunnett placed on public record the view that Boyle was one of several members of the Fulton Committee who made little impact on its work (Hennessy et al., 1988, p.47), and in discussion with the author Sir Edward described himself as having had insufficient time to make the contribution that he would have wished.

Sir William Richard Joseph Cook (1905–87) was Deputy Chief Scientific Officer in the Ministry of Defence between 1964 and 1970, and this was the post that he held during his membership of the Fulton Committee. Cook first entered the Civil Service as a scientist in 1928, and his career involved research and development work relating to a number of weapons systems conducted in various of the defence departments, as well as the civil application of nuclear energy when employed at the UK Atomic Energy Authority (*The Times*, 19.9.87). Cook was not an important member of the Fulton Committee, and Sir James Dunnett chose to put on public record his view that while he had 'a great regard for Cook . . . he really did not make much contribution to the discussions' (Hennessy et al., 1988, p.47).

Sir Ludovic James Dunnett (b.1914) was Permanent Secretary to the Ministry of Labour at the time the Fulton Committee was appointed, becoming Permanent Under Secretary of State at the Ministry of Defence in June 1966, a post that he held until 1974. Following success in the Administrative Class Open Competition, Sir James had begun his Civil Service career in the Air Ministry in 1936, subsequently serving in the Ministry of Civil Aviation and then the Ministry of Transport of which department he became the Permanent Secretary in 1959, before coming to hold posts at the same level at the Ministry of Labour in 1962 and then at the Ministry of Defence. Robert Sheldon said that 'Ned Dunnett was the most forceful of the civil servants on the Fulton Committee' (Interview, 1988). Dunnett was unimpressed by his own contribution, emphasising that 'Sir Philip Allen and myself had heavy duties in our government departments' (Interview, 1988).

Dr Norman Crowther Hunt (1920–87) had been a Fellow of Exeter College and a University Lecturer in Politics at Oxford since 1952. Hunt's involvement in the *Whitehall and Beyond* broadcasts as an interviewer did not seem to have made much of an impression at least on some Treasury officials. When the letters of invitation to serve on the Fulton Committee were sent out, James Callaghan, who signed them as Chancellor of the Exchequer, later recalled that 'an invitation was nearly sent to the wrong Norman Hunt but was intercepted just in time' (letter to author, 27.10.1988). Norman Charles Hunt, the then Professor of Organisation of Industry and Commerce in the

University of Edinburgh, the only Norman Hunt in the contemporary *Who's Who*, would have been the recipient. It was not as surprising as perhaps it now seems that such an administrative error almost occurred, because, in 1966, Norman Crowther Hunt's best known published work was called *Two Early Political Associations. The Quakers and the Dissenting Deputies in the Age of Sir Robert Walpole* (Oxford, Clarendon Press, 1961). Hunt was not an academic authority on the Civil Service at the time that he was appointed to the Fulton Committee. At Oxford, he lectured on British Constitutional History since 1660, which would mean that he would have a background knowledge of the history of the Civil Service, and his tutorial responsibilities on the Political Institutions course would have required him to keep abreast of recent developments in the British Civil Service as well as in the Civil Services of France and the United States Federal Government. Research and scholarly publication had not resulted, and, on the Civil Service, in those days Hunt would not have been considered to be in the same academic league as, say, D. N. Chester, W. J. M. Mackenzie, W. A. Robson, or Brian Chapman. Indeed, Chapman's book, *The Profession of Government* (London, Allen and Unwin, 1959), prominent on the Oxford reading lists in the first half of the 1960s, may well have been the main source of such information as Hunt, like others, had about the Civil Services of continental Europe at that time. Norman Hunt owed his place on the Fulton Committee to the friendship that he had formed with Harold Wilson at the time of the *Whitehall and Beyond* discussions; and when granted a year's sabbatical leave on generous terms by Exeter College, Oxford, to work on this Committee and its Management Consultancy Group (PRO: BA1/96) Hunt took full advantage of the opportunity.

Robert Ralph Neild (b.1924) was a professional economist. He recalled: 'While I was a member of the Fulton Committee I had a full time job as Economic Adviser to the Chancellor of the Exchequer, James Callaghan, after which I was busy establishing the International Peace Research Institute in Stockholm, which curtailed my attendance at the Fulton Committee's meetings.' Neild added,

> I'd thought about Civil Service reform. I'd been Chairman of a Fabian group on the subject for two years not long before the Fulton Committee was set up. I'd been in and out of the Civil Service quite a lot. After I was invalided out of the Royal Air Force, I had been a junior Scientific Officer doing operational research. Then, after I had done my Economics degree at Cambridge, I took the Civil Service examination, going through country house and all that. I passed and was offered a job at the Board of Trade but I turned it down. Later between 1951 and 1956, I worked in the Economic Section of the Treasury. By then, the squeeze on the economists was on. With decontrol, out went the economists, and it was back to the Old School. I had a fixed term contract and I was told that if I wanted to become permanent I would have to take a late entry

examination, even though I had passed the Administrative Class examination before. So I went into university life.

He said: 'When it came to the reform of the Civil Service, I started with some rather clear views formed in the Fabian group and before' (Interview, 28.10.88). The Secretary of the Fulton Committee, Richard Wilding, reflected the general opinion when he said that 'Robert Neild was a good member of the Committee. He was an active reformer with Fabian views. He kept up with the material, and he was a perceptive questioner' (Interview:, 29.9.88).

Robert Sheldon (b.1923) had been Labour MP for Ashton-under-Lyne since 1964, having previously worked in private industry. Sheldon observed, 'The Fulton Committee had started work before I became a member, replacing Shirley Williams. I did not know much about the Civil Service. My main interest was in economic policy. So, being on the Committee involved me in a vast amount of work. I stayed up half the night doing it. My main contribution was to press for unified grading, and to lend support to the advocacy of preference for relevance' (Interview, 1988).

Thomas Spensley Simey (1906–69), created Baron Simey of Toxteth in 1965, was Charles Booth Professor of Social Science at Liverpool University at the time of his membership of the Fulton Committee. Lord Simey had held this post since 1939, having previously been the Leverhulme Lecturer in Public Administration at the same university since 1931. Simey's book, *Principles of Social Administration* (London, Oxford University Press, 1937) had contained material about the organisation of central government departments, and reference was made to official reports on the Civil Service. The book related the study of public administration and social administration in a manner that was to be rare in subsequent works once the scale of state social provision had become more extensive, and also perhaps academic restrictive practices had set in. Indeed, the research for the book had been aided by a grant from the Institute of Public Administration. Lord Simey was not, though, an academic authority on the Civil Service and he did not see himself as such. Margaret Simey recalled that 'Tom was not happy with the Fulton set up. It was not really his subject and he only went on under pressure. He had complained to Wilson that he was wasting his time in the Lords. Harold Wilson offered to make him Black Rod as a sop. Having rejected that with great fury, it was difficult to refuse Fulton when it came his way' (letter to author, 10.3.90). Eventually, illness limited Simey's contribution to the work of the Fulton Committee, but before this happened Sir Philip Allen's recollection was that 'Simey could come up with the unorthodox, the unexpected' in discussion (Interview, 1988), and, of course, there was to be Simey's note of reservation to the opening chapter of the Fulton Report.

John Edward Wall (1913–81) was Deputy Chairman of the Post Office between 1966 and 1968, a post to which he was appointed during the period when he was already a member of the Fulton Committee, being knighted in

1968. Wall worked in private industry before joining the Ministry of Food in 1939, eventually becoming an Under Secretary in that department, before leaving the Civil Service in 1952 to join Unilever. Wall was Managing Director of Electrical and Musical Industries from 1960 to 1966 (*The Times*, 3.1.81), and had been a member of the Plowden Committee on the Control of Public Expenditure. Wall's contribution to the work of the Fulton Committee was limited once he was involved with the translation of the Post Office into a public corporation.

'The Fulton Committee was an outstandingly able committee, abler than any I can think of in my experience,' one of its members, Robert Sheldon, was later to observe. Though the Committee had been divided on several issues, he thought that only ' a few thin skinned people' would see it as having been an unhappy body and this was certainly not his view (Interview, 1988). Both its Secretary, Richard Wilding (Interview, 1988) and Sir Philip Allen, another of its members, explicitly described the Fulton Committee as 'an unhappy committee.' Allen said that 'there was an undercurrent of unease and distrust' (Interview, 1988). Wilding recalled that: 'We used to meet every Tuesday, and every time as regular as clockwork there would be a bit of a row. Norman Hunt would charge the Secretariat with doctoring the minutes. He was convinced that Michael Simons and myself were trying to water down what was being said. Hunt was full of mistrust of the Secretaries' (Interview, 1988). The verdict of Sir James Dunnett was blunt: 'The Fulton Committee was not a heavyweight committee. Indeed, it was not really a committee at all, given the quality of the Chairmanship' (Interview, 1988).

The Committee was 'led from behind' according to Robert Neild (Hennessy et al., 1988, p.45), and Sir James Dunnett's opinion was that 'things were largely run by Norman Hunt, whose Oxford college granted him sabbatical leave, which gave him time' (Interview, 1988). 'What did seem to worry Lord Fulton and to embarrass him was that Norman Hunt seemed to come to the Committee armed with the Prime Minister's approval', Allen observed (Interview, 1988), having on another occasion said that both Hunt and Fulton 'used to go and see Harold Wilson and together they would get their instructions', presumably about how the Committee's work should proceed. Allen added that the rest of the Committee 'were not party to these instructions' (Hennessy et al., 1988, p.45). Not all the members of the Committee knew about the meetings between their Chairman, Hunt, and the Prime Minister, and not everybody considered that they had much importance for the manner in which the Committee operated. The minutes for the meeting on August 1st 1967 recorded that

> the Chairman reported an informal discussion with the Prime Minister. He had given a general indication of the way the Committee were thinking, and the Prime Minister had had no particular comment to make. He had however shown enthusiasm for a Civil Service Training College on a large scale. The Chairman had pressed the Prime Minister

on whether he felt the need for a larger staff, in particular to co-ordinate forward planning. The Prime Minister had said no: the Cabinet Office had been strengthened and he was now adequately served (PRO: BA1/10). Lord Fulton's papers contain only one reference to a meeting between the Prime Minister, Hunt and himself to discuss the progress of the Committee on the Civil Service, and this took place over dinner at Chequers on Sunday, 21 May 1967. Marcia Williams's recollection was that 'there were certainly meetings both at Chequers and at Number 10, but Harold Wilson did not directly intervene in the workings of the Fulton Committee. His links with it were through his Principal Private Secretary, Michael Halls. Norman Hunt was also extremely close to Harold and saw him a great deal anyway. Lord Fulton was a friend of Harold's from Oxford days, but saw him less than Hunt did' (Interview, 1989).

'In the manner in which he behaved on the Committee Norman Hunt did seem to see himself as having a remit from the Prime Minister,' Richard Wilding observed, adding that 'Norman Hunt worked extremely hard, both on the Fulton Committee itself and on the Management Consultancy Group. He was hyper-active. How he got through all the things that he did in a day nobody knows'. Wilding said that Hunt, Neild and Dunnett constituted a radical troika on the Committee (Interview, 1988). Besides the Chairman, the membership of the Committee divided into three main groups, Michael Simons believed. The first comprised those who made the smallest contribution, and this included Anderson, Cook and Wall. The second group was an intermediate one, consisting of Boyle and Simey. Then there was the main group which included Allen, Dunnett, Sheldon, Neild, Hunt and Kipping. Simons added that until Dunnett became disenchanted with the Committee's activities he was one of its radicals (Interview, 1989). 'In terms of diagnosis, Sir James Dunnett was a radical, but in terms of specifics he was more conservative,' Richard Wilding observed; 'Dunnett was conservative in the sense of knowing what was feasible in terms of Civil Service management' (Interview, 1988).

It is not necessary to share the bleak opinions about the overall ability present on the Fulton Committee that Dunnett (Interview, 1988) and Allen (Interview, 1988) expressed in order to recognise that the Committee did not merit the descriptions of it as being 'strong' and 'powerful' that it initially attracted. It was not really in the same league as, for instance, the MacDonnell Royal Commission on the Civil Service of 1912–15, which had Graham Wallas and Philip Snowden as ordinary members. That said, though, given the scale of investigative activity that was taking place at that stage of the 1960s, the Fulton Committee seemed to have its fair share of such talent as was available in what was treated as being the pool from which it had to be drawn. For all the subsequent criticism of Fulton as Chairman that was later advanced by some members of the Committee and by those who worked with it, in principle he was a good choice for that role. Lord Fulton had an impressive record as a university administrator, and, as he had pointed out himself, he had been an Administrative Class civil servant and he had some academic background knowledge of the Civil Service too (*The Times*, 11.2.66). 'Lord Fulton was a nice man who got the Committee working together,' Robert Sheldon considered (Interview, 1988), even if others thought differently. Michael Simons encapsulated their views when he described Fulton's style of Chairmanship as being diffuse (Interview, 1989). One thing that the Committee did not lack was practical knowledge of the Civil Service. The presence of Dunnett, Allen and Cook ensured that, of course, as did that of Neild; and, in fact, seven of the ordinary members of the Committee had worked in the Civil Service at some time in their careers, though Boyle's experience at the Foreign Office during the war had not been as a conventional civil servant.

Though there were too many strong characters around the table for Norman Hunt to have dominated the Fulton Committee, as Walter Anderson remarked, his fellow member risked little in describing Hunt as the most active member of the Committee (Interview, 1988). On the Fulton Committee, Hunt fulfilled two of the roles that David Donnison, a veteran of several inquiries, once identified as types of committeemen, namely that of advocate of a particular philosophy and that of 'fusebox', blowing up if the way that the Committee was going threatened to depart in any way seriously from his assumptions and attitudes (Bulmer, 1980, p.16). While Hunt brought no academic expertise on public administration to the Fulton Committee, he did bring to the Committee a set of highly critical opinions about the Civil Service and particularly its Administrative Class. Hunt adhered to these views with remarkable tenacity in pursuit of the goal, which he shared with several other members of the Committee, of ensuring that the Fulton Report would be what he and his allies perceived to be a truly radical document.

Chapter 2

Organisation of the Committee's Work

Precedents for the Fulton Committee

The Fulton Committee was not 'a classic good and great exercise', according to one of its members, Sir Philip Allen, who did not disguise his view that such an 'exercise' would have been a better means of reviewing the Civil Service: 'There had never been a committee like this; Callaghan said it was an experiment of mixed insiders and outsiders. On reflection, he thought there ought to be more outsiders than insiders but I'm not conscious of any precedent for it – I don't think anyone was at the time' (Hennessy et al., 1988, p.45).

The Plowden Committee on the Control of Public Expenditure of 1959–61 was a fairly obvious and then relatively recent example of a committee of inquiry composed of a mixture of insiders and outsiders even though the balance between them was different from that of the Fulton Committee. It will be recalled that Sir Laurence Helsby mentioned the Plowden Committee as a possible model for an inquiry into the Civil Service in his evidence to the Select Committee on Estimates in 1965. If the Plowden Committee was not thought to represent a precedent because it was internally conducted, there were other examples that could be cited of committees of insiders and outsiders, both as regards reviews of the machinery of government and of the Civil Service in particular, as well as more generally. As K. C. Wheare wrote, in a famous essay on the British Constitution, about the presence of serving civil servants on committees of inquiry:

A most striking example was the Committee on Ministers' Powers appointed by the Lord Chancellor in 1929. Upon it sat no less than three heads of important departments – the head of the Lord Chancellor's Department itself, Sir Claud Schuster, the Permanent Secretary to the Treasury, Sir Warren Fisher, and the Permanent Under Secretary of State at the Home Office, Sir John Anderson. The Royal Commission on Licensing in England and Wales of 1929 included a high official of the Home Office, Sir John Pedder. The Inter-Departmental Committee on Children and the Cinema which reported in 1950 included among its members an official from each of the three departments which jointly established the Committee – the Home Office, the Ministry of Education, and the Scottish Office (Wheare, 1955, p.73).

Professor Wheare was himself the chairman of that large committee of insiders and outsiders (Cmd. 7945, 1950, p.ii).

The chairman of 'the small committee' set up in 1943 to undertake 'a survey of the remuneration and conditions of service of scientists in government departments' was Sir Alan Barlow, a Second Secretary to the Treasury; and the other members of this committee were Sir Edward Appleton, Secretary of the Department of Industrial and Scientific Research, W. F. Lutyens of ICI, and Professor E. K. Rideal of the University of Cambridge (Cmd. 6679, 1945, p.2). Of the other examples that Wheare might have mentioned, one notes that the Haldane Machinery of Government Committee, which reported in 1918, included among its members Sir Robert Morant, who was a serving official, being the Chairman of the Insurance Commission at that time (Cd. 9230, 1918, p.2). As the Haldane Committee and the Donoughmore-Scott Committee on Ministers' Powers of 1929–32 were widely recognised as having conducted important inquiries into the workings of British government, the Fulton Committee was not inherently disadvantaged in seeking to produce a report of comparable standing by also having serving officials in its ranks.

Around the time that the Fulton Committee was established, there seemed to be no consistent pattern to decisions about whether it would be a Royal Commission or a departmental committee that would conduct the major inquiries into British institutions that the then Labour Government believed to be needed. According to the classic study of committees of inquiry in British government, 'the only difference between a departmental committee and a Royal Commission, for all practical purposes, is that the former lacks the aura of dignity and eminence to be derived from the title of "Royal Commission" and the possession of a royal warrant of appointment' (Clokie and Robinson, 1937, p.207). While recognising the distinction in terms of prestige between departmental committees and Royal Commissions, another observer once suggested that 'membership of a departmental committee *may* be confined to persons whose sole qualification is that they understand the subject referred to them', whereas 'members of a Royal Commission *may* understand the subject upon which they are to report, but they *must* – or at least a majority must – be persons whose names can be found in *Who's Who*. This requirement is usually expressed by the phrase that the names must command public confidence' (Greenwood et al., 1937, p.399). Several people who had served on or who had worked in support of committees of inquiry in the 1960s and 70s have expressed the view that the formal distinction between a Royal Commission and a departmental committee did have implications for financing. Royal Commissions were thought by them to be in a better negotiating position for getting money than departmental committees. Though the latter could use the research resources of the sponsoring department or departments and those of the Government Social Survey too, there was a belief that the committees of inquiry that had done insufficient research had tended to be departmental committees kept on a tight financial rein by their departments (Bulmer, 1983, p.304). Whether this was the case or not with the Fulton Committee is difficult to establish, given that there was no separate heading for research in its accounts (PRO: BA1/97). If one treats research as having what Michael Simons called, in a letter to Lord Simey on 1 February 1968, 'an elastic definition embracing the Management Consultant Report' (PRO: BA1/74), it could be safely said that the Management Consultancy Group was not stinted financially. Of the academics who conducted research for the Fulton Committee, Dr J. F. Pickering found the payment made to him to be 'eminently reasonable' (PRO: BA1/75). A. H. Halsey originally undertook to do research work for the Fulton Committee without a fee, and it was the Committee itself which suggested payment to ensure that 'Halsey's report was the Committee's property not his' (PRO: BA1/79). Halsey described the total fee paid to him as 'generous' (PRO: BA1/84). Another academic researcher, Richard Chapman, with some cause, was less impressed with the money made available to him, and suggested in a letter to J. A. Lewry of the Treasury on 23 December 1966 that the subsistence allowances were of an order that made it a matter of regret that 'the Treasury did not send me a list of cheap hotels' (PRO: BA1/74).

While the Fulton Committee was at work, no less than five Royal Commissions investigated other areas of prospective institutional reform. A Royal Commission on Trade Unions and Employers' Associations, under the Chairmanship of Lord Donovan, was appointed in April 1965, and its report was published in June 1968 (Cmnd. 3623, 1968). A Commission on Tribunals of Inquiry under the chairmanship of Lord Salmon was appointed in February 1966, and its report was published in November 1966 (Cmnd. 3121, 1966). Another on Local Government in England under the Chairmanship of Lord Redcliffe-Maud was appointed in May 1966, and reported in June 1969 (Cmnd. 4040, 1969). A Commission on Local Government in Scotland under the chairmanship of Lord Wheatley was appointed in May 1966, and its report was published in September 1969 (Cmnd. 4150, 1969). That on Assizes and Quarter Sessions under the chairmanship of Lord Beeching was appointed in November 1966, and reported in September 1969 (Cmnd. 4153, 1969). On the other hand, it was the Home Secretary, the Secretary of State for Education and Science, the Minister of Housing and Local Government, and the Minister of Health who, in December 1965, appointed the Committee on Local Authority and Allied Personal Social Services, under the Chairmanship of Frederic Seebohm, which published its report in July 1968 (Cmnd. 3703, 1968).

That a departmental committee of the Treasury and not a Royal Commission was assigned the task of reviewing the Civil Service did not represent an innovation. There had been no less than four Royal Commissions on the

Civil Service, namely those chaired by Sir Matthew White Ridley (1886–90), Lord MacDonnell (1912–5), Lord Tomlin (1929–31), and Sir Raymond Priestley (1953–5): but there had also been departmental committees which had conducted Service-wide inquiries. There was no rule that a general review of the Civil Service required a Royal Commission, or, given the restrictions placed on the terms of reference of the Priestley Commission, that the appointment of a Royal Commission meant that such a review was envisaged. It was as a Treasury departmental committee that Sir Stafford Northcote and Sir Charles Trevelyan produced their famous Report on the Organization of the Permanent Civil Service published in 1854. The Playfair Commission of 1874–5, sometimes listed as a Royal Commission on the Civil Service (e.g. by Cartwright, 1975, p.26), was actually a Civil Service Inquiry Commission and effectively a departmental committee of the Treasury. The Inquiry Commission comprised two MPs, Lyon Playfair and Lord Claud Hamilton, and six serving officials (*The Times*, 4.5.1874). Though obviously the composition of the smaller Playfair Commission differed from it in having a majority of insiders among its membership, the Fulton Committee could not be said to be the first body comprising both insiders and outsiders that had reviewed the Civil Service. It was the case, too, that the membership of the MacDonnell Royal Commission on the Civil Service of 1912–15 included a serving official, Sir Kenneth Muir Mackenzie, who had been Permanent Secretary to the Lord Chancellor since 1880 (*The Times*, 14.3.1912), a post that he continued to hold until 1915.

Royal Commissions 'take minutes and waste years', Harold Wilson had observed when Leader of the Opposition (*Report of the 96th Annual Trades Union Congress*, 1964, p.384), but the Labour Government of 1964–70, of which Wilson was Prime Minister, appointed no less than seven such Commissions (Rhodes, 1975, p.17), and, with this scale of activity being undertaken, a Royal Commission on the Civil Service would not have looked out of place. 'Royal Commissions by their very nature take a very long time to report', Marcia Williams commented about the Labour Government's decision to appoint a body like the Fulton Committee to make recommendations about the reform of the Civil Service; 'Harold Wilson wanted this Report to be produced more speedily, so that action could follow' (letter to author, 19.9.90). Eighteen months to two years was what the Government had in mind for the Committee to complete its task, its Chairman said publicly (*The Times*, 11.2.66), and in his opening remarks to the Committee itself (PRO: BA1/2), but the Committee did not meet its target. Two years and four months elapsed between its appointment and the publication of its Report. If speed was to be a test of virtue, the Priestley Royal Commission on the Civil Service of 1953–5 had taken only two years to complete its task; and the Tomlin Commission of 1929–31, although criticised for its supposed 'failure to take advantage of a great opportunity' (Laski, 1931, p.506) in the midst of an economic blizzard, and for the alleged mediocrity of its membership (Hanser, 1965, p.177), produced its Report in just twenty-one months. The average time taken by committees of inquiry in the 1960s and 70s generally seemed to be of the order of two and a half years (Bulmer, 1983, p.18). This made the matter of months, which the Salmon Royal Commission on Tribunals of Inquiry took, look all the more exceptional. It meant, too, that the Fulton Committee completed its task marginally faster than most investigatory committees and certainly more swiftly than, for instance, the contemporaneous Royal Commissions reviewing local government. The Wheatley Commission, in particular, though, did a thorough job.

It will be remembered that the Select Committee on Estimates had recommended that a committee of insiders and outsiders 'on the lines' of the Plowden Committee on the Control of Public Expenditure should be appointed to research and report upon the Civil Service, preceding Government action and the possible subsequent establishment of a Royal Commission. A Plowden style of inquiry would have had to have been internally conducted, otherwise the analogy was misleading. In establishing the Fulton Committee in the form that it did, the Labour government chose to have an external committee of inquiry, but one that had a composition that broadly resembled the Plowden Committee and one that was to be a surrogate for a Royal Commission on the Civil Service and not a precursor for such a review body, being expected to produce its findings speedily, and with narrowly drawn terms of reference that would make such an outcome attainable. The Labour Government's appointment of the Fulton Committee did not represent 'tribal dance' or 'medicine hut' activity (Greenwood et al., 1937, p.408) on its part, or 'anything but action' (Herbert, 1961, pp.251–302). The Labour Government had Fabian guidance about the reforming 'action' that it needed to take, but it felt the need for this to be proposed by a review body that would be seen as being independent, and which was able to include, among others, two Permanent Secretaries to associate the Civil Service with the inquiry's findings. It is a matter of outlook whether one construed the use of such a review mechanism as evidence of concern for the maintenance of the non-political character of the career Civil Service or, alternatively, of deference to an established interest.

Task of the Fulton Committee

Effectively, the task that the Fulton Committee was given was to analyse and to make recommendations about several aspects of the Civil Service that the Priestley Royal Commission of 1953–5 had been precluded from considering properly. That Commission had complained about 'the restricted nature of our terms of reference', which confined it to pay and conditions of service and made 'no mention of a variety of matters such as structure, grading, complementing and their relationship to the size of the Civil Service; nor are we called upon to make recommendations about recruitment, training and promotion procedures. Though we have not felt debarred from enquiring into these questions, we have found it extraordinarily difficult to examine and advise on the pay rates of an organisation so complex as the Civil Service without the opportunity of making positive proposals on these intimately related matters' (Cmd. 9613, 1955, paras 54–5).

The Fulton Committee was able to consider these matters, but, as we have noted before, it was denied the opportunity to review fully others that were relevant. 'That the terms of reference of the Fulton Committee excluded the machinery of government and the convention of ministerial responsibility was deliberate,' Sir Philip Allen observed, 'It is difficult to see any modern Government allowing an outside body to review machinery and what Ministers do. Even if such a review body was thought to be suitable, it would have to have been a different and much weightier body that the Fulton Committee could ever hope to have been. The Haldane Committee had been such a body but it didn't achieve very much' (Interview, 1988). Walter Anderson thought that the terms of reference of the Fulton Committee were 'widely drawn' as they stood: 'we had a big enough job anyway' (Interview, 1988). Robert Sheldon's view was that 'if the terms of reference of the Fulton Committee had embraced the machinery of government and the doctrine of ministerial responsibility it would have been a vast undertaking that would have taken several years to complete. The Committee might even still be sitting. The Fulton Committee had an extensive enough task as it was' (Interview, 1988). Sir James Dunnett did not consider that the Committee's terms of reference were unduly restrictive: 'The Fulton Committee was simply charged with looking at the constitution and working of the Civil Service' (Interview, 1988). Robert Neild said of the Committee that 'our terms of reference gave us a limited mandate' – and at times he found the formal exclusion of the machinery of government and the convention of ministerial responsibility to be frustrating – but 'in retrospect I think this was just as well because lack of leadership of the Committee meant that we could not have done a bigger job' (Interview, 1988). Norman Hunt thought that the restrictions on the terms of reference meant that the Civil Service had 'managed to chalk up a couple of victories' even before the Committee started work. The exclusion of the doctrine of ministerial responsibility was the more important 'victory', in Hunt's opinion, because it meant that the Committee 'could not directly concern itself with the power of the Civil Service.' Hunt said that the Civil Service's 'victory' in narrowing the Committee's terms of reference to exclude the machinery of government later enabled the Service to argue that this restriction invalidated much of what the Committee had to say. Hunt himself believed that the exclusion of the machinery of government was 'a sterile controversy' because 'the Committee's main recommendations were concerned with the type of civil servant you needed to undertake the tasks of modern government irrespective of the precise way Whitehall might organise itself to carry out these tasks' (Kellner and Crowther-Hunt, 1980, pp.27–8).

The reform of the Civil Service, the doctrine of ministerial responsibility, and the machinery of government were bound to be closely related matters. There was nothing 'sterile' in the 1960s in considering whether or not the machinery of British central government was that which was needed in the era of the Keynesian welfare state, an economic and social order which had the support of the contemporary political consensus. Furthermore, one did not have to have to believe in supposed conspiracies about protecting 'the power of the Civil Service' to see that requiring the Fulton Committee to examine that Service, while abstaining from fully reviewing the current working of the convention of ministerial responsibility, which conditioned the manner in which government departments operated, certainly risked the Committee's work being rendered 'sterile.' The contemporaneous conversion of the Post Office from being a government department into a public corporation (with which, as we have noted, one of the members of the Fulton Committee, Sir John Wall, was involved) was an obvious example of the continuing importance not only of issues such as political control and accountability, but also of differing organisational forms and the implications that they had for what types of public servant were needed. Inevitably, as will be seen, the Fulton Committee had to trespass into the forbidden territories of machinery of government and ministerial responsibility, although, of course, such incursions could not have the same authority as established rights of access would have provided. As for what was undisputedly supposed to be the Fulton Committee's territory, the Committee began its work with the knowledge that a Treasury Working Party on Management Training had been established in November 1965 and that the resulting report was always likely to be available before its own.

The Fulton Committee had not been given an 'extensive', 'big', even 'massive' task, as some of its members seemed to believe, but a relatively restricted one compared with, say, the Haldane Committee, which had reviewed a machinery of British government that had been very substantially extended by the demands of total war before recommending a form of re-ordering of it for the purposes of peacetime organisation. To take a more recent example, as a former Permanent Secretary, Dame Evelyn Sharp, pointed out approvingly at the time, the remit of the Fulton Committee was much more limited than that of the Canadian Glassco Royal Commission on Government Organisation of 1960–2 (Sharp, 1967, p.283).

'The British go about these things in a much more amateur way; which is not to say that it is necessarily a worse way,' Dame Evelyn Sharp observed; 'I don't think we should ever conceive of a single commission reviewing the organisation and methods of all the departments – we would think them too different in function for this to be successful.' Dame Evelyn emphasised what she saw as the differences between the Glassco Commission and the Fulton Committee, writing of the latter:

Its members are mostly, if not all, very busy men, who must carry the

work of the Committee on top of their ordinary loads. They are unpaid.
And they have a very small secretariat. They could commission inves-
tigators if they want to, but I should doubt if they will do much of that.
They hear whatever evidence people care to put to them; they invite
people whom they think may have ideas to contribute to come and talk.
This is the traditional British way of tackling such problems – a sort of
adaption of the jury system; and it can work very well. But I sometimes
wonder whether it doesn't ask too much of the members of these commissions. Maybe we over-do the amateur method. Certainly the idea of
asking management consultants to examine our Civil Service has not
yet crossed our minds. No doubt this is partly because management
consultancy has not yet achieved the standing in Britain that it has in
North America. But it is also, I think, because we should instinctively
mistrust the business efficiency approach to problems of government. In
our philosophy one achieves efficiency in government by getting the right
men, training them rightly, and picking the right ones for the top jobs.
And that, I think, will prove to be the Fulton Committee's main concern
(Sharp, 1967, p.283).

Though Dame Evelyn Sharp was one of the more unconventional of
modern Permanent Secretaries, her view may well have reflected a more
general expectation among higher civil servants, and others too at the time,
that the Fulton Committee would rely solely on the traditional means of
inquiry, but this was not to be the case.

Procedures of the Fulton Committee

The Fulton Committee's first meeting was held on the afternoon of Thursday,
10 March 1966. Aside from the press conference convened to mark the
publication of the Fulton Report on 26 June 1968, what was officially recorded
as being the final meeting of the Committee took place on Wednesday, 19
June 1968. The work of the Committee involved the holding of a conference
at the Civil Defence Staff College at Sunningdale during the weekend of 24–6
June 1966. A similar weekend conference was held at the White House in the
Island of Thorns, a residence owned by the University of Sussex in the
Ashdown Forest on 22–3 July 1967. This latter conference was treated as
being the twenty-seventh meeting of the Committee in 1967, but that held
earlier at Sunningdale was not officially listed as a meeting. The Fulton
Committee had thirty-two meetings formally recorded as such in 1966, thirty-
five in 1967, and eighteen in 1968. The Committee agreed at the outset that
it should expect to meet on the same day every week, starting at 9.30 a.m. and
ending at about 4 o'clock (PRO: BA1/2). Though there were some exceptions of
the kind noted above, the Fulton Committee normally met on Tuesdays, and
the drafting committee that was eventually formed from its ranks followed
the same practice.

Initially, the Secretary of the Fulton Committee was Mary Loughnane, a

Principal in the Treasury, who had been Assistant Secretary to the Priestley Royal Commission on the Civil Service of 1953–5. From the fourth meeting, on 5 April 1966 until the end of its work, Michael A. Simons, an Assistant Principal from the Ministry of Labour, acted as Assistant Secretary to the Committee. At the ninth meeting held on 19 May 1966, the Chairman announced that, at her own suggestion, Miss Loughnane was being relieved of the Secretaryship on grounds of health and that she was being succeeded by R. W. L. Wilding, a Principal from the Treasury. Miss Loughnane, Wilding and Simons all attended that meeting, and the tenth held on 17 May 1966 (PRO: BA1/2), but after that the secretariat comprised Wilding and Simons. 'Most Secretaries learn the job by doing it' according to one informed study of committees of inquiry, although there were perfunctory *Notes for the Guidance of Secretaries* available (Bulmer, 1983, p.1). 'I took over the Secretaryship from Miss Mary Loughnane in May 1966', Richard Wilding recalled, and 'she had already made some plans and laid some foundations. That was certainly a help. Molly had learnt the job by being Assistant Secretary to the Priestley Commission. Otherwise, it was a question of applying thought and commonsense; in a *technical* sense, the task is not difficult' (letter to author, 24.3.89).

'The Fulton Committee was fairly chaotic', according to Wilding; 'The taking of oral evidence went on far too long, and certainly beyond the point where diminishing returns had set in. For the first fifteen months, the Committee wasted an awful lot of time. Things got better when Norman Hunt produced his first draft, as this concentrated the Committee's mind' (Interview, 1988). Michael Simons too, thought, that the Fulton Committee wasted a lot of time.

> Certainly, it took too much time taking oral evidence from a randomish selection of witnesses. After all, only two views of the Civil Service really mattered. One was that of the public, which got the rough side of it, as in the Department of Health and Social Security, although whether it had informed views about the Civil Service may be doubted. The other view of the Civil Service that mattered was that of Ministers. Of the Ministers and former Ministers who gave evidence, Reginald Maudling and Enoch Powell were the most pro-Civil Service, and Richard Crossman was the only really hostile witness among the politicians, possibly as a consequence of having had to deal with Dame Evelyn Sharp when he had been Minister of Housing and Local Government. Crossman was the witness that the Committee took most notice of (Interview, 1989).

Its terms of reference required the Fulton Committee to review the career Home Civil Service *qua* Service, and so its consultations had to be wider than those with ministers, even if it did not choose to find out what the public at large thought of the Civil Service. When the question was put at the opening meeting of the Committee about why it had been appointed, Sir James Dunnett suggested that one of the reasons was the malaise felt and expressed, particularly about the Higher Civil Service, in various quarters. He agreed to write on the matter, and he did so the next day, 11 March 1966, in a letter to Fulton. A copy of this letter was circulated to each member of the Committee. For some reason, a copy was not retained among the Committee's papers, even though discussion about the letter took place at the meeting on 15 March 1966 (PRO: BA1/2).

In his letter Dunnett doubted that there was much public interest in the Civil Service, but he did think that academics and, as a consequence, journalists perceived there to be a malaise which, to some extent, was felt within the Service's ranks too. He thought that what had developed into a criticism of the Higher Civil Service as a whole owed its origin and was largely based on academic criticism of the way that the Treasury was running the economy. This had led other academics in such fields as public administration to think that because France's economic performance had come to be better than that of Britain this was attributable to French administrative superiority. He doubted how far this deduction was valid, but added that his personal view was that

> our public administration did not do particularly well in the period from about 1951 to 1956/57. I think that this was in part due to the fact that during this period Permanent Secretaries were allowed, if not actually encouraged, to stay until 65, and that at any rate in some departments the higher direction was somewhat out of touch with the problems that needed tackling. I can give examples from my own experience of the way in which (it seems to me) there was a substantial advance from 1957 onwards in various fields, e.g. economic targets for the nationalized industries, which was due in part at least to the policy laid down by Sir Norman Brook that Permanent Secretaries should normally retire at 60. Sir James thought that the greatest impediment to efficient and vigorous administration, certainly in those departments that can be broadly called economic, is the lack of qualified statisticians and economists.

As for a sense of malaise within the Civil Service, Dunnett did not detect this in the Administrative Class outside the defence area, though the pressure of work at Principal and Assistant Secretary Level had grown considerably in recent years, with the risk of adverse effects on morale. Sir James recognised that what he called 'the present split between the Administrative Class and the Executive Class' might be a cause of discontent among members of the latter; and he wrote too that, despite changes in recent years, there was 'little doubt that in those departments that employ a large number of scientists and engineers there is a real problem of the relationship between these people and administrators' (Simey Papers: Box 5337).

At its first meeting there was general agreement on the Committee that all of its meetings, including those at which oral evidence was heard, should be held in private and that the proceedings should be treated as confidential to the Committee. It was agreed provisionally that in general written evidence should be published and that oral evidence should not, although this might need to be modified in the light of the actual evidence received and the views of particular witnesses about publication. At its second meeting, the Committee drew up a list of persons and organisations to be invited to give evidence, which was not to be substantially expanded later. At the opening meeting, Sir Philip Allen said that the Treasury hoped to let the Committee have by the end of March a factual memorandum which would describe the organisation of the Civil Service and would contain a good deal of information about the recruitment (including educational qualifications), numbers, duties, pay and conditions of service of the various classes. Allen added that the Treasury had also done some preliminary work on collecting information about the Civil Service as it was organised in France and in the USA, and that this could be made available very quickly. This latter material, together with some prepared by Norman Hunt on the same subject, was made available for and discussed at the Committee's sixth meeting on 19 April 1966 (PRO: BA1/2). At that meeting, too, the Treasury's factual memorandum was circulated in page proof form (PRO: BA1/13), and by the Committee's ninth meeting on 10 May 1966 a Treasury paper on the future structure of the Civil Service had been made available too (PRO: BA1/2).

The manner in which the Fulton Committee treated the oral evidence that was presented to it was peculiar. There had been instances even of Royal Commissions not publishing oral evidence before, and, in some instances, written evidence too, with the saving of money being a motive for this practice in the inter-war period (Clokie and Robinson, 1937, p.180). Economy of this kind was not a consideration in the Keynesian 1960s. Most of the individual departmental reports supporting the thesis of the Northcote-Trevelyan Report had been published, and no other committee of inquiry before the Fulton Committee that was seen as conducting a general review of the Civil Service had not published its formal evidence in full. Treasury and Civil Service Commission witnesses and other civil servants, who had appeared before the House of Commons Select Committee on Estimates as part of what, at the time of Fulton, were its then recent reviews of Civil Service organisation and work, had their oral evidence published. While the Plowden Committee on the Control of Public Expenditure had been intentionally an internal inquiry, the role of the Fulton Committee, aside obviously from status, had more in common with that of the Select Committee on Estimates. When the Chairman told witnesses that they could speak freely before the Fulton Committee because what they said was not for publication, it was unclear what they were at all likely to say that merited such reassurance when earlier inquiries into the Civil Service had felt no need to offer it.

The taking of oral evidence began at the third meeting of the Committee, held on 22 March 1966, when Sir Richard Way and Sir Herbert Andrew, two Permanent Secretaries on a list of such prospective witnesses drawn up by Allen and Dunnett, appeared separately before the Committee. Early witnesses included other Permanent Secretaries, together with 'witnesses representing the two main lines of criticism of the Civil Service: dilettantism and inequality of opportunity for the scientist and professional as compared with the administrator'. Thomas Balogh made two early appearances, having swiftly produced memoranda. The view of some members that the Committee should concentrate on taking oral evidence from civil servants and ex-civil servants, ministers and ex-ministers, and academic witnesses before going on to take evidence from what it saw as the Service's 'customers' and other organisations was the practice broadly followed (PRO: BA1/2). When it came to the selection of ministers and ex-ministers to appear before the Committee, Allen at least became anxious about the matter of political balance. Boyle proposed that Reginald Maudling should give evidence. Allen pointed out to him that, if Maudling did so, this meant that a Conservative ex-Chancellor of the Exchequer would appear before the Committee whereas there was no Labour counterpart. The current holder of the post, James Callaghan, would wish to reserve his position. Allen's solution to what he perceived as a problem was to invite Lord (formerly R. A.) Butler to give evidence on the basis of his 'uniquely wide experience of Ministerial office', and for discussion with Maudling to take place 'on a rather less formal basis, perhaps by arranging for some members of the Committee to meet him over a meal.' Such an arrangement would avoid 'any awkwardness which might arise when we came to publish the list of witnesses who had actually appeared before the Committee at formal sessions' (Boyle Papers: MS 660/36765). Lord Butler did not give evidence to the Committee, but Maudling did, and on a formal basis too. Boyle, in effect, insisted on this, pointing out, for instance, that Maudling had been 'Chancellor at the time of the major reorganisation of the Treasury in 1962' (Boyle Papers: MS 660/36766). Privately, in a letter to William Whitelaw, who was also to give evidence, Boyle observed: 'Sir Philip [Allen] is a nice and admirable man, but one cannot help being a little amused when one is reminded of the "style" of these worthy knights: anyone would think he was writing about some really weighty issue like defence expenditure or the balance of payments!' (Boyle Papers: MS 660/36767).

The Fulton Committee displayed an amateur method in dealing with its oral evidence. Initially, most members of the Committee even believed that there was no need for a verbatim record, provided that a full note was taken by the Secretary (PRO: BA1/2). As there was to be a full record available of all the other formal evidence, effectively this policy was to treat the oral evidence as being of lesser importance. If this was actually the belief of the Committee, or at least most or some of its members, the amount of oral evidence taken was remarkable, as, indeed, was the fact that such evidence was still being heard as late as March 1968. Inevitably, it was not long before the practice of not keeping a verbatim record had to be modified. There were complaints as early as the Committee's sixth meeting on 19 April 1966 about the manner in which the evidence of the Permanent Secretaries that had appeared before the Committee was being recorded (PRO: BA1/2); and at the Committee's twelfth meeting on 31 May 1966, Hunt complained that some of the points made by Nicholas Kaldor when giving evidence seven days earlier had been omitted from the summary submitted by the Secretariat. The Committee agreed that the oral evidence of most of those who came to talk informally with the Committee should continue to be recorded in précis form, which would inevitably be to some extent selective, but that it would be desirable to take a verbatim record of some of the meetings, and the Committee would decide in advance which should be handled in this way. The first verbatim record was taken at the fifteenth meeting on 21 June 1966 (PRO: BA1/3). At the thirty-first meeting, held on 13 December 1966, the Secretaries were instructed to prepare and circulate summaries of the evidence given at future sessions, in addition to any verbatim transcripts which were also taken (PRO: BA1/5).

Norman Hunt eventually pressed for the publication of the oral evidence (PRO: BA1/55) to the alarm of the Secretariat. Richard Wilding circulated a note which said that

> in practice those giving oral evidence have been assured virtually always in writing when being invited to attend and very often orally by the Chairman at the beginning of the session as well, that the record which was being taken was for the Committee's domestic use only and was not for publication; they were invited to take advantage of this to speak frankly and informally. These assurances covered both sessions with individuals (which have been mainly recorded by secretarial summary) and with representatives of bodies (many verbatim). In answer to enquiries by witnesses about the verbatim records, I have said that while the Committee have not yet taken decisions on publication, my understanding is that the records will not be published as such but that the Committee may wish to quote particular statements; and that if they do, the witnesses will be consulted first (PRO: BA1/46).

At its meeting on 5 December 1967 the Committee agreed that 'because of the assurances of confidentiality which, as decided by the Committee from the beginning, had been given to witnesses, and because of the character of the records, it could not publish the records of oral evidence, where the only records were the summaries prepared by the Secretaries from their notes. In cases where a verbatim transcript had been made, the same assurances had been given. It was thought nevertheless that the possibility of publishing these transcripts was worth consideration' (PRO: BA1/10). The Committee took no decision on this, though, and in February 1968 it had to be asked to take one by the Secretariat (PRO: BA1/49). Consultations took place with the Treasury, and on 2 April 1968 the Committee decided not to publish any of the oral evidence presented to it (PRO: BA1/11).

This outcome was always likely, given that assurances about confidentiality had been given to witnesses from the outset, and that the oral evidence was recorded in an incomplete form. Unless it was in imitation of the Northcote-Trevelyan exercise, quite why the Fulton Committee felt that, unlike other earlier inquiries into the Civil Service intended to be of a broad kind, it could dispense with fully recorded oral evidence remains a mystery. The contemporaneous Redcliffe-Maud, Wheatley, and Donovan Royal Commissions took and recorded oral evidence in the traditional manner and with advantage. Of course, the conventional wisdom about the value of oral evidence to committees of inquiry had become that of the Webbs who had observed that 'of all recognized sources of information . . . oral "evidence" . . . has proved to be the least profitable. Considering the time spent in listening to it, or even in rapidly reading and analysing these interminable questions and answers – still more, the money spent over them – the yield of solid fact is absurdly small' (Webbs, 1932, p. 142). In practice, though, when it suited their interests, the Webbs made considerable use of what had been said in oral evidence, as was the case, for example, with the Minority Report of the Hamilton Royal Commission on the Poor Laws and Relief of Distress of 1905–09 (Cd. 4499, 1909, pp.719–1238). The reports of Royal Commissions on the Civil Service have certainly benefited from taking account of oral evidence. Indeed, the oral evidence that W. J. Brown gave to the MacDonnell Commission and that which Sir Warren Fisher presented to the Tomlin Commission was the most telling of all the evidence that those bodies received.

As things turned out, the Fulton Committee's oral evidence, even in summary, tended to have more originality than the general run of written evidence. It remains unclear from Norman Hunt's papers, and other papers too, why against the odds he pressed so hard for the publication of the oral evidence. One reason that could have been advanced was that, given that the Committee was always unlikely to be able to resist making recommendations in favour of less secrecy in the conduct of public policy, it was open to the criticism that it did not practice what it preached. After all, if, despite the contrary examples of the past, the Committee accepted that, without assurances about lack of publicity, witnesses would not speak frankly before it even though it was only a committee of inquiry, it was difficult (to put the matter mildly) to sustain an argument that a substantial measure of confidentiality was inessential to the actual and successful conduct of government.

Though the list of persons and organisations to be invited to present written evidence was decided by the Fulton Committee fairly early on, the Committee displayed a lack of urgency about obtaining this evidence, which was behaviour that was in some contrast with, for instance, the manner in which the Redcliffe-Maud Commission chose to operate (Cmd. 4040, 1969, p.7). Those asked by the Fulton Committee to submit written evidence tended to reply that they needed more explicit guidance than the initial approach to them gave about what it actually was that the Committee wanted to know. What was perhaps impolitically called 'a cockshy draft' questionnaire (PRO: BA1/13) was submitted by Miss Loughnane to the Committee's tenth meeting on 17 May 1966. Amendments were suggested, mainly by Sir Norman Kipping (PRO: BA1/2). A revised questionnaire was drawn up with draft covering letters (PRO: BA1/14) which, at its twelfth meeting, a fortnight later, the Committee disliked, believing that the questionnaire needed to be radically shortened and made more general; while at the same time agreeing that a more detailed form of the questionnaire should be preserved and enlarged for its own use (PRO: BA1/3). Richard Wilding then submitted an outline of a general letter to be sent to those asked to submit written evidence, together with a draft note on the Committee's terms of reference which might be enclosed with the letter in place of a detailed questionnaire (PRO:BA1/15). At its thirteenth meeting, held on 7 June 1966, the Committee made more revisions, some in conflict with its earlier wish for economy of words. Those asked to submit written evidence were to be requested to do so as soon as possible after the end of September and not later than 1 December 1966 (PRO: BA1/3). The amount of overall correspondence involved in the obtaining of written evidence proved to be substantial (PRO: BA1/88, BA1/89) with, as might be expected, even the Committee's later deadline not always being observed.

The Research Commitment

At the opening meeting of the Fulton Committee there was general agreement that 'there would probably be need both for research to be undertaken by the Committee's own full time staff and for some larger scale projects to be commissioned from outside agencies.' The point was made in discussion, too, that 'the results of research undertaken or commissioned by the Committee clearly ought to be published.' At the second meeting, the need for a job analysis of Civil Service work was agreed, and the possibility of hiring management consultants to undertake it was raised (PRO: BA1/2); but, as will be seen, it was only really as a result of Norman Hunt's persistence that the Committee eventually established a Management Consultancy Group to support it. The Fulton Committee never did have 'all the help, statistical and otherwise' that it needed; but then there is no record of the Committee having asked for such help. The Redcliffe-Maud Commission appointed L. J. Sharpe of Oxford University as its Director of Intelligence, with the status of Assistant Commissioner, and the Commission was clear that its work was 'greatly assisted by the research programme that he organized for us' (Cmnd. 4040, 1969, p.7). The Fulton Committee made no such appointment and it had no full time research staff of its own, and the projects conducted by academics that it encouraged did not constitute a coherent research programme. The Committee was in no position to quantify its proposals, and it chose neither to promote original research into the history of the British Civil Service nor into the development and current organisation of the Civil Service of other countries.

The Committee agreed at its second meeting that it needed to acquaint itself not only with the Civil Service systems in the USA and France but also with those of Holland, Sweden, Western Germany, and Canada. The Committee recognised that it would be desirable for some members to visit these countries at a later stage in its investigations (PRO: BA1/2). Both the Treasury and Norman Hunt swiftly produced introductory material about the French and American Civil Services (PRO: BA1/12), which was discussed at the Committee's sixth meeting on 19 April 1966 (PRO: BA1/2). A reading list about foreign Civil Services, again of an introductory nature, compiled with the aid of Norman Hunt and very largely concerned with French, American, and Swedish arrangements, was circulated to the Committee in mid-May 1966. About that time, too, a Treasury background paper about the Canadian Civil Service was circulated (PRO: BA1/13). As its fifteenth meeting on 21 June 1966, the Committee heard oral evidence from Professor Marver Bernstein of the University of Princeton about the Civil Service in the USA (PRO: BA1/3). At the end of the same month, a note from the Treasury about the staffing and organisation of the EEC Commission was circulated (PRO: BA1/17). The Committee received other material about arrangements in the USA (PRO: BA1/34), and particularly France, including a meeting between some members of the Committee (Sir Philip Allen, Sir James Dunnett, Sir Norman Kipping, Robert Neild and Norman Hunt) and officials at the French Embassy on 27 July 1966 (PRO: BA1/19), and an interesting note by Sir Malcolm Henderson, the Deputy Chairman of the Civil Service Selection Board, about the *Ecole Nationale d'Administration* (PRO: BA1/31). Though the Fulton Committee did not lack general information about foreign Civil Services, it cannot be said that co-ordinated research into the subject took place under its aegis.

In some contrast with its earlier aspirations, the Committee concentrated its attention on the Civil Services of the USA, France and Sweden, and made its visits abroad on that basis. The visit to the USA was made by Lord Fulton and Sir Philip Allen over five days in September 1966. An undated note about it was circulated to the Committee by the latter, it would seem in November 1966 (PRO: BA1/25). The visit to France took place between 7–10 November 1966, and was made by Fulton, Dunnett, Hunt, Kipping and Neild, accompanied by Michael Simons. A note about it was circulated by Simons in February 1967 (PRO: BA1/30). The visit to Sweden took place between 6–9 February 1967, and it was made by Fulton, Anderson, Dunnett, Hunt, Kipping, Neild, Sheldon, and the Committee's Secretary. In March 1967, Richard Wilding circulated a note to the Committee about the visit which included material prepared by himself and Hunt (PRO: BA1/32).

The visits abroad would seem to have been too brief to be of much utility, but most members of the Committee and its Secretary thought differently. 'I was against prolonged foreign visits myself and I still am,' Allen observed, 'Brief visits of the kind we made give you a fair idea of what was going on' (Interview, 1988). Dunnett said that,

No useful purpose would have been served by lengthy visits to study foreign systems. To have looked at the American arrangements in much depth would have risked going outside our terms of reference. As for Sweden, after my time in the Ministry of Labour, I had got a bit bored with the Swedes. After all, Sweden is a much smaller country than Britain. France, though, was interesting. Three of us on the Committee, including myself, interviewed Michel Debré, who told us how the French had reconstructed their Civil Service after the War. He thought that it had been a mistake not to have abolished the *Grand Corps*, who were now more powerful than ever. It amazes me that the French tolerate such an elitist system. I doubt whether we would here (Interview, 1988).

Robert Neild thought that

the visits to France and to Sweden were brief but they were useful. I knew a bit about both systems, learnt from reading and from friends. My ideas were considerably sharpened by the visits. Actually visiting the ENA and the *Ecole Polytechnique* lent precision to what had been a hazy picture. We learnt too how much the different Civil Services were the product of different national histories. For example, the Swedish autonomous boards had been established when Gustav Adolphus had gone off to war and had wanted to diffuse power. What was also interesting about the Swedish system was its reliance on people with legal qualifications, although, of course, law is taught much more broadly there. It is a different tradition from our own (Interview, 1988).

Walter Anderson recalled that 'the trip to Sweden that a group of us made was very useful. The value of it was in demonstrating the difficulty of translating Swedish arrangements into our system'. Anderson said that they met a thirty-year old official who had got to the top of their Civil Service already – he was spent. There was not much point in copying such arrangements, Anderson believed, but the structure of Swedish central government had been interesting to see, and he thought that all the foreign visits had been useful ones to make (Interview, 1988). Richard Wilding considered that the foreign visits were of value (Interview, 1988), but Michael Simons did not. He said that 'Sweden seemed to be included because Robert Neild had a bee in his bonnet about the virtues of the system of government there. Neild was very impressed by the French system too, its elitism apparently not bothering either him or the rest of the Committee.' As we have noted, this was not the case with Dunnett. Simons himself was critical of the French arrangements, and some of the French higher civil servants with whom he talked were hoping that the Fulton Committee would be critical too and thus help them to promote change.

Appendix C of the Fulton Report, which was about the visits abroad and the foreign Civil Services studied, contained no criticisms of the French system, and Simons said that he was not proud to be associated with the material presented there (Interview, 1989). At one stage, the Secretariat did suggest that, given what it described as the 'amateur' nature of the material on the US Federal Civil Services, the 'best course' would be to 'publish nothing' about it (PRO: BA1/58). Independently, Robert Neild argued for this outcome too, but Wilding came to the view that not to have a note about the American visit 'would look very odd' (PRO: BA1/59). Eventually, Sir Philip Allen wrote a revised note which was circulated as late as 10 May 1968, a diffident early sentence about its value not surviving to publication (PRO: BA1/52). There seems no reason to dissent from Simon's view that 'the foreign visits that the Fulton Committee undertook did not result in serious studies of other Civil Services' (Interview, 1989).

Both the Majority and Minority Reports of the MacDonnell Royal Commission on the Civil Service of 1912–15 had included an 'historical sketch' of the development of the Service, but none of the other Royal Commissions had felt the need for such material and the Fulton Committee was slow to promote any historical research. At its sixth meeting on 19 April 1966, Fulton himself suggested to the Committee that 'it might be illuminating to commission an analytical study of the contribution made by one or two outstanding civil servants of the past.' At the next meeting, 'the general feeling was that a study showing how an outstanding individual had changed the Civil Service from inside would be extremely interesting and would be relevant to the Committee's main task of making recommendations which would attract the progressive kind of man into the Service.' Historical research of any kind did not feature on the list of research projects that the Committee drew up at its tenth meeting on 17 May 1966 (PRO: BA1/2), although the subject was discussed again at the Sunningdale Conference in June 1966 (PRO: BA1/17).

Fulton and Hunt approached various academic historians about doing research for the Committee only to be met with a lack of enthusiasm for the work involved, which the most persistently courted historian did not choose to disguise (PRO: BA1/4). On July 21st 1966, Boyle and Dunnett, on the Committee's behalf, did have a discussion with Sir Thomas Padmore about the career of Sir Warren Fisher, and a note about it was circulated to the Committee (PRO: BA1/18). Following up a suggestion originally made by its Secretary (PRO: BA1/15), the Committee agreed at Sunningdale to commission what were called 'historical essays by departments' (PRO: BA1/17). The Ministry of Defence (PRO: BA1/25), the Board of Inland Revenue (PRO: BA1/31) the Scottish Home and Health Department (PRO: BA1/32), and the Ministry of Public Building and Works (PRO: BA1/36) produced these 'essays': but, in fact, they tended to be case studies of how particular areas of work were organised and contained little history. Of more potential use to the Committee were biographies of contemporary Permanent Secretaries that the Secretariat was instructed to produce for it (PRO: BA1/14), especially when supplemented by material from the same source about the educational background and career record of Permanent Secretaries in post in 1936, 1946,

1956, as well as in 1966 (PRO: BA1/20). In response to discussion at its Sunningdale Conference, the Committee also required the Secretariat to produce details about whether or not the recommendations of past committees of inquiry into the Civil Service had been implemented (PRO: BA1/17), and the relevant summary was submitted to it in April 1967 (PRO: BA1/34).

Sir James Dunnett had found the 'historical sketch' at the beginning of the MacDonnell Majority Report to be 'an interesting account' of how the Civil Service had developed between 1853 and 1912, and in September 1967 he suggested to his fellow members of the Fulton Committee that they might benefit from reading it (PRO: BA1/43). The Committee never did commission any comparable historical research, but Dunnett, as a member of its drafting committee, did ensure that such work was undertaken. John Bourn, a member of the Administrative Class, was assigned the task, and he has since recalled:

> At the time that the Fulton Committee was at work I was a Principal and the Private Secretary to the Permanent Under Secretary of State for Defence, Sir James Dunnett, who was of course a member of the Committee. I used to put together the Fulton papers for him. One day, Sir James Dunnett came back from the committee and said that it had been discussing previous Reports on the Civil Service and, as the Secretariat was hard pressed, he asked me if I would produce an historical summary of past Reports. As I had done the BSC (Economics) degree at the LSE I knew about the earlier Reports on the Civil Service, but only in the vaguest possible way. In one sense, doing the research was a straightforward task because the Ministry of Defence Library had all the past Reports, and they were simply wheeled up to the room across the corridor that was set aside for me to do this work. Of course, I had to do my ordinary job as well, and so, during the normal working day, the research had to be fitted in between meetings. I completed the research in eight weeks, mainly by means of getting up very early in the morning and by working weekends on it. Then I sent the draft along to the Fulton Committee. They liked it, and published it. As an historian, Norman Hunt was interested in my research work, but I don't think that it had any influence on the Fulton Committee's findings (Interview, 1989).

Dr Bourn's memorandum, which was called 'The Main Reports on the British Civil Service since the Northcote-Trevelyan Report', was placed in the second part of the third volume of the published work of the Fulton Committee. As the memorandum was dated May 1968, it came too late to be of direct use to the Committee. As a summary, Bourn's work was excellent, but it was not a substitute for the large scale historical survey that the Committee had ideally needed much earlier as a basis for recommendation. As it was, it took some skill on Bourn's part to introduce what had to be brief references to Sir Warren Fisher's role as Head of the Civil Service in the inter-war period, whereas Fisher's philosophy and practice of administration was at the heart of the criticisms that many members of the Fulton Committee had of the Civil Service, and so needed to be addressed directly by them.

Of the ten Surveys and Investigations that were included in the two-part third volume of the Fulton Committee's published work, only five had been commissioned by the Committee itself, and Bourn's historical summary was one of them. The other work was done under the aegis of the Treasury, partly in response to the recommendations made by the Estimates Committee following its review of recruitment to the Civil Service. The Fulton Committee did have a role in the planning of the Executive Class Follow Up Survey (PRO: BA1/92), but none in the Survey of Wastage of Executive and Clerical Officers, or the Study of Ability, Efficiency and Job Satisfaction among Executive and Clerical Officers, or the study called Recruitment of Graduates: Survey of Student Attitudes. The memorandum entitled School Background of Members of the Administrative Class had been originally submitted by the Treasury in 1967 to the Newsom-Donnison Commission on the Public Schools of 1965–70 (PRO: BA1/62).

The Fulton Committee drew up a list of possible research projects at its tenth meeting on 17 May 1966 (PRO: BA1/2), having been informed by the Treasury during the week before about surveys and inquiries in progress following the Report of the Estimates Committee (PRO: BA1/13). At that tenth meeting the Secretariat was instructed to discuss with the Civil Service Commission the practical possibility of research being done into the relationship between performance in the various forms of competitive entry into the Administrative Class and that of their progress later on in departments (PRO: BA1/2). The Committee was then informed that Dr Edgar Anstey, Senior Principal Psychologist and head of the Commission's Research Unit, had done research of this kind although it would need to be expanded and brought up to date to meet the Committee's needs (PRO: BA1/16). At its Sunningdale Conference, the Committee made it clear that it wanted such work to be done (PRO: BA1/17), and the Administrative Class Follow Up Survey 1966 was made available to the Fulton Committee in the summer of 1967 (PRO: BA1/93) and later published in the second part of its third volume.

In his written evidence to the Estimates Committee in 1965, W. J. M. Mackenzie had suggested about recruitment to the Civil Service that 'a follow up study of unsuccessful applicants is logically necessary to complete the picture, but it is technically a very difficult job. It might however be worth trying a separate experimental study of a sample of "near misses" of various types' (HC 308, 1964–5, p.138). The Fulton Committee was reminded of this idea by Mary Loughnane (PRO: BA1/13). Professor Mackenzie had not had a study limited to the Administrative Class in mind. That was, though, what the Committee wanted. The Committee had been informed about research into recruitment to the Administrative Class that was then being done at Durham University by Dr John F. Pickering together with C. H. Dodd, and which was later published (Dodd, 1967, pp.55–80; Pickering, 1967, pp.

169–99). At its tenth meeting on 17 May 1966, the Committee decided that, after the Sunningdale Conference, Lord Simey and Norman Hunt should approach Pickering about following up its version of Mackenzie's idea (PRO: BA1/2).

Though Sir Norman Kipping, for one, found Pickering's project to be 'unattractive', it was nevertheless proceeded with on the assumption that the resulting report would be ready to be circulated to the Committee by not later than 1 April 1967 (PRO: BA1/75). In fact, the final version of the report was circulated on 19 May 1967. In an accompanying note, Richard Wilding observed that

> Dr Pickering has been remarkably successful in tracing the candidates of 1951 and the response rate has been high. He has also devised an ingenious method of comparing the 'success' achieved by people in different employments. The validity of the method is a matter of judgment, but there is, I think, a sufficient amount of fact in the report to justify his conclusion that those who did not enter the Service in 1951 have done about as well as those who did. It is however interesting – and reassuring – to note that there is a correlation between subsequent success and performance in the entry competition. Those who were successful but declined appointment (whom the study also covers) have done particularly well, and broadly speaking the closer an unsuccessful candidate came to being selected, the better he has done since (PRO: BA1/36).

Pickering was not asked to discuss his findings with the Fulton Committee and there is no formal record of discussion of them on the Committee's part.

The Committee 'discussed the possibility of commissioning a sociologist to do some work on the Administrative Class' at its Sunningdale Conference in late June 1966. The Committee was divided about the utility of such a research project and about what form it should take, although it was agreed that 'any commissioned study would have to be done quickly.' Lord Fulton and Lord Simey were asked to take soundings among prominent sociologists (PRO: BA1/17). In the meantime, Lord Simey took an initiative of his own. Writing from the University of Liverpool on 27 June 1966, Simey told Fulton that 'I saw my colleague this morning, Dr Chapman of the Department of Political Theory and Institutions, late of the Civil Service ... I told him about my idea that we might do a survey of the age group of Assistant Principals over the last ten years and he was strongly attracted by it. I think he would do the job himself if asked.' The Chairman replied on 29 June 1966:

> On the question about Chapman, I have talked to Wilding. He tells me that the Civil Service Commission is producing the statistics on the Assistant Principals over the last ten years. I have said to him that in principle I am in favour of Chapman being given this material and asked him to do a survey on it. He will be writing to you to make one or two further enquiries about the nature of the survey you have in mind in

order that there should be no crossing of wires with the research that we have commissioned last weekend. Unless any snag occurs I think you should be free to rope in Chapman for the job you suggest. It is very good of you to take the trouble over it (Simey Papers: Box 5337).

There was no conflict between the research work commissioned at the Sunningdale Conference and Simey's proposal, which he then put to the Committee's seventeenth meeting on July 5th 1966. Simey informed the meeting about his discussion with Chapman and the research project envisaged:

The idea would be to take the direct Assistant Principal entry of 1956 and trace their history through their first ten years in the Service. Each of those concerned would be sent a questionnaire, to be followed up by personal interview, the departments would not need to play any part beyond agreeing that the exercise should be undertaken, and the Civil Service Commission would be asked simply to supply the names of the 1956 entry and their departments. The object would be to examine the sort of people who came into the Administrative Class by direct entry, what happened to them, and what they thought of their experiences.

The Committee agreed that it would be a useful project (PRO: BA1/3).

The Treasury learnt that there was to be 'one more research project' from Wilding in a letter dated 8 July 1966, which described the exercise as 'fairly painless' (PRO: BA1/74). Richard Chapman's study, *Portrait of a Profession. The 1956 Entry into the Administrative Class*, proved to be a professional piece of work in the best sense. For a start, he met his deadline, which was the end of February 1967. Indeed, his report was circulated to the Committee on 27 February 1967. In an accompanying note, Wilding described Chapman's study as 'an interesting and useful report,' and among the 'careful findings' that, with some justice, Wilding thought to be particularly interesting, was the material on the political opinions of Civil Servants and on their attitudes towards their work, especially on when they decided to join the Civil Service, which was relevant to the question of whether the Committee should recommend certain first degree courses as preferred educational background (PRO: BA1/31). Chapman was not invited to discuss his research findings with the Fulton Committee: the Committee was simply made aware of them. Lord Simey, at least, was pleased, believing Chapman's work to be 'valuable and useful' and suitable for publication in its own right (PRO: BA1/74). This was just as well, given the delays in the completion of the Social Survey of the Civil Service that the Committee commissioned, a saga which merits separate consideration.

The Social Survey of the Civil Service

The Social Survey of the Civil Service, which formed the first part of the third volume of the Fulton Committee's published work had a troubled history from its conception to its eventual, and very late, publication. The Committee had not envisaged commissioning such a Survey either at the meetings at which it drew up its original list of research projects or at its Sunningdale Conference. The idea for a Survey arose out of meetings held in the summer and early autumn of 1966 initially convened to mainly discuss the details of the Chapman and Pickering projects. These meetings were attended by Lord Simey and Norman Hunt and by Chapman and Pickering, as well as by what Hunt called 'sociologists.' A. H. Halsey of the University of Oxford, R. K. Kelsall of the University of Sheffield, and Tom Burns of the University of Edinburgh would seem to attract such a description without the inverted commas, even if F. F. Ridley of the University of Liverpool, who attended some of the meetings, did not. Statistical advice was produced by Louis Moss of the Government Social Survey, Richard Layard of the LSE who had assisted Claus Moser in his work for the Robbins Committee on Higher Education of 1961–3, and W. Tjaden of the Treasury's Management Statistics Division.

Of a meeting held on 16 September 1966, and attended by all of the above apart from the statistical advisers, Hunt told the main Fulton Committee at its twenty first meeting four days later that two things had been agreed. The first was that the Committee needed a 'sociological picture' of the Civil Service as a basis for its work, and that

> this could be done by sending a carefully drafted questionnaire to a sample of each of the different classes of the Civil Service, which would be designed to elicit both demographic facts (social class, educational background, career in the Service etc.) and attitudes to the Service. The processed results should then be written up for the Committee by a professional sociologist with a paid research assistant.

Hunt said that this exercise was to be co-ordinated with the Chapman and Pickering projects 'in order to provide integrated results.' It was also important that the material collected should be related to 'what was known about other professions.' The second thing that Hunt and Simey, Chapman and Pickering, and the 'sociologists', had agreed about had been that the Committee needed to have details of 'the supply and demand for qualified manpower for and by the various professions' (PRO: BA1/4). In fact, at its Sunningdale Conference, the Committee had already identified the need for such information (PRO: BA1/17), and the Treasury and the Civil Service Commission had already made relevant material available in the summer of 1966 (PRO: BA1/19). Further material about the output of the educational system and the demand for qualified manpower was to be forthcoming, including some from the Department of Education and Science (PRO: BA1/49) that was to appear in the fourth volume of the Fulton Committee's published work.

News of the 'proposed Sociological Investigation' was received without enthusiasm in the Treasury. K. E. Couzens wrote to Richard Wilding on 27 September 1966 about 'our doubts and the pitfalls.' Couzens observed that 'if we complete our own survey into efficiency/job satisfaction of Executive Officers and Clerical Officers by mid-1967 (as we hope so to do) it will have taken us two years to plan, execute, and bring it to fruition. You are being asked to consider doing a much wider ranging project in six months.' Couzens added that 'departments already are assisting with three management surveys-wastage, the E.O. follow up survey and the efficiency/job satisfaction survey. They will not be keen to take on a fourth.' Then there was the problem of the response rate. Couzens said that 'M.S.(G) has sweated blood (on follow up work) to obtain an 80–90 per cent response to our own survey' even though it was about 'job attitude and job satisfaction and respondents could see that they might obtain some benefit (however small and long term) from participating.' Couzens doubted 'whether individuals will respond sufficiently well to questions on social background, outside activities etc,' and said 'our experience has also shown that officers forget or become confused about their own background.' Wilding replied to Couzens on 6 October 1966 that 'I take the point that some people may not like saying that their fathers were bricklayers, but I would hope that the fact that the Fulton Committee not the management were asking these questions might be helpful, especially if a covering letter took care to explain why the Committee had a genuine interest in the extent to which the Service reflected the society it was serving' (PRO: BA1/76).

Wilding wrote to both Lord Fulton and Norman Hunt on 13 October 1966 to try to get the business moved along and to have the matter of the socio-logical investigation settled one way or the other: 'May I in confidence as between Secretary and Chairman send you a copy of a letter which I have written to Norman Hunt about our proposed sociological investigation?' Wilding told Fulton that Hunt was pursuing this with very great energy.

> A good deal of work is going into it by way of meetings and examining the possible sources of information etc; and if this exercise gets launched, this will be due in very large measure to him. The same is true, as you know, of the large scale management consultant exercise which is now under way and in which he is taking the leading part. But while I feel sure that the management consultant exercise is now soundly based and ought to produce some valuable results, I feel some uneasiness about the sociological investigation for the reasons set out in the enclosed letter. If I may say this without impertinence, I have come to form a great respect for Norman, but he is an enthusiast and is apt to override other people's hesitations. My impression is that he may to some extent have ridden over those of Halsey and Kelsall in relation to this project. They may now be fully converted and my fears may be completely set at rest at next week's meeting. But I do not feel sure about this, and, while I am a complete novice in this field, I have been impressed by what more knowledgeable people have said to me about the pitfalls and dangers of hastily constructed questionnaires, especially if they deal with attitudes and the building up of multi-dimensional pictures (PRO: BA1/76).

Wilding's letter to Hunt was simply headed 'Sociology', and it related to 'the possible reception of a Report which is partly based on a sociological investigation which, as we all agree, can only be a limited one in the time available.' (PRO: BA1/76).

'I may be allowing a personal scepticism about sociology to erect unnecessary fears' Wilding wrote to Sir Philip Allen on 13 October 1966 (PRO: BA1/76). Whether this was the case or not, the meeting with 'the sociologists' on 18 October did not take the form anticipated. Though he had 'not yet recovered from the shock' of the meeting held the previous day, Simey displayed some 'scepticism' of his own in a letter written to Wilding on 19 October. What had 'shocked' Simey was what he saw as 'the highly unpleasant criticisms' of the eventual Fulton Report that had been 'threatened yesterday' by some of those present at the meeting if the sociological investigation did not proceed. Simey found their line to be 'irresponsible' and 'most dangerous' and to require 'avoiding action' on the part of the Committee. Simey said that he could see that the 'Fulton Report could not be based solely on miscellaneous conversations with people like Sir Antony Part and most of the other witnesses we have seen,' even though this oral evidence had been 'illuminating and often pleasant.' This did not mean, however, that the proposed sociological investigation was needed. 'We should, I think, drop the idea completely forthwith,' Simey wrote. This was because the work could not be done properly in the time available, and because of Simey's own belief that 'all these detailed researches of the kind Kelsall has been involved in concerning correlations between different kinds of education and progress in the Civil Service are old hat, and I don't think that much more can be got out of that. I would prefer to look at the problem of correlating output from the educational system in general with the entry to the Civil Service, and leave things at that.' Simey said that the Committee needed 'as much material based on mild research' as it could get in order to 'forestall criticisms,' and he thought that 'a substantial volume of statistics' derived from Treasury enquiries and published possibly some months after the main Report itself would help (Simey Papers: Box 5337).

Wilding replied to Simey's letter about the proposed sociological investigation on 24 October:

> I am sorry, if not altogether surprised, that you felt upset about last Tuesday's meeting. On the value of this exercise I must, as Secretary, be neutral. But I do think it most important that the decision should not be taken without a thorough and searching discussion on 1st November, and I am leaving room for this in the programme. I hope, therefore, that you will press your point of view. A paper will be coming round containing the proposal as it was put together after you had left us last Tuesday. One point which we must bring out is that the project will involve a great deal of work against a very tight timetable. In my judgment, we should have about a fifty-fifty chance of producing valid results by next May; allowing for the hitches that always bedevil such

operations, I doubt if the prospects can realistically be assessed in much more optimistic terms than that. On the other hand, Halsey and Kelsall are now convinced that the exercise is desirable and possible; and we must reckon that they will criticize us and stimulate others to do likewise if we now drop it (PRO: BA1/77).

It was obvious by this stage that the sociological investigation was going to proceed whatever the objections to it. As Wilding wrote to A. Collier of the Treasury in a letter dated 20 October 1966, 'Lord Fulton in particular is enthusiastic for a project in this field', and as Simey wrote to Wilding on 25 October, 'Hunt seemed to wish to go on anyway.' Nevertheless, given that in his opinion the project was still 'in a state of some confusion,' Wilding felt the need to write to Fulton on 27 October to say that 'I have come to the conclusion (and Tom Simey told me a little time ago that his was the same) that I ought to recommend to you that the project in this form should be dropped.' Wilding said that there was 'a serious danger that the project would break down' meaning that it would not be 'ready in time to influence the Committee's thought, and will be unsatisfactory when it does emerge.' Wilding gave several reasons for being pessimistic about the project, but the main one was that Halsey had too many commitments at Oxford and in advising government departments to provide 'the directing mind' that the project needed in its vital preparatory period. Furthermore, the survey work itself would have to be completed with unusual smoothness and speed, given that Halsey had only the Easter vacation 1967 in which to write up the findings. In a letter to a Treasury colleague, Dr S. Rosenbaum, on 28 October 1966, Wilding said that he had some hopes that the project would now be dropped: 'If not, I fear that we shall have to revert to the idea that the Treasury should do what it can to help and hope for the best. If however it is dropped, I should expect the Committee to want to substitute a more limited exercise based on the records of the Civil Service Commission.' In a letter to Simey the same day, Wilding told him that he had come to the conclusion that 'whatever the merits of the project in principle it is almost certainly unworkable in practice.' Simey was also told the unsurprising news that Hunt did not share this view (PRO: BA1/77).

At the Fulton Committee's twenty-sixth meeting on 1 November 1966, Norman Hunt outlined the proposal for a 'Sociological project', and informed it that A. H. Halsey had offered to write up the results of the questionnaire for the Committee. This would produce 'a skeletal outline of the profession rather than a full portrait,' but Hunt thought there were two main arguments in favour of proceeding with the questionnaire. The first was that

> it might produce information which would be directly relevant to the Committee's recommendations. For example, if it showed the Civil Service to be out of touch with the rest of the world, this would lend weight to the recommendations for secondments to industry etc.; gaps in the social and geographical origins of recruits might suggest untapped

sources of talent or a need to give young civil servants training in the provinces. More generally, one could not tell in advance exactly what practical implications might be suggested by the results, but the Committee could not conclude that a sociological questionnaire would be barren in this respect unless they tried it.

Hunt's second main argument was that 'it would be important from the presentational point of view to show that the Committee had done their best in the time available to examine the sociological aspects of the Civil Service.'

Hunt then indicated some of the practical problems that the project involved, and a discussion followed which revealed that the Committee was divided about the merits of proceeding with this work (PRO: BA1/5). Michael Simons recalled: 'In the case of the Halsey exercise, Lord Fulton summed up against the sense of the meeting. He wanted the Halsey thing and he was supported by Norman Hunt, Edward Boyle, and Ned Dunnett who said that the Committee would look naked without something of this kind. Robert Neild presented a devastating case against having the Halsey exercise done. Neild was backed by Sheldon, Simey, who was after all a social scientist, Cook, Anderson, and Philip Allen. Kipping and Wall were absent but there was no cause to assume that they would support the idea of the Halsey survey. So, on a count of heads, a majority of the Fulton Committee was against the Halsey exercise, and the balance of reasoning power was against it too, but Lord Fulton still summed up the sense of the meeting as being in favour' (Interview, 1989).

Though the Chairman obviously has a special role to play on a committee of enquiry, Lord Fulton's behaviour in this instance did depart from the ground rules laid down by the Balfour Committee in 1910, which stated that appointment in that role 'does not impose upon a Chairman responsibilities or duties of a nature which would justify him at any time in attempting to disregard, still less to override, the deliberate opinion of his colleagues or of dictating to them what shall or shall not be done' (Cd.5235, 1910, para. 17). There was no call either for the use of a casting vote by the Chairman (ibid, para. 18), six of the ten members of the Fulton Committee present being against the Halsey survey. Nevertheless, once the Committee had decided in principle that it would produce a research-based Report, as it did at its opening meeting, Fulton and those who thought like him may well have been right in believing that in the intellectual context of the 1960s such a Report that did not at least have associated with it something resembling the Halsey survey would be commonly considered to have wilfully disregarded an obvious source of research information. In principle, too, given that, at much the same time, the Redcliffe-Maud Commission was conducting extensive survey work without any risk of damage to its credibility, it was difficult to take the full parade of official objections to the Halsey survey as such entirely seriously.

If a Director of Research had been appointed by the Fulton Committee, the need for an exercise of the Halsey kind in any modern programme of research relating to the Civil Service would most probably have been recognised at the outset. At it was, November 1966 proved to be too late a date for the Committee to be commissioning this sort of study. Moreover, while few administrative arrangements guarantee success, those made regarding this exercise invited disappointment. Richard Wilding wrote with prescience to Lord Simey on October 28th 1966:

> It is now clear to me that the project is not something that Halsey can run by remote control from Oxford. It needs a Director (not a directing Committee) who is in immediate charge of the machine and who alone can take the continuing flow of necessary decisions about the tabulations he will need, the design of the questions which will elicit them, and the grouping of the population to be questioned. You will know already how complicated these operations are and how especially important it is to get all this right in a postal questionnaire which cannot be piloted and which allows no time for interviews. I did not, but, since I have come to have some idea of it, I have become convinced that the proposed set up is most unlikely to get valid results against a very tight timetable which allows no time for hitches and misunderstandings (PRO: BA1/77).

'Mr Halsey will need a research assistant, mainly to dig up and organise for him whatever comparative material already exists about other professions and the population at large,' Wilding informed the Treasury on 2 November 1966, 'One has been found: Mr Ivor Crewe, a postgraduate student at the LSE. He will need a fee' (PRO: BA1/77). Crewe's recollection was that

> Norman Hunt was central to the exercise. A survey was his idea; he recruited Halsey and myself (I was a student of his at Oxford); he provided the main headings for the survey questionnaire; he commented on the questionnaire drafts; he suggested subjects for analysis; he requested special analyses after the main findings had been presented; he read and commented on the more important chapters; and he constantly championed the use of the survey when his colleagues on the Fulton Committee seemed sceptical or – more frequently – indifferent (letter to author: 26.11.88).

Halsey recalled Norman Hunt's recruitment of Crewe and himself to do the survey and said of Hunt that

> we had to explain at length to him what could and could not be done with survey material. He wanted very much to get at attitudes. We (I) insisted that in the short time available it would be better to concentrate on 'factual' data about careers, origins, and destinations. This gave a usable profile of Civil Service careers and their social and educational antecedents. I imagine that other members of the Fulton Committee (ie. other than Hunt) were in any case chary of incorporating attitudinal material. Norman Hunt didn't help us in any of the technicalities of the survey or its analysis (because he was inexperienced in this kind of work). His contribution was to persuade [the] Fulton [Committee] of the

desirability of the survey. Don't forget that he also persuaded them to do other in-house studies (letter to author: 1.1.88).

'Time was short. The results were required by the end of 1967 if they were to be of serious value to the Committee before it formulated its Report.' Thus runs an early sentence on the first page of the published version of the Social Survey of the Civil Service, as Halsey's report eventually came to be called. 'We were lucky,' the report added, 'the civil servants responded promptly to give us a 97 per cent response rate and the computer, exceptionally and mercifully, did not break down.' In Annexe I of the report, the questionnaire was reproduced which had been sent to 5,187 civil servants in January 1967 and which had been returned by the end of February. Norman Hunt told the Committee at its eleventh meeting of 1967 held on March 21 that 'the sociological investigation of the Civil Service was well under way.' Halsey and Crewe were said by Hunt to have received nearly all the material that they had asked for from the Government Social Survey and the Management Statistics Division of the Treasury, and they had begun writing up their findings (PRO:BA1/38).

The timetable that the Fulton Committee had in mind, though, as Wilding had told the Treasury on 2 November 1966, had been the submission of Halsey's draft report by the end of April 1967 (PRO: BA1/77). So, time was intended to be even shorter than it was later assumed in the published report to have been. Well past the deadline, Halsey was asking Louis Moss of the Government Social Survey for more material. 'We really must draw the line somewhere', Moss wrote to Wilding on 5 June 1967, though there was little prospect of this if Halsey insisted on having the information requested, which he did in a letter dated 22 June. Moss complained to Wilding on 6 July: 'Nothing in Halsey's letter explains why these extra tables are essential, and, as he himself agrees, they cannot affect the conclusions which are relevant for the Committee's purposes. The situation appears to be that he has sketched out the broad headings of a report, and without regard for the need for particular tables assumes that anything he wants to fill in under these headings can be provided' (PRO: BA1/79). So it was, eventually. What, understandably, Halsey seemed to be aiming to be aiming for was a report, publishable in its own right; and what the civil servants seemed to fear was that this report would be of a particular kind, and that some of its findings would be disagreeable.

The first draft chapters of the Halsey survey were made available to the Fulton Committee in July 1967 (PRO: BA1/33), and there was some consideration of them at the Committee's twenty-seventh meeting, which was held on 22 and 23 July at the White House, the Isle of Thorns (PRO: BA1/10) or Crown of Thorns, as Lord Simey preferred to call the location (Simey Papers: Box 5335). At that meeting it was agreed that Halsey's material would need to be read by other academics, and at the twenty-ninth meeting on August 8th 1967 it was further agreed that 'people with a knowledge of the world of business' should read it too. The Committee noted that some of Halsey's findings seemed to conflict with other evidence, and the Secretariat was instructed to check up on this (PRO: BA1/10). There then began consultations with Professors Asa Briggs, Tom Burns, R. K. Kelsall, and W. J. M. Mackenzie from academic life, and with Lord Heyworth (Unilever), Sir Henry Wilson Smith (Powell Duffryn), Dr E. G. Woodroofe, Dr T. Wilson, M. Zinkin (Unilever), and Sir Peter Runge (Tate and Lyle) from business. A batch of outside comments was circulated to the Committee in November and then early December 1967 (PRO: BA1/46), and Professor Briggs made available his observations on 28 December 1967 (PRO: BA1/47). Sir Norman Kipping chose to refer to the industrialists who helped the Committee as 'the wise men,' but the main contribution that was to be forthcoming from any of them was the making available, for the purpose of comparison, of material about Unilever, which was the 'large industrial organisation' referred to in the final report (PRO: BA1/82).

'Frankly, it is a very awkward sample design,' Claus Moser wrote of the Halsey survey in a letter to Wilding on 20 November 1967, when successfully recommending that Dr Martin Knott of the LSE should be hired to test the findings for statistical significance (PRO: BA1/81). The statisticians in the Treasury and in the Government Social Survey were very critical of the draft version of Halsey's report, and, in particular, Chapter III, which was about the Administrative Class. According to the draft, only 10 per cent of the Administrative Class as opposed to the commonly assumed 40 per cent were shown to have been promoted from the Executive Class, the difference supposedly being accounted for by transfers across from other Classes. The Fulton Committee itself picked up this mistake at its meeting on 8 August 1967 (PRO: BA1/10), and the next day Richard Wilding took the matter up with D. J. Hodgkins of the Treasury, asking for the records to be checked, and suggesting that the error followed from Halsey's 'naturally small knowledge of the Service.' Eventually, Halsey wrote to Wilding on 18 September 1967:

> Ivor Crewe and I have been thinking about the points you and Simons have raised on the distinction between 'promotees' and 'transfers' in Chapter III and of the meaning to be attached to and the conclusions to be drawn from them. It is clear that many 'transfers' on our analysis are 'promotees' in reality. We have to recognise that about half of the 'transfers' were Clerical Officers or in even more lowly positions when they first entered the Civil Service and that we ought to revise our analysis accordingly.

Richard Wilding himself spotted a flaw in the means which Halsey used to show that the post-1946 Administrative Class had become more socially exclusive than the pre-1946 Class had been, a thesis which Wilding described in a letter to Sir James Dunnett on October 3rd 1967 as being dear to Halsey's and Norman Hunt's heart. As one Treasury statistician, S. Rosenbaum, put it in an internal minute dated 28 September 1967, 'Halsey should be comparing *entrants* at two different dates, rather than cross-sections of those in post, where the youngest group is still practically all direct entrants.' When the point was put to Halsey, he recognised its validity, and, in a letter to Wilding dated 12 October 1967, he changed the divide to 1940 and asked for more information with which to make ' a more direct analysis on the lines you suggest.' Halsey emphasised that 'the analysis that we have already under-taken is sufficient to support the general interpretation of a narrowing social and educational recruitment to the Administrative Class in more recent years' (PRO: BA1/80).

The Fulton Committee devoted three of the eighteen meetings that it held in 1968 to consideration of the Halsey survey. At its second meeting of 1968, held on 23 January, the Committee had a discussion with Halsey, Crewe, and the businessmen who had commented on the draft. It has to be a matter of opinion whether the authors of the survey took much notice of Sir Edward Boyle's observation that 'in presentation it was desirable to avoid the appear-ance of an anti-middle class bias, about which a lot of people were increasingly sensitive.' At its fifth meeting, on 2 February 1968, which Crewe also attended, the Committee discussed the Halsey survey with W. J. M. Mackenzie. Little seemed to be achieved at these meetings, with discussion being mainly about direct entry recruitment to the Administrative Class.

At the Committee's seventeenth meeting, on 6 June, the draft report of what had now come to be referred to as the Social Survey of the Civil Service was discussed, and 'it was agreed that it would require substantial amendment before it could be published.' In response to critical comments made by Sir Norman Kipping, Norman Hunt said that 'there was interesting and impor-tant material in the Survey.' Hunt agreed, though, that 'it was not yet suitable for publication; in addition to mistakes of fact, logical errors, obscurity, and turgidity, of expression, and the other criticisms that had been made, it showed insufficient understanding of the Civil Service.' For example, the authors of the Survey 'did not appear to appreciate that much of its findings about the pattern of educational qualifications were attributable to the Ser-vice's requirements for entry at different levels.' Hunt said that the Survey needed re-drafting, but he doubted whether Dr Halsey would have time to do it during the coming months. Hunt then volunteered to prepare drafts for Halsey if the Committee wished, which it did, and if Halsey himself agreed, which he was later to do. The re-drafting work was expected to take two or three months. Once the Fulton Report itself had been published, a sub-committee was to be kept in existence to clear the eventual draft. The Com-mittee thought that 'it would be wrong to hold up the other studies to be published in Volume 3 until the report of the Social Survey was completed. It was therefore agreed that the Volume should be divided into two parts to be published separately' (PRO: BA1/11).

Under the heading 'Halsey Survey', Richard Wilding wrote to the members of the Fulton Committee from the Civil Service Department in April 1969 (the precise date not being recorded):

> You will no doubt have been wondering what has become of this Survey, which is to be published as Volume 3 (1) of the evidence to the Fulton Report. Here at last is the revised text and tables with covering note by Norman Hunt who has laboured long and strenuously with Halsey to make improvements over the version which you last saw. As Norman says, he has not been able to do as much as he had wished and you may notice things that still seem capable of improvement. I hope however that you will agree that we should now get the report printed without seeking to amend it further, for two reasons. First, a lot of time has been spent on improving the report this far, and its non-appearance is already causing embarrassment, notably to the Committee which is conducting the inquiry into Method II recommended in our Appendix E and whose work is being held up. Secondly, Halsey has, as Norman reports, made quite a number of alterations. He is not prepared to make further alterations to meet the points on which the Civil Service Commission are not satisfied, and I suspect that if we raise additional points that occur to members of the Committee, this will certainly take time and may not in the end produce results.

In an accompanying note, Norman Hunt wrote, 'I had hoped to be able completely to reorganize and rewrite the Halsey Survey,' but this 'proved impossible,' not least because 'it would have meant omitting a great deal of material to which Crewe and Halsey attached considerable importance.' Hunt said that the most that he had been able to achieve was 'some tidying up of the text,' and 'mediating between Halsey and the Civil Service Commission as a result of which Halsey has made substantial modifications to the text to meet many (but not all) of the points which the Commission raised.' Hunt had also managed 'to produce a summary of the main findings of this report. This is the new Chapter XIII – though even this Chapter has now become longer and more detailed than I would have liked as a result of a good deal of to-ing and fro-ing between Halsey and the Civil Service Commission' (PRO: BA1/84).

Controversy dogged the Social Survey of the Civil Service all the way down to publication. Even the Press Notice was one source of contention. 'Crewe and Hunt are now cooking up some additional paragraphs which sounded as if they might be a little controversial,' B. Strong of the Civil Service Commission wrote to another official there on 11 September 1969; 'Our dilemma here is just another result of our unfortunate role as both publisher and victim of the author.' Strong added: 'Do we really want to say the conclusions were unexpected? Apart from the fact that it makes us sound as if we did not know what kind of people we were recruiting (and, after all, much of the critical data was supplied to Halsey by the Commission), my impression was that the Survey brings out the very conclusions Halsey expected to find.' The revised Press Notice included Crewe's textual changes and was enlarged to place less emphasis on the Administrative Class (PRO: BA1/84). Then, again, there was a long delay in publication of the Halsey Survey between April 1969 when the final version was made available, and September 1969 when it was actually published. No explanation for this delay is to be found in the Fulton Committee's papers. Ivor Crewe has since suggested that 'the Treasury deliberately waited until the Davies Report, which said much kinder things about selection procedures, was ready for simultaneous publication' (letter to author: 26.10.88). Even if the Treasury did behave in this manner, the opportunity would not have presented itself had there not been earlier delays.

The Social Survey of the Civil Service seemed at the time and it seems now to be an interesting piece of research, even though, in its preparation, its authors had to run the gauntlet of criticism, some of which, at times, savoured of undue trepidation about what the researchers might discover. The Survey did include some uncomfortable facts about the social composition of the direct entry to the Administrative Class, but there was no suggestion that it was any more exclusive than either higher management in the British private sector or the Higher Civil Services of other countries. The much mulled-over Chapter III about the Administrative Class proved to be less interesting than some of the other chapters, notably those relating to the often otherwise neglected Executive and Clerical Classes, and Chapter VII on the Works Group of Professional Classes dealt well with a commonly ignored area of the Civil Service. Much of the supporting material that accompanied the Survey's findings was known to specialists in the public administration anyway, but information was also published that might well not have been elicited except by an investigation associated with an official committee of inquiry. When it was finally published, the Social Survey of the Civil Service did represent a contribution to knowledge, but Halsey's self-indulgent attitude towards deadlines neither furthered the Fulton Committee's work nor helped his fellow researchers. To take one example, Richard Chapman would have preferred to have done a comparative cohort study of Administrative Class entrants in 1951, 1956, and 1961, but his deadline, which he observed, did not make this seem feasible (letter to author: 21.5.90). As things turned out, there would have been plenty of time in which to do this work.

None of the surviving members of the Fulton Committee, nor the members of its Secretariat, nor the researchers themselves believed that the Halsey, Chapman or Pickering projects had any influence on the Committee's Report. Ivor Crewe observed that 'I remember thinking that the survey research seemed very much a separate and unconnected exercise, something tolerated by the Committee members as one of Norman Hunt's whims, but also something that major Committees were then expected to do (cf. Donovan, Robbins)' (letter to author: 26.10.88). Halsey thought that the Social Survey of the Civil Services was 'an afterthought, reflective of Robbins, pressed by

Norman Hunt,' and such influence as it had was on the Davies Committee
on recruitment to the Administrative Class (letter to author: 1.11.88). 'The
Halsey survey was interesting and it was a useful way of looking at the Civil
Service as a whole,' Robert Sheldon recalled, but he added that by the time
it was made available to the Fulton Committee 'we had already made up our
minds' (interview: 1988). Another member of the Committee, Robert Neild,
was much more critical:

> The research activity was not integrated with the Fulton Committee's
> main work. Because the Committee lacked leadership, its work was not
> organised. There was no strategy. We asked for pieces of information
> from the Treasury and from the Civil Service Commission. Halsey was
> commissioned to do his Social Survey because some people on the
> Committee felt that a Report that wasn't based on some kind of social
> research would be inadequate or unfashionable. I was sceptical through-
> out. We knew the social origins of civil servants by schools pretty well
> and what newspapers they read (Interview: 1988).

Taking Simons' 'elastic definition' of research to embrace the activities of the
Management Consultancy Group, that Group, as Neild like others acknowl-
edged, was to make an important contribution the Fulton Committee's work.
It is to the activities of that Group that we now turn.

Chapter 3

The Parallel Inquiry: the Management Consultancy Group

The Establishment of the Management Consultancy Group and its Mode of Operation

'There was general agreement that the Committee would need to undertake or commission some sort of job analysis of Civil Service work. Without a clear picture of what the various grades did or ought to be doing it would be impossible to decide what qualities were required or what changes might be needed in the structure.' Thus ran the minutes of the second meeting of the Fulton Committee held on 15 March 1966. The view was also expressed that 'in order to equip themselves to consider the question of greater mobility between the Civil Service and outside employment, the Committee would also need to make some study of work in relevant fields outside the Civil Service.' The extent to which 'the Committee should undertake these studies themselves and how much help they might be able to get from e.g. the Civil Service Pay Research Unit or firms of managements consultants' was left for later decision (PRO: BA1/2).

'The use of management consultants was relatively rare in the public sector in those days', as John Garrett, a member of the Fulton Committee's Management Consultancy Group was later to observe (Interview, 1989). The Fulton Committee was aware, though, that the Post Office, then still within the Civil Service, was currently employing McKinsey to review its postal services from its headquarters organisation downwards (HC 340, 1966–7, p.48; HC 340–I, 1966–7, pp.25, 389). The Committee expressed interest in this at its fourth meeting on 5 April 1966, as it had done in the McKinsey review of Shell at its third meeting a fortnight earlier (PRO: BA1/2).

Though no action followed, one member of the Committee, Norman Hunt, seemed to be determined that there was going to be a management consultancy exercise. In the afternoon following the Committee's ninth meeting on 10 May 1966, Hunt went to see the Postmaster General, Anthony Wedgwood Benn, about the matter. Benn recalled: 'In strictest confidentiality, I lent him a copy of the McKinsey Report on the Post Office and he took it away, promising to bring it back by hand' (Benn, 1987, p.410). At the tenth meeting of the Fulton Committee on 17 May, 'Dr Hunt suggested that the

Committee should commission a firm of outside consultants to carry out a study of a sample field of Civil Service work. He thought the Committee would be open to criticism if they did not have a detailed study made and if it were not made by an independent body.' Hunt also pressed the case for a study of staff management practice outside the Civil Service, which idea, when developed by another member, J. E. Wall, the Committee found attractive. Though doubts were expressed by some members about the benefits that would follow from employing management consultants in the planned exercises, the Committee did agree to consult Ivor Young of Urwick, Orr and Partners, then seconded to the Civil Service, about what form their involvement might take (PRO: BA1/2). In his evidence to the Fulton Committee on 31 May 1966 (PRO: BA1/3) and in a subsequently circulated letter to the Chairman dated 8 June, which had followed discussions with Norman Hunt, Young said that a mixed team including management consultants 'might produce something useful' in terms of a study of Civil Service work (PRO: BA1/15).

The Fulton Committee settled the matter at its Sunningdale Conference held from 24–26 June 1966. Young's evidence and letter were used as the basis for discussion in a note circulated by the Secretary, Richard Wilding, on 15 June (PRO: BA1/15), and at Sunningdale the Committee agreed that

> the investigations should concentrate on blocks of work in the Civil Service without paying detailed attention to outside analogues, but that the ability of the team to make comparisons with business practice should be strengthened where appropriate by the inclusion in the team of a representative of industry and commerce with experience which could be relevant to the examination of the block of work in question (PRO: BA1/17).

Ivor Young had suggested that the investigating team should submit draft terms of reference for the Committee's approval (PRO:BA1/15). Norman Hunt, though, did some pre-emptive drafting himself, presenting the following:

> 1. The basic scheme is that a mixed team composed of a member of the secretariat, one or two members of the Committee, one or more businessmen selected *ad hoc*, and two management consultants might examine in detail a number of small blocks of work in the Civil Service. The team would concentrate particular attention on the following:
>
> > a. The amount and kind of responsibility held by each officer within the block; the number of grades in the hierarchy and the flow of work (both with reference to speed and to over- and under-loading).
> > b. The specialist content of the work and the way in which specialist skills (inside and outside the block) are brought to bear.
> > c. The nature of the supporting services provided.
> > d. The qualities and skills which the work calls for.
> > e. The previous training which it calls for and how much those concerned have had.

2. In part the operation would be a detailed consideration of Civil Service work and practice matched against the knowledge possessed by members of the team of the work and practice in efficient business firms.

3. The hope would be that such an investigation would throw light on:

a. What precisely are the actual tasks performed by the Administrative Class.

b. The nature of the division between Administrative and Executive Class functions.

c. Whether there are the right number of grades in the hierarchy.

d. The relationship between administrators and specialists.

e. The extent to which an individual's skills and abilities match the needs of his job.

f. Whether there is scope for the application of business methods of personnel management.

g. The extent of the burdens imposed by accountability to Parliament and how that affects the nature of the jobs.

h. Whether the pattern of responsibilities and expertise really is best designed to secure the efficient achievement of the block's objectives.

4. As a by-product the survey could well throw some light on:

a. New *trends* in Civil Service work (it's difficult to imagine such an investigation not taking into account the directions in which the work is changing);

b. problems of interchange between the Civil Service and business;

c. Frustrations (justified or not) at all levels.

5. The next step would be for a group composed as at paragraph 1 above to meet and draw up precise terms of reference, and consider what blocks of work might be tackled. For these meetings it is essential that a Committee Permanent Secretary should be added to the group (PRO: BA1/17).

The Fulton Committee accepted Hunt's draft without amendment, and its Secretary, Richard Wilding informed the Treasury by letter on 4 July 1966 that 'the Committee has decided that it would like to set up a small team to examine in some detail a few reasonably small but representative blocks of Civil Service work'. Wilding said that it was the Committee's intention that the team should comprise two of its members, Norman Hunt and Robert Sheldon, its Assistant Secretary, Michael Simons, 'two management consultants with general experience of analyzing other employments' who would be 'members of the team throughout', and 'where appropriate, a businessman with expertise of analogous work' who would be 'selected *ad hoc* for each block where this was thought desirable'. Wilding added that the Committee had also agreed that the two Permanent Secretaries among its membership, Sir Philip Allen and Sir James Dunnett, should take responsibility for selecting the blocks of work to be investigated (PRO: BA1/70).

'Obviously we could not stop the Fulton Committee doing this if we wanted to, and I am far from sure that we would want to stop them', T. H. Caulcott of the Treasury replied on 7 July

> We have discussed this proposal in the E.M. Divisions and while Mr Ross and I are both uneasy about the approach, chiefly I think because it is evidence of the Committee being unwilling to trust us to say what happens in the Civil Service and wanting to have their own investigations, nevertheless we have no positive suggestions to make on the project itself . . . I could say that this is another indication of how far the Committee is slipping behind its original timetable for its Report. The Committee is still at the stage of initiating quite a large scale of enquiry projects. This one is certainly going to take a good time (PRO: BA1/70).

When the letters went out from the Treasury to four firms of management consultants on 13 July inviting them to tender for the work, the timetable envisaged was that a start should be made towards the end of September 1966, and that the work should be completed by the end of January 1967, with the report reaching the Fulton Committee by early March. There was an idea at one stage that two firms of consultants might be employed in harness (PRO: BA1/70). The four firms of management consultants were interviewed by Norman Hunt. Robert Sheldon attended some of the interviews and the Secretariat were present. As Michael Simons reported to the full Committee:

> McKinsey's although stimulating in some respects, ruled themselves out for three reasons: they were very expensive; they were not prepared to work in harness with another management consultant firm and it would have looked bad to employ an American firm alone; most fundamentally, they were reluctant to accept the idea of a joint team headed by Dr Hunt in which management consultants would work under his ultimate direction and preferred that it should be a McKinsey investigation producing a McKinsey report with full responsibility for the results resting solely with the firm.

Of the three British firms, Urwick, Orr and Partners ruled themselves out on grounds of cost, and, though there was little difference in price between PA Management Consultants and Associated Industrial Consultants, the latter were prepared to quote a fixed price whereas PA proposed in effect to charge on a time basis, and AIC made the better impression both on paper and in person. So much so, that it was decided to offer the job to them alone (PRO: BA1/20).

The suggestion from within the Treasury that the Fulton Committee's desire to establish a Management Consultancy Group was indicative of its distrust of being made dependent on official evidence may not have been an accurate judgment of the Committee as a whole, but according to E. K. Ferguson (Interview, 1989), who was loaned to the Group by British Petroleum, and John Garrett, it was true of Norman Hunt. As Garrett said, 'Hunt soon recognised that the evidence being presented to the Fulton

Committee risked being dominated by the submissions of entrenched interests, and especially by Treasury memoranda suggesting that Britain had the
best of all possible Civil Services. Hunt believed that it was imperative that
the Fulton Committee possessed a means of finding out how the Civil Service
really worked, and he pressed for the establishment of a Management Consultancy Group to be led by himself' (Interview, 1989). 'Hunt was the chairman of the Group', S. D. Walker recalled, 'and he led the discussions, but in
no way did he dominate them. Our independence was treasured' (Interview,
1989). Besides his part in setting up the Group, 'Hunt was the leading figure
too in the sense that he was a member of the main Fulton Committee and
acted as our messenger to it', E. K. Ferguson observed; 'Then again, when
we went to the government departments whose work we studied, it was Hunt
who would usually do the political stuff of making the introductions. So, he
would be the Group's leader in that sense as well. There was also the fact
that Hunt was a friend of the Prime Minister' (Interview, 1989). Though this
friendship existed, John Garrett was clear that 'Hunt was not Harold Wilson's
placeman on the Fulton Committee or on the Management Consultancy
Group. Contrary to what some people in the Civil Service said later, neither
Hunt nor myself were "got at" by the Prime Minister to produce a particular
type of Management Consultancy Report' (Interview, 1989).

When the Group began its visits to government departments in October
1966, it was only in general terms that its membership took the form initially
expected, and this membership was also to change. Robert Sheldon from the
Committee did not in fact take part in the Group's work as had been anticipated, and the involvement of Michael Simons was short lived. By early
December 1966, one of the management consultants, David Morley-Fletcher
had left the Group. According to another of the Group's members, E. K.
Ferguson, 'Morley-Fletcher . . . did not coalesce with the Group. He was a
very senior management consultant with AIC, and he seemed more suited to
dealing with the politics of large business organisations rather than the down
to earth workings of the Civil Service' (Interview, 1989). John Garrett said
that 'Morley-Fletcher left the Group as a result of personal differences with
Norman Hunt' (Interview, 1989). Morley-Fletcher's replacement was Dr R.
F. Ferguson, also from AIC, who worked with the Group for a short time,
helping it with its examination of the scientific and professional areas of the
Civil Service.

'Though Hunt was not simply an academic, he had no knowledge of the
private sector of the kind that John Garrett and I possessed', E. K. Ferguson
observed; 'John Garrett was a pretty powerful member of the Group. Johnny
Walker was very impressive too, having worked his way up from the bottom
of the Civil Service. He had wide experience of the work of government
departments, and he kept the Management Consultancy Group's feet on the
Civil Service ground' (Interview, 1989). S. D. Walker had in fact joined the
Board of Customs and Excise as a Departmental Clerical Officer in 1935, and

been promoted into the Executive Class; and after a spell at the Pay Research Unit, he was Chief Executive Officer in the Treasury's Organisation and Methods I Division at the time that the Group was established (Interview with S. D. Walker, 1989). 'Johnny Walker was incredibly able', in John Garrett's opinion; 'He was the best management consultant I ever knew'.

Garrett himself had spent five years as a management consultant before joining the Group, having earlier had management experience with the Rootes Group and with ICI. Garrett said that, 'I knew mostly about control systems, and something about personnel management. Most important of all, though, I had been a Visiting Fellow at the Graduate Business School at the University of California in Los Angeles, and what I learnt there gave me what was then a fairly novel way of looking at government organisation. What are the aims of the organisation? What is its strategy? How can that strategy achieve the organisation's objectives? How can you assess performance? Once you asked these questions, a number of things fell into place' (Interview, 1989).

E. K. Ferguson was appointed to the Management Consultancy Group to provide it with a member who was currently a business manager. In the relevant discussions, the Civil Service Pay Research Unit had suggested to the Committee's Secretariat that a private company should be asked if they would lend the Group a 'structures' man of about Assistant Secretary or Under Secretary equivalent. Ferguson, who was a member of British Petroleum's Central Staff Department, was lent by that company free of charge (PRO: BA1/71). Before moving to BP, Ferguson had worked in the Civil Service at the Cabinet Office and then in the Ministry of Defence (Interview, 1989).

The Management Consultancy Group treated Hunt's original draft as forming its detailed terms of reference, and, in fulfilling that remit, between 12 October 1966 and 6 April 1967, the Group examined twenty-three blocks of Civil Service work in twelve government departments and in detail the tasks of 576 individual civil servants defined as providing a representative cross-section of the work covered by those blocks. As planned, the two Permanent Secretaries on the main Fulton Committee selected the blocks of work, and they did so from a list drawn up as the combined result of suggestions made by the Pay Research Unit, talks with the staff associations involved and the Staff Side of the National Whitley Council, and consultations with the Treasury and the Permanent Secretaries of the government departments concerned. It was Sir Laurence Helsby and Sir William Armstrong, for instance, who chose the Public Enterprises Division of the Treasury as being the most suitable for investigation (PRO: BA1/71).

The various blocks that were selected were listed in Appendix II of the published Report of the Management Consultancy Group. The selection was criticised at the time. For example Sir Clifford Jarratt, the then Permanent Secretary at the Ministry of Social Security, pointed out in a letter to the Treasury dated 31 August 1966 that absent from the list of blocks was 'administrative work with a high legislative, as distinct from general Parliamentary, content'. S. P. Osmond, replying on 8 September, conceded this, observing that 'while we could not very well choose the work of a Division which was currently putting through major legislation, since this would be an intolerable strain, I think the inclusion of the Distribution of Industry Division of the Board of Trade will mean that the team see a Division which has had a fair amount of legislation in its time. We certainly hope that this will give the Committee a picture of that type of work' (PRO: BA1/71).

As it was, the Management Consultancy Group had been set a formidable task, and one that it was soon obvious could not be completed by early March 1967 as had been initially planned. 'It must be confessed that we underestimated the time that this job would take', Richard Wilding, the Committee's Secretary, told the Treasury on 21 December 1966, citing two factors. One was that 'Dr Hunt has turned out to be so much the dominant figure in the team that it is not practicable (as was originally intended by all concerned) for it to function in his absence – on Committee days and during visits abroad.' The other factor was that 'the amount of relevant material which the exercise is yielding is much more than we originally thought, and much more time is having to be set aside for review and discussion between the expeditions to departments.'

Wilding's view of how the Group operated was necessarily derived from the observations of the Committee's Assistant Secretary, Michael Simons, who had worked with the Group at one stage. Simons had not in fact described Hunt as 'dominant' but as seeing himself as 'the leader of the team and its principal figure', which as we have recorded was how the other members saw him too.

Simon's description of the Management Consultancy Group's working methods was as follows:

> First, there is a review of each investigation after the team has completed it. The idea is to produce a report on each block of work investigated; these reports are for the team's use as source material on which the report to the Fulton Committee on the exercise as a whole will be based. To prepare these reports it is necessary first of all, because the team deploys in each block for detailed investigations with each member doing a side of the block's work and staff, for them to get together to exchange their findings and their views as to the moral to be drawn. Then one of the management consultants goes away and prepares a draft report, which is discussed, amended and adopted. The least that Dr Hunt is prepared to allow for that kind of thing is one whole day for each block of work – fourteen days in all . . . He also wants four weeks at the end of the investigations for the joint preparation of the report for the Fulton Committee. Although it seems a great length of time, I do think from experience of the team's methods and manner of working that they will need it (PRO: BA1/72).

The timetable, revised in December 1966 and envisaging a final report from the Management Consultancy Group by the end of April 1967, could not be kept to. A brief Interim Report dated 7 May 1967 setting out conclusions was circulated to the Fulton Committee (PRO: BA1/35), at the meeting of which on 2 May Hunt had said that a further six to eight weeks would be needed for the full report, and the Committee had instructed the Secretariat to seek the necessary financial authority for the employment of the management consultants during the period concerned (PRO: BA1/8). When complying, Simons said to the Treasury that 'the matter has really been beyond our control because Hunt has been beyond our control. Only the Committee is in a position to control Hunt and, although we took care on this occasion that matters should be put to the Committee, the Committee chose to approve what Hunt wished to do.' That was written on 5 May, and on 7 July Wilding wrote to Hunt: 'Michael Simons has told me that you now think that in order to complete the report of the management consultant exercise you will need up to 20 more consultant days after 15th July, the date we had been aiming at . . . The prolongation of the exercise has obliged us to apply to the Treasury for further financial authority . . . This is of course embarrassing: it is now the fourth time that we have had to apply to them for authority for revised expenditure, and it brings the total increase over the original estimate to 83 per cent' (PRO: BA1/72).

Norman Hunt seemed determined to produce the best possible Management Consultancy Report irrespective of the time taken or the cost, and, though draft material was made available earlier to the Fulton Committee, in fact it was 29 December 1967 when John Garrett sent the Final Report to Wilding (PRO: BA1/73).

The Report was accompanied by an Annex called 'Some Aspects of the Work of the Public Enterprises Division, HM Treasury'. Having read it, the Fulton Committee instructed its Secretary to approach the Treasury to obtain permission for its publication. Apparently Hunt was the moving spirit here too; at least Wilding wrote to the Treasury on 5 February 1968 that ' I underestimated his desire to get this Annex published'. Why Hunt wanted publication was ascertainable from another letter which Wilding had sent to the Treasury, that of 31 January 1968:

> The main Report criticizes what its authors see as the inadequacy of the qualifications and experience which many administrators bring to their jobs, but cites neither P. E. nor any other division as specific examples of this. The Annex which we are now discussing is the only place in which the qualifications and experience of the members of a specific administrative division is referred to. It thus seems fair to say that the discussion of P. E. in the Annex provides from the Committee's point of view a useful illustration of what will be one of their main themes; from P. E.'s point of view the doubtful privilege of supplying this ammunition.

In fact, from the perspective of radicals like Hunt the material in paragraph

20 of the Annex alone was worth publishing since it showed, among other things, that only one of the administrators in the Public Enterprises Division had an economics degree; that the average length of time that administrators had spent in their present post was two years; that, though some had previously held jobs in the Service with an economic content, none had previously served with a sponsoring department, a nationalised industry, or in private industry or commerce; and that the Under Secretary in charge had been in post for two years, had held eleven completed posts since 1949, and had since moved on to other work in the Civil Service. Given that there had never been any undertaking to allow the publication of specific studies of the kind made of the Public Enterprises Division, it was unsurprising that the Treasury both resisted publication and that its resistance was successful. Norman Hunt only dropped the idea in early June 1968 with about three weeks to go before the Fulton Report was published (PRO: BA1/73).

In the meantime, the Fulton Committee had taken evidence from the Treasury, B. W. R. Mooring and P. D. Ince from British Petroleum, Roger Morrison from McKinsey's, and the Management Consultancy Group itself about grading structure and related issues (PRO: BA1/11); and the Group's Report had survived, subject to some very minor drafting alterations submitted by Richard Wilding and Sir Norman Kipping, and with the addition of one paragraph to the original 379 (PRO: BA1/73), to become the Fulton Committee's Volume 2. The additional paragraph was that numbered 364 in the published version which saw 'a particular need for the formation of high level departmental units concerned with strategic planning'. It is not clear from the papers from what source this addition was derived.

Unlike the Social Survey that it commissioned, the Management Consultancy Group's findings reached the Fulton Committee in plenty of time to influence its recommendations, while remaining a sufficiently distinct piece of work to have been seen as having made a contribution of its own to the debate about what future shape the Civil Service should take.

The Management Consultancy Group and Reform of the Civil Service

'The Report of the Management Consultancy Group was a superb piece of work', John Garrett has said, adding that: 'The Civil Service has never been able to rubbish the Management Consultancy Group's Report in the way that it has been able to do this to the Fulton Report itself. We had the evidence to support our findings . . . The Management Consultancy Group's Report was way ahead of its time. Volume 2 changed the climate and the agenda within which the reform of the Civil Service was thereafter discussed' (Interview, 1989). 'The Management Consultancy Group studied the Civil Service closely for the first time and it came up with radical proposals for change', was S. D. Walker's assessment of the Group's achievement (Interview, 1989); and another member of the Group, E. K. Ferguson, who described its Report as 'a conscientious piece of work', said that 'what we recommended was the introduction into the Civil Service of attitudes of mind and practices that were common in private industry and commerce and the adoption of which we believed would make for a more efficient Civil Service' (Interview, 1989).

Having been conceived in the heyday of market philosophy, the career Civil Service had plenty of practice by, say, the days of the Geddes Axe in the 1920s, of learning to live with the economic liberal view that government departments would be more efficiently run by 'business methods' than by its own procedures. The exigencies of parliamentary government, involving as these did potential detailed external examination of the work of civil servants and the need to account publicly for administrative behaviour, militated against the minimisation of running costs in government departments, as the majority signatories of the MacDonnell Report pointed out in 1914. Costs were raised, too, by the political expectation that the state should act as an enlightened employer (Cd. 7338, 1914, chapter IX, paras 85–7).

For all the differences in environment, and the attraction of foreign examples met in competition, it may have been that the Civil Service eventually did become a model for large scale British business organisation in some respects. Only military organisation, elegantly translated into management theory by no less than Colonel Urwick, provided much of a British alternative. Writing in the 1960s on the basis of personal experience, the former and highly successful businessman, Peter Nettl stressed both the dependence of the business community on the Civil Service for ideas on organisation and the relative inferiority of its own procedures (Nettl, 1965, p.32f). A different view was that of John Garrett who observed that 'the trouble with O. and M. in the Civil Service had been that it was overwhelmingly about M. and never thought about O'. (Interview, 1989). A more extensive range of studies of different British companies would be needed to test Nettl's argument properly; and also to assess the influence of American management ideas. The grading structure of British Petroleum was said by one of its representatives, P. D. Ince, in evidence to the Fulton Committee in 1968, to have been modelled on that of other international oil companies, and he also said that the example of the US Federal Civil Service had been an influence on the American oil companies in the related practice of job evaluation (PRO: BA1/11).

The status of the Civil Service, of course, and its separateness from the private sector was of a different order in the USA compared with Britain. With a lesser divide to surmount, it was natural that management ideas should be seen as being in common there. As the introduction to one well known American collection of readings in personnel administration put it in 1964: 'In any organization, management's task is to develop and co-ordinate the willing efforts of employees in accomplishing organizational aims. This is just as true in government agencies and non-profit organizations as it is in private enterprises' (Pigors, Myers, Malm, 1964, p.1). Even New Deal thinking on public administration was not divorced from business ideas (Waldo, 1948, p.71). Though the Report of the President's Committee on Administrative Management of 1937, written by Louis Brownlow and others, was 'generally displeasing to the business community' at the time, it was correctly observed by Dwight Waldo that the Report 'mirrored rather faithfully the form and spirit of current business thought on organization and management' (Waldo, 1948, p.9: cf. Polenberg, 1966). The same could be said of the Hoover Commissions of 1947–9 and of 1953–5 (Moe, 1982). It was thus unsurprising that from its first edition in 1953, a text on American public administration such as that by Marshall and Gladys Dimock should refer to the management thinking of, say, Peter Drucker (Dimock and Dimock, 1953, p.79) and that later editions would take up the 'management by objectives' ideas that Drucker advanced in *The Practice of Management* (Dimock, Dimock and Koenig, 1958, pp.375–8; Dimock and Dimock, 1964, pp.231–3).

In the different British context, traditionally, as we have seen, the advocacy of importing 'business methods' into the Civil Service had prominently emanated from economic liberals. Bodies like the Geddes Committee, though, did little about the introduction of such 'methods', in effect establishing a ceiling for administrative costs and leaving the Civil Service to organise itself. Ironically, the Fulton Committee, owing more in inclination to Fabianism, appointed a Management Consultancy Group which, while sharing the constraints placed on the main Committee, did demonstrate how 'business methods' could be applied to the organisation of the Civil Service.

The Management Consultancy Group put forward for the Committee's consideration possible major lines of reform and development of the Civil Service based on its analysis of the evidence that it had gathered and its knowledge of industry and commerce (Report, 1968, para.344). The Group favoured 'the abolition of the present class system' in the Civil Service and 'the creation of a classless uniformly graded Service' informed by job evaluation (ibid., para. 346). E. K. Ferguson observed: 'The Management Consultancy Group's ideas about unified grading did not derive exclusively from the example of British Petroleum, although I worked for that company at the time and I would refer to it. Unified grading was common practice in the private sector and it made for greater flexibility in the use of staff than the existing Civil Service structure permitted' (Interview, 1988). John Garrett said that

> the idea of a unified grading structure came from the evidence. The case for it kept being made all the time as we examined the adverse effects on the efficient organization of the work that the career class system led to. It confined a whole lot of people into cages that they couldn't get out of. Kim Ferguson, like myself, could not see the need for the Civil Service to have a career class system, and we thought that the Service should adopt the private sector approach in which people came in to do a specific job and they progressed if they did it well (Interview, 1989).

What was 'essential for the Civil Service of the future', the Management Consultancy Group believed, was 'the development of a new managerial style' promoted by 'the evolution of organizations in which more scope is given to managerial initiative, with proper safeguards; in which this initiative is encouraged and rewarded; in which suitable controls are devised so as to permit management by objective; in which there is as clear a delegation of authority and responsibility as possible and in which management is judged according to its skill in achieving the objectives for which it is responsible' (Report, 1968, para.374)

E. K. Ferguson said that

> The Management Consultancy Group saw accountable management not in terms of heads rolling but in terms of personal responsibility for an area of work. Somebody carries the can when things go wrong. Of course, we realised that what is called in management theory the time span of discretion would apply in some cases and that things might not go openly wrong until long after those really responsible had moved on. Security of tenure would not necessarily conflict with accountable management. We found clever, intelligent people in the Civil Service who seemed to have been shunted into a non-job, having carried the can for past failures. Not reaching a career grade in the Civil Service, say, being kept down to Principal in the Administrative Class, would be an unpleasant thing to experience in relation to one's peer group (Interview, 1989).

John Garrett recalled that 'what we wanted was a fairly benevolent system of accountable management, not the type leading to dismissals and so on. The kind of accountable management that we had in mind was that of a manager clearly designated as being in charge of a unit and for there to be measures of outputs'. It was intended to be a managerial system 'with minor sanctions but a fair bit of preferment' (Interview, 1989).

The Management Consultancy Group's main target was the Administrative Class, with 'its lack of continuity in the job, its relative isolation, its lack of management skills and experience, and its largely irrelevant educational background' (Report, 1968, para.68). More generally, the introduction of the managerial arrangements that the Group favoured were aimed at modifying 'the unique constraints upon the line manager in the Civil Service' to which the Whitley system contributed, that meant that 'he cannot hire or dismiss, he cannot reward merit by any form of payment, he cannot promote, he cannot reprimand formally, he cannot even stop the annual increment of an unsatisfactory subordinate' (ibid., para.335).

As the machinery of government and the convention of ministerial responsibility, and in effect a large Civil Service and the Whitley system, had to be treated by it as given, to make a distinctive contribution the Fulton Committee needed a different approach to the staple questions of Civil Service reform. To the extent that there were novelties in the Fulton Report, the

Management Consultancy Group would seem to have been the author of many of them. The analysis and recommendations contained in Chapter 5 of the Fulton Report, dealing with the structure of departments and the promotion of efficiency within them, would appear to be one example, and Chapter 6, about the structure of the Civil Service, would be another.

Influence cannot be proved, of course, and one surviving member of the Fulton Committee, Charles Anderson, believed that 'the Management Consultancy Group's work was unimpressive, and added little or nothing to what we knew already. We got all we really needed to know out of the general evidence that was presented to us, of which there was rather a lot' (Interview, 1988). Robert Sheldon thought that the work of the Management Consultancy Group was presented too late to have much impact on the Fulton Committee's thinking, although he appreciated the support that its findings gave to his own ideas on management (Interview, 1988). On the other hand, Sir James Dunnett considered that 'the Management Consultancy Group, through Hunt, was influential'. Dunnett's view was that 'Hunt became obsessed with the way that things were done particularly at British Petroleum. He seemed to be heavily influenced by John Garrett and the work of the Management Consultancy Group, whose findings had a very considerable bearing on what was said in the Fulton Report' (Interview, 1988).

'The Management Consultancy Group was very much Norman Hunt's initiative', Robert Neild recalled; 'It was a separate exercise from the work of the main Committee, and it was an exercise about which Hunt became very excited. Most of the rest of us were rather detached but accepted the Group's main recommendations. My impression was and remains that it was a useful piece of work' (Interview, 1988). Sir Philip Allen thought that 'the work of the Management Consultancy Group was important and its report was better and more restrained than the Fulton Report itself' (Interview, 1988).

Richard Wilding observed that

> The Management Consultancy Group did make a difference to the brickwork of the Fulton Report, adducing the supporting evidence. The Management Consultancy Group was influential in pointing towards the drafting of Chapter 1, though the Final Report taken as a whole and that of the Group differed in some respects, such as treatment of management by objectives. There was a more pragmatic tone to the report of the Management Consultancy Group than there was to the Fulton Report itself, although they were both trying to do the same thing.

He added that, 'Accountable management was an idea that followed from the work of the Management Consultancy Group. The consonance between what the Group said and the Fulton Committee said was incomplete, but Hunt came back from the Group saying "we must press for accountable management", and Sir John Wall and Sir Norman Kipping, with their industrial experience, backed him firmly, and it was accepted by the rest. The ideas got through comfortably' (Interview, 1988).

'Nobody on the Committee seemed much interested in accountable management until the Management Consultancy Group came up with the idea', Allen recalled (Interview, 1988), and Robert Sheldon thought that 'it was inherent in appointing the Management Consultancy Group that it would advocate accountable management' (Interview, 1988). The term 'accountable management' made its first appearance in a draft of what eventually became Chapter 5 of the Fulton Report that was submitted to the drafting sub-committee by Norman Hunt in December 1967 (PRO: BA1/58). The phrase did not appear as such in the Group's report, and one of its members, S. D. Walker said that it was 'a non-expression' because 'there is no such thing as "non-accountable management"' (Interview, 1989). Established civil servants were protected from the most disadvantageous of managerial initiatives. Structures involving 'cost centres' and 'accountable units' meant less than they did in the private sector because of security of tenure and standardised pay scales and promotions, which largely rendered costs as given, and because of the effects of the doctrine of ministerial responsibility.

If we take the McGregor private enterprise management model of Theory x and Theory y, by contrast the Civil Service had its own arrangements that, to emphasise the point, one could characterise as Theory ws, meaning the Whitley system, and Theory wf, meaning the Warren Fisher system. Of course, a sustained political initiative from the elected Government aimed at changing substantially the organisation and methods of the Civil Service would constitute 'direction and control through the exercise of authority', namely the Theory x approach (McGregor, 1960, p.49). The Thatcher government acted in this manner later. More familiarly, the Civil Service was left to govern itself, although this did not mean that its practices closely resembled the integrative Theory y approach, whose application was concerned with 'the creation of an environment which will encourage commitment to organizational objectives and which will provide opportunities for the maximum exercise of initiative, ingenuity, and self-direction in achieving them' (ibid., p.132). Given the existing structure of government departments, there was ministerial responsibility for what Civil Service managers did.

Theory y was described by its author as being 'a special and not at all typical case of the conventional conception of management by objectives' (ibid., p.61). A government department was bound to be a special case when it came to applying that concept. After Peter Drucker had developed the idea in *The Practice of Management* in the 1950s, 'management by objectives' had become conventional wisdom in management theory by the time that the Fulton Committee's Management Consultancy Group was appointed, as a knowledge of the contemporary literature makes evident (e.g. Schleh, 1961; Schaffer, 1964; Hughes, 1964; Humble, 1965; Odiorne, 1965; Batten, 1966; Forrest, 1966; Knight, 1966; Miller, 1966; Stewart, 1966; Valentine, 1966;

BIM, 1967). The Management Consultancy Group made no original contribution to management theory. Its role was the pragmatic one of demonstrating how the best of current management practice could be adopted in British central government departments in a manner that would not only be supportive of a large scale career Civil Service while encouraging what the Group deemed to be greater professionalism within that Service and promoting more efficient organisation and methods of work.

It did appear to be the case, as S. D. Walker observed, that 'the Fulton Committee seemed to treat the Management Consultancy Group's volume almost as if in competition with it, and made very few direct references to our Report, although if you compare the two volumes you can see how influential the Group was on the Committee's findings' (Interview, 1989). As we have seen, not all the surviving members of the Fulton Committee conceded that what Norman Hunt (1968, p.101) once called 'my Management Consultancy Group' made a major contribution to the work of the Committee and its Report. Nevertheless, nobody doubted that Hunt made a contribution. Given that his experience and academic training left Hunt dependent on the Group for his knowledge of private sector management, it seems reasonable to assume that the Group at the very least was indirectly influential, even if, inevitably, the extent of this influence remains unclear.

Chapter 4

Central Management of the Civil Service

The Context for Change

Whether or not the central management of the Home Civil Service should continue to be the responsibility of the Treasury was always going to be one of the core issues facing the Fulton Committee. The Tomlin Royal Commission on the Civil Service of 1929–31 had been able to treat the location of central management as being one of the 'ancillary questions' facing it. That Commission had recognised that 'the control of the Treasury over staff matters' had 'developed out of the power of the purse', and, in an era in which the mores of economic liberalism were dominant, it was only to be expected that the Commission would recommend 'no change in the present system' (Cmd. 3909, 1931, pp.169 ff). Thirty years later, the Plowden Committee on the Control of Public Expenditure of 1959–61 described the traditional means of Treasury control of such expenditure as having been rendered inadequate by, among other factors, the advent of the Keynesian Welfare State, and it made recommendations for different and supposedly more effective and, in form, more sophisticated arrangements.

The adoption of Keynesianism had also required the Treasury to take on the role of macro-economic management. By the first half of the 1960s, critics such as Robert Neild had come to be unhappy with the Treasury acting as both a Ministry of Finance and a Ministry of Economic Affairs. In January 1962, Neild told a Labour Party committee:

> One Ministry . . . inevitably has one philosophy and one set of touchstones by which it judges policy from day to day. In the Treasury, which holds the purse strings, this is bound to be defensive, restrictive, and conservative. It always has been so. It would be wrong if it were otherwise, just as it would be wrong if bank managers started living riotously. If we want some planning, expansion and courage, we must create another set of men, probably with another Minister, who think about real things – production, investment, living standards. Most other countries have two Ministries. And I think we would probably do best to follow their example (*Minutes of the Finance and Economic Policy Sub-Committee of the Labour Party 1958–66*, R D 202).

The establishment of the separate Department of Economic Affairs in 1964 was in accord with such thinking. Further, the belief that the Treasury's 'defensive, restrictive, and conservative' outlook made it the wrong department to be charged with the management of the economy was only a short step away from also considering a Treasury with such characteristics to be an unsuitable department to be responsible for the central management of the Home Civil Service, and, again, it was known that some other countries had different arrangements.

The first overt sign that 'the Treasury had a central responsibility for the Civil Service' had been the Treasury minute of 1868 that made Treasury sanction necessary for any increase in staff numbers', Sir Laurence Helsby told the Select Committee on Estimates in 1963; adding that by 1919 this responsibility had 'developed to the point where the Treasury set up within its own organisation a department whose express function it was to watch over the staffing of other departments and their internal organisation' (HC 228, 1963–4, evidence, 12).

The majority of the MacDonnell Royal Commission on the Civil Service of 1912–15 (Cd. 7338, 1914, pp.86–7), the Haldane Committee on the Machinery of Government of 1917–18 (Cd. 9230, 1918), and the Bradbury Committee on the Organisation and Staffing of Government Offices of 1917–19 had all made recommendations in favour of the creation of what in the first instance was called the Establishments Department of the Treasury. The Bradbury Committee had rejected the idea that a separate government department was needed for the role of central management of the Civil Service because this would lead to 'friction and duplication of work' with the Treasury (Cd.62, 1919, p.5). Then in 1920, the practice began by which the Prime Minister's approval was needed for appointments to Permanent Secretary, Deputy Secretary, Principal Establishment Officer, and Principal Finance Officer posts in all government departments. The Permanent Secretary to the Treasury was designated Head of the Civil Service and became the Prime Minister's principal adviser on Civil Service appointments. The Treasury itself was empowered by Order in Council in 1920 to 'make regulations for controlling the conduct of His Majesty's Civil Establishments, and providing for the classification, remuneration and other conditions of service of all persons employed therein, whether permanently or temporarily' (HC 228, 1963–4, evidence, p.2). Sir Laurence Helsby thought that 'in 1920 one sees the high water mark of the notion of Treasury control – the Treasury imposing its judgement on other departments. Shortly afterwards one sees beginning to emerge the idea that other departments must take the primary responsibility for what went on within their own organisations'. Sir Laurence pointed to the emergence of the Standing Committee of Establishments Officers as illustrating 'the spirit of co-operation between the Treasury and other departments being given importance' (ibid., q.17). That said, though, aside from the Post Office after 1933, as the Treasury itself observed, 'the tight control exercised over grading and complements by the Treasury during the nineteenth century continued up to 1939 – no post could be created or shifted to another part of the office without Treasury authority' (ibid., p.2).

The range of powers accorded to the inter-war Treasury made it a natural target for criticism, and this was not diminished by the manner in which Sir Warren Fisher, the Permanent Secretary to the Treasury, conducted himself as Head of the Civil Service. One member of the Fulton Committee, Sir Philip Allen, though not of the generation of higher civil servants whose careers were affected, did not disguise his distaste for Fisher on the grounds that 'Fisher promoted his chums' (Interview: 17.10.88). That Fisher had any say even in principle in senior promotions in the Foreign Office and the Diplomatic Service was objected to there, especially by those who believed their careers to have been blighted. Fisher's prominent involvement in the formation of public policy in matters of defence and foreign affairs, of which he had no more than general knowledge, invited controversy (Fry, 1969a, pp.52). Fisher's behaviour was one factor that led to the Eden-Bevin reforms of the 1940s which created a united Foreign Service 'entirely separated from the Home Civil Service' and 'treated as a self contained and distinct Service of the Crown' (Cmd. 6420, 1943, p.3), thus bringing to an end the only period in the Civil Service's history when the Treasury or, come to that, any government department, had formal responsibility for the central management of the Civil Service as a whole.

'In the period between the wars the response of the Treasury to the demand that expert knowledge and study should be brought to bear on the problems of departmental organisation was meagre in the extreme', the House of Commons Select Committee on National Expenditure stated bluntly in 1942 (HC 120, 1941–2, para.56) in the course of a report on the Organisation and Control of the Civil Service which an official study team described in 1980 as 'dispassionate and accurate though critical' (Hawtin-Moore Report, 1980, p.11). The criticisms made were of a different kind from those advanced by the staff associations comprising the Staff Side of the Civil Service National Whitley Council in evidence to the Tomlin Commission, and by their natural academic allies like Harold Laski, and which therefore were the suggested remedies. Laski wrote: 'A separation will have to take place between the financial and establishment functions of the Treasury. A separate Minister of Personnel is required to whom all questions of recruitment, training, promotion and pay and other conditions of service will be entrusted. The present fusion of functions in the Treasury has the undesirable result of making financial considerations unduly influential in personnel problems' (Laski, 1942, p.11). Laski wanted the Civil Service Commission to be the body assigned responsibility for central management of the Service, observing that 'we do not want an organisation concerned essentially with scientific management and labour saving devices' (Laski, 1931a, pp.514–15). By contrast, the Select Committee was firmly of the opinion that central management functions should remain with the Treasury, and that, despite its unpromising record since 1919, the establishments work of the Treasury in general, and Organisation and Methods work in particular needed to be expanded (HC 120, 1941–2, paras 98–107).

The Keynesian re-writing of the rules by which the economy was supposed to be managed gave the Treasury at one and the same time important, onerous and extended responsibilities, as well as helping to create a financial climate and bureaucratic expansion which made the practice of the traditional Treasury functions even more difficult than they had been under economic liberalism. The growth of the Civil Service in wartime and afterwards had overwhelmed the arrangements for close Treasury control over complementing which was formally abandoned in the main part of the Service in 1949 for all but the highest grades. Sir Edward Bridges from 1945 until 1956, and then Sir Norman Brook from 1956 to 1962, were uncontroversial in the role of Head of the Home Civil Service, certainly by comparison with Fisher, even if some critics like Thomas Balogh found the powers that they exercised over promotions in the Higher Civil Service to be excessive. Public lectures that Bridges was given to delivering about the work of the Treasury and the Administrative Class provided critics with ammunition.

The changes in 1956 had only really affected the top of the Treasury, but the post-Plowden reforms of November 1962 did represent a major reconstruction of the Treasury as a whole, with the abolition of the mixed divisions which had dealt with both the supply and establishments aspects of a department's activities, the amalgamation of Home and Overseas Finance, and the integration of the Economic Section with the main part of the Treasury. The arrangement dating from 1956 of having two Joint Permanent Secretaries to the Treasury, one responsible for economic and financial policy, and the other acting as Head of the Home Civil Service continued, and these roles were to be carried out by Sir William Armstrong and Sir Laurence Helsby respectively. The most important difference was that the 1962 changes meant that the departmental structure below them had been subject to a large scale reorganisation which on the Establishments side, and in line with the Plowden Report's recommendations, involved an emphasis on and development of management services in addition to the more familiar concerns such as pay and conditions of service (Chester, 1962, p.423).

The reorganisation of the Treasury in 1962 was launched against a background of considerable outside criticism of the department, and with, as it turned out, insufficient time for the revised structure to prove itself before further changes were politically deemed to be necessary in the form of the DEA. In 1962 itself, such was the climate of opinion that even a well disposed observer such as D. N. Chester could not resist remarking of Helsby's early training as an economist that 'no doubt this element of expertise was condoned or overlooked as he was to be concerned not with economic and financial policy, but with establishment and management matters' (ibid., p.425). In 1964, the Fabian authors of *The Administrators*, including of course Robert Neild, were dismissive of the changes that had been made on the Establishments side of the Treasury, seeing what had happened as 'another game of musical chairs . . . with most of the same people circulating round the old jobs, some slightly regrouped under new names.' It was still the case, the Fabians maintained, that there was 'no suitable organ of personnel management in the Civil Service'. Their 'solution to this problem', said to be 'a radical one', was in fact that suggested many years before by Laski, namely to 'take personnel management and concern with the structure of the Civil Service out of the Treasury altogether' and to give it to an 'enlarged and reformed Civil Service Commission', for which arrangement there were 'useful precedents and parallels' in other countries (Fabian Group, 1964, pp.32 ff). Though an unflattering review conducted by the Select Committee on Estimates in 1965 of how the Civil Service Commission carried out its existing functions (HC 308, 1964–5) cast doubt on the Commission's suitability for a wider role, by the time that the Fulton Committee had been appointed it seemed inevitable that another department than the Treasury would be assigned the task of central management of the Home Civil Service.

Review of the Main Evidence

The information that some members of the Fulton Committee brought back from Sweden, that there was 'no central personnel management of the Civil Service' there (PRO: BA1/32), was one of the few invitations to radicalism present in the evidence that the Committee had before it about central management of the Home Civil Service; aside, that is, from the predictably forthright views of Thomas Balogh and Jeremy Bray. The bulk of the evidence was concerned with discussion about where the central management of the Service should be located, what its nature and extent should be, and the machinery for promotions at the highest levels of the Service.

1. The role of the Head of the Home Civil Service and the machinery for making appointments to the highest posts

The procedures by which appointments were made to Permanent Secretary, Deputy Secretary, Principal Establishment Officer, and Principal Financial Officer posts in government departments were described by Sir Laurence Helsby in his evidence to the Fulton Committee about the role of the Head of the Home Civil Service. As might be expected, the Treasury was said to have a detailed knowledge of the field, consultation was wide and informal and, especially in the case of appointments to Permanent Secretary posts, acceptability to ministers was 'one of the most important factors'. Helsby saw no advantage in advertising leading posts within the Civil Service, and he was opposed to establishing a formal board to make recommendations about promotions to the highest grades. In his opinion, a formal committee would damage flexibility in two ways: 'first, it would be bad to have to take to the Prime Minister a firm remit which he could not depart from without going back to the board. Secondly, it would be impossible to pick a board with a definite membership which would be the best source of advice for all appointments over the whole field' (PRO: BA1/6).

Lord Bridges told the Fulton Committee that when he first became Permanent Secretary to the Treasury he had considered the idea of establishing a board for senior appointments but he had decided against it (PRO: BA1/8). He had three main reasons for preferring informal consultations. One was that the persons who from their own experience could give the fullest and best advice differed from one case to another. The second was that he found by experience that, while Permanent Secretaries would speak to him personally with frankness and candour, if he collected a small group of them they did not speak with the same frankness in front of their colleagues. The third reason was that

> every recommendation for appointment as Permanent Secretary requires the approval of the Prime Minister and of the Minister of the department concerned. The appointment is indeed made by the latter. Obviously the Head of Civil Service must be prepared not merely to make a formal submission of a name, but to discuss the various possibilities, and the reasons for preferring a particular candidate, with the Minister and the Prime Minister. All this could certainly become much more difficult and might indeed present considerable embarrassment if a formally constituted board had made a firm recommendation that Mr x should be appointed Permanent Secretary of a particular department (PRO: BA1/29).

Bridges said that 'he had adopted a pragmatic method of consultation on senior appointments; he had always regarded the recommendations he put to the Prime Minister as representing the best Service view and not just a personal view.' In answer to a question, he agreed that a board for senior appointments might have advantages from the point of view of morale; and he observed that 'there had been times in the past when the appointment of Principal Establishment Officers and Principal Financial Officers had not received enough attention from the Treasury. The Treasury had exercised a negative rather than a positive check. Some departments used to put in their old fossils as Principal Establishment Officers.' He added that he had tried to improve standards, and on occasion he had turned down a department's first recommendation and asked them to think again (PRO: BA1/8).

'The long and at times acrid dispute over the title "(Official) Head of the (Home) Civil Service"' was one 'which has now burnt itself out', Bridges commented in his written evidence to the Fulton Committee (PRO: BA1/29). The role that the holder of the post played, though, remained a matter for debate, with the most controversial contribution coming, of course, from Thomas Balogh. 'So long as advice to the Prime Minister on appointments was given by a single man (a system which would turn a Saint into a Machiavellian), there would be a monolithicism based not on opinion but on ambition', Balogh told the Committee. 'The post of Head of the Civil Service was a thoroughly bad one', he believed,

> and the most important reform needed was to put it into commission. The British had a long tradition of doing just this in order to get rid of over-mighty subjects . . . No one person should have the professional job of picking people for appointments. It meant that the choice would be made for personal reasons rather than because a man was the right man to carry out the policy work attaching to the post. It would be much better for the selection of people to fill Permanent Secretary and other senior posts to be made by a committee of four or five of the most senior civil servants. They should be serviced by lowly but intelligent staff who would have no possibility of becoming a hidden power. The reports on candidates for selection should be made objectively in writing (PRO: BA1/2).

'The Home Civil Service should have a Head to give leadership – someone to whom Permanent Secretaries could turn for advice on such problems as relations with their Ministers', Lord Normanbrook told the Fulton Committee in his evidence (PRO: BA1/3). The idea of actually abolishing the post of Head of the Home Civil Service seemed to appeal only to Balogh among those presenting evidence; but the same could not be said about the greater formalisation of the procedures for making senior appointments. Dame Evelyn Sharp told the Committee that

> the key to a good Service was to get the top jobs right and that this was still done too haphazardly. There had always been *ad hoc* consultation about senior appointments between the Head of the Civil Service and some of his senior colleagues, but she wondered whether that might not be formalized by setting up a council with real responsibility for senior posts. In effect such a council might amount to putting the Headship of the Service into commission as far as senior appointments were concerned, but the Head of the Civil Service could take the chair (PRO: BA1/4).

Another Permanent Secretary, Sir Eric Roll of the DEA, thought that 'there should be a committee of Permanent Secretaries with a rotating membership for senior appointments; there was already informal consultation on those lines but it should be systematized'. The former Conservative minister, Aubrey Jones, made the same suggestion (PRO: BA1/3). The Institution of professional Civil Servants wanted promotions at Permanent Secretary level to be made by a committee comprising the Head of the Home Civil Service, a representative of the central management organisation, and a member nominated by the Civil Service Commission from a panel of persons of eminence. The IPCS wanted ministers to be closely involved in promotions at Permanent Secretary, Deputy Secretary and Under Secretary levels, in the latter instances with the Permanent Secretary replacing the Head of the Home Civil Service on the board (PRO: BA1/30).

A much more ambitious role for ministers in the making of appointments in the Higher Civil Service was envisaged by Jeremy Bray, the then Parliamentary Secretary at the Ministry of Power, in his evidence. Bray advocated a system under which the minister would write the job description and either select a promotion panel or make nominations himself for the Prime Minister to make the appointments. Vacancies were to be circulated and advertised throughout the appropriate levels of the Civil Service. Outside selectors were to form a majority on promotion panels. Bray's object was to increase ministerial control and outside influence so as to break the self-perpetuating nature of the Civil Service at its highest levels (PRO: BA1/28).

Another ministerial witness, Richard Crossman, told the Fulton Committee that he shared Balogh's antipathy to the development since the time of Lloyd George's Prime Ministership of 'a unified Civil Service centrally controlled by the Treasury . . . The effect was that men who reached the top had to be Treasury types; ambitious civil servants knew that their promotion and success depended on pleasing certain key figures in the Treasury' (PRO: BA1/6). In his diary Crossman complained about the high priority that he believed Harold Wilson gave in April 1966 to finding Sir Bruce Fraser another senior post in the machinery of government: 'Interesting that a Prime Minister in considering our out legislative strategy should be mainly preoccupied with the convenience of one of the Permanent Secretaries, or, as Harold would put it, the relationships between the Government and the Higher Civil Service' (Crossman, I, 1975, p.499: cf. castle, 1984, p. 114). Though Crossman actually drew the attention of the Committee to this particular example, he had no proposals to make, institutional or otherwise, for changing the system of Higher Civil Service appointments; and indeed he told the Committee that he had no regrets that ministers did not have more say in appointments in departments. He said he did not think it was important, and personally he would be prepared to take whoever was appointed provided that the set-up was right (PRO:BA1/7). In his diary Crossman wrote about his role as Minister of Housing and Local Government: 'I took practically no part in appointments. True enough I kept the Dame as my Permanent Secretary longer than the Prime Minister wanted, and then, greatly to his perturbation, put a veto on Bruce Fraser succeeding her . . . I can only claim that I played some role in the appointment of the Permanent Secretary to succeed Evelyn Sharp. Down below I had no influence at all' (Crossman, I, 1975, p.621). Dame Evelyn Sharp's view was that 'Ministers should be consulted about senior appointments. A Minister's opinion was important but not all important, because of his limited point of view, and his ephemeral tenure' (PRO: BA1/4).

2. Nature and extent of central management of the Home Civil Service

As for the nature and extent of central management of the Home Civil Service, Sir Laurence Helsby told the Fulton Committee that contemporary opinion among the leading civil servants had come to favour a high level of central intervention; and he anticipated that, in future, developments such as the proposed merger between the Executive and Administrative Classes would mean more deliberate career management on the part of the Treasury because 'only central management could manage the managers' (PRO: BA1/6). S. P. Osmond of the Treasury said in his evidence that the expanded graduate intake that such a merger would mean made for 'a big managerial job' on the part of departments (PRO: BA1/4), and he concurred with the view of a colleague, Louis Petch, who had observed that the Treasury would have to take a good deal more responsibility in the future to try to ensure as much uniformity of treatment of entrants as was practicable (PRO: BA1/5). A 'greater degree of central management' was envisaged by the University Appointments Boards if more graduates were recruited (PRO: BA1/21); and, in his evidence, Sir George Abell, the First Civil Service Commissioner, said that a larger graduate entry to the Service would require obtrusive and interfering staff management from the centre (PRO:BA1/3).

'We see a need for a great deal more training and career management centrally, which I think in the past has been done by the Treasury on a shoestring and quite inadequately', R. B. M. King of the First Division Association told the Fulton Committee (PRO: BA1/5); and several of the other staff associations in giving evidence also advocated the strengthening of central management with, as might be expected, the improvement of their members' career expectations being the main motive. The Society of Technical Civil Servants, representing the drawing office grades in the Civil Service, was explicit about this:

> differences between careers in different departments ought to be avoided. It is substantially a matter of chance which government department a new entrant comes into. There ought not to be such a heavy penalty (and, at the time of entry, a quite unknown penalty) attaching to going into one department rather than another. In the Executive Class there is an arrangement, by way of departmental quotas, for, to some extent, levelling out promotion opportunities. This is at least as necessary in the draughtsman class. There ought to be a thorough going review of complements with a view to ironing out the enormous differences which exist between departments, and also with a view to providing an adequate career structure (PRO: BA1/24).

J. R. M. Dryden of the Society of Civil Servants, whose Executive class members benefited from the Treasury promotion pooling arrangements so envied by its fellow staff association, wanted central management to have additional machinery to remedy the mis-allocation of officials to posts and departments for which they were ill suited (PRO: BA1/5). The Institution of Professional Civil Servants argued for more central management intervention in the careers of scientists and professionals, and for civil servants with such backgrounds to administer the machinery (PRO: BA1/30). When asked by Sir

Philip Allen about the absence of such specialists currently, Louis Petch of the Treasury replied that

> while the Treasury has no scientists or any professionals other than economists, when we are operating in this field we work very closely in co-operation with the other departments of Whitehall who have plenty of them. So we get our professional advice, though at one remove. But we would not rule out the fact that there is something to be said for scientists and other professionals being attached to the Management Division of the Treasury. But you might find it jolly difficult to do this, as it would be perhaps rather a dreary job compared with others they could do.

After Sir William Cook had observed that this was 'a very valid point', Petch added: 'We have, of course, a scientific management panel to advise us on this.' Sir Laurence Helsby thought that such arrangements were sufficient, adding that 'transplanted scientists would dwindle in scientific stature and would become rather cut off from their base' (PRO: BA1//8).

More provision for central personnel management and for inter-departmental movement of staff was advocated by A. F. Earle, the Principal of the London Graduate School of Business Studies, in his evidence (PRO: BA1/24); but an insider, Sir Burke Trend, the Secretary of the Cabinet, was of the opinion that 'the Service tended to go in for too much central control and for moving people about too much' (PRO: BA1/4). Sir Maurice Dean, the Permanent Secretary at the Ministry of Technology, believed that 'Treasury control over departments should be reduced. There must be a central authority to maintain consistent treatment and standards, but delegation could and should be further extended in the interests of giving departments a proper self respect and building up people's sense of personal responsibility'. Not entirely consistently, as he recognised, Sir Maurice also observed that his experience in having established two new government departments had been a grim one, because although 'the Treasury had been very helpful . . . they had only limited powers to coerce departments to release good people. This applied not only to senior posts but also to typists.' Of course Sir Maurice could see that giving the centre more power 'to move people around the Service compulsorily . . . would be incompatible with allowing departments the maximum freedom' (PRO: BA1/2). F. J. Doggett of the Establishments Branch of the Ministry of Aviation told the Committee that the Treasury was 'receptive and reasonably quick in approving new posts and complements.' Doggett, thought, however, that the Treasury 'did not always know what they were doing and would be better advised to give more delegated authority and concentrate more on ensuring that departments had effective systems for controlling themselves. Big departments could play ducks and drakes with the Treasury if they wished, since the Treasury simply could not know enough about the work load in different parts of the department to ask the right questions' (PRO: BA1/7).

That government departments had been 'among the first organizations in the UK to make use of automatic data processing for administrative work' was emphasised by the Treasury in early evidence to the Fulton Committee, as indeed was the Treasury's own belief that, well before the Plowden Report on the Control of Public Expenditure, it had 'played a positive role in encouraging departments to use these techniques' (PRO: BA1/13). The obvious expansion in the central provision of management services in the Civil Service since the Plowden Report had made the Treasury a more difficult target for critics than in the past, but the practice of largely leaving O. and M. work to members of the Executive Class did attract adverse attention. One member of the Committee, Robert Neild, found such arrangements 'very odd', to which S. P. Osmond of the Treasury replied that 'there is an expertise in getting blocks of work sensibly organised . . . and on this, good Executive Class civil servants, who are pretty intelligent chaps, can make a real contribution.' Neild was openly sceptical:

> Are these higher executives really in a position, at the end of examining all the material, statistics and so on to say 'I think this is the best way of organising it', not to say 'You should have x clerks', and so on, but to say: 'probably you do not need a lot of this information anyway. The whole job should be done in a different manner'? This is the critical point I think in getting a really good organisation. You can have two sets of terms of reference, one where you can tell the sergeant major to do it, and at the other extreme you can say 'This is all rubbish, we do not need to know this, that and the other'. Are your O. and M. people in a position to and do they often adopt the latter approach?

Osmond replied: 'They are certainly in a position to do that. They might very well, rather than formally saying it off their own bat, come back and talk to their Assistant Secretary about it, but this kind of point can certainly be brought out' (PRO: BA1/4).

Otherwise, the Treasury witnesses got off rather lightly when being questioned about that department's management functions. The only interesting evidence on that subject was that submitted by the IPCS, which, while not hostile to the Treasury, advocated the establishment at the centre of the Civil Service of management teams 'with a wide range of experts, analogous to management consultancies in the business world. It should be a function of these teams to visit and report on departments not only in the organisation and methods held or on staffing, but generally on all matters affecting efficiency.' The IPCS thought that, besides reviewing government departments, these management teams could be made available to firms and organisations outside the Civil Service on a strictly commercial basis (PRO: BA1/30).

3. Location of the central management of the Home Civil Service

What the central management of the Home Civil Service actually did, and how the performance of that role could be improved, seemed to interest the

Fulton Committee and those who gave evidence to it less than the matter of which department or organisation ought to be assigned the role. Support for leaving central management with the Treasury was a minority position among those presenting evidence. It was one not shared, for instance, by Dame Evelyn Sharp, though she recognised that whatever was done, the Treasury would still have to have a say on salaries and on major questions of manning and the like which had important financial implications. In any rearrangement of responsibility for the management of the Service the danger of duplicated responsibility for such matters would have to be recognised in order to be minimised. Some alternatives to the present position would be a change for the worse, notably a glorified Civil Service Commission, an idea mooted from time to time. She thought that the best solution to the problem would be to set up a Prime Minister's Department responsible amongst other things for the management of the Civil Service (PRO: BA1/4).

The extent of Prime Ministerial involvement in any new arrangements, and the allocation of other Ministerial responsibilities, as well as the special position of the Civil Service Commission, complicated discussion of the future location of the central management the Home Civil Service that was to be found in the evidence presented to the Fulton Committee. The Royal Institute of Public Administration informed the Committee that there were only three main possibilities when it came to locating central management elsewhere than in the Treasury. The first was to have 'a Minister for the Civil Service with a normal department'. The second was to have 'a Civil Service Board responsible to the Prime Minister'. The third was to have 'a Civil Service Board responsible mainly to a Minister, who is the holder of one of the sinecure offices, but for certain purposes to the Prime Minister' (PRO: BA1/28). Those giving evidence, though, did not always confine themselves to these categories. Indeed, the range of views was such that in presenting a digest of evidence to the Committee, the Secretariat could do little more than list them, and draw particular attention to those advocates of change who favoured establishing a Public Service Commission to run the Civil Service and the 'greater number' who proposed that central management should be moved out of the Treasury but kept under ministerial responsibility (PRO: BA1/38).

The Public Service Commission idea surfaced early in the Fulton Committee's deliberations. Sir Maurice Dean, giving evidence at its fourth meeting on 5 April 1966, said that on the question whether the management of the Civil Service should remain with the Treasury the arguments were nicely poised, but he was in favour of investing functions in a Public Service Commission or Civil Service Department which would be independent of the Treasury. There was no reason why economic and financial control and personnel control should go together – in industry and in the Armed Forces they were separated – and he agreed with the view expressed by some members of the Committee that the present system could produce a kind of schizophrenia in the Treasury because of conflict between their two functions as managers of the Civil Service and guardians of incomes policy. Such a Commission would deal with recruitment, training, pay, complementing, promotion policy and other central management matters, without interfering with the responsibility of departments to manage their own affairs to the greatest possible extent (PRO: BA1/2).

In early evidence, too, Thomas Balogh told the Committee that 'the personnel management of the Civil Service should be handed over – on the model of most Commonwealth countries – to the Civil Service Commission' (PRO: BA1/12). In its evidence, the Labour Party wanted the same institutional change, saying that in addition to 'its present functions of recruitment and selection', a strengthened Civil Service Commission's role ought also to comprehend 'conditions of service questions and training' and responsibility for 'some degree of career planning and for higher appointments in the Service. The new Commission would retain the independence of the old, and enhance its status. It would negotiate with the Treasury for the funds necessary to carry out its functions as would any other spending department of the Government. It would accordingly be able to approach its managerial functions with efficiency rather than economy as its watchword' (PRO: BA1/27). Similarly the Liberal Party, in its evidence, advocated 'extending the work of the present Civil Service Commission into that of a Public Service Commission concerned with the general planning of recruitment and training in the Civil Service' (PRO: BA1/25). B. R. Crick and W. Thornhill of the University of Sheffield (PRO: BA1/27) and A. F. Earle of the London Graduate School of Business Studies (PRO: BA1/24) were others presenting evidence who wanted the responsibility for central personnel management to be transferred from the Treasury to an expanded Civil Service Commission without specifying ministerial responsibility for the new organisation.

The establishment of a Public Service Commission of a kind was also part of the evidence submitted to the Committee by J. H. Robertson, a former Private Secretary to the Head of the Civil Service and Secretary of the Cabinet, who had since become a management consultant. Robertson envisaged the establishment of a Prime Minister's Department comprising the Prime Minister's Office, the Cabinet Office, the Cabinet Secretariat, and the management side of the Treasury. 'Much of the day-to-day work of the Civil Service management now done in the Treasury should be devolved to the Civil Service Commission', Robertson wrote; 'In due course, the Civil Service Commission should merge with the Diplomatic Service Administration Office and expand into a Public Service Commission.' Robertson said that

> the twentieth century growth of public service bodies outside the Civil Service – national boards, corporations etc – has presented new opportunities for political and personal patronage. Without suggesting that these opportunities have been abused by recent Governments, it is clear that some sort of institutional arrangement will soon be necessary to bring appointments to these boards, etc., under orderly control. A Public

Service Commission would be the twentieth century equivalent of the nineteenth century Civil Service Commission (PRO: BA1/28).

Proposals for an independent Public Service Commission, with central managerial responsibility for the Home Civil Service and not for the public sector as a whole, were what critics of this proposal for change concentrated their attention on when giving evidence to the Committee. Sir Laurence Helsby told the Committee as early as its eleventh meeting, on 24 May 1966, that

> he thought that the management of the Service ought to be linked with its general work. It was a mistake to isolate management from the formulation or carrying out of policy. Many other countries had entrusted management to a Public Service Commission, but the disadvantages of this were becoming apparent, and had recently come to a head in Canada. Isolation of the management function led to the overcodification of rules on promotion, discipline etc., to the risk of a quasilegalistic system, and to the risk of a conflict between management and those who were getting on with the job (PRO: BA1/3).

In later evidence, Helsby observed that Canadian and Australian experience of the Public Service Commission arrangement had shown it to be 'a hindrance to have a body the purity of whose principles exceeded their knowledge of the work', and he thought that 'the day was long past when management could be given to a body outside Ministerial control' (PRO: BA1/6).

The Civil Service Commission itself, though not initially in favour of the retention of Treasury control of the Civil Service, had no enthusiasm for the Public Service Commission alternative. Sir George Abell told the Committee that a Public Service Commission was 'not feasible in our society', and that 'the only thing for which you can claim a constitutional independence is the actual selection, and that in the context of our democracy, anyhow, to ask Ministers to have practically nothing to do with questions like job classification, organisation, training, and staff management generally would really be a democratically retrograde step. It would be going back to something which flourishes rather more in the new Dominions' (PRO: BA1/5). Like Helsby, Lord Normanbrook thought that 'the Treasury should continue to be responsible for the management of the Civil Service. Because of its central role in the other fields of financial and economic policy, there was a store of knowledge within the Treasury about individual members of the Service which no other department had. A Public Service Commission would have to rely almost entirely on written reports' (PRO: BA1/3). Sir Eric Roll 'did not think that the Civil Service should be managed from the Treasury because it was now too large and complex, but that it should be managed somewhere where there was contact with departments in their day-to-day activities. Therefore he was against the idea of a Public Service Commission. Perhaps it should be put into a Prime Minister's Department' (PRO: BA1/3).

There was 'no reason in logic why the central management of the Civil

Service should be the responsibility of the Treasury', Reginald Maudling, the former Conservative Chancellor of the Exchequer, told the Fulton Committee in one of the few pieces of evidence presented by a minister or former minister which referred to the subject. Maudling continued:

> Indeed, the other burdens on the Chancellor and his senior officials were too great for them to do very much on that side. If management of the Civil Service were taken away from the Treasury there might be problems about responsibility for Civil Service pay but perhaps there was no reason in essence why the Treasury should not have the same relationship on the matter with a department responsible for the Civil Service as it did on doctors' pay with the Ministry of Health, on teachers' pay with the Department of Education and Science etc. . . . He did not see that it would be a satisfactory solution to make it the responsibility of a Prime Minister's Department, because the Prime Minister had quite enough to do already. A Cabinet Minister was needed as the head of whatever department was made responsible but he did not think that the Minister should intervene in personnel management questions in other departments, except on the most important questions. A separate Civil Service Department might well be the solution (PRO: BA1/6).

Another former Conservative minister, Aubrey Jones, saw

> no reason why control of expenditure must be combined with control of staff. There were two positive disadvantages in Treasury control of senior posts: first, officials of other departments who had to do battle with the Treasury might be inclined to pull their punches; and, secondly, it led to the suspicion, which, whether well founded or not, was bad for morale, that the Treasury favoured its own men . . . The control of Civil Service staff in general might be put into a Prime Minister's Department (PRO: BA1/3).

The serving Labour junior minister, Jeremy Bray, told the Committee that

> staff management is a perfectly definite function for a separate Staff Department. Ministerially, responsibility for the higher level appointments rests with the Prime Minister already, and there is something to be said for making the Staff Department responsible to him. The Prime Minister might invite a non-departmental Minister like the Lord President to assist him in looking after the general business of the Staff Department (PRO: BA1/28).

Besides Sir Maurice Dean and Dame Evelyn Sharp, whose views we have already noted, the advocates of change had further support from a minority of serving or former higher civil servants. The most important support came from Sir William Armstrong, who said of his role as Joint Permanent Secretary to the Treasury that 'on the whole it was a disadvantage to be a joint head. It relieved him of a considerable burden but on the other hand there was the feeling that, in spite of good relations with the other side, he was not in charge of his staff to the extent he would like.' Armstrong thought that 'the management of the Civil Service should be carried out outside the Treasury in a Public Service Department reporting to the Prime Minister but with its own Minister. The Chancellor of the Exchequer already had enough to do without the extra chore of managing the Civil Service' (PRO: BA1/3).

Another supporter of change was Sir George Mallaby, who, when he was still first Civil Service Commissioner, had written about the difficulties of the existing relationship between the Treasury and the Civil Service Commission (Mallaby, 1964, pp.5ff). In his evidence to the Committee he envisaged the role of central management being removed from the Treasury and assigned to what he eventually referred to as a Civil Service Department under a responsible Minister, preferably the Prime Minister, and including the Civil Service Commission (PRO: BA1/5).

C. H. Sisson, the Principal Establishment Officer at the Ministry of Labour, under questioning from Dunnett, told the Committee that when it came to running central management 'neither the Treasury nor the Civil Service Commission were what the doctor ordered'. Replying to Simey, Sisson thought that what he later referred to as a Ministry for the Civil Service was feasible, preferably staffed by civil servants seconded from other departments and reporting to a Treasury minister but outside the Treasury. Until Fulton suggested to him that the Prime Minister might act as Minister for the Civil Service with the support of a Minister of State, Sisson's main concern, expressed in replies to Simey and Kipping, was that a Ministry for the Civil Service would degenerate into little better than a Civil Service lobby (PRO: BA1/7).

Understandably, this was not a matter of great concern for the leading Civil Service staff associations, all but one of whom favoured the removal of central management functions from the Treasury. The FDA wanted 'a new organisation charged with overall managerial responsibility for the Civil Service' to be established with a senior cabinet minister as its political head. The organisation was to incorporate the Civil Service Commission, and; in order to safeguard the independence of the recruiting authority, they suggested that the permanent head of the new organisation should combine the roles of Head of the Civil Service and First Civil Service Commissioner, and that he should have his duties statutorily defined. 'Without having very strong views', the FDA was 'slightly inclined to favour the transfer of pay to the new organisation' (PRO: BA1/21). In oral evidence, G. W. Watson, a member of the executive committee of the FDA said that 'there is a fairly strong feeling of dissatisfaction with the way in which the Treasury runs the Civil Service. There is a feeling – which existed long before the war – that people in the Treasury or known to the Treasury get preferential treatment'. T. S. Pilling, the Chairman of the FDA told the Committee that there was also 'quite strong feeling' that the weight of the reforms needed in the Service called for 'a definitely more expert – more professional if you like – body of people to carry them out. To leave the responsibility with the Treasury management divisions, where people are posted in the main only for a spell in the course of a Treasury career, might be inferior to setting up a separate department which would establish its own professional method, its own kind of management specialism, and might approach the problems with a new outlook in that regard' (PRO: BA1/5).

The SCS, in its evidence to the Committee, said that the aim of any reconstruction of the central management of the Service should be 'to bring together under unified control the whole range of Civil Service affairs and to build a strong central leadership which will fight for the resources it requires and provide assistance and firm guidance to employing departments in carrying out their personnel and career management responsibilities.' The Society thought that the Treasury was too negative in its outlook for such a role, and it wanted to see established a 'combined central management organisation (covering recruitment and personnel management, including pay and conditions)', possibly to be 'linked with the Cabinet Office or the Prime Minister's Office.' The Permanent Secretary of this organisation was also to be 'Head of the Civil Service with direct responsibility to the Prime Minister who might be assisted by a Minister of State for Civil Service affairs.' The Society believed that 'such an arrangement would ensure that the new central management organisation had sufficient power and authority and the support of the Head of Government' (PRO: BA1/20).

The CSCA favoured 'the establishment of a new department, under a senior Cabinet Minister, to deal with all central personnel management matters' in the Service, sharing responsibility for central post-entry training with a Training Board, and leaving recruitment to a still independent Civil Service Commission (PRO: BA1/24).

Leaving the central management of the Home Civil Service with the Treasury was recommended to the Fulton Committee by R. A. Hayward, the Joint Secretary of the Staff Side of the National Whitley Council (PRO: BA1/5), and by one staff association, the IPCS. Of the other associations' proposed alternatives, the latter observed: 'Quite simply, if the central management organisation has to go to the Treasury for financial approval on all topics, the Treasury becomes the effective voice and the central management organisation is correspondingly weakened. Conversely, if the central management organisation is given financial independence, Treasury control is weakened to the point which we believe would be unacceptable to Parliament' (PRO: BA1/30). Nevil Johnson, a former civil servant, said in his evidence that compared with foreign practice, having an arrangement whereby 'the principal finance and economics department' had 'so much responsibility for the management of the Civil Service' was unusual, but it was one which was 'deeply embedded in the structure of British administration and in British thinking about financial control.' So, Johnson thought that 'it would be impracticable, at least in the near future, to divest the Treasury of large slices of its Civil Service responsibilities', although he did think that management functions such as training and education, which had little financial significance, could be transferred to the Civil Service Commission (PRO: BA1/24).

That Lord Normanbrook and Lord Bridges were firm advocates of the Treasury retaining its central management responsibilities was unsurprising. Bridges said that

> it was true that for many years Chancellors of the Exchequer, because of their other pre-occupations, had not done very much on the Civil Service side but there were other Ministers at the Treasury who could be brought into Civil Service matters. A Ministry for the Civil Service, even if it was also responsible for the machinery of government, would not provide enough work for a senior Minister, since very few of the questions arising from the management of the Civil Service were questions of policy appropriate to a Minister. Moreover, if there were a Minister for the Civil Service it would make more difficult the Head of the Service's access to the Prime Minister which was very important. He saw no reason why the recruitment responsibilities exercised by the Civil Service Commission should not be moved closer to central management and brought under Ministerial responsibility, provided it was laid down that Parliamentary Questions were out of order and Ministers did not intervene in individual cases. The management side of the Treasury should have its own separate staff made up largely by borrowing from other departments. The Treasury should not use its role in central management and its pre-eminent position to pinch all the talent from the rest of the Civil Service; it was necessary to strike a balance between the needs of the Treasury and the needs of departments. In his experience there was no foundation for the belief that to have rows with the Treasury on behalf of his department was a disadvantage to a man's career.

Lord Bridges also observed that 'in his day the combination of jobs as Head of the Treasury and of the Civil Service and Secretary of the Cabinet had been a very heavy burden and clearly it would be quite impracticable nowadays. Three men were needed for the three jobs. He would be against the remarriage, which was sometimes mooted, of the Secretary of the Cabinet with the Head of the Civil Service. The Secretary of the Cabinet was too much at the Prime Minister's bid and call to devote much time to the needs of the Service' (PRO: BA1/8). Lord Normanbrook said in his evidence that 'the sheer burden of work' in being both Secretary of the Cabinet and Head of the Home Civil Service had been 'too heavy' to enable the latter role to be carried out 'as satisfactorily as he would have wished' (PRO: BA1/3).

Naturally, the main task of defending the Treasury's position fell to the current Head of the Home Civil Service, Sir Laurence Helsby, whose memorandum on central management was circulated to the Fulton Committee in November 1966. This eventually appeared in the first part of the fifth volume of the Committee's published material, but at the time it was neither intended for publication nor shown to the staff associations (PRO: BA1/24).

In his oral evidence before the Committee, presented on 17 January 1967, Helsby said that

> ten years ago many Permanent Secretaries would have favoured minimal interference by the centre in the affairs of departments. Now, however, they all agreed that the work of the government had become so complex that the central management of both human and non-human resources was essential. It must moreover be co-ordinated; it would be chaotic if separate agencies dealt with each and spoke with different voices. The two sides of the Treasury were now rightly separated for many purposes, but they were co-ordinated and consultation was easy. Departments did not find that they could make one single application for both money and staff. But the two answers to the two applications were consistent . . . One Permanent Secretary had thought that the Treasury was too powerful. But this was a minority view; most found that the Treasury's replies were sensible and helpful (PRO: BA1/6).

To judge from the other evidence, the odd man out in this instance was Sir Maurice Dean.

Describing his own views, Helsby said that

> the ministerial structure of the Treasury was very convenient. Certain subjects were necessarily reserved to the Prime Minister; machinery of government, security, top appointments, and honours. He performed these functions as First Lord of the Treasury and not as Chairman of the Cabinet. The convention whereby the Head of the Civil Service dealt directly with the First Lord on the reserved subjects and with other Treasury Ministers on the rest was well understood and worked smoothly. If central management were removed from the Treasury, the question was: what Minister should be in charge?

If the Prime Minister kept the reserved subjects, which Helsby saw as being inescapable, then he believed 'there was not enough left in the management job to engage the full interest and activity of a strong senior Minister who could be an effective spokesman for the Civil Service in the Cabinet.' As Sir Laurence put it, 'the plums in the pie were reserved for the Prime Minister; the rest lacked glamour and political importance.' He accepted that it might be possible to give the job to the holder of one of the ancient offices such as Lord President of the Council, Chancellor of the Duchy of Lancaster, or Paymaster General, but

> such Ministers were appointed for a variety of reasons – which were unlikely to include their suitability for the job of managing the Civil Service. More important was the inevitable involvement of the Prime Minister; the interposition of any other senior Minister would be awkward. Admittedly, there was already a division of roles here between the Prime Minister and the Chancellor of the Exchequer but this convention had worked smoothly for many years. A new one might not.

So, 'if there were to be a change,' he believed, 'it should be to a department which was directly under the Prime Minister with a Minister of State in charge of minor matters' (PRO: BA1/6).

Of course, Helsby did not wish to see central management removed from the Treasury. Indeed, his view (supported by the experience of having once been First Civil Service Commissioner) was that the Civil Service Commission could be absorbed into the Treasury without producing a material change. On pay, 'the Chancellor of the Exchequer could put the Civil Service case as well as anyone else,' he said, believing that 'there would always be a tendency for the Civil Service to lag behind in pay, because the public watched like hawks for any signs of Government favouritism towards their own employees.' He did not accept that a Minister for the Civil Service would be in a similar position vis-à-vis the Treasury as the Secretary of State for Education and Science was when representing the interests of teachers, or the Home Secretary was in relation to the police. 'There is a difference,' Helsby said, 'In each of these cases, the staff concerned were a body of people used for a single purpose of government. The Civil Service reflected the totality of government activity, in which finance represented the main common element.'
Helsby

> did not attach great importance to the argument that the Treasury got a unique knowledge of departments through the exercise of their financial functions. The management side relied on the expenditure side to some extent; he would not think of recommending the appointment of a Principal Finance Officer without consulting the expenditure side. But this reliance was diminishing as the management side built up its own direct knowledge. There was, however, a kinship between the management of men and the management of money, and it was important to keep these functions closely linked whether in one department or in two working closely together.

He thought that 'more important was the organisation side. O. and M. was increasingly concerned with techniques for decision making. These particularly involved new methods of financial appraisal, cost benefit analysis, input/output budgeting etc. O. and M. needed considerable development on this side and it was very closely linked to the expenditure side of the Treasury.' Helsby argued that greater continuity of administration would be achieved if the financial and management sides of the Treasury were put into separate departments. He believed that 'it was healthy for the financial controllers to have experience of management and for management staff, who were necessarily concerned with the finance aspects of management, to have experience of financial control.' Then again 'the two sides of the Treasury were relatively small. There were 700 in management and 1,000 in finance. In each case only a fraction were graduates. The management function would certainly have to grow but he did not foresee a vast increase in staff. It would, therefore, be difficult to maintain good career management in two separate departments of this size.'

Summing up, Helsby said that 'the removal of central management to a department under the Prime Minister was feasible. He did not know whether it would work better than the present arrangements. In his view the strongest argument in favour of a change was the present image of the Treasury. Those who had experience of Treasury know that the image was false; the picture of parsimony ignored the recent development of the management side and the concept of partnership. But many believed that the Treasury was restrictive, and this belief must be reckoned with' (PRO: BA1/6).

Sir Laurence Helsby's arguments against the transfer of central management functions away from the Treasury did have the effect of changing the outlook of the Civil Service Commission. In his evidence to the Committee, presented on 7 June 1966, the First Civil Service Commissioner, Sir George Abell, had spoken in favour of the establishment of a separate Civil Service Department which would include the Civil Service Commission retaining its independence in its selection work (PRO: BA1/3). In his evidence on 7 December 1966, the First Civil Service Commissioner, while, naturally, insisting that the Commission would 'continue to claim independence for selection', told the Committee that he and the other Commissioners had found 'the Treasury memorandum' to be 'convincing' and that 'in fact it would not improve things by taking out management into a new department' (PRO: BA1/5). Unlike Abell and his fellow Civil Service Commissioners, Fulton and his Committee did find it possible to resist Sir Laurence Helsby's advocacy.

The Fulton Committee's Deliberations

The location and role of the central management of the Home Civil Service was not a subject that greatly divided the Fulton Committee. As we have seen, the balance of the evidence that the Committee received was in favour of taking central management away from the Treasury. In its deliberations, material from the foreign visits that members of the Committee had made was noted. So was a Treasury memorandum on Canadian arrangements for the central management of the Civil Service that was circulated as early as May 1966 (PRO: BA1/13), and Sir Laurence Helsby's evidence drew attention to Canadian as well as Australian experience. When R. A. Hayward of the National Staff Side said in his oral evidence that it would be an advantage for the Committee to meet D. Love of the Canadian Treasury Board, who had been associated with the Glassco Commission, and who was an admirer of the British system of central management of the Civil Service (PRO: BA1/5), action was taken. On 10 April 1967, Sir Norman Kipping, Sir Philip Allen, Norman Hunt, and Robert Neild talked informally with Love about the central management of the Canadian Civil Service, with a note being circulated subsequently by the Secretariat (PRO: BA1/34). Six days earlier, in oral evidence to the Committee, William McCall, the General Secretary of the IPCS, recognising that the staff association was in the minority in wanting the location of central management to be kept in the Treasury, pointed out that in the previous month the Canadians had changed their arrangements, and that 'of all the other alternatives available they chose to come back to the present British pattern of organisation' (PRO: BA1/8).

Sir James Dunnett's reaction at the time to McCall's information was unwelcoming. Sir James was an advocate of change, and twenty years later he observed: 'There was a widespread feeling among senior civil servants against Treasury control of the Civil Service, some of it dating from the Bridges line on pay which had been to keep it at low levels. Evelyn Sharp, who had served briefly in that department and had disliked it, was one leading civil servant who was very critical of the Treasury, and she was not alone in this. Like many other senior civil servants, I thought that it was necessary for a time to have a Civil Service Department to take a new view of things' (Interview, 1988).

Another member of the Fulton Committee with decided views was Robert Sheldon: 'Locating central management in the Treasury is no good. All the Treasury sees is gaping mouths. On every committee, it is the Treasury versus the rest. The Treasury has no time to be interested in man management. Its job is to keep spending down.' Looking back on ministerial experience in the 1970s, Sheldon said: 'I remember the lino was terrible in the Treasury. We found out in the C.S.D. that the cheapest way to replace it was with wall to wall carpeting, but that, of course, would have looked too ostentatious. So, the Treasury replaced the old, rotting lino with red lino that was actually more expensive than the wall to wall carpeting would have been, but it had the virtue of looking cheap. That is the Treasury outlook. The Fulton Committee thought, and I still think, that a separate Civil Service Department was needed to look after the Civil Service as a whole. The Treasury is not up to this' (Interview, 1988).

With attitudes like these present on the Fulton Committee, Sir Laurence Helsby had little hope of maintaining the Treasury's position, especially when the level of support that the existing arrangements were said by him to command among the Higher Civil Service was diminished when his fellow Permanent Secretary to the Treasury, Sir William Armstrong, lined up with the advocates of change. At its meeting on 9 May 1967, the Committee generally agreed that the central management of the Service should be taken out of the Treasury. It was also agreed that it would be necessary to have a Minister responsible for the Civil Service;

> the idea of an independent, non-ministerial Public Service Board as in some other countries was not supported. The question therefore was where should central management be located. Sir Edward Boyle thought that there were two sides of central management. The first was pay for which some economic Minister, such as the Chief Secretary or the Financial Secretary, or even a DEA Minister, could still be responsible. The second was personnel management and the machinery of government which might be made the responsibility of a senior Minister such

as the Lord President or the Chancellor of the Duchy. In answer to the point that such Ministers were often appointed on other grounds and given other, often heavy, duties, Sir Edward said that the arrangement could be flexible, the Lord President at one time, the Chancellor of the Duchy at another time and so on. Some members were not happy about the suggested division of pay and management and were not sure that it was necessary for an economic Minister to be responsible for pay; non-economic Ministers were responsible for the pay of doctors, teachers etc. An alternative suggestion was to put the management of the Civil Service under a Minister of State attached to the Prime Minister. Sir Edward thought that it would be a novelty in British government to have a Minister in a special, subordinate relationship to the Prime Minister. It was generally agreed that it was important that the official Head of the Civil Service should have access to the Prime Minister even though there was another Minister with a general responsibility. The Minister for the Civil Service should be a full-time job and, where practicable, should be a Minister who had had experience of the government machine. Doubts were expressed as to whether it would be within the Committee's terms of reference to make specific recommendations about Ministerial responsibility for the Civil Service. It would be better to set out the considerations but not to make a final, specific recommendation (PRO: BA1/8).

At its meetings on 3 and 4 July 1967, the Committee discussed the central management issue again. This time, while agreeing once more that this role 'should be the responsibility of a department, not the Treasury', the Committee also agreed that such a department should have 'a part-time senior Minister in charge and a Minister of State with responsibility for day-to-day management' and that 'the subjects now reserved to the Prime Minister should so continue.' There was agreement too that 'the Civil Service Commission should be part of the central management department but it should be independent in regard to the conduct of competitions.' The Committee also agreed that 'the central management department should be largely manned by staff coming in temporarily and permanently from the operating departments, but a good proportion of these should be staff making a speciality of establishments work in their own departments. When the central management department was first set up there might be advantage in bringing in some staff from outside the Service.' Further, the Committee agreed that 'consultations on top appointments should be formalized into a committee which should have a frequently changing membership with a mixture of administrators and others. There might be advantages in having outside members provided they were in a minority and were not ex-civil servants' (PRO: BA1/9).

Though there was early agreement on the Fulton Committee about the broad lines along which it thought that the central management of the Home Civil Service should be changed, discussion continued until the meetings on 13, 14 and 15 May 1968 (PRO: BA1/11). What was going to be said about the future relationship between the Treasury and the Civil Service Department was not really settled until after a meeting between Sir Philip Allen, Sir Edward Boyle, Norman Hunt, Sir Laurence Helsby and Sir William Armstrong, also attended by Richard Wilding, that was held in Helsby's room at the Treasury on 28 March 1968. This meeting had before it an informal note prepared by the Treasury which was not formal evidence to the Committee and which was not for publication. In this note, the Treasury referred to itself as the Public Expenditure Department and to what was to be the Civil Service Department as the Public Service Department. The following main points were made in discussion.

Firstly, 'in the allocation of functions between the two departments, a problem would be posed by those public services (e.g. police and local government) whose pay and numbers were now of some concern to the financial side of the Treasury, but which did not come within the direct purview of the pay and management side as teachers, National Health Service staff, and the Armed Forces did.' The Treasury note proposed that the Treasury's functions in relation to the latter should be transferred to the Public Service Department (PSD). Its functions in relation to the former could be considered later.

Secondly, 'overall manpower considerations – e.g. the forecasting of the manpower demands of different parts of the economy – would be a matter in which the DEA or the Ministry of Labour would take the lead. It would be the job of the PSD to speak for the public services on the question, and for its Minister to represent the public service interest on appropriate Ministerial committees.'

Thirdly, 'the remaining Treasury or Public Expenditure Department (PED) would continue to develop and disseminate techniques of financial analysis and systems of financial control. It would deal directly with the finance discussions of departments etc. on these matters (though it would be the responsibility of the PSD, after discussion with the PED, to arrange suitable training or to supervise departmental reorganisation in the interest of better financial control). The development and dissemination of managerial and administrative techniques, on the other hand, would lie with the PSD. Where these areas overlapped the two departments should work together. But this should be on the basis of joint teams set up *ad hoc* rather than of shared units; it was important to distinguish the separate responsibilities of the two departments as clearly as possible.'

Fourthly, 'on pay, the Treasury thought it most important that the PSD should have the final authority as employer; if a "faceless" PED stood behind, the Civil Service unions would want to negotiate with it rather than the PSD. The PED, like the DEA, would retain a big interest in incomes policy generally. But the administration of incomes policy in relation to public service employers should be the sole responsibility of the PSD. The relative position of the various public services vis-à-vis the central authority on pay would thus remain as it was today, with this authority vested in the PSD: the Civil Service would deal with it directly, the other services at one remove through the Ministers responsible for them. Ministers collectively would continue to have such overriding powers to upset agreements or insist that they should be staged as they possessed today; but the PED as such would have no special position in this.' Fifthly, 'machinery of government questions should pass wholly to the PSD'; and sixthly, 'the two central departments would need to co-operate closely,' and the Treasury hoped that 'the Committee's Report would indicate in very broad terms the way in which the split might work, and in particular assure the unions that the PSD should have full "employer" authority in pay matters.' The Treasury saw 'no objection to the idea that the Report might mention the transfer of the Treasury's "employer" functions vis-à-vis other services to the PSD in general terms, but should refer to the new department as a "Civil Service Department" in the context of its own terms of reference.' It was agreed too that Sir William Armstrong and Sir Laurence Helsby would see the relevant material before it was put into final form (PRO: BA1/50).

The Fulton Committee's published findings about the central management of the Home Civil Service were unsurprising, apart from references to the Whitley system of joint consultation and the role of the staff associations which were less reverential about Whitleyism in particular than conventional reformist wisdom commonly allowed. Otherwise, the Committee set out the reformist case much as it agreed at its meetings in July 1967. In a phrase that recalled evidence submitted to it by the SCS, the Committee advocated the establishment of a Civil Service Department to run the central management of the Home Civil Service, which Department would be in 'a position to fight, and to be seen to be fighting, the Treasury on behalf of the Service' (Cmd.3638, 1968, para.252). The Committee emphasised that the CSD which was to absorb the Civil Service Commission (ibid., para.254) needed to be staffed by 'men and women who have knowledge and experience of personnel management and organisation, both inside and outside the Civil Service' (ibid., para.255). The Committee wanted the Permanent Secretary of the CSD to become the Head of the Home Civil Service (ibid., para.258), while recommending that in giving evidence to the Prime Minister on appointments at Deputy Secretary level and above that official should be assisted by a committee of rotating membership consisting of 'two or three Permanent Secretaries, an approximately equal number of scientists or other specialists, and not more than two eminent people from outside the Service' (ibid., para.260). The Committee also added that 'we hope that we are not exceeding our terms of reference too much if we recommend that, outside the area for which he is directly responsible already, the Prime Minister should delegate day-to-day responsibility [for the CSD] to a non-departmental Minister of appropriate seniority who is also a member of the Cabinet. His part will be of vital importance, especially during the period of reorganisation' (ibid., para.261).

The Fulton Report's discussion of the future working relationship between the CSD and the Treasury benefited from the discussions that had taken place with the latter department in March 1968. What the Fulton Committee never did in its Report, though, was directly to confront the arguments against change of the kind marshalled by Sir Laurence Helsby in earlier memoranda. There seems no cause to doubt that the Committee was convinced of what it perceived to be the case for establishing a Civil Service Department, and that it was not merely seeking what the then Head of the Home Civil Service called 'some presentational advantage' (PRO: BA1/24).

Chapter 5

Organisation of Central Government Departments

The Context for Change

Though the Fulton Committee was required to abstain from making recommendations about the general organisation of the machinery of central government and about the current working of the doctrine of ministerial responsibility, the internal structure of central government departments and the promotion of efficiency in them were matters within the Committee's terms of reference. As there were not always clear boundaries that could be drawn between these subject matters, the Committee, like some who presented evidence to it, was bound to stray into territory that was forbidden.

This was always likely to happen given that, in the years leading to the appointment of the Fulton Committee, complacency about the manner in which the British system of government was organised had come to be in relatively short supply. It may well have been the case, as one distinguished academic observer has written, that if the projected White Paper of the Anderson Committee on the Machinery of Government had been published in 1945, 'it would have contained a clear message in favour of British methods of government and a firm faith in the established Constitution' (Lee, 1977, p.143). Such sentiments were understandable at the end of the Second World War in which Britain had secured a moral victory and shared in a military one. Ten years and more later, a climate of opinion more conducive to institutional change had been created. By that time, the political costs of the War were more obvious. The Crichel Down affair had cast doubt upon the efficiency of the core constitutional convention of ministerial responsibility in modern conditions. Perhaps most importantly, the Keynesian Welfare State, though still politically sacrosanct, was already in difficulties as an economic and social order capable of success in international competition.

The reorganisation of government departments, like the reform of the Civil Service, was never going to play a major part in reversing or even arresting relative national decline. Like their counterparts in the first decade or so of the twentieth century, the 'national efficiency' reformers of the period from the late 1950s onwards thought otherwise, of course, with the ubiquitous Thomas Balogh leading the way. At the time, the Haldane Report on the

Machinery of Government of 1918, the last act of the earlier 'national efficiency' movement (Searle, 1971, pp.239, 259–60), was still the main domestic blueprint for change. There still seemed point to the Haldane Committee's observation that 'in the sphere of civil government the duty of investigation and thought, as preliminary to action, might with great advantage be more definitely recognised' (Cd. 9230, 1918, p.6).

A quarter of a century later, citing the Haldane Report, PEP had proposed that a Planning Group should be established in all major government departments to engage in policy planning and research. The head of this specialised division was to have high status and direct access to the Permanent Secretary, with the Planning Group's work being directed by a standing Policy Committee in close touch with the Minister (PEP, 1943, pp.5). In the same month that the Fulton Committee was appointed, the Prime Minister's Parliamentary Private Secretary, Peter Shore, criticised 'the lack of research centres or policy planning units in the Ministries. Even at the lowest level of information, there is quite inadequate feedback arrangements through which departments can evaluate the effects of their own actions. As for long term policy, the need for organized thinking and research has been virtually ignored.' Shore thought that the 'fundamental problems' of policy would 'never be seriously and sensibly tackled until thinking and research is more adequately organized' (Shore, 1966, p.154).

'The most important reform of all is to make the power of Ministers more effective in their own departments,' Shore went on to say; 'Deluged by work, largely cut off from Ministerial colleagues, separated from supporting MPs by the Official Secrets Act, accessible on a day-to-day basis only to top officials, none of which they have appointed, Ministers have a relationship with their civil servants which is dangerously unbalanced and dependent.' Shore believed that the power of ministers would be strengthened 'by ensuring that top advisers, knowing the Minister's policies and able to watch over the main fields for which he is responsible, are brought into the departments' (ibid., p.155).

Balogh similarly portrayed ministers as being 'overworked and isolated' and unable to control their departments. Balogh suggested that

> all major departments . . . should be put under a Committee of equal Permanent Officials who are to advise the Minister as a body on all major questions. Each of these civil servants, as in America, should be in charge of a part of the office (or certain functions entrusted to it if they can be separated). In this way there is hope that the advice tendered will be informed and not merely inspired. The power position between Ministers and civil servants will begin to approach the picture painted in constitutional fiction.

Though Balogh believed that 'the American system which replaces the Heads of Divisions with politically trusted experts whenever the Party in power changes has worked much better than the British', the 'relatively minor reform' that he proposed was the 'compromise' that 'Ministers in charge of large departments must at least be armed with Private Offices and experts recruited from outside and dependent on the Minister' (Balogh, 1959, p.121f).

Continental European rather than American models of public administration tended to be more in vogue with 'national efficiency' reformers in the years before Fulton. Of the structure of British central government departments, for instance, Brian Chapman wrote in 1963: 'The Minister's constitutional responsibility for the entire work of his department inevitably results in an administrative pyramid with the Permanent Secretary at its apex. It is by no means certain that this is the best organizational form for a Ministry, and, with a few exceptions, it is not found in European government' (Chapman, 1963, p.40). Chapman thought that in British government 'the logic' of what were then 'the recent internal reforms in the Treasury' would probably lead 'to Ministries operating on the basis of directorates and a *cabinet*' (ibid., p.42). Enthusiasm of this kind for French-style arrangements was matched in others by admiration for the way things were done in Sweden, where there was the institution of the Ombudsman, a form of 'open government', and a structure of central government departmental organisation one feature of which was what Chapman called 'the purest type of board administration, a system by no means unknown in Britain in the eighteenth and nineteenth centuries' (ibid., p.35).

The Board of Admiralty in Britain, of course, as Balogh knew, functioned as a Ministerial board in the twentieth century and, indeed, all the way down to March 1964, with the Permanent Secretary being one member of it (Roskill, I, 1968, p.25f; Hampshire, 1975, p.224; cf. Greaves, 1947, p.106). Balogh's advocacy of a collegiate structure for decision making in government departments recalled the endorsement in the 1930s, by F. A. A. Menzler of the IPCS, of 'the Bridgeman Committee's remedy for the weaknesses it discovered in Post Office administration, viz. the creation of a functional Board' as being 'a simple panacea of general application.' With the Permanent Secretary, like the Director General of the Post Office, being no more than *primus inter pares*, Menzler wrote that 'the Minister would have the opportunity of hearing first hand the view of his expert advisers'; and it was his belief that 'the establishment of the Board system with adaptions to suit particular departmental needs would be . . . the fundamental step towards the emancipation of the expert' (Menzler, 1937, p.181f). The Post Office, though, more generally tended to be perceived as being *sui generis* among government departments rather than having a structure worth copying, and by the time of the Fulton Committee it was on the way to becoming a public corporation.

In reviewing the internal organisation of government departments, the Fulton Committee conducted its work when the climate of opinion was still that engendered by the Plowden Committee on the Control of Public Expenditure with its emphasis on departments from the Permanent Secretary downwards giving more priority to and seeking greater efficiency in Civil

Service management and to the promotion of the relevant services. The findings of the Fulton Committee's Management Consultancy Group ensured that the possible adoption of private enterprise practices in departments formed part of the review.

Review of the Main Evidence

1. The hiving-off of executive activities of departments

The formal exclusion of the general organisation of the machinery of government from the Fulton Committee's terms of reference did not prevent the possible hiving off of activities from government departments to autonomous boards from being considered in evidence. As would be expected, too, it proved impossible to review how individual government departments themselves should be organised, which had to be a concern of the Committee, without reference to the practice of ministerial responsibility.

The main arguments advanced in evidence to the Committee in favour of hiving off were fairly described by the Committee's Secretariat as being that (a) it would 'take executive activities outside the ambit of detailed Parliamentary scrutiny'; that (b) it would 'free the policy making element in departments from executive responsibilities'; that (c) it would 'free executive activities from central management of recruitment, pay etc.'; and that (d) it would 'introduce a new concept of accountability for performance into the management of executive activities' (PRO: BA1/38).

'It might be right to move in the direction of "hiving off" purely managerial functions from the Civil Service proper', Sir Burke Trend, the Secretary of the Cabinet, had told the Committee; 'But he would advocate looking very carefully at each case on its merits. Too sharp a distinction would cut policy making off from one of its roots, and the ambiguous position of nationalized industries vis-à-vis Ministers, though it had settled down to some extent, was still uncomfortable' (PRO: BA1/4).

The Joint Permanent Secretary to the Treasury, Sir William Armstrong, said in his evidence that it was necessary to ask whether the executive management of public services was best carried out within the traditional framework of a Ministerial department or whether it should not to some degree approximate to the pattern of the BBC or the nationalised industries. He suggested that there might be services, e.g. health and education, the executive management of which could be delegated to official boards or commissions, while retaining Ministers' responsibility for major policy and forward thinking.

> The boards would have public accountability for the efficiency and humanity of the working of the service. They would also have delegated financial responsibility within the framework of an overall budget decided upon by Ministers. The Inland Revenue and the Customs and Excise were already run rather on these lines. He had not thought out which other services could be run in this way, although National

Insurance suggested itself as an example. The system certainly could not be applied to the whole of the work of the Service; there were departments, such as the Home Office, where much of policy emerged from case work. He did not suggest that the Committee could identify all the areas in which this solution would be practicable. But the principle was worth examination. Such a new system would change the role of the civil servants concerned. He had no blueprint to put forward but he thought that a new kind of structure would be needed, and a new concept of accountability; he saw the head of an executive board as a public figure in his own right (PRO: BA1/3).

Another serving official, W. S. Ryrie, an Assistant Secretary at the Treasury, wrote in his evidence that 'a drastic reorganisation and simplification of the central departments' was needed with 'responsibility . . . delegated to subsidiary bodies with well defined functions wherever possible, removed from day-to-day Parliamentary scrutiny' (PRO: BA1/31).

When asked for her views on the possibility of taking some kinds of work out of the immediate ambit of ministerial departments and putting them under semi-autonomous boards, Dame Evelyn Sharp said that whenever possible this should be done (PRO: BA1/4); and the former Head of the Home Civil Service, Lord Normanbrook observed that

> there were in the Service blocks of executive management work which could well be 'hived off' from Ministerial departments and put under boards. The Ministry of Pensions and National Insurance was an example which suggested itself. If the board system were brought back into fashion, there might be the further advantage of relief from business arising from day-to-day accountability to Parliament – especially if the Ombudsman partly replaced Parliament as the protector of the interests of individuals (PRO: BA1/3).

Lord Franks thought that hiving off was

> practicable where the Government could frame a reasonably permanent policy, for example in an Act of Parliament, and then hand it over to others for execution. The US Interstate Commerce Commission was an example. The Inland Revenue could conceivably be an example in this country. But there were many areas where the reality of policy lay in the continuous working out of means to the desired end; here he thought it would be very much more difficult (PRO: BA1/3).

'The basic case for "hiving off" was the simulation of a business situation,' Professor W. J. M. Mackenzie suggested to the Committee in his evidence, not himself being convinced of the need to follow the example of Swedish central government arrangements (PRO: BA1/6). Sir Ronald Edwards, an academic who combined this role with being Chairman of the Electricity Council, 'did not believe that it was possible to distinguish between those decisions which were for Ministers and those which were not.' He envisaged the civil servant who would be the head of a hived off executive service being 'a public figure like the head of a nationalized industry' (PRO: BA1/4). Lord Reith, who, of course, had been such a figure at the BBC, was 'strongly in favour of "hiving off" some central government services to the control of public corporations. The constitution of the Civil Service, the pressure of the Parliamentary question, and the civil servant's security of tenure were not conducive to managerial efficiency. A public corporation could provide decent and flexible conditions of service and, he guessed, a fifty per cent increase in efficiency' (PRO: BA1/26). An existing public corporation, British European Airways, suggested in its evidence that Civil Service executive services should be hived off (PRO: BA1/25). The Confederation of British Industry in its oral evidence maintained that it would be easier to set objectives and measure success in reaching them if services were hived off to independent boards, which would also allow greater opportunities for personal responsibility and flexibility in operating programmes (PRO: BA1/5).

There was scepticism about the virtues of hiving off expressed in some of the evidence submitted by serving and former civil servants. Sir Alexander Johnston, Chairman of the Board of Inland Revenue, told the Committee in June 1966 that having a board system was 'a good arrangement within its own field and might be capable of application elsewhere where the work consisted of administering a detailed code, for example, in the MPNI. However, it was significant that at one time there were a number of boards in the government service which had now vanished and become government departments' (PRO: BA1/3). In evidence presented in March 1967, he emphasised the difficulty of copying the Inland Revenue example: 'One reason was that they were in a statutory position and not answerable to Ministers on the affairs of individual tax payers: the tax payer's remedy lay in an appeal and not in a Parliamentary question. It was difficult to see the same system working in the Ministry of Social Security (as the MPNI had become), even though they too operated an appeal system on a limited scale' (PRO: BA1/8).

Lord Bridges said that 'there were areas in which "hiving off" was feasible and areas in which it was not. He was a bit sceptical about it because he saw very few areas in which policy was so fixed that it was not at the play of current events. The example of the Inland Revenue was worth considering because it had been done not by an attempt to differentiate between policy and execution but by the devolution of decision making' (PRO: BA1/8). Though he thought that a move in the direction of the Swedish system was a worthy matter for debate, Sir Lesie Rowan, a former Treasury official who had moved into private industry, said that 'it would not be possible to separate thinking and doing in his company', and he was 'opposed to complete separation' of these roles in central government 'because it would lead to disunity within the Service.' He observed that 'there was a relationship, which should not be forgotten, between executive actions on the part of the Government and the ballot box;' and he added that 'it had to be borne in mind that the agencies within the United States Federal Government Service were by no means immune from public examination and criticism' (PRO: BA1/4).

There were reservations about the virtues of 'hiving off' expressed by the few ministers and ex-ministers who discussed the subject in their evidence to the Committee, with the exception of Aubrey Jones who thought that 'the removal of blocks of Civil Service work from the immediate ambit of Ministerial departments' would be 'a welcome relief to Ministers' (PRO: BA1/3). Another Conservative, William Whitelaw was 'not clear what advantages "hiving off" might have within the Civil Service, but, as regards relations between the Civil Service and Parliament, he thought that it would tend to be a theoretical exercise, because any major issues which aroused political attention would go back into Parliament whatever the organizational relations that had been made' (PRO: BA1/5).

Jeremy Bray thought that hiving off appeared 'attractive at the present time because of the way in which the administration operated, but if the mode of operation were made more loose-limbed, he would be against it' (PRO: BA1/6). Another Labour minister, Richard Crossman, said that 'there must be a number of subjects of public administration which it would be profitable to "hive off."' He had been very glad to push rent assessment out of the Ministry of Housing and Local Government. That suggested that the pattern might be to use the machinery of a Ministerial department to set a public activity going, and then get rid of it and let it run itself as soon as it was capable of doing so. However, he did not think 'that agencies should be completely out of the control of Ministers; one must beware of the dangers of a Corporate State. For instance, it would perhaps not intrinsically be a good thing to "hive off" pensions from the Ministry of Social Security.' He added that

> as to the argument that 'hiving off' would free Ministers and senior officials from a lot of day-to-day responsibilities and enable them to devote more time to policy formation, it was certainly true that Ministers would long to 'hive off' as much departmental work as they could do so long as their lives were so organized that they had no time to think. However, it might in fact be preferable to deal with this problem not by 'hiving off' but by reorganizing the top structure of Ministries in order to relieve Ministers and senior officials of much of their burden of day-to-day administration' (PRO: BA1/7).

The Fulton Committee received little evidence about which specific activities should be 'hived off', as its Secretariat remarked (PRO: BA1/38). An exception was the evidence presented by the North East Metropolitan Regional Hospital Board which wanted the internal running of the National Health Service to be delegated to a 'General Staff' recruited mainly from the health services under the direction of a Ministry similarly staffed (PRO: BA1/29).

The CBI initially put forward the NHS as a candidate for hiving off, although its representatives did not stand up too well to questioning from Norman Hunt and Sir Philip Allen in particular when asked about what this actually meant; and the CBI's final position seemed to be that hiving off was most suitable for the Export Credits Guarantee Department and the road programme and activities generally that were more akin to industrial tasks (PRO: BA1/5).

The scepticism which Crossman and, eventually, Johnston had expressed about the feasibility of hiving off social security was shared by Professor Mackenzie (PRO: BA1/6); and the Committee took most interest in proposals about the relationship between Whitehall and the NHS. Lord Bridges had told the Committee that 'his impression was that the departmental set up of the Ministry of Health did not suit them at all, that the department was not sure of its ethos and lacked a single soul. However, he was not sure what the solution was' (PRO: BA1/8). Before giving oral evidence, Sir Arnold France, the Permanent Secretary of the Ministry of Health, was asked by Richard Wilding to put in a paper about the practicability of having an hived off NHS Board. Sir Arnold's paper pointed out that the running of the NHS was already hived off to a large extent to hospital boards and local executive councils and so on, and it was doubtful whether further hiving off would be politically acceptable, given not least the scale of public expenditure, or whether it would be conducive to greater efficiency (PRO: BA1/9, BA1/32).

2. Ministers and their departments: ministerial cabinets and the use of irregulars

Though, like the overall structure of the machinery of government, the current working of the doctrine of ministerial responsibility had been placed outside the Fulton Committee's remit, evidence submitted to the Committee similarly did not always respect this limitation on the field of review, and not surprisingly so, given that the internal organisation of government departments was deemed to be the Committee's legitimate concern.

Whether government departments were subject to effective political control was doubted by the Labour Party in evidence that was 'drafted in the Party's Research Department in consultation with a number of people in the Party and our Fabian colleagues, representing a very wide and varied experience of the Civil Service.' The Labour Party alleged that higher civil servants deliberately concealed vital information from ministers to ensure favoured policies were pursued (PRO: BA1/27). As the Prime Minister and some of his cabinet colleagues were members of the Labour Party's National Executive, Harold Wilson took the opportunity, when presented, to dissociate himself from the allegation (Wilson, 1967, p.184; 739 HC Deb. 5s. c.1267–8).

The Home Secretary, Roy Jenkins, in discussion with Lord Fulton and Sir Philip Allen, 'certainly did not agree that there was deliberate withholding of information from Ministers.' Jenkins said that 'in his career as a Minister he had not found any difficulty about getting his policies carried out. Civil servants would argue with him about the merits and demerits of a particular proposal, but once the issue had been thrashed out and a decision taken he had found complete loyalty in carrying out the decision' (PRO: BA1/30).

Richard Crossman told the Committee that 'the Higher Civil Service was a coherent and cohesive oligarchy presenting Ministers with narrow alternatives of choice.' He said that

> civil servants had no loyalty to their Ministers; their loyalty was to their colleagues in the Civil Service, to whom they passed on information about their Minister. For instance as Minister of Housing and Local Government he had found that his officials passed on everything about what he was planning, including his consultations with his allies in the Cabinet, to the Treasury, that is, from the point of view of a Minister of Housing and Local Government to the enemy. All this had the effect of separating a Minister from his colleagues, and of preventing any united front of Ministers to counterbalance the united front of civil servants. He did not blame civil servants for the way that they operated. He had no evidence that civil servants treated Labour Ministers differently from Conservative Ministers. If there was a conspiracy it was a conspiracy of the permanent against the impermanent; no doubt civil servants felt that they had to behave as they did in order to preserve a departmental continuity in the face of frequent changes of Minister. In his opinion nothing devalued Ministers in the eyes of the public as well as those of the Civil Service more than frequent changes of office.

When he was asked whether the passing on of information from a department like the Ministry of Housing and Local Government to the Treasury might not in fact be the way in which the officials of the spending departments tried to soften up the Treasury to take a favourable attitude, Crossman agreed that this 'might often be the case, but thought that it underlined the need for a civil servant ambitious of success to be in good standing with the Treasury, which he considered to be undesirable' (PRO: BA1/6).

In order to strengthen political control over government departments, the Labour Party proposed in its evidence that an incoming Minister should have the power to appoint his own *cabinet*, 'a political brains trust,' which would have research and liaison functions, and the role of 'transmitting the political impulse from the Minister to officials working in the department who may rarely or never see him' (PRO: BA1/27). The Labour sympathiser and academic, Roger Opie, told the Committee that there was 'no alternative to the formation of something along the lines of the *Cabinet du Ministre* system in France. To argue that this will only encourage a Minister to bring people who agree with his views is of course the whole point' (PRO: BA1/37). Another Labour sympathiser, at the time Director General of the Economic Planning Staff at the Ministry of Overseas Development, Dudley Seers, without being so institutionally specific, wrote that 'it should be accepted practice that a Minister brings his own immediate advisers with him when he takes office'

(PRO: BA1/33); and Thomas Balogh made a similarly generalised proposal (PRO: BA1/2). The serving official, Sir Eric Roll, thought that

> French practice was particularly interesting because it did not involve a wholesale change every time the Government changed (which he thought would be highly undesirable in this country) nor were the political advisers for the most part brought in from outside the Civil Service. Senior civil servants in France tended to be identified with particular policies to a much greater extent than here. However, he agreed that that was easier in France because of the absence of a two party system; identification with a policy did not necessarily mean identification with a whole party programme and ideology (PRO: BA1/3).

The Secretary of State for Education and Science, Anthony Crosland, remarked in his evidence to the Committee about 'the Minister's sense of political loneliness', and said that

> before and on first becoming a Minister he had thought that the answer might be to set up a Ministerial *cabinet* as in France. However, whatever the general merits of that kind of system, in his department a Ministerial *cabinet* would have to be manned by educationists and the nature of educationists was such that they would create antagonisms and disarray in the department. He now got the advice he needed from various sources. His PPS was a former school teacher. He was in close touch with the Chairman of the back bench education group, also a former teacher. Both had also served in local education authorities. He invited groups of helpful people to his house in an informal way. His Permanent Secretary quite welcomed all that (PRO: BA1/4).

Denis Healey told the Committee that when he first became Secretary of State at the Ministry of Defence 'he had thought of having a Ministerial *cabinet* on either the French or the American model. However, he had decided against it, first, because it would injure the morale of the permanent Civil Service, and, secondly, because it would act as a buffer against direct personal access to the senior men [in the Ministry]' (PRO: BA1/3). Roy Jenkins was 'against the Minister having his own separate *cabinet*. He himself had the part time services of a special adviser, and found this valuable. But he did not want more than this. He did however attach very great importance to having a strong Private Office' (PRO: BA1/30). Richard Crossman said that 'the introduction of a *cabinet* system on the French model would be nonsense. An outsider could not do the job, whereas if he tried hard a Minister could get a Private Office which would give him the right service.' Crossman, though, saw 'the need for one outsider in a Minister's Private Office in order to do political speech writing and letter writing. Ministers needed outside advice and he had encountered considerable opposition in getting it' (PRO: BA1/6).

Besides the introduction of Ministerial *cabinets* into government departments, the Labour Party also proposed that there should be short term political appointments to a limited number of 'posts of confidence' located at strategic points in departments, with the aim of ensuring the implementation of particular policies. The holders of these 'posts' were to have privileged access to Ministers (PRO: BA1/27). This proposal, as did that for *cabinets*, looked like an attempt to systematise and, in some respects, to extend the practice of importing politically sympathetic 'irregulars' into government departments as various Labour Ministers had been doing since 1964. The experience of this practice, which the Fabian Society, helpfully for the Committee, analysed in favourably inclined evidence (PRO: BA1/31), tended to be the main focus of a discussion in which several of those giving evidence drew a distinction between the desirability or otherwise of bringing political appointees into departments, and the temporary recruitment of more disinterested specialist advisers or, as the academic, Trevor Smith, called them, 'agnostics' (PRO: BA1/27).

Sir Laurence Helsby told the Committee that he took 'a pragmatic attitude' to the importing of political advisers into departments, observing that: 'It would be possible to go so far in introducing special advisers attached to Ministers as to endanger the concept of a non-political Civil Service. But he thought that the importance of recent appointments from this point of view could easily be exaggerated; and many recent imports would probably stay in the Civil Service even if there were a change of Government' (PRO: BA1/3). Sir William Armstrong saw 'no great principles at stake in the practice of bringing in special advisers to Ministers from outside the Service.' He said that 'the Service had accommodated itself to the introduction of these people without any serious embarrassment,' although he did associate the advisers with 'a considerable slowing down in the working of the machine' (PRO: BA1/3). Sir Burke Trend thought there was room for outside advisers, always provided that the permanent core and structure of the Civil Service was retained. With American experience in mind too, he observed that 'the gains' from the use of such advisers 'lay in the virtue of the fresh eye,' and among 'the losses' was 'the fact that those who merely hopped in and out could have no sense of continuing responsibility' (PRO: BA1/4). Lord Franks considered that 'the temporary adviser's best role was as a person who was around and with whom the Minister could rub minds; he could come fresh and with unexhausted physical energy (one not minor point) and could be used as a valuable extension of the Minister's own personality in the department. All this was good and more use could be made of it. But he thought it essential to avoid substituting the temporary adviser for the regular machinery of the department. This could not work' (PRO: BA1/3). Lord Bridges said of the British Civil Service that 'we had perhaps been rather stuffy compared with the Americans in bringing in outside advisers. However, he would be alarmed if outside advisers were chosen not as experts but as the Minister's confidants' (PRO: BA1/8). Dame Evelyn Sharp's view on irregulars was that 'she sympathised with Ministers' need for advice from outside the Civil Service machine and undoubtedly outside advisers were very useful at times. However, there was a difficult problem of choice; the wrong man could cause harmful strains in a department. On the whole, she thought that outside advisers should be specialists with specific terms of reference brought in to advise on a particular subject. She did not like the sort of outside adviser who was brought in merely to wander around the department and tell the Minister what was happening' (PRO: BA1/4).

The Special Adviser to the Chancellor of the Exchequer between 1964 and 1968, Professor Nicholas Kaldor, told the Committee that

> the experiment of bringing in temporary advisers to Ministers from outside the Service worked well. The advisers worked with officials but had their own access to Ministers. They usually agreed with the official brief but it was valuable that they were free to dissent. Official briefs were necessarily synthesized, even though in their formulation there might at earlier stages have been considered divergence of views. The outside adviser was able to give the Minister alternative views. There was also the important consideration of sympathy of political outlook. The adviser's presence was also stimulating to officials. Therefore he hoped the practice would be maintained by future Administrations of all parties. Usually one such adviser to a Minister would be enough, but the adviser might need two or three men under him (PRO: BA1/3).

Thomas Balogh, naturally, stressed in his evidence the importance of Ministers having 'their own advisers, not necessarily in their Private Offices, upon whom they can depend personally, and who at the same time share the political orientation of the Minister' (PRO: BA1/12).

Serving Labour cabinet ministers said relatively little in their evidence about the practice of using outside advisers, although, as we shall see, Anthony Crosland had institutional ideas which involved their deployment. It was interesting that former Conservative ministers tended to be unenthusiastic about the use of irregulars. Reginald Maudling, for instance, said in evidence that 'expert advice from outside the Civil Service was valuable and should be available to Ministers and senior officials, but he thought that it was dangerous to bring experts into the Service temporarily from outside, because they did not stay in long enough to adapt themselves and acquire the administrative *savoir-faire*' (PRO: BA1/6). It was surprising that the Civil Service staff associations generally made little comment about the introduction of outsiders into government departments. The IPCS was an exception. That association could see a role for outside experts, though one which would have to 'fit into the appropriate place in the machine'; but it dismissed the use of 'general political advisers' as having been 'adapted from foreign practice without sufficient consideration of the fact that our political and constitutional system is different from those in other countries' (PRO: BA1/30). The anxieties about the confidentiality of advice given by irregulars, which Sir Leslie Rowan expressed in his evidence (PRO: BA1/4), exemplified the

British outlook. Sir Burke Trend observed that 'the danger of the temporary adviser . . . lay not so much in the breach of anonymity while he was in the Service but in his natural tendency to self justification when he went out again. If decisions were taken during his time with which he must be expected to have disagreed, he might feel that his own reputation required him to explain how he had been overborne' (PRO: BA1/4).

3. *The Official Secrets Act, openness, and the anonymity of civil servants*

'The Official Secrets Act and the tradition of anonymity' were 'powerful forces in retaining the real power in the hands of officials,' Roger Opie wrote in evidence that argued that the balance needed to be redressed in favour of ministers (PRO: BA1/37). Arguments that the anonymity of civil servants in the making of public policy should be relaxed were a familiar feature of evidence submitted to the Fulton Committee, being a view expressed by, among others, Professor W. J. M. Mackenzie (PRO: BA1/6), Professor David Donnison (PRO: BA1/5), Sir Ronald Edwards (PRO: BA1/4), Jeremy Bray (PRO: BA1/28), the Shell International Petroleum Company (PRO: BA1/28), the Consumer Council (PRO: BA1/24), and the Liberal Party (PRO: BA1/25). The IRSF took the opportunity to argue for the relaxation of rules constraining party political activity on the part of civil servants (PRO: BA1/25).

Most of those who presented evidence in favour of greater openness, though, did so on the grounds that public policy-making would benefit from this, and that change was taking place anyway. Sir John Maud, a former Permanent Secretary, said that 'the philosophy of anonymity had become unreal' and the development of specialised parliamentary committees would make it even more so (PRO: BA1/5). Sir Andrew Cohen, the Permanent Secretary at the Ministry of Overseas Development, told the Committee that 'everyone who knows anything knows that senior civil servants in practice have to take personal responsibility for a great deal of what goes on,' which meant that 'the proposition, often hotly defended, that civil servants should be anonymous in the sense that they should not take part in public discussion' was 'a sacred cow.' Cohen wrote that

> this hiding under the blanket of anonymity seems to me both unnatural, hypocritical and perhaps dangerous to the public interest . . . I can see no real difficulty about retaining one's reputation for impartiality and objectivity even if one ceased to be anonymous. It is perfectly possible to talk publicly about things which are controversial politically without oneself indulging in political controversy. In the United States there is a shadowy line between people regarded wholly as politicians and those regarded wholly as civil servants. Those on the borderline, e.g. Assistant Secretaries and Deputy Assistant Secretaries in the State Department, manage very well on the whole without complete anonymity. I believe that senior civil servants here in Britain could do the same (PRO: BA1/22).

The academic and former civil servant, Nevil Johnson, wrote in his evidence that

> the linking of neutrality and anonymity has been willed by politicians. It is they who have encouraged so extensive an interpretation of the doctrine of Ministerial responsibility that it is no longer conceivable that a civil servant might give information and express opinions simply as a servant of the State without any implication that he is thereby committing his Minister. Undoubtedly, if the relations between the higher levels of the Civil Service and the world outside Government are to become closer and less inhibited, this situation must gradually be modified. Both civil servants and Ministers need to take a more relaxed view of what civil servants can say and write without infringing the principle of political neutrality or involving Ministers in political commitments. (PRO: BA1/24).

The only serving cabinet minister to say much directly on the subject, Roy Jenkins, was of the opinion that 'perhaps the anonymity of the civil servant was overdone', and that he 'would not see serious objection to civil servants appearing before House of Commons specialist committees on a rather greater scale than hitherto and in public.' However, Jenkins added that 'this could not be taken too far, since a civil servant who was associated openly with a particular line of policy would clearly be in a difficult position if there were a change of Administration and a Minister came in who followed another policy' (PRO: BA1/30).

The FDA, in evidence specially requested by the Committee, wrote of anonymity that higher civil servants took a more prominent part in the discussion of public policy than was commonly realised, notably in giving evidence to the committees of the House of Commons, and the Association believed that anonymity could be further relaxed. More informed public debate would result, but there were risks involved, including the starting of rumours about future policy developments, the identification of civil servants' views which might be at variance with those of Ministers, and the implication of dissent from settled policy. The FDA thought that the risks were worth taking and that they would be minimised if officials confined themselves mainly to professional and academic forums rather than the artificial confrontations of television journalism, and limited themselves as well to long-term policy issues rather than current ones (PRO: BA1/29).

> Lord Bridges said that
>
> in considering whether a relaxation of anonymity was desirable and practicable one should reflect on what would happen on a change of Government if a Permanent Secretary had become publicly identified with the policies of the outgoing Minister. A Permanent Secretary should not be the advocate of Ministerial policy but should confine himself to explaining the details of agreed policies. Another point to be considered was how far would Ministers like it if senior officials became public

figures. The late Sir Godfrey Ince had at times attracted the limelight and had rather acquired the public image of a policy maker. Ministers were not altogether pleased.

Presumably with his own practice in mind, Bridges saw no difficulty in senior officials making speeches, giving lectures, and writing articles, always provided that the subjects were chosen carefully (PRO: BA1/13).

William Whitelaw pointed out in his evidence that, however desirable in principle it was to relax anonymity,

> it was very difficult for civil servants to make any public pronouncements without entering into controversial and party political matters (or, what was as bad, being so interpreted) and that would impair the vital principle of political neutrality . . . it had to be recognized that what would interest the press, television and so forth would be anything indicative or capable of being interpreted as an advance statement of Ministerial policy or – even more exciting in the Fleet Street scale of values – evidence of disagreement between officials and Ministers (PRO: BA1/5).

4. The office of Permanent Secretary

Of the various proposals that the Fulton Committee received relating to the reorganisation of central government departments, among the more radical was advocacy of the abolition of the office of Permanent Secretary and its replacement by a board system.

As in his writings, Thomas Balogh proposed institutional changes of this kind in his evidence to the Committee in which he said that he 'believed strongly in the collegiate system of government' on the basis of the experience of university life. Balogh recognised that replacing 'the present monolithic structure of departments' by a board system 'might detract a little from efficiency but it would be worth it. He did not see the need to have one top official in charge in the same way as one had to have one Minister. It was not for any one permanent official to submit a departmental view to the Minister, but for the Minister to take a decision on the views submitted by several officials.' Asked by the Chairman and Sir John Wall whether the collegiate system might not paralyse decision making and the carrying out of policy, Balogh said that

> it was not for officials to make decisions but for Ministers. It was wrong to look on the Permanent Secretary as the Managing Director with the Minister as Chairman of the Board. It was the Minister who was the Managing Director with the Prime Minister as Chairman. The Minister was not just the spokesman and publicity officer for the department. He was the man who had to take the rap. The knowledge of this meant that advice given him by officials was always cautious, because everybody tended to be cautious in advising about something for which somebody else was to take the responsibility. If caution was what one wanted,

the present system might be alright. If one wanted something more adventurous, the system must be changed. The change might make for less comfort but it would make for greater liveliness and interest and would keep up the intellectual tensions.

Sir Edward Boyle observed that

although he agreed that it was very important for a Minister to see different opinions . . . he could think of two sets of circumstances where it was helpful to have a single chief adviser taking a clear line. One was when the Minister was trying to get his colleagues to agree to something, and the Permanent Secretary could do a great deal in persuading the Permanent Secretaries of the other departments concerned. The other was when a question involved technical factors on which there was a difference of view within the department, and it was a great help for the Minister to have an unequivocal view from the Permanent Secretary.

In reply, Balogh said that

there would always in practice be a chief adviser because, although the Joint Permanent Secretaries would be equal, some would be more equal than others. There would be one of them who was most in sympathy with the Minister, and, if only there could be less whirligig movement of Permanent Secretaries between departments – and if there were several Joint Permanent Secretaries in a department there would be less political pressure to move people around – there would always be people with long experience of the department to give the Minister the assurance he wanted.

Sir William Cook commented that 'in practice Mr Balogh's suggested collegiate system would be like taking away the Permanent Secretary and leaving the Deputy Secretaries in charge of their own parts of the department.' Balogh said that 'this was not quite so because at present a Deputy Secretary would feel inhibited from expressing views on something which was another Deputy Secretary's baby. The Joint Permanent Secretaries would all have a wider view and would be free to comment upon things which were not their immediate responsibility.' On the practical question of who would represent the department in dealings with people outside on matters on which two sides of a department held different views, Balogh was recorded as not giving a clear answer (PRO: BA1/2).

'The office of Permanent Secretary is a peculiarly British invention', Nevil Johnson told the Committee; 'It has no place in the bureaucratic organization of many countries in Western Europe nor in the USA. In Western Germany, where departments are headed by an official known as the State Secretary, the post corresponds to Deputy Minister rather than that of Permanent Secretary. In France the office exists in only two or three departments, and then in somewhat diluted form.' Johnson said that the radical step of abolishing the office of Permanent Secretary in British central government departments should be taken and there should be the phased introduction into departments of a Management Board system for their direction and control. This in effect means learning from the example of those few departments which already have something on these lines, and from public and private corporations. At the top of the departmental hierarchy there should be a number of posts, roughly equivalent in status and salary to a Deputy Secretary in the present structure. Each post would carry responsibility for a broad segment of the work of a department.

The minister would take over formally as chairman of the Management Board, and 'the need for an official arbitrator of issues which cannot be resolved by individual members of the Board (and with which Ministers ought not to be troubled) could be met by making the member for organization and personnel the senior member of the Board, with the status of Vice-Chairman' (PRO: BA1/24).

Professor P. M. S. Blackett said in his evidence that 'the old ideal prototype of the top structure of a department could be described as 111N (1 Minister, 1 Permanent Secretary, 1 Deputy Secretary, and N Under Secretaries). This was a suitable structure for running a block of routine work but was unsuited to continuous innovation from within . . . The result of a narrow pyramid at the top was to overburden the top individuals with detail, and there was a serious lack of top people who had time to think.' Blackett wanted to see 'the introduction of some top officials who would be professional policy makers without detailed responsibilities and without a mass of subordinates – a type of merit promotion.' He noted that the Ministry of Technology had 'a broader structure than the 111N formula' and that it was 'more like a Board', but that it did not have his preferred arrangement of having 'a number of Deputy Secretaries without executive responsibilities' (PRO: BA1/7).

'The load on the Permanent Secretary was very heavy but not intolerable,' Sir Laurence Helsby said in evidence to the Committee, adding that 'where it was too great, Second Permanent Secretaries had been introduced,' with examples being the Ministry of Defence and the Board of Trade. The basic principle that final responsibility should rest with the Permanent Secretary should be preserved, he believed, and there ought to be one 'Managing Director'. He did not think that the substitution of a collegiate structure for the Permanent Secretary would produce a livelier dialogue within departments.

> Some comments on the Civil Service suggested that the Permanent Secretary collected the opinions, formed his own view, and then gave only that view. This was a travesty. He must of course give his own view, but he would equally give opposing views, and usually in the form in which they had been expressed. Ministers would then hold meetings with the Permanent Secretary and their professional advisers together to sort out the various possible courses of action. Ministers varied in the extent to which they wanted to be in on the formative stages of policy. Most

now did. But others sometimes wanted not six differing views, but one definitive recommendation. Departments had to gauge what their Minister would want in each case; they certainly did not wait to consult him until a firm view had emerged if he made it clear that he wanted a dialogue at the formative stage. It was not therefore necessary to change the structure to achieve this end.

As far as interdepartmental questions were concerned, Helsby said, committees were in a sense collegiate. The Ministers often took an interest in how their work was proceeding, and he did not think that it was difficult for them to find this out and make their views known. Certainly a Permanent Secretary would not take a line in committee on an important matter without first consulting his Minister. And it was not his experience that interdepartmental differences were played down in reporting back. Helsby recognised that 'some scientists and professionals thought that a collegiate structure would improve the status of their own disciplines. But this was another, and mainly psychological point, and he did not think that it outweighed the need for a single Managing Director at the top, or that a collegiate structure would make any marked difference to the contribution which scientists and professionals were already making' (PRO: BA1/6).

The FDA thought that the office of Permanent Secretary, the holder of which 'would normally be an administrator', ought to be retained, given the need for departments to have a 'chief housekeeper' (PRO: BA1/5); and, as might be expected, similar sentiments were also expressed by several serving or former higher civil servants in their evidence. Sir John Maud, for instance, said that

> he would be against putting Permanent Secretaryships into commission; the Permanent Secretary was a very necessary animal. He was aware that in many other countries the Civil Service contained no equivalent of the Permanent Secretary, but that was in the setting of different constitutions and systems of government. Moreover, he was not convinced that the absence of a Permanent Secretary in those countries did not give rise to practical disadvantages; the French, who had the most notable example of a Civil Service without Permanent Secretaries, often deplored the lack. He thought it right that the three functions of a Permanent Secretary – as the Minister's senior policy adviser on policy, as the executive head of a department, and as Accounting Officer – should be united in one man . . . The accountability of the Permanent Secretary was logically derived from his managerial role. He recognised that in practice a Permanent Secretary could not have an immediate supervision and control over all the financial transactions of his department, but the same was true of Ministers, and the Permanent Secretary's accountability before the Public Accounts Committee was not fundamentally different in principle, and was indeed an extension of the Minister's answerability in the House of Commons (PRO: BA1/5).

Sir Gordon Radley, a former Director General of the Post Office, told the Committee that he preferred having a Permanent Secretary to a collegiate structure (PRO: BA1/8), as did for example, Sir Henry Benson, a former Director of Ordnance Factories (PRO: BA1/7), and the serving Permanent Secretary, Sir Douglas Allen (PRO: BA1/9). Sir Antony Part, the Permanent Secretary at the Ministry of Public Building and Works since 1965, clearly with the former Ministry of Works in mind, said that the ministry had 'a low reputation', to some extent 'deservedly', and 'it could only be built up into an efficient machine with a high reputation if there was a single, strong directive drive from the top.' Co-equality had been tried before and it had failed, and, although Part did not rule out a successful arrangement in the future, he thought 'it was desirable to have one person in charge' – the Permanent Secretary: 'the Minister could not really fulfil this function; he was more like a part time Chairman' (PRO: BA1/37). The only Minister to say much on the subject, Richard Crossman, wanted the office of Permanent Secretary to continue and for its holder to be the Accounting Officer. Crossman said that 'it was better to have a single person to do the Whitehall in-fighting on the Minister's behalf'; but he also observed that 'there was no reason why a more collegiate top structure, such as already existed in some degree at the Ministry of Defence, should not be applied to other departments' with the advantage of 'promoting free discussion in front of the Minister' (PRO: BA1/7).

The evidence that the Fulton Committee received about the origin, length of tenure, and movement of Permanent Secretaries did not always take the form that might have been expected, even if it was predictable that 'Mr Balogh was filled with amazement at the way departments were taken over by Permanent Secretaries with no previous experience of the department' (PRO: BA1/2). Sir Laurence Helsby thought it wrong for a Permanent Secretary to stay in his post for more than five to seven years:

> Departments needed a solid core of continuity. But this was best provided a little lower down. He personally thought it dangerous to have a Permanent Secretary who had been there so long that he knew all the answers. Permanent Secretaries often did their most productive work when they were relatively new to the department and asked the probing questions which could come from a man who had both the experience and the skill to ask them and the ignorance of detail that made them necessary. This situation was the biggest contribution to a constructive dialogue. It was not however true that after five to seven years a Permanent Secretary had lost his usefulness and should be retired. It was right to retire them in good time, say at 60 or a little over. But a man who had been Permanent Secretary in one department could then bring an important breadth of professional wisdom to the job of Permanent Secretary in another. The view that Permanent Secretaries should be retired at 50 or so depended on the assessment that the principal qualities

were quickness of wit and energy. This in his view implied the denial of the professional element in the job, which he thought crucial (PRO: BA1/6).

Sir Edward Playfair, who had been Permanent Secretary at the War Office and then at the Ministry of Defence, was in favour of appointments being made to Permanent Secretaryships while the civil servants concerned were relatively young and had the energy and ability to innovate. Then they should be retired early on full pension (PRO: BA1/27). Dame Evelyn Sharp was 'against moving Permanent Secretaries between departments' (PRO: BA1/4) and Sir Burke Trend thought that 'it was a reflection on a department if it was incapable of producing its own next Permanent Secretary, and there was too much top level appointment from outside. Continuity was an underrated virtue' (PRO: BA1/4). Sir Charles Cunningham, the Permanent Under Secretary at the Home Office saw 'no great advantage in movement at Permanent Secretary level. A Permanent Secretary could not hope to make a major impact on a department in less than seven years, and nine years did not seem to him too much' (PRO: BA1/2). Sir Leslie Rowan told the Committee that he had been 'in charge of the Overseas Finance side of the Treasury for six years and at the end of that time he was just beginning to learn the job. The philosophy of shifting Permanent Secretaries and Deputy Secretaries about departments was nonsense and the practice was damaging in several ways. It took a long time to build up a capital of expertise and it was wasteful to dissipate it. Constant chopping and changing was bad for the image of the Service in the outside world; it looked unserious. It imposed an unfair strain on the persons concerned' (PRO: BA1/4).

5. Policy planning units

It was implied in a wide range of the evidence submitted to the Fulton Committee, and specifically stated by Professor Peter Self in his written submission, that half a century on there was still substance in the Haldane Committee's criticism that government departments were poorly organised in relation to long term policy planning. 'The creation of a planning unit within each principal department would provide most desirable assistance for the administrator in his role of policy adviser,' Self observed (PRO: BA1/25); and Dudley Seers was another advocate of planning units (PRO: BA1/33).

Giving oral evidence in March 1966, Sir Herbert Andrew, the Permanent Under Secretary at the Department of Education and Science, said that he would expect any administrator to devote some of his time to dealing with long-term policy problems, and 'he did not consider that the Department should set up a small unit to conduct its own research. This was better left to outside organizations' (PRO: BA1/2). Six months later, the Secretary of State at the same department, Anthony Crosland, having complained about the 'lack of long term planning and rationality in decision making' as one of the weaknesses of government departments generally, told the Committee that he was 'setting up a long term planning branch' in the DES. This was to be headed by an Under Secretary, with other administrators under him. Crosland had considered that 'to bring in an outsider as head would cause too much friction,' but he had recruited other outside experts. He said that the principal initiative for setting up the planning branch had come from himself, and 'he thought that there was a moral to be drawn applicable to any large spending department, namely, that there should be a special branch responsible for long term planning which was not weighed down with day-to-day business' (PRO: BA1/4).

The Home Secretary, Roy Jenkins had a different attitude:

> He saw some difficulty in striking the right balance between coping with immediate problems and engaging in long term planning. He saw the advantage of the department being ready with new proposals in case a new Minister with a particular interest or a change of political circumstances, suddenly presented an opportunity of taking up a new scheme on which the department had been working. He certainly thought it right that long term thinking should go on, but considered that it could make for difficulties if this . . . were not related pretty closely to the philosophy and intentions of the Minister in power. To take an extreme example . . . it would obviously be very distasteful to him if preparations were going on in the Home Office for legislation restoring capital and corporal punishment just in case at some future date a right wing Tory administration came into office and wanted to put the clock back in these respects (PRO: BA1/30).

6. Personnel management by departments

When it came to evidence submitted to the Fulton Committee about the broad organisation of the work of individual government departments, as might be expected in relation to any inquiry into a career Civil Service, there was plenty written and said to the Committee about personnel management. Predictably too, so soon after the Plowden Report on the Control of Public Expenditure, there was no shortage of evidence about the necessity of placing more emphasis on managerial responsibility generally and the use of the latest management techniques, some to be adapted from private business.

The Committee itself invited evidence from Principals on loan to government departments from industry, commerce, and the universities under a scheme introduced in 1965 and, in summary, their views about their experience in the Civil service were that

> responsibility for decision making was not clearly allocated. There was too much horizontal sub-division of responsibility, necessitating constant consultation with other branches. There was not enough delegation of responsibility down the hierarchy, especially below the level of Assistant Secretary. Most thought that they had less responsibility as Principals

in the Service than in their jobs in industry and commerce. The practice of progressive drafting was strongly criticized. The tendency was for matters of relatively unimportant nature to go too high up, and for important matters to begin too low down. It led to delay, was a misuse of highly paid staff, and was irksome to individuals. It was thought that there were too many stages in the vertical structure and that the pyramid was too narrow. One witness said that it appeared that departments were made to fit the traditional organizational structure rather than suitable structures devised to fit the job in hand. Several comments were made on the time and effort devoted to problems of co-ordination, on the proliferation of committees, and on the great amount of paper that came one's way. The desire to achieve perfection, mainly in written work, on the part of members of the Administrative Class was sometimes overdone, but it was thought that this and other practices and procedures were in large measure due to the Service's accountability to Ministers and Parliament.

Some of the imported Principals thought that 'the Service was poor in applying management techniques and, in particular, that no attempt was made to use financial information as a vital tool of management,' but others saw the Service as showing 'a willingness to try new ways of improving efficiency.' Some Principals said that there should be more O. and M. and one suggested that job evaluation should be applied to all posts. The overall quality of personnel management in departments was criticised, with the suggestion being made that Establishments work should be professionalised and 'not treated as just another job' (PRO: BA1/65).

Lord Normanbrook, whose career as an official began in 1925, told the Committee that

> when he entered the Service management was neglected. The Establishment Officer was usually the weakest Assistant Secretary in the department, and probably only employed part time on establishment work at that. The Service got through because departments were very much smaller. As departments had become larger, management had become more important. There was a need for more management training and for a knowledge of the management practices of other organizations. However, he would not favour the separation of management from the other work of the Administrative Class, and the setting up of management specialists (PRO: BA1/3).

Though appointments to the post of Principal Establishment Officer in major departments needed the approval of the Head of the Home Civil Service and ultimately that of the Prime Minister, naturally the Permanent Secretaries of departments normally got the appointee of their choice; and, in his evidence, Harry Pitchforth, a Treasury Under Secretary, said that 'occasionally, Permanent Secretaries have taken the easy way out in the past – I do not think it happens so much now because Permanent Secretaries have tended to realize that this is a chap who works direct to them, and if they pick on a chap who is not terribly bright they get the load on their shoulders. Normally I think the Permanent Secretary will look around for a man who has had a fairly wide experience in the department, if possible with some kind of managerial experience as well.'

When asked by Lord Simey if there was not a need for a more professional approach to personnel management, S. P. Osmond, a Third Secretary in the Treasury, said that 'we do not believe on the whole that it is a good thing for people to spend the whole of their lives in personnel management in the Civil Service. I think that if, for example, I had spent my whole time working in Establishments Divisions – I have spent quite a bit of it one way and another – I would probably do my job even worse than I do it, because I would not understand at first hand what the problems of the people are who have to run other divisions of the department' (PRO: BA1/4).

In his evidence, L. T. Foster, the Principal Establishment Officer at the Ministry of Public Building and Works, said that 'he would be very much against making a profession of establishments work, and especially against making the Director of Establishments a professional. This would lead to remoteness from the actual work of the department' (PRO: BA1/7). R. C. Elkington, the Principal Establishment Officer at the Ministry of Technology, told the Committee that 'the work required some specific qualities,' and that 'spells in establishment work should be longer (five years or more) than they had commonly been in the past,' but 'in general he would be against making personnel work too much of a specialism.' For one thing, 'if personnel work were professionalized, those outside the Establishments Branch might well become less inclined to take their own personnel management responsibility seriously and leave this to the professionals' (PRO: BA1/7).

A. R. Bunker, the holder of that post at the Home Office, thought that a Principal Establishment Officer should not stay too long on that job; a fresh outlook was required from time to time. Specialized knowledge of various aspects of Establishments work, such as training, conditions of service, was provided lower down mainly by officers in the middle ranks of the Executive Class. A Principal Establishment Officer need not necessarily have previous experience of that work, but he should be picked carefully with an eye to such qualities as fairness, an interest in people, and he should be prepared to regard himself as the servant of the department and of its efficient running and not its master. Few men, taking his colleagues in the Home Office as an example, had the right combination of qualities. This was rather an unsatisfactory situation and it was probably right to say that every senior manager should have many of the qualities required. The reason was that that generation had not been brought up to think of staff management as part of their work. It was necessary to breed up the younger generation in the idea that it was. The Home Office tried, often with some difficulty, to impress on Assistant

Secretaries that they had full management responsibility, including responsibility for staff management (PRO: BA1/8).

The serving Permanent Secretaries, Sir Antony Part (PRO: BA1/22), Sir Andrew Cohen (PRO: BA1/22), and Sir William Armstrong (PRO: 1/3) either stated or implied in their evidence that departmental personnel management would need to be more professional and systematic in the future. The former Permanent Secretary of the Ministry of Land and Natural Resources, F. A. Bishop told the Committee that departments needed 'much more elaborate machinery than now existed for spotting the fliers. One could never be sure that some able men would not be left mouldering in backwaters (as sometimes happened now, especially in the Executive Class), but it should reduce the risk and give people more hope' (PRO: BA1/2). Dame Evelyn Sharp was critical of current personnel management arrangements which she perceived as wasting a lot of talent because of ill-considered postings. She seemed to have the Executive Class particularly in mind, and said that 'management ought not only to pick out the fliers, to which a good deal of attention was given already, but also to discover the special aptitudes of people who were not fliers, and to put them into jobs where they were properly used' (PRO: BA1/4). Treasury witnesses recognised that an expanded general graduate entry to the Service would have to mean a more sophisticated approach to career management on the part of departments in monitoring the progress of the middle order graduate entrants (PRO: BA1/5).

That evidence of the Institute of Personnel Management stated that personnel work should be a specialism in the Civil Service (PRO: BA1/29) was as unsurprising as the view of the IPCS that its members among the specialist classes should have a greater role in Establishments work (PRO: BA1/30). 'Without going so far as to say that personnel management should form . . . a completely separate career,' the CSCA believed that such management should stop being 'a "tour of duty" in a general purpose career' and it should be 'recognized as a specialization' (PRO: BA1/24). The SCS said that 'many administrators regard Establishments work as a diversion from the mainstream of departmental policy work,' and only those who had been promoted from the Executive Class had personal experience of staff management on any substantial scale. The Society argued that the status of Establishments work needed to be raised, and that 'in the larger departments one of the Deputy Secretaries should . . . have special responsibility for organization and management' (PRO: BA1/20). Sir Henry Wilson Smith, a former Permanent Secretary at the Ministry of Defence and Treasury official who had moved into the private sector, and who was Vice-Chairman of the Council of the British Institute of Management, said that personnel management was increasingly being treated as a specialism in industry, and though he emphasised that he had no recent experience in government departments, he doubted whether people of comparable drive and enthusiasm were doing personnel work in the Civil Service (PRO: BA1/2).

At Sir John Wall's suggestion, the Fulton Committee decided as early as its tenth meeting in May 1966 to find out for itself about private sector staff management practice (PRO: BA1/2). A sub-committee shared by Sir Norman Kipping had discussions with ICI, Marks and Spencer, Shell, and Unilever. Sir William Cook attended all the meetings, as did the Secretary; and Sir Philip Allen and Norman Hunt came to some of them. From the resulting note, which was undated but which must have been circulated in December 1966, it was evident that though Marks and Spencer had 'a deliberate policy of formal training for their personnel staff,' ICI, for instance, did not. Indeed, ICI 'insisted that the Personnel Director, both at the centre and at divisional level, should combine this with another function, if possible of a profit making character.' The Central Personnel Director of ICI was also Director for Organisation and Services at that time, and, while Unilever preferred to keep the activities separate, there was general agreement among the other companies that organisation and personnel work should go closely together (PRO: BA1/26).

7. *Management services, techniques and responsibilities*

Though the Fulton Committee was inevitably told by the CBI of the advantages of applying 'business methods' to the work of government departments (PRO: BA1/25), it was also informed in early evidence from Ivor Young, a management consultant with recent experience in the DEA, that 'a distinction between management and administration, analogous to that in the Civil Service, was now developing in the larger industrial firms: small groups were being assembled at the top into whose hands the main threads of policy were drawn.' The principal difference in his view between management and administration was that 'responsibility could be allocated and performance measured more precisely in management. This was closely related to the idea that responsibility and performance could be measured only where a clear and identifiable objective could be established for the relevant part of the organization.' He agreed that the Civil Service was too large and multifarious for its overall objective to be defined, 'though a number of minor objectives could of course be defined within the Service, especially where the implementation of policy decisions was concerned.' Young had found that 'the quality of thought was high' among the civil servants that he had worked with, but they 'lacked expertise in the implementation side of management' and they 'seemed unfamiliar with what an industrialist would regard nowadays as the stock tools of management.' Young's view was that 'the manpower resources which the Civil Service devoted to management techniques were slim compared with those devoted by big industrial concerns' (PRO: BA1/3).

That the Civil Service devoted more resources to management services and techniques than even in the relatively recent past was clear from the Treasury's evidence to the Committee, although, inevitably, arguments in favour of the need for the Service to do more, and criticisms of its working methods, were present in other evidence. To what became familiar complaints in the evidence about what the Treasury official, W. S. Ryrie called 'the time wasted in the ever growing jungle of inter-departmental committees in Whitehall,' Ryrie's solution of 'a reorganization of functions and a drastic streamlining of the government machine as a whole' (PRO: BA1/31) was, of course, outside the Committee's terms of reference. The criticism that 'decisions which could perfectly well be taken lower down were passed all the way up the ladder,' which several witnesses made and which F. A. Bishop, a former official, most clearly articulated was, of course, explained, as Bishop added, by the operation of the convention of ministerial responsibility (PRO: BA1/2), another excluded subject. Ryrie observed:

> We see our political masters overburdened with detailed work on day-to-day issues, and unable to give proper attention to the basic and long term issues of policy which should be their main concern. At the same time we feel frustrated. Government departments grow larger and responsibility tends to get pushed up. Officers at the level of Assistant Secretary and Principal feel they have much less responsibility than their predecessors twenty or thirty years ago and they are right. They are advisers and drafters, yes, and that requires intelligence and con-scientiousness. Very few have much sense of responsibility for decisions. The whole ethos of the Civil Service discourages the taking of responsi-bility. All the pressures are in the direction of referring upwards if in doubt: anyone who errs on the side of taking too much responsibility will soon discover that everything can be of political interest and needs to go to the top. Hardly ever is a civil servant reproved for putting too much up, for not taking enough responsibility. All this is not the fault of individual civil servants nearly so much as of the way the machine works and especially of the way in which the whole of government, in every detail, is under the surveillance of the national Parliament (PRO: BA1/31).

The former minister, Aubrey Jones, believed that 'there was a need for the Service to work out and use techniques of management development as a substitute for the tests of financial performance and so forth applying in business' (PRO: BA1/3). The British Institute of Management told the Com-mittee that

> the need for cost consciousness, budgetary control and performance targets, however obvious these may be as essential disciplines, is not invariably a feature of the operations of government departments and they should be instituted throughout and at all levels. Target setting and 'management by objectives' are common features of management in industry. Techniques of staff control and staff measurement as practiced in large scale multi-unit groups in industry could well lead to more economical use of staff resources in certain departments.

The Institute said that 'the practice in many large industrial concerns of setting up a "Management Services" unit, charged with a wide range of responsibilities aimed at achieving maximum efficiency at all levels, should be studied for its possible application within the Civil Service as an extension of the existing O. and M. services. In any such development it might be advantageous for some of the staff to be on temporary assignment from industry to ensure periodic infusion of new ideas and experience (PRO: BA1/26).

Though the Fulton Committee did not lack submitted evidence that emphasised the need for the Civil Service to keep abreast of the latest developments in management science and technology, some of which ignored the Service's leading role in promoting the latter, it did need evidence of practicality in relation to the actual work of government departments which was where the Committee's Management Consultancy Group made its contribution.

The Fulton Committee's Deliberations

The terms of reference of the Fulton Committee explicitly precluded it from making general recommendations about the machinery of British central government. 'The restrictions on the terms of reference only mattered on two occasions,' Richard Wilding recalled, 'One was when it came to "hiving off" the Civil Service Department. Of course, this did change the machinery of government, but in this case the recommendation concerned did seem to be within the Committee's remit, and nobody objected to this. Secondly, when 'hiving off' was discussed as such, some members would have liked to have gone more deeply into it, but there was general agreement that the Committee had to limit its subject matter somehow' (Interview, 1988).

Robert Neild has since said that he found the restrictions placed on the terms of reference of the Fulton Committee to be inhibitive at some points. This was particularly the case with the question of 'hiving off'.

> I think I started off the discussion of the topic because of my knowledge of the Swedish arrangements, and because I disliked the nonsense of our own system of everything being done in the name of Ministers. This is one of the means by which the Civil Service controls things. The notion of officials being able to 'enter the Minister's mind' and thus to fulfil his wishes even when he is unaware of their actions, and the notion that there is a 'departmental view' or tradition on policy, when taken together, are incompatible. The scale of modern government demanded change, and I wanted to import a Swedish style structure with small policy-making Ministries and the executive activities 'hived off' to agencies answerable to Parliament by others means than through Ministers. Edward Boyle and Robert Sheldon, the two MPs on the Committee were uneasy about such a structure because it would mean that, in relation to the 'hived off' agencies, the public would lose some of its right to appeal through the Parliamentary Question. Other people on the Committee said that 'hiving off' was simply outside our terms of reference. So we

ended up by recommending that another committee should look at 'hiving off'. No such committee seems to have been established (Interview, 1988).

Neild was the only surviving member of the Fulton Committee to express any regret at the limitations on the Committee's terms of reference. The Committee may not always have been so ready to respect these constraints. In a note addressed to the Assistant Secretary to the Committee dated 16 August 1966, Wilding recorded that: 'I took the opportunity to speak pretty firmly about the Committee's terms of reference - i.e. that as far as I could see "hiving off" particular services, and Ministers' responsibilities to Parliament generally, lay outside them' (PRO: BA1/74).

Though the organisational structure of government departments in general was deemed to be outside the Fulton Committee's terms of reference, the organisational structure within them was not so defined, and the Committee gave a great deal of attention to the role of the Permanent Secretary and to the possibility of a collegiate structure at the top of departments. Kipping and Dunnett circulated papers on the subject (PRO: BA1/33) which were discussed at the Committee's meeting on 18 April 1967. Introducing his paper, Kipping said that

> at present the load on the Permanent Secretary, who combined the functions of the Minister's principal policy adviser and the manager of a department, was too heavy. As a policy adviser, the Permanent Secretary was a professional, expert in politics, Parliament, the machinery of government etc. The proposals were intended to enable him to devote himself to that undistracted by the day-to-day execution of policies and programmes. On the other hand, the majority of the departments had large scale executive responsibilities; these were the great spending activities of government, very major jobs, which needed to get more senior attention. Apart from the impracticability of effectively bearing two loads, there was no reason to suppose that Permanent Secretaries were the best men by aptitude and expertise for running large executive programmes (PRO: BA1/8).

In his paper, Kipping suggested that, with a few exceptions dictated by the needs of the work, each ministry should be headed, under the Minister, by a board containing three essential elements: the Permanent Secretary, the Chief Executive, and the Director General of Services. In some ministries there might be two or even three joint chief executives. All would attend meetings of the board, with their deputies present when their own subjects were being deal with. The chairman would be the Permanent Secretary or Chief Executive with the greater seniority of service. The Minister would be in a position similar to that of a part time chairman. When the board met under his chairmanship, it would constitute the Minister's Council. On those occasions, the Junior Minister(s) in the department would also be present, and any special advisers designated by the Minister would attend for their own subjects. Sir Norman envisaged the Permanent Secretary as being 'in charge of the Secretariat of the Ministry': the Chief Executive as being 'responsible for the organization and management of all the executive activities for which the Ministry had powers': and the Director General of Services as being 'responsible for the provision of all the common services required in the department.' Kipping saw this different structure as providing 'a ladder reaching to the top, that is to Permanent Secretary or Chief Executive, for any member of the department's staff, whatever his background.' The proposals were also described by him as providing 'a businesslike Board for the co-ordination of the department's work, and for reaching agreement about organization and priorities,' and as enabling the introduction of 'a system of budgetary control and management by objectives' (PRO: BA1/33).

Whereas Kipping, understandably, seemed to wish to reorganise government departments so that they more closely resembled the private sector organisations which he knew best, Dunnett's proposals reflected his own experience in the Civil Service. He wrote that it was

> dangerous . . . to dogmatize about the proper organization of all departments since they vary greatly as between themselves. The problem of the position of the Permanent Secretary seems to me to be the most acute in those departments which employ a large number of professionals, e.g. the Ministry of Technology, the Ministry of Defence, the Ministry of Public Building and Works and, to some extent, the Ministry of Housing and Local Government and the Department of Education and Science. There is also, I think, a problem in the economic departments. On the other hand, I do not think that there is a problem at all in departments such as the Ministry of Pensions and National Insurance and the Ministry of Labour.

Dunnett concentrated on what he called the technological departments:

> In the Ministry of Defence . . . the department is headed effectively by a triumvirate (theoretically by a quadrumvirate) consisting of the Chief of the Defence Staff, the Permanent Under Secretary of State, and the Chief Adviser (Projects) (the fourth member of the team is the Chief Adviser (Studies)). In some ways this is a fairly clumsy form of organization and I know some of my predecessors regarded it as intolerable and inefficient. On the other hand it can be made to work. No other department has quite the same problem in that it does not have large numbers of military personnel as well as large numbers of engineers and scientists. I deduce, however, from my experience that a system under which there was in parallel with the Permanent Secretary a chief professional officer with the same status as the Permanent Secretary and with direct access to the Minister could be made to work. I know that it will be argued that when systems of this kind have been adopted in the past, e.g. in the Ministry of Works, there could be a clash of personalities and that the system did not work. This is a danger one faces in any form

of organization. On the other hand, I do not think that we can advocate a system under which we pretend that the post of Permanent Secretary can be filled by anybody, when in practice it will be filled nine times out of ten by an administrator.

He added that: 'It does not, of course, automatically follow that work would be better done with a chief professional officer in parallel with the Permanent Secretary . . . On the other hand I have the firm impression that the scientists and engineers suffer from the feeling that they are second class citizens and that any step which made them feel that they enjoyed parity of esteem with the administrator would definitely be good for the Civil Service' (PRO: BA1/33).

The papers submitted by Kipping and Dunnett were not well received by the other members of the Fulton Committee at its meeting on 18 April 1967. Dunnett was asked to produce a further paper dealing with the various points raised in the discussion (PRO: BA1/8). When the second paper appeared, it proved to be very largely a critique of Kipping's ideas on the basis of a case by case demonstration of how a distinction between policy and execution would not be a suitable basis for departmental organisation. Dunnett was unenthusiastic about the idea of there being a Director General of Services, believing that the work concerned should come under the Permanent Secretary; and he also took the opportunity to record his doubts about the use of the grade of Second Permanent Secretary, 'first introduced to deal with the particular problem of the Ministry of Defence when the three Service departments and the old central Ministry of Defence were put together' and since extended to the Board of Trade and to the Ministry of Technology (PRO: BA1/34). At its meeting on 3 and 4 July, the Committee agreed that it was not in favour of a Chief Executive co-equal with the Permanent Secretary (PRO: BA1/9).

The Committee agreed at its meeting on 1 August that as 'different structures would be appropriate to different departments at different times, [it] should not, therefore, try to prescribe a single pattern for departments to follow, but should set out principles by which the top structure appropriate to a department might be determined. It was generally agreed that even in Ministries with a collegiate top structure one man should be *primus inter pares* with the final responsibility for running the office.' Robert Sheldon argued that 'because in the foreseeable future Ministers would generally be transient, they would be very dependent on the Permanent Secretary who, by virtue of that relationship, would inevitably become the most powerful civil servant in the department.' It followed that the Committee should not recommend structural patterns which ran counter to this reality. Sheldon said that 'good Ministers would still reach down in the department and ensure that they were not restricted to a single channel of policy advice.' Some members thought that

if the Permanent Secretary was the Minister's right hand man in the

> way described, he would not be able to spend much time running the department and therefore there was a need for deliberate, planned and understood delegation of responsibilities; it would be necessary for the Permanent Secretary, as *primus inter pares*, to be head of the office in the sense of having the final responsibility, but if he was concentrating on advising the Minister he would need a senior person or persons to whom the day-to-day work of management could be delegated.

This seemed to be resurrecting the idea of there being a Chief Executive which the Committee had rejected only four weeks earlier.

Other members of the Committee, 'while accepting that one man should be formally in charge, preferred a more collegiate structure at the top, and thought that the possibility of a weak Minister supported rather than weakened this case; he should be exposed to more strong voices than one. The term "Permanent Secretary" should go. If the head of the office were, as he might be, a professional or primarily a policy adviser, he would need a right hand man to do much of what the Permanent Secretary now did, but his title would have to be different.' Allen and Dunnett were of the opinion that 'the job of a Permanent Secretary was not an intolerable burden for one man, provided that he delegated as much as was practicable. They pointed out that in most departments there had in recent years been an increase in the number of Deputy Secretaries, to whom senior responsibilities could be delegated. But a more collegiate structure, especially in technological departments, could raise the morale of scientists and professionals.'

Dunnett repeated his dislike of the use of the grade of Second Permanent Secretary, an arrangement 'which did not work very well,' while at the same time considering that 'there was a need for a grade between Permanent Secretary and Deputy Secretary in very big departments.' Some members thought that 'if, even in Ministries with a collegiate structure, one man was to be *primus inter pares* and head of the office, he would also be the Accounting Officer. The Accounting Officer should however be accompanied to the Public Accounts Committee by his senior colleagues who should answer for their own areas of responsibility.' Kipping said that 'he believed that those parts of a department which could be so organized should be run as separate, accountable entities; in his opinion it would then follow that the heads of the management entities should be made answerable to the PAC' (PRO: BA1/10).

In its Report, as will be seen, the Fulton Committee rejected a board structure at the top of departments and reflected Dunnett's views in recommendations about the status accorded to the leading specialists within departments, and in regarding the Second Permanent Secretary grade unfavourably (Cmnd.3638, 1968, para.179) before recommending that 'the Permanent Secretary . . . should still be head of the office under the Minister' (ibid., para. 187). If the Committee had simply recommended – as the same paragraph of its Report put it – that 'there should be one person who has the overall responsibility under the Minister . . . for all the affairs of the department, and that this person should, as now, be the Permanent Secretary,' who was to be Accounting Officer and 'ultimately in charge of the departmental machine,' then its lengthy discussions about the organisation of the top structure of departments would have yielded little. As it was, the related idea of there being a Senior Policy Adviser or Advisers in government departments derived from those discussions.

'Members saw value in a chief policy adviser in certain departments,' according to the record of the Fulton Committee's twenty-fourth meeting of 1967. The holder of this post 'would have the departmental planning unit under him. It was hoped that he would often be a relatively younger man. Provided that he had his own access to the Minister and was not under the Permanent Secretary's direction in formulating issues and giving advice to the Minister, it was less important that he should be the Permanent Secretary's equal in pay and status, or in the running of the office' (PRO: BA1/9).

As we have seen, there was evidence presented to the Committee and advocacy beforehand relating to the creation of policy planning units in government departments. Sir Edward Boyle told the author that he had been the prime mover inside the Committee in proposing Senior Policy Advisers and policy planning units, and the example that he (as a former Economic Secretary to the Treasury) and the Committee had in mind had been the Economic Section of the Treasury and the Economic Adviser to H.M. Government in the person of Sir Robert Hall who had held that post between 1947 and 1961. 'Policy planning units and Senior Policy Advisers were Sir Edward Boyle's idea,' Richard Wilding recalled, expressing doubt about the realism of the proposal. 'The Economic Section of the Treasury was not much of a model,' Wilding observed; 'What Boyle seemed to have had in mind was a single individual acting as the principal source of policy advice on the whole range of the department's activity. This, the Economic Section never pretended to do. Nobody would dream of funnelling all the economic advice in the Treasury through the Economic Section' (Interview, 1988).

To judge from the semi-official history of the Economic Section (Cairncross and Watts, 1989), and Sir Robert Hall's dairies (Cairncross, 1989; Cairncross, 1991), and as one would expect, that institution did not have an exclusive role in policy advice. Led by Hall, what it did have was a position of independence. Wilding considered that 'in pressing for the Senior Policy Adviser and policy planning unit idea, Sir Edward Boyle had the Economic Section of the Treasury less in mind than the Department of Education and Science which had a Planning Branch, and Boyle seemed to see the Senior Policy Adviser as a glorified Chief Inspector of Schools who could act as a professional source of wisdom. Boyle used to frequently refer back to Education, which struck a chord with Fulton and with Hunt' (Interview: 29.9.88).

Michael Simons's recollection was that 'the idea of policy planning units was in the air anyway. Sir Edward Boyle did not initiate the discussion. All he did was to take part in it, citing the Economic Section as a possible model' (Interview, 1989). Dunnett said that 'several members of the Fulton Committee had been interested in policy planning units and he had no recollection of Sir Edward Boyle being the originator of proposals relating to them' (Interview, 1988). Allen observed that

> the idea of policy planning units was much canvassed. It wasn't Sir Edward Boyle's idea. There was general agreement that more brain-power needed to be applied to long term policy issues in government departments. Of course, some applications would be unwelcome to Ministers. When he was Home Secretary, Roy Jenkins would not have welcomed a policy planning unit looking at capital punishment. The Economic Section at the Treasury was a good idea for the department, but not a model for others to copy. The idea of policy planning units and policy analysis generally was never thought out. The Rothschild outfit came to a sticky end (Interview, 1988).

In the Committee's consideration of policy planning units, Robert Neild recalled that there were

> several analytical starting points. One was that the Minister should have his own *cabinet*, and another was that the planning of policy should be done with a longer view than those submerged in the day-to-day running of policy can manage. The Swedish agency set up achieves of this in quite a good way. The Minister lets his bright boys try things out on the board, and then he can judge what emerges. With a Ministerial *cabinet* system, the cabinet may not take such a long view. The Fulton Committee went round these ideas. Interest in *cabinets* died down and that in policy planning units survived (Interview, 1988).

In its Report, the Fulton Committee proposed that 'a department's responsibility for major long term policy planning should be clearly allocated to a planning and research unit.' In some departments, such as the Home Office, with widely separated fields of activity, more than one planning unit might be needed. The main task of planning units was 'to identify and study the problems and needs of the future and the possible means to meet them.' The planning units ought to be 'relatively small' (Cmnd. 3638, 1968, para.173) and 'staffed by comparatively young men and women' from both the Civil Service and outside (ibid., para.175) who would be 'aware of' and able to 'contribute to new thinking in their field' (ibid., para.174). The Committee envisaged that these units might need central co-ordination, given that policy problems extended beyond departmental boundaries and that there was a need for a consistent approach (ibid., para.177). When the draft material was circulated (PRO: BA1/48), Lord Simey thought that the Civil Service Department might have this central responsibility (Simey Papers: MS16.9), but the Committee decided that it was a general machinery of government question and so beyond its terms of reference (Cmnd. 3638, 1968, para.177).

The Committee considered that its proposals 'for accountable management and for enlarging the role of departmental personnel and organization division will inevitably add still further to the burdens of the Permanent Secretary. He will have to devote more time to his managerial function' (ibid., para.181). The Committee therefore recommended that 'in most departments, if not all, there should be a Senior Policy Adviser to assist the Minister. The Adviser should be head of the planning unit. His prime job, like that of the unit, would be to look to, and prepare for, the future and to ensure that day-to-day policy decisions are taken with as full a recognition as possible of likely future developments.' The Committee hoped that 'the Adviser would often be a relatively young man,' sometimes an outsider brought in by the Minister, but most commonly a career civil servant, preferably with outside and expert experience. Where the department's responsibilities were particularly wide in range, the Committee thought that as there would be a need for more than one planning unit it would be necessary to have more than one Senior Policy Adviser in such cases (ibid., para.182). The Committee considered that 'for the proper discharge of his duties . . . the Senior Policy Adviser must have direct and unrestricted access to his Minister, both personally and in writing. He should also be free to determine, after consultation with the Permanent Secretary, but subject only to the Minister, what problems his planning unit should tackle. While the Adviser should have the chief responsibility for planning the longer term departmental policy, he should not have responsibility for the day-to-day operations of the department; these should remain under the day-to-day control of the Permanent Secretary' (ibid., para.183).

'No doubt the long term pattern' of responsibilities as between the Permanent Secretary and the Senior Policy Adviser 'should vary according to the needs of different departments at different times,' the Committee observed, while suggesting that the rank of the Adviser 'should not normally be below that of Deputy Secretary' (ibid., para.184), and going on to say:

> In some of the big technical departments there may well be a case for a further top post. For example, where a department is engaged on large scale scientific research or on major building or engineering projects, it might be right to appoint a Chief Scientist or a Chief Engineer to be in charge of these operations. His job would be to take the chief responsibility for the direction of the department's technical work; he would have direct access to the Minister as his main adviser in these matters; he would also be the professional head of the specialist staff. In exceptional cases there might be a need for two such posts (ibid., para.185).

The Committee said that 'we do not propose that these senior officers together with the Permanent Secretary, should constitute a formal board. The working arrangements should be informal and variable from department to department and from time to time; different Ministers' individual ways of working will do much to determine the pattern' (ibid., para.186).

The possibilities of the wider adoption of private sector forms of organisation and practices in government departments interested both Sir Norman

Kipping and Sir John Wall on the Fulton Committee as we have seen, and the Committee also received evidence, most cogently from the British Institute of Management, for instance, along the same lines. The most important thinking about managerial arrangements in departments, though, came from the Committee's Management Consultancy Group. The Group's arguments for a changed style of management were a sophisticated attempt to reconcile what it recognised as existing constraints on line management in the Civil Service with the need to devise 'new organizational forms related not to classes but to the task in hand,' and to define 'the objectives and priorities for areas of the organization' as a means of 'delegating responsibility clearly to individuals,' as well as 'increasing the use of management controls' and finding means of 'measuring managerial effectiveness.' Though the Group suggested that how this was to be done was matter for a further management review of departmental organisation, in fact, as when proposing the intro-duction of 'responsibility centres', analogous to budget centres, within depart-ments, the Group was clear about the future form which it considered devel-opments should take (PRO: BA1/73). One member of the Group, John Garrett, was later to observe that 'the main Fulton Report did show signs of the Management Consultancy Group's findings having been misrepresented. Norman Hunt was unable to explain satisfactorily to the Committee the Group's recommendations on career specialization and on management by objectives, or the Committee just could not grasp them' (Interview, 1989). Whether this was so or not, the section of the Fulton Report which was about 'accountable and efficient management' was plainly heavily influenced by the findings of the Management Consultancy Group, even in some places using similar phrases such as in the remarks made about budget centres and the need for 'flatter' departmental hierarchies (Cmnd. 3638, 1968, paras 150–62).

The Fulton Committee responded to criticisms made in the Management Consultancy Group's Report and in the general evidence submitted about the work of Establishment and Organisation divisions and the relative neglect of management services. Taking up a suggestion in the evidence presented by the British Institute of Management, the Committee recommended that 'each major department should contain a Management Services Unit with wider responsibilities and functions than are given to O. and M. divisions today' (ibid., para.165), citing the criticisms of the Management Consultancy Group. As, in its opinion, the term 'establishment' carried 'implications of stuffiness' and had 'bad effects both on the status of the work and on the way it is done' which were not specified, the Committee recommended that the term 'should be used no longer.' Thereafter it referred to 'personnel and organization' divisions or branches, and believed that, if implemented, its reform pro-gramme would 'enlarge their future responsibilities and thus improve their status. This should help to attract those who are capable of rising to the highest posts. At the same time this work will call for high expertise and thus for greater specialization. We welcome this prospect. We wish to add two riders. Those specialized in personnel work should from time to time get experience of work in this field outside the Service. They should also have experience of working in operating divisions and of the effect of personnel and organization work upon them' (Cmnd. 6368, 1968, paras 121–122).

The Committee's recommendation that 'an early and thorough review' should be conducted to examine the possibility of a considerable extension of 'hiving off' the executive activities of government departments (ibid., para.190) was one of three further inquiries relating to the organisation of the work of departments that it proposed. The Committee also suggested that 'the Government should set up an inquiry to make recommendations for getting rid of unnecessary secrecy in this country. Clearly, the Official Secrets Act would need to be included in such a review' (ibid., para.280). The Committee recognised that the traditional anonymity of civil servants might be eroded. This the Committee as a whole welcomed (ibid., paras 283–284). In a letter to Richard Wilding, which was later circulated, Sir John Wall observed that 'senior civil servants must expect to be in the limelight from time to time, and they should not be worried if they are. Certainly, such a person must not indicate the relationship between his advice and what the Minister has really done' (PRO: BA1/32). Quite how this was to be achieved under a system of 'open government' was not stated. As the Committee believed that the Whitley system of joint consultation operated 'in ways that hamper effective management' (Cmnd. 3638, 1968, para.271), another inquiry that it recommended was into that system because 'it is clearly essential that the pattern of joint consultation should reflect, not determine, the results of the changes we propose' (ibid., para.274).

While the Fulton Committee welcomed the increasing use that ministers had come to make of importing a small number of political appointees into government departments, the Committee neither recommended the translation of this activity into a large scale practice along American lines nor the introduction of ministerial *cabinets* (ibid., para.285). For all its concerns about the efficient and economical use of the staff that the Civil Service employed (ibid., paras 294–301), the Fulton Committee plainly envisaged the career Civil Service continuing to be of a similar scale to that which it reviewed, while wanting it to be organised along different lines.

Chapter 6

Structure of the Civil Service

The Context for Change

Whatever the limitations that were otherwise placed upon the Fulton Committee's field of review, the structure of the Home Civil Service was one of the subjects about which, in principle, the Committee had considerable freedom to make recommendations for change. In practice, as was inevitable in any attempt to reconstruct an existing career Civil Service, the Fulton Committee had to cover ground that was occupied or contested by interest groups, often represented by staff associations, and in relation to which there was a familiar reforming agenda, much of it derived from academic writing about the Civil Service. Of course, the Committee was not bound to respect the wishes of the various interests, some of which conflicted anyway, and neither was there any need to defer to what, in broad terms, might be called the reformers' case. The Fulton Committee had an opportunity to make its own mark.

The task facing the Committee in its review of the structure of the Home Civil Service, and the related evidence submitted to it, was bound to be broadly concerned with five main subject areas. The first was the concept and the desirability of there being a career Civil Service. The second subject area was consideration of the overall structure of the Home Civil Service and the extent to which it could or should be treated as a unity. The third subject area was the structure of the Higher Civil Service. The fourth such area was the structure of the General Classes of the Home Civil Service, and the fifth was the structure of the Specialist Classes of that Service.

As the doctrine of ministerial responsibility had to be treated by the Fulton Committee as given, then so had the continuance of a non-political career Civil Service in some form. 'It has been the supreme good fortune of Great Britain that she has, during the past century, developed a Civil Service of exceptional capacity and integrity,' the Webbs had declared when assigning it a prominent role in their administrative plans for the future (Webbs, 1920, p.67). With recruitment by open competition, and a formalised structure of Classes and grades with promotion according to rules and involving merit, and identifiable salary scales with regular increments, and security of tenure for the staff and pension rights, the established career Civil Service that the Webbs and their fellow Fabians as well as others admired so much in principle resembled Max Weber's ideal type of advanced bureaucratic organisation in many respects, even if the manner of the Official Secrets legislation and that forbidding corrupt practices and the restrictions placed upon the political activities of Civil Servants made for a code of conduct that was more particularistic (Robson, 1937, pp.12ff; cf. Gerth and Mills, 1948, pp.196–244). The various types of unestablished staff, at times substantial in numbers, employed by government departments, whose position had been a matter of concern for earlier committees of inquiry, did not so easily fit in with the common perception of the Civil Service developing as if in a straight line from the Northcote-Trevelyan Report and the Order in Council of 1870.

For all the general agreement in public discussion that there was 'no substitute for a career Service of high quality' (Robson, 1937, p.16), not always consistently the 'closed' nature of that Service at times attracted the critical attention of Fabian and other reformers; as did, even more fundamentally, the supposed political preferences of higher civil servants. The experience of the Labour governments of 1945–51 was thought, not least by the Prime Minister concerned, Clement Attlee, to have seen off earlier concerns expressed by Harold Laski that a government of Socialist intent would find the Administrative Class to be obstructive (Attlee, 1954, p.308; Laski, 1938, pp.84, 315–22). Though admiring the 'vitality and audacity' of the politically imported administrators of the Washington of the New Deal (Laski, 1942, p.9), Laski had not advocated the introduction of a politicised Higher Civil Service into Whitehall (Laski, 1951, p.176f). Like other Fabians, Laski was within the mainstream tradition of outside criticism of the Civil Service which was concerned not with displacing the career Service, but with 'improving' it by means of reforms of its structure, recruitment, and training, and, following the liberalisation of pension arrangements, the encouragement of greater movement in and out of the Service (e.g. Laski, 1942, pp.10–15). The Fabian authors of *The Administrators* took up those reforms in the 1960s, but their advocacy of explicit and systematic provision being made for political appointments to advisory positions within government departments was a departure from conventional reformism that the authors' search for earlier individual precedents, and sensitivity to the charge that such appointments would be 'immoral', only served to emphasise (Fabian Group, 1964, pp.39ff). Of course, what such advocacy, and Labour Government practice after 1964, signalled was renewed distrust of and controversy about the role of the Administrative Class.

The difficulties of undertaking a review of the structure of the Civil Service of the kind that the Fulton Committee had been assigned, as well as some idea of the likely fate of any proposals made, was illustrated by the experience of the wartime Crookshank Committee. This had been appointed in June 1942 by the then Chancellor of the Exchequer, Sir Kingsley Wood, under the chairmanship of the then Financial Secretary to the Treasury, H. F. C. Crookshank, 'to conduct a general survey of the form of, and conditions of service in, the Home Civil Service after the War'. The other members of the Committee were Sir Donald Fergusson, the Permanent Secretary of the Ministry of Agriculture and Fisheries, Sir Thomas Gardiner, the Director General of the Post Office, Sir Perceval Waterfield, the First Civil Service Commissioner and Henry Wilson Smith, the Principal Establishment Officer at the Treasury. The Committee held sixteen meetings before submitting its Report in February 1943. The Committee took account of outside opinion, including that expressed in what it called 'Professor Laski's Twenty Point Plan,' meaning that academic's views in their 1942 form, and took soundings of Civil Service opinion too.

The Crookshank Committee was not short of ideas itself, proposing 'the institution of what is sometimes described as a "one class Service",' as a Treasury memorandum submitted to Wood's successor as Chancellor, Sir John Anderson, on 17 July 1944 put it:

> The proposal here was that while the Service should continue to be recruited at the three main educational stages – from those leaving school at 16 (who enter the Clerical or Clerical Assistant Class), from those leaving school at 18 (who enter the Executive Class), and from those leaving University at 22–24 (who enter the Administrative Class) – all recruits should, at some stage post-entry, meet on a common grade from which the best would be selected for the senior posts, irrespective of the source of entry. It was not part of the proposal that Administrative or Executive Class recruits should start on work considered appropriate to the Clerical Class; but that instead of the existing three ladders of promotion, passage from one to the other of which can be made only exceptionally, there should be one common ladder, Clerical Officers coming in on the bottom rung, Executive Officers on the second, Administrative Officers on the third. Thereafter (in theory) the best man would climb the fastest.

The Crookshank Committee had in fact also observed that 'there should be opportunities for interchange between the Administrative and the Professional, Technical and Specialist Classes. Neither outside nor Civil Service experience suggests that the latter will qualify for the highest posts in the Service; on the other hand nothing but good can come of a policy founded upon a clear understanding that the Administrative Class is not a closed preserve, but is held as open to the best brains from the rest of the Service as to the recruit from outside.' When, on 5 July 1943, a meeting of the Heads of Departments discussed the Crookshank Committee's proposals, Sir Thomas Phillips, the Permanent Secretary of the Ministry of Labour, proved to be 'more favourably disposed than his colleagues to the idea of a one grade Service because it seemed to him to promise greater fluidity, between Treasury Classes and Departmental Classes.' Otherwise, while there was no dissent about the need to make use of the Executive Class, there was general agreement among the Permanent Secretaries that 'the idea of a one grade Service was not attractive' (*Report*, 1943).

Nothing resembling a 'one grade' or 'one class' structure followed from the work of the official committees and those connected with the Whitley system of joint consultation that reconstructed the Home Civil Service during the latter part of the Second World War and the years immediately afterwards. The Scientific Civil Service, the Works Group of Professional Classes and the Professional Accountant Class were all established following Reports from committees headed by Sir Alan Barlow and Sir Thomas Gardiner, and the former also chaired a committee which reorganised the Legal Class. The Medical Officer Class was reorganised too, latterly by a committee chaired by Sir Harold Howitt. Only the Statistician Class, though, was given a structure that was closely related to that of the Administrative Class (Fry, 1969a, pp.208–32). As for the structure of the General Classes, the main change which took place was that indicated by the title of Treasury Circular 5/47, namely the *Extended Use of the Executive Class*. Promotion to the Executive Class became the natural career outlet for the Clerical Officer (*Whitley Bulletin*, March 1947, pp.36–38). The Administrative Class remained separate, although there was promotion into its ranks from the Executive Class and transfer across from the specialist groups. The Administrative Class and the Higher Civil Service did not continue to be more or less synonymous, as they had been in the inter-war period; but the most prestigious posts in government departments still tended to be dominated by members of the Administrative Class, and more especially by its direct entrants, which made them and their Class the natural targets for critics both inside and outside the Civil Service.

There was much that was recognisable from 'Professor Laski's Twenty Point Plan' in the reforming agenda that characterised the debate about the future structure of the Home Civil Service in the period leading down to the appointment of the Fulton Committee, and similarly familiar were the arguments of the staff associations, sometimes taken up by outside reformers with apparent innocence. Conventionally advanced were proposals favouring a unified Higher Civil Service, and the removal of the barriers between the Administrative and Executive Classes, as well as better opportunities generally for the specialist groups, particularly economists. The position of the Administrative Class was under challenge on several grounds, not least that of what the Fabian authors of *The Administrators* called 'the central issue of amateurism versus professionalism' (Fabian Group, 1964, p.18), and also because one basis of the Class's exclusivity was threatened by university expansion. Though the scale of criticism of the structure of the Home Civil Service did not diminish as the 1960s progressed, one general limitation on their advocacy that critics tended

to observe was that a centrally organised career Civil Service should continue
to exist.

Review of the Main Evidence

1. The concept and desirability of a career Civil Service

'The British type of democracy was the basic determinant of the character of
the Civil Service,' Sir Burke Trend observed in his oral evidence to the Fulton
Committee; 'We had chosen to make Ministers responsible for giving effect
to the will of the people. They were helped and supported by a Public Service.'
The Secretary of the Cabinet said that ' "Service" was the word to be stressed'
and 'three principles were cardinal in this.' The first was anonymity: 'The
civil servant submerged his identity in an anonymous machine. This was
not irreconcilable with personal ambition, but carried wide implications for
structure, management, and recruitment.' The second principle was political
neutrality: 'The civil servant accepted the political decisions of Ministers.
This had implications for in and out movement, interchange, and the question
of personal advisers for Ministers.' The third principle was incorruptibility:
'This was often taken for granted but should not be. The moral standard of
the Civil Service was of the first importance.' Trend considered that 'these
principles were all characteristic of a Service under discipline; they implied
leadership, authority and a hierarchical structure. He very much hoped that
they would be left intact in any changes; if they were touched, we should
move towards a different sort of Service, and one which he thought unsuited
to our kind of democracy' (PRO: BA1/4).

The concept of a Permanent Civil Service was 'fundamental to our present
Civil Service organisation and to the morale of the Civil Service,' Lord Bridges
told the Fulton Committee (PRO: BA1/37) in one of the relatively few pieces
of evidence that explicitly discussed the matter. When the former official,
Nevil Johnson wrote that 'our political system and the demands of an efficient
public service require a career Civil Service, most of the members of which
are committed to a lifetime in it' (PRO: BA1/24), he was taking care to spell
out in his evidence what most others making submissions seemed simply to
assume. When Leslie Williams, the General Secretary of the SCS, told the
Committee that 'our basic philosophy is a career Civil Service' (PRO: BA1/5),
his view was representative not only of the position of the Service's staff
associations but also of most individuals and organisations presenting evidence.

While there were few submissions to the Fulton Committee that explicitly
opposed the concept of a career Civil Service, there was also no shortage of
evidence from those who wanted a loosening of the career and who proposed
an increase in later recruitment and movement in and out. While many of
those submissions stated that support for such developments was not intended
to impair the concept of a career Civil Service, as the Committee's Secretariat
observed in its digest of evidence, 'it is not clear among the others where the

line is to be drawn between those who merely want a relaxation of the present practice and those who really envisage a dilution of the concept of a career Service. On the far side of the line one might place those who propose that posts should be open to competition both from inside and outside the Service' (PRO: BA1/38). Certainly, the Society of British Aerospace Companies was clear that the problems of the Civil Service were 'inherent in what has been the fixed concept of the Civil Service being staffed, at all important levels, by a *permanent* body of individuals who have sought to make a career by being a *civil servant.*' The Society's solution was for there to be recruitment to specific jobs in government departments and for employment to be based on specific contracts (PRO: BA1/26). The politician, Jeremy Bray, was one individual giving evidence who made proposals which amounted to the abandonment of a career Service. Bray said that 'it was not sufficient merely to voice well intentioned aspirations, nor would piecemeal reforms such as a broadening of recruitment, the merging of classes and so forth effect the necessary radical change. What was needed was a powerful tangible reform.' In Bray's opinion this would be brought about by arrangements under which 'appointments to senior posts would be open, in a sense that vacancies should be advertised and everyone, civil servant or not, should be eligible' with selection being undertaken by 'an advisory panel composed mainly of non-civil servants.' Bray also favoured 'more fluidity of careers lower down in the Civil Service.' He thought that 'it was questionable whether the old concept of a career as a set of tramlines along which one drove for the whole of one's working life was still attractive to the youth of today. He did not see why the Civil Service should not make appointments for limited terms, with provision for renewal if need be, as other undertakings did' (PRO: BA1/6).

As it was 'the policy in some larger companies to look for a proportion of their senior men from outside their own ranks in order to prevent inbreeding,' the CBI suggested in its written evidence to the Committee that 'the opening to the outside world of some of the more senior posts in the Civil Service might well bring similar advantages,' which led it to recommend 'more recruitment into the Service at ages and stages senior to normal university recruitment' (PRO: BA1/25). In oral evidence, though, J. Whitehorn, representing the CBI, emphasised that 'it is a small yeast we are looking for' (PRO: BA1/5). The British Institute of Management wrote that 'the present limited recruitment of post-experience entrants into the Civil Service at all levels should be extended' (PRO: BA1/26), but it did not quantify this proposal any more than the Labour Party did its suggestion favouring 'the advertisement of specific senior posts both inside and outside the Service' (PRO: BA1/27).

The Chairman of the Electricity Council, Sir Ronald Edwards believed that

> in general large organisations, including the Civil Service, should throw posts at the middle levels more open to competition from outside as well as inside. It would provide a valuable infusion of new blood, and would

widen the range of experience available in the staff of an organisation. However, it should not be carried too far because of its effects on morale, and there might also be practical difficulties with trade unions and staff associations. The Civil Service should be sparing in bringing outsiders in at the highest levels and should do so only when it was absolutely clear that the men being brought in were really outstanding (PRO: **BA1/4**).

The Permanent Secretary at the Ministry of Overseas Development, Sir Andrew Cohen, wrote that

> obviously the Civil Service needs people who will spend a whole career in it. But it also needs people for shorter periods . . . I believe that we should get substantially more of the best young people if we were prepared to offer shorter periods of service as an alternative to recruitment for a whole career. With full employment, mobility is more attractive and we ought to aim more at the adventurous. There is, I think, a good deal of evidence that young men are deterred from coming into the Service because they do not want to commit themselves for a whole career.

Cohen, therefore suggested that 'recruitment for a period should be an alternative to recruitment for a career. The numbers of each type selected would have to be watched, so as to keep up an adequate flow of people who would remain for a working lifetime.' The period that he thought in terms of was probably 'not less than seven years and might be ten years,' and, subject to the agreement of the employing department, 'it should be open to those coming in for a period to convert to a career basis later' (PRO: **BA1/22**).

That 'the Civil Service might move towards a system in which men, both from within and from outside the Service, applied for specific jobs' was suggested to the Committee by Professor W. J. M. Mackenzie on the grounds that

> while some very able men preferred their careers to be planned for them once they had made the initial choice, the majority of able young men today, particularly the managerial types, like to plan their own careers. Leaving aside the man with a drive towards research work, the normal pattern was for the ambitious and able young man to plan his own career, but to keep a safety net under him, that is, most professions had safe routine work to fall back on. After taking his degree and perhaps doing some post-graduate work, such a man sought to choose a job aligned to his speciality; after three or four years he moved on, having shaped further qualifications for himself. By the age of 45 or so the best men had come out on top while the others for the most part had reached their career peak. The old style Administrative Class, whereby a man sold himself to the service of the State and in return received a career structure shaped for him did not fit the new pattern' (PRO: **BA1/6**).

Professor David Donnison also observed in his evidence that 'the young were less attracted by continuity in their careers than they used to be' which made them less interested in a permanent career of the type that the Civil Service conventionally offered to established staff (PRO: BA1/5). At least as far as the Administrative Class was concerned, there was some confirmation of this from discussions about undergraduate attitudes that, at the request of the Committee, Michael Simons, its Assistant Secretary, had with Assistant Principals at the Centre for Administrative Studies (PRO: BA1/18).

The evidence submitted to the Fulton Committee about the career Civil Service and discussion about movement in and out of that Service was inevitably mainly related to the Administrative Class and included material from the Treasury about current arrangements (PRO: BA1/13 and BA1/20) and about foreign practice. The Committee learnt that there was little movement between the Civil Service and outside employment in Sweden (PRO: BA1/32); a considerable amount of movement out at senior levels in the French Civil Service but little movement in after the early career stage (PRO: BA1/19); and that in the American system there was a great deal of movement both ways and only partly because of political appointments (PRO: BA1/3). In his evidence, Lord Franks told the Committee that 'it was difficult to draw a moral from US practice. Their loose structure was related to the looser nature of United States Government, the continental size of the country, and the fact that Americans were used to living in a goldfish bowl.' Plainly referring to the Administrative Class, Franks said that 'the British Civil Service had suffered from seeming to be a self enclosed priesthood.' This impression was 'largely mistaken, but it existed,' and, while he thought that 'the main core of the Civil Service would have to remain permanent', and he had no wish to copy American arrangements, he also believed that 'there was room for some loosening up by taking some recruits later in life and some for short periods' (PRO: BA1/3).

That there should be greater movement in and out of the Civil Service was effectively a conformity in the evidence presented to the Fulton Committee, whether it was submitted by active or former politicians or civil servants, academics, Regional Hospital Boards, local authority associations, the CBI and other private sector groups, and even some Civil Service staff associations. 'Civil servants thought that the Administrative Class was more self sufficient than it really was,' the former minister, Aubrey Jones, observed; 'This sprang from a narrowness of experience. In this country, there was a greater gulf between the Civil Service and the outside world of business, the universities and so forth than, for instance, in the US. In spite of the ever increasing involvement with industry, since the War men had not been brought into the Civil Service from industry until the DEA was set up. Communications should be opened up.' He would not advocate the recruitment of a different type of man to the Administrative Class, but a wider training with 'secondments outside to industry and the universities. In the other direction, there should be temporary movements from outside into the Civil Service.' He realised that the present rules on pay, pensions and conditions of service put obstacles in the way of these movements but 'believed that these obstacles could be overcome once the attitude of mind changed' (PRO: BA1/3).

The Secretary of State for Defence, Denis Healey, having found that 'few civil servants had much of idea of the world of business and industry' told the Committee that interchange with the private sector would be valuable. He thought that 'such exchanges should be for about three years' and that 'the level should be Principal to Under Secretary.' He also believed that 'the exchanges should be two way,' being of the opinion which few other witnesses expressed, that 'in the lack of understanding between industry and the Civil Service the faults were by no means all on the side of the Service' (PRO: BA1/3).

The relative absence of opposition in principle to greater movement in and out of the Civil Service did not of course prevent the practical difficulties being emphasised in some of the evidence to an extent that was undermining. The Treasury's note of caution expressed in M. E. Johnston's remark that 'you have to compromise between the needs of the Service and the desire for more mobility' (PRO: BA1/7) was as predictable as the rider that the SCS attached to its approval of increased mobility that 'in order not to disturb career expectations a balance should be maintained between movements in and out of the Civil Service' (PRO: BA1/20).

Sir Richard Way, the Permanent Secretary at the Ministry of Aviation, thought that the ideal would be for the Administrative Class civil servant to spend five of his or her first twenty years outside the Service, but

> there were practical obstacles in the way of interchange between the Civil Service and outside employment. It was not easy to spare civil servants at a time of shortage, for example of Principals. Nor was it easy to find people from outside willing to come into the Service for a term of years. Many outside concerns were relatively small and could not easily release people, and the individuals concerned were often worried about what would happen to them when they returned to their old employment. In the Ministry of Aviation there was a particular difficulty arising from the department's relations with the aircraft industry. Ministry officials were party to the secrets of every firm in the industry, and could not do their job properly if this were not so. Confidence would be undermined if a firm had reason to think that a civil servant who had knowledge of their secrets was likely to become the employee of one of their rivals (PRO: BA1/2).

When Sir Wilfred Morton, Chairman of the Board of Customs and Excise, and G. Imms of that department gave oral evidence, and there was questioning from Lord Fulton about interchange with industry and commerce, the latter replied that the Board would not be hostile in principle, but it was 'a little difficult to visualize this as a practical programme' not least because of the 'poacher and gamekeeper' risk in switching roles (PRO: BA1/8). The Principals on loan to government departments from industry and commerce also tended in their evidence to the Committee to approve of exchanges of staff in principle 'in order to help to remove the idea that civil servants are a race apart' as one of them put it; but they also stressed the practical difficulties such as that 'good men will be the ones which companies can least afford to spare,' and the differences in the jobs to be done and the levels at which they could be most usefully undertaken (PRO: BA1/25 and BA1/26). When, under the Chairmanship of Sir Norman Kipping, some members of the Fulton Committee held talks with ICI, Marks and Spencer, Shell and Unilever, they found that on the subject of interchange with the Civil Service 'nobody showed enthusiasm. ICI in particular thought the scope very limited . . . They had occasionally taken in a university teacher for a short spell, and had found it quite interesting but an infernal nuisance' (PRO: B1/26).

Though a more fluid career Civil Service in the future was the least that many organisations and individuals submitting evidence to the Fulton Committee seemed willing to contemplate, the related issues of the established and temporary status of Civil Servants and their pension arrangements were practical matters which attracted less attention. 'An established Civil Servant is one who has been admitted to the Civil Service with a certificate from the Civil Service Commission or, more rarely, holds his appointment direct from the Crown e.g. the Civil Service Commissioners themselves,' the Treasury informed the Committee. The Superannuation Act of 1859 provided that 'with certain exceptions, no person should thereafter be deemed to have served in the permanent Civil Service of the State for the purposes of that Act unless he should have been admitted with a certificate from the Civil Service Commissioners.' Thus, the Treasury wrote, 'at an early stage "established" and "pensionable" became associated to such an extent that in many people's eyes they were virtually synonymous.' The Treasury recognised that arrangements could be devised for civil servants to become eligible for a pension at the appropriate time in their service without the present formalities attached to established status: 'If the concept has value – which we suggest it has – this is for other reasons than pensionability.' One reason was that 'there is still a need for the Civil Service Commission to operate their selection procedures openly and fairly.' Above all, though, the Treasury believed,

> establishment remains necessary for the great bulk of the staff, since it carries with it the assurance that, given competence and reasonable conduct, they will have a permanent career in the Service as a whole, and not necessarily confined to the department to which they may first be allocated. With the frequent changes in the machinery of government which are now a feature of life in the Service, some such status is necessary in order to recruit or transfer officers who might otherwise feel unwilling to join an organization which could well have a limited life (PRO: BA1/20).

'The present superannuation system was highly immobilizing,' Sir Arnold Hall, Managing Director of the Hawker Siddeley Group and a former Director of the Royal Aircraft Establishment at Farnborough, told the Committee in early evidence. Indeed, he wondered whether the present concept of establishment, originally introduced to protect civil servants against improper pressures, 'was not in some respects out of date, even, although he did not claim to be able to speak of them with inside knowledge, for the Administrative and Executive Classes' (PRO: BA1/2). 'There were divided views about the transferability of pension rights' on the Staff Side of the National Whitley Council, its Joint Secretary, Richard Hayward informed the Committee; 'It was sometimes argued that it would lead to two Civil Services: men who made their career in the Civil Service: and men who merely worked there. There was not much pressure for transferability among the Administrative and Executive Classes, but quite a lot in the Professional and Scientific Classes. Personally he believed in a career Service, but he thought that the rules of transferability of pensions and gratuities should be eased to some extent' (PRO: BA1/5).

In fact, the FDA representing the Administrative Class (PRO: BA1/29) and the SCS representing the Executive Glass (PRO: BA1/20) both presented evidence to the Committee which favoured either full or greater transferability of Civil Service pensions, as did the Inland Revenue Staff Federation (PRO: BA1/25). L. A. Wines, the General Secretary of the CSCA, wondered 'whether it really is necessary and wise to make establishment and superannuation synonymous,' and, in reply to a question from Sir Philip Allen, he said that 'personally, I am very much attracted to a wise contributory scheme, that is, a much more wise scheme than was recommended by the Tomlin Commission of 1929–31, that seemed to me to be a half baked effort' (PRO: BA1/4). The IPCS, which was critical of the distinctions that the Civil Service made between permanent and temporary and established and unestablished staff, and wanted these differentiations abolished, told the Committee that 'there should be general transferability, or preservation, of accrued Civil Service superannuation benefits as of right, and that the superannuation system should be modified to enable transfer values to be paid in respect of any new entrant who has accrued superannuation service with another employer' (PRO: BA1/30).

Sir Laurence Helsby told the Committee that 'he would rather welcome a contributory pension scheme in order to bring Civil Service pension practice in line with the majority of other pension schemes in this country, if this were practicable. The main difficulty was that a change would involve a lot of complicated legislation, which he thought should be avoided unless the case for a change was clearly and strongly made out' (PRO: BA1/8). Believing that 'there should be more movement in and out of the Civil Service,' Dame Evelyn Sharp said in her evidence that 'civil servants should be free to leave with their notional pension contributions credited to them.' She realised that under present superannuation arrangements this gave rise to problems to which she did not know the answer: 'It was often argued, particularly by specialist departments, that if movement out of the Service were made easier

there would be too much wastage. That attitude was too timid. She thought
that the misfits would go, and the belly-achers would stop belly-aching' (PRO:
BA1/4).

Sir Alexander Johnston, Chairman of the Board of Inland Revenue, one
of the departments which would be at risk of a loss of important staff if
restraints on pensions were eased, told the Committee that he was not against
transferability but thought that there should be managerial discretion to
refuse it in certain cases (PRO: BA1/8). C. H. Sisson, as Principal Establishment Officer at the Ministry of Labour, argued both for a more exacting
form of probation before a civil servant became established, and for the
retention of restraints on transferability of pensions because Civil Service
rigidities on grading and pay made it uncompetitive in relation to staff that
the Service needed to retain. Sisson was satisfied with the arrangements
for getting rid of misfits in the Service, if unenthusiastic about using such
procedures (PRO: BA1/7), and this was a subject that interested several of
those who gave evidence or had discussions with the Committee. The Home
Secretary, Roy Jenkins, in conversation with Sir Philip Allen, made it clear
that he wanted 'rather better arrangements for early retirement for those who
no longer fitted in' (PRO: BA1/30).

The Committee was told in evidence by Sir Colin Crowe of the Diplomatic
Service Administration Office that 'Section 45 of the Superannuation Act of
1965 (originally part of the Foreign Service Act 1943) gave the Diplomatic
Service a power not enjoyed by the Home Civil Service to retire people early
in the interests of the Service. This was used to remove those who had slowed
up or were not likely to go further.' Crowe said that 'on the whole Section
45 worked satisfactorily. If anything it improved morale since younger people
knew that the dead wood above them was being pruned' (PRO: BA1/4).
The Treasury subsequently distributed a background paper on premature
retirements in the interests of efficiency from the Home Civil Service, which
meant those effected under the provisions of Sections 9 and 10 of the Superannuation Act of 1965, and there was discussion of adopting in addition
arrangements similar to those of the Diplomatic Service (PRO: BA1/22). As
the Treasury's paper was deemed to be of a confidential character, the note
circulated from that department on the same subject in January 1968 (PRO:
BA1/48), which was eventually published as Memorandum No. 22 in the
fourth volume of the Committee's evidence, was simply of a factual kind. In
discussing in oral evidence what Robert Neild called these 'divorce laws',
Louis Petch of the Treasury said he thought that in practice the Diplomatic
Service found itself as inhibited in using Section 45 as the Home Civil Service
did in using its existing powers to retire on grounds of inefficiency (PRO:
BA1/7).

Discussion about essential features of a career Civil Service such as superannuation and the 'divorce laws' did not entirely take the form of the Treasury
versus the rest, even if that department was given to emphasising the 'diffic-

ulties' of change. Thus, Louis Petch told the Committee: 'I see no particular advantage in having a completely statutory scheme as we have at the moment and I would have thought you could work a pension scheme equally well with the sort of Estacode regulations which we have for pay, agreed with the Staff Side . . . On the other hand this is something which Parliament has always had, and one has to think very carefully before recommending that we take the privilege away from them.' Then, again, and also on the pension scheme, Petch said, 'I think if we started from scratch in the Civil Service we would probably go contributory there now, but we have a non-contributory system at the moment and I do not think the advantages of changing over would in any way justify the difficulties involved.' When he was asked by Walter Anderson if there was 'any reason why temporaries should not have a pension?' Petch replied: 'There is no reason of principle at all, but the thing has just grown up this way. It would cost a considerable amount to bring in a pension scheme for temporaries. It is difficult to estimate how much, but the figure I have been given is that something like 10% of the cost of the superannuation scheme would be added if all temporaries were to be brought into the pension arrangements' (PRO: BA1/7).

When Walter Anderson observed, in exchanges with Louis Petch, that 'it seems strange' for a civil servant 'to be temporary with twenty years' service' (PRO: BA1/7) his remark emphasised the peculiarity of an arrangement that could not be expected to survive a review of the type that the Fulton Committee conducted, while at the same time exemplifying the assumption, which the Committee as a whole acted as if it shared, that, aside from explicit political appointments, the career Civil Service should be all-embracing.

2. Unity versus diversity in the structure of the Home Civil Service

Whether the Home Civil Service should have a unified structure or whether departmentalism should be emphasised more was a continuing matter for consideration in the mass of evidence that was submitted to the Fulton Committee about that Service's overall structure. The Treasury submitted evidence to the Committee as early as May 1966 entitled 'The Future Structure of the Civil Service', the presentation of which had the presumably desired effect of heavily influencing the agenda for subsequent discussion. Despite its broad title, though, the Treasury's paper was almost entirely concerned with proposing the merger of the Administrative and Executive Classes on a particular basis and about a form of unified Higher Civil Service. The Treasury thought that 'it would then probably be right to abolish the word "class" throughout the Service, and substitute some less emotive word such as "group"; and the replacement of the somewhat archaic, and little understood, titles of the grades in the present Administrative and Executive Classes merits further consideration' (PRO: BA1/13). The 'ancient, honourable but mysterious titles' of these grades were 'quaintly baffling to the outside world,' the International Publishing Corporation wrote in its evidence, observing that: 'A considerable step forward would be achieved if accepted business terms were used; if the Permanent Under Secretary were to be named Managing Director; the Deputy Under Secretary, Deputy Managing Director; the Assistant Under Secretary, a Director; the Assistant Secretary, Senior Manager; the Principal, Middle Manager; the Assistant, Junior or Trainee Manager' (PRO: BA1/27). The Secretariat recorded the opinion that the IPC had been 'genuinely funny at the expense of the present system' (PRO: BA1/38) and one can see that any humour must have been welcome to them amidst the mass of evidence. Tales of the 'I don't deal with Under Secretaries – give me the Higher Executive Officer' variety had been told before, of course (e.g. Walker, 1961, p.258), and changing the names of grades had to be a minor matter.

In terms of the overall structure of the Home Civil Service what was of paramount importance was the issue of unity versus diversity. Explicitly or implicitly, all the evidence submitted to the Committee, barring that of the Society of British Aerospace Companies (PRO: BA1/26), assumed that some type of categorisation of the Service was essential. Though, as would be expected, there was plenty of opposition to particular sorts of change, it seemed to be generally recognised that the future structure of the Service would not take the existing form, thus opening the way for discussion about the shape that it should take.

'A marked feature of the British Civil Service, particularly as it has developed in this century, is that it is a structure of separate classes, and that accordingly people are recruited to and make their careers within a class', observed the former official, Nevil Johnson, in the only piece of evidence that the Committee received which successfully attempted to take an overview of the structure of the Service. Johnson considered that 'this class structure does justice to certain functional needs. It expresses the belief that the efficiency of the Civil Service is enhanced if staff are recruited for a range of work within their competence rather than for specific posts. In contrast, position classification as developed in the USA and Canada, requires the public services to think more in terms of filling posts than of securing groups of staff qualified for a relatively rude range of duties.'

Johnson believed that a class structure of the kind that the British Civil Service had developed afforded 'considerable flexibility in the use of staff within the classes' and that it was 'neither practicable nor desirable to abandon to any significant extent the principle of the class structure.' He did think, though, that some modifications were needed, and one that he suggested was the superimposing on the existing classes of 'a unified structure of grades and salaries' and cited the West German example as a possible model. What he envisaged was a three-level Service with the levels simply labelled A, B and C, in which

> salary scales might then run something like 1 to 4 in level C, 5 to 9 in level B, and 10 to 18 in level A. It would then be necessary to decide what

the points of equivalence are between Classes, after which salaries could then all be brought into line within given ranges of the scale. Some reduction in the number of grades in some Classes would be required. In practice, it would then be possible, to give a few examples, to put the Executive Class on exactly the same grading and salary scale as the Experimental Officer Class, members of the Legal Class on the same scale as Administrative staff, and members of the Works Group on the same scales as the Scientific Officer Class. If the highest level were that of Director General . . . the post would be classified as Class A, salary group 18. The professional attachment of occupants would be immaterial (PRO: BA1/24).

The Treasury supplied the Fulton Committee with early evidence about the American system of common grading (PRO: BA1/12) and the Canadian system of occupational categories (PRO: BA1/13). There was no shortage of evidence suggesting the integration of the specialist groups with general management, which necessarily carried the implication of at least unified grading for the Higher Civil Service. The abolition of class divisions in the Home Civil Service was proposed by both the Royal Institute of Chemistry (PRO: BA1/29) and the Labour Party (PRO: BA1/27) without discussion of the structural consequences. In its evidence, the Engineers' Guild expressed the hope that 'the Committee will feel able to recommend an "across the board" classification of Civil Service posts' (PRO: BA1/25).

The Civil Service Union, representing the Messengerial and Ancillary grades of the Service, meaning many of 'those in the lower salary bands outside the Clerical field,' told the Committee that the main need was for 'the replacement of the present rigid structure of watertight general service and linked departmental classes and miniature departmental grades by an integrated Civil Service in which men and women of ability and character can make use of and extend their potential for service and leadership without being held back by artificial barriers, whether of class or age' (PRO: BA1/22).

The UK Atomic Energy Authority, once part of the Ministry of Supply, stated in its evidence that for the structural problems of the Civil Service

a radical solution would be to have – as with the Authority's Senior and Band Staff – a single pay structure for officers of all classes – Scientific, Technological and Administrative. An officer would be recruited to the section of the single promotion ladder appropriate to his qualifications and merit. His career would similarly proceed through successive grades (with common pay scales and conditions of service for all disciplines) according to qualifications, ability and responsibilities. A structure on these lines should provide maximum flexibility to find the right man for each job and maximum adaptability to changing needs and work programmes. Similar structures are already operated by some major employers in the UK by a number of international organizations (PRO: BA1/27).

Specific examples would have been useful. When the Committee had discussions with ICI, Marks and Spencer, Shell and Unilever, it learned that it was the practice of those companies to 'recruit graduates for a range or class of jobs' (PRO: BA1/26), but there was no evidence of sophisticated grading structures being available which could serve the Committee as examples for the Home Civil Service to follow. It was only late on in the Fulton Committee's existence that material about British Petroleum was made available, and unified grading was a subject that was more prominent in the Committee's deliberations than it was in the main body of evidence submitted to it.

For those critical of Treasury control of the Civil Service, of course, that Service was too unified already in important respects, although replacing the Treasury by another central department would not necessarily diminish what was presumed to be the coherence of the Service's structure. This made room in the evidence submitted to the Fulton Committee for discussion of the virtues of a structure of general as opposed to departmental classes, greater professionalism, and of a structure based on the grouping of departments.

'Government departments can be differentiated according to the organizational structure and the nature of the decision making process,' the academic, Trevor Smith, observed in his evidence to the Committee: 'Thus Whitehall does not constitute a single monolithic bureaucracy but rather a complex of bureaucracies at various stages of development; and it follows that Ministries have differing manpower needs. Hence the present practice of staffing them from a corps of general administrators is inappropriate.' Smith advocated that 'administrators should be recruited and allocated to groups of related Ministries' (PRO: BA1/27).

The Society of British Aerospace Companies believed that 'departments whose role is essentially to work within and assist industry and commerce should be organized and staffed in a manner compatible with the pattern and purposes of industry. This is likely to mean that such departments may well differ in character from others having entirely different objectives' (PRO: BA1/26). Dr A. F. Earle of the London Graduate School of Business Studies was alone in suggesting groupings of the more important departments. Category I comprised 'Ministries whose work involves management of the national economy and/or the influencing of management in industry and commerce,' and included the Treasury, the Board of Trade, the Department of Economic Affairs, the Ministry of Technology, the Ministry of Agriculture, Fisheries and Food, and the Foreign Office trade services. Category II comprised 'Ministries whose work involves managerial techniques similar to those of industry and commerce', and included the Ministry of Power and the Post Office. Category III comprised 'Ministries whose spending is substantial and for whom cost effectiveness criteria are important, and whose spending powers can be used to influence industry and commerce', and included the Ministry of Defence, the Ministry of Aviation, the Ministry of Housing and Local Government, the Department of Education and Science, and the

Ministry of Health. Category IV comprised 'Ministries whose work is difficult to measure or of a social nature', and included the Foreign Office diplomatic services, the Ministry of Overseas Development, the Home Office, the Commonwealth Relations Office, and the Ministry of Pensions and National Insurance. Earle considered that the need for a knowledge of modern managerial techniques was high in Categories I, II and III, but less important in Category IV (PRO: BA1/24).

The Home Secretary, Roy Jenkins, in conversation with Sir Philip Allen, said that 'he was against grouping of departments for the purposes of recruitment and movement of staff. He thought that this would introduce artificial barriers' (PRO: BA1/30). The former Minister, Aubrey Jones, told the Committee that he was

> not attracted to the idea of grouping departments for purposes of recruitment, training, careers and so forth. It might appear *prima facie* that departments could readily be divided into groups but on closer examination it would be found that there was a very complicated network of affinities. Moreover, grouping would militate against mobility over the whole Civil Service, because the groups would tend to create their own frontiers. He did not mind that more interdepartmental mobility for the Administrative Class might mean less specialization (PRO: BA1/3).

In answer to a question on the grouping of departments, Professor Richard Titmuss, an academic authority on social policy and administration, said that 'he would be seriously concerned if that had the effect of, for instance, dividing off the economic departments or of making the social service departments a closed area. Since, after all, the Treasury made decisions about the social services it was important that there should be some men in the Treasury with direct experience of that kind of work; they . . . should have a spell working as a counter clerk in Newcastle' (PRO: BA1/4).

Not surprisingly, suggestions for a similar career pattern were absent from the evidence of serving or former higher civil servants. Lord Normanbrook told the Committee that 'he was very doubtful of the advantages of putting departments into groups. To the extent that it was necessary it already happened *de facto*, but he did not wish to encourage the artificial fragmentation of the Service which would be against recent trends towards more integration of the Service' (PRO: BA1/3). Lord Franks doubted the utility of the grouping of departments, saying that 'his impression was that the need for a more quantitative and practical approach was Service wide. For example, the Home Office had many problems which involved this and could benefit from a gentle introduction to the quantitative approach. Moreover, it would be a mistake to man, say, the Ministry of Labour exclusively with sociologists. He thought it better to man the Service as a whole and then allocate its manpower sensibly' (PRO: BA1/3). Sir George Abell, the First Civil Service Commissioner, 'doubted whether it would be right to sort departments into groups and to recruit people for a specific group. This might make the Service more attractive to some recruits but it would complicate the problems of the Service if more divisions and compartments were erected. The Commission already tried to start people off in suitable departments or kinds of departments' (PRO: BA1/3). Sir Laurence Helsby thought that 'the special skills of the manager were needed over the whole field. It was over-simple to divide departments into groups; the differences were shadings of degree, not cut-offs of kind. For example, no department was more than 80 per cent economics in its subject matter, or less than 20 per cent' (PRO: BA1/8). Sir Leslie Rowan was 'not attracted by the idea' of grouping departments for career purposes. Even in

> a group of departments with an industrial sponsorship role – the Board of Trade, Ministry of Technology, Ministry of Aviation, . . . it took a long time to get to know really well, for example, the aircraft industry, so that mobility even within such a group would militate against the acquisition of the necessary expertise. He would not advocate a hard and fast rule of keeping senior officials to one department because in some cases it might hold up deserved and valuable promotions, but as far as practicable the object should be depth of experience beyond a certain level (PRO: BA1/4).

Dame Evelyn Sharp took a slightly different line, which was that

> while she was opposed to moving Permanent Secretaries between departments, she was not against moves at lower levels provided they were planned and deliberate, taking into account a person's aptitudes and the need to widen his experience. In most cases, such moves should take place between comparable departments. But she was against the formal organisation of the Service in groups of departments: in the first place, groups overlapped; secondly, some individuals might profit by a complete change to an entirely different department (PRO: BA1/4).

Though the question of whether the structure of the Home Civil Service should be organised on a General Service Class basis, or departmentally, or, like the current arrangements, as a combination of the two, would seem to be an issue that would attract a broad discussion, a disproportionate amount of attention was given in the evidence to the existing Departmental Class organisation in the Executive and Clerical field in the Board of Customs and Excise, the Board of Inland Revenue, and the Ministry of Labour. In its evidence on the Departmental Classes, the Treasury did try to introduce some wider considerations, recalling that the Reorganisation Committee of 1920, 'whose recommendations led to the establishment of the Administrative, Executive and Clerical Classes in the present form,' had

> suggested that Departmental Classes engaged on duties analogous to those assigned to the General Service Classes should be brought within the scope of the revised classification and recommended that the possibility of assimilating these Classes should be explored departmentally at an early date. A number of Departmental Classes were so absorbed,

but a number remained. Their position was confirmed by the Tomlin Commission who, while agreeing with the view that unnecessary differences between departments in relation to grading and organisation should be avoided, concluded that the clerical work of many departments required for its proper performance a departmental form of organisation which, by having regard to the nature of the work, might differ from department to department. However, many of the pre-war departmental grades were absorbed into the General Service Classes during 1945–1947. Since then it has not been the practice to establish new Departmental Executive and Clerical Classes, despite the setting up of a number of new departments. In general, the number of Departmental Classes is less than before the war, but there are still some big and important ones.

It was the Treasury's view that 'there is little doubt that the flexibility of the Civil Service, and its abilities to move quickly to meet the changing demands of different Administrations, would be seriously at risk if a pattern of Departmental Classes emerged on any more widespread scale than exists at present.' The Treasury's suggestion to the Committee was that 'the main criterion against which both existing Departmental Classes and any new proposals for the creation of new Departmental Classes should be judged is the necessity to train their members in skills specific to the department, usually with the requirement of a definite qualification, either externally or internally acquired' (PRO: BA1/29).

Aside from the views of one Minister, William Rodgers, who was opposed to departmentalism on the basis of experience of difficulties in staffing the DEA (PRO: BA1/5), the evidence about the comparative advantages of General Service or Departmental Class structures tended to be dominated by officials in departments with the latter form of organisation and by the staff associations and their representatives.

Inevitably, some of the evidence was narrowly drawn, and this was certainly the case with that submitted by Richard Hayward, who said that the Staff Side of the National Whitley Council whom he represented was

> particularly concerned about the large number of departmental grades. First, the "lags and leads" in the pay scales of the Departmental Classes were a great nuisance in staff pay negotiations. Secondly, the proliferation of Departmental Classes inhibited movement between departments. For instance, the problem of setting up the Ministry of Social Security would have been many times greater had there been departmental grades in the then Ministry of Pensions and National Insurance and National Assistance Board, or if, as had at one time been suggested, a part of the Ministry of Labour had been absorbed in the new Ministry. It was fortunate that there were no departmental grades in the Administrative Class and that facilitated movement between departments.

Hayward's preference for 'broader based' General Service Classes, however, also followed from his belief that

the existence of departmental grades led to departmental staff associations, and, because of vested interests, that created a vicious circle.
There were 65 unions in the Civil Service and it was fair to say that the
small ones profited from the central agreements on pay and conditions
obtained mainly by the larger unions, and yet kept their own little
privileges. It was sometimes argued that Departmental Classes and
departmental staff associations were good for *esprit de corps*; however,
it was not sufficiently appreciated that, while they might do something
for departmental *esprit de corps*, they were bad for morale throughout
the Service at large (PRO: BA1/5).

There would seem to be wider considerations affecting the future structure
of the Home Civil Service than making pay negotiations easier and effecting
the rationalisation of the Service's staff association movement, and some of
the staff associations addressed these broader issues, if, predictably, in a self
interested manner. Thus, Leslie Williams, the General Secretary of the SCS
could not have surprised the Committee when he said that there was 'a very
good case for extending the General Executive Class more widely.' This Class
was 'highly specialised in some areas' but it was also 'easily moved from one
quarter to another. Conversely to that, if you were to extend the system of
departmental gradings to more departments than we have now it would
become increasingly difficult to make these dispositions.' Williams added that

> if you create small classes of a specialised kind, the Information Officer
> Class might be an example, you do get difficulties in time of creating a
> proper career structure within it. Another example would be if we decided
> to create a special class for ADP, automatic data processing work. There
> was a lot of talk in the Treasury about doing that. In fact, instead, it is
> absorbed today in the General Executive Class, and we can throw up
> enough reserves to train and specialise and do that work, who later on
> can go back into the main career stream, so another problem is sorted
> out.

Williams said that 'if one was looking for some formula, it would be that,
unless the work of the department was so highly professionalised as to require
some intensive technique of specialisation which cannot be acquired within
the Service, one ought to look on the General Service pattern as being the best'
(PRO: BA1/5). In written evidence, the SCS made it clear that the application of
this formula would mean that, of the existing major Departmental Classes,
only the Tax Inspectorate would survive, while losing some headquarters
posts (PRO: BA1/34).

Len Wines of the CSCA told the Committee that

> our bias or prejudice is in favour of General Service. We have not been
> absolutist on this, because cases vary in degree. If we were pushed we
> could see a rather better case for a special structure in the Inspectorate
> of Taxes Branch of the Inland Revenue, for example, than we could see
> in the Collection Service of Inland Revenue or in the Customs and Excise

Outdoor Service, or in the Ministry of Labour regional and local service. So we are not absolutist, but we think there is a great deal to be said for a General Service multiple system of grading, which has flexibility in this direction: it facilitates the manning up of new work, and it is perhaps significant that when new departments or big new branches of departments are set up, within my experience none of them have been set up on anything but a General Service basis (PRO: BA1/24).

'Because of growing specialisation and the need for more selective recruitment in the future we would strongly argue that the trend must be away from General Service uniformity and towards more departmentalism,' the Inland Revenue Staff Federation told the Committee (PRO: BA1/25). The Association of Her Majesty's Inspectors of Taxes stated in its evidence that

> we do not think that a uniform pattern of lower and middle management organisation or complete freedom of interchangeability at all levels throughout the Civil Service is possible . . . We suggest that greater freedom for departments to evolve structures based on increased professional/technical specialisation might indeed improve Civil Service efficiency in the face of similar developments outside and by virtue of giving greater definition to the kind of job a graduate would have within the Civil Service it would improve the prospects of recruiting him.

As might be expected, the AIT wanted 'the special position of the Tax Inspectorate' to be maintained (PRO: BA1/25), and on behalf of the Official Side of the Board of Inland Revenue, Sir Alexander Johnston said that 'we are very much in favour of Departmental Classes remaining,' and that if there had to be change in the manner in which the Board was staffed it should be in the direction of greater departmentalism (PRO: BA1/8).

Between sixty and seventy per cent of the Executive and equivalent grades in the Board of Customs and Excise were doing work that differed from that of 'the normal office-bound or chair-bound Executive Officer,' J. E. Morrish of the Customs and Excise Preventive Staff Association told the Committee, which meant that the civil servants concerned were 'employed upon work that could be sufficiently distinguished in a number of different aspects from the generality to justify a separate and somewhat specialist set up' (PRO: BA1/6). 'The case for maintenance of a Departmental Class is in our view unanswerable,' declared the Customs and Excise Federation, representing the Officer Grade which was the main grade of the Outdoor Service of the Board, asserting that to organise the staff otherwise would lead to 'a loss of efficiency and an increase in manpower' (PRO: BA1/38). E. J. Hoskin, representing the Customs and Excise Surveyors' Association, said of that body that 'we have come out quite positively for the grades of Customs and Excise to be treated as Treasury grades. We can see no advantage whatsoever in the maintenance of a Departmental Class' (PRO: BA1/6). That there were marked differences of view and of interest among the staff and their associations in the Board of Customs and Excise was acknowledged by Sir Wilfred

Morton, when representing its Official Side before the Committee. He also emphasised the 'perceptibly high morale amongst the members of the ex-Headquarters staff groups' with their 'sense of being separate' and in 'individual charge of a geographical area' with 'responsibility for the work of the department there.' Morton observed that 'it used to be said that you have the squire, the vicar, and the Excise Officer, and this was the group which led, and this obviously continues.' He believed though, that the case for Departmental Classes rested on the nature of the work, and that of the ex-headquarters branches of the Board of Customs and Excise was distinct in character from the general run of Executive Class work. It demanded an expertise which came only from experience, and it required a certain kind of personality of an independent, active kind, different from that required by the desk-bound work of the General Executive Class (PRO: BA1/8).

'To work effectively in the Ministry of Labour you have to acquire the expertise to deal with both workers and employers, and the knowledge of a great deal about industry, its structure, the pay arrangements in industry, its methods of industrial relations, and many other things which, on the whole, are not required in most other Civil Service departments,' M. R. Booth of the Association of Officers of the Ministry of Labour told the Committee in oral evidence which emphasised that this work required staff with 'a particular personality' as well as training. Booth said that the Ministry of Labour had 'a very real *esprit de corps*,' which he ascribed to the Departmental Class arrangement, and the Association wanted that also to embrace what Booth called 'the Ministry's watertight departments' such as the Factory Inspectorate (PRO: BA1/7).

The Ministry of Labour Staff Association made much the same points about the Ministry's work having a distinctive character requiring special qualities in its staff. J. L. Tindall, the Association's General Secretary, stressed that members of the Departmental Class had 'a special pride in doing the work' which was 'like a regiment of the line taking pride in itself.' While being opposed to an integrated Departmental Class within the Ministry of Labour of the kind proposed by the AOML, and wanting Departmental Class arrangements in the Ministry limited to regional and local office staff, Tindall and the MLSA saw 'nothing wrong' in 'the extension of departmentalism' elsewhere in the Civil Service (PRO: BA1/7). Much of the evidence submitted by the Principal Establishment Officer at the Ministry of Labour, C. H. Sisson, about that Ministry was concerned with its practice of having a graduate Cadet entry set just below Assistant Principal level, which was of particular interest to the Committee, given the Treasury's structural proposals. Speaking of the Ministry of Labour in general, Sisson said that 'there is no doubt of the tremendous loyalty, enthusiasm and liking for the job which very large numbers of the staff have,' while describing the advantages of having a Departmental Class as 'marginal but important' (PRO: BA1/7).

The special nature of the work, and of the qualities needed to do it, unusual conditions of service, and the *esprit de corps* that separateness was believed to promote were, then, the main arguments that were advanced in evidence to the Fulton Committee in favour of there being Departmental Classes. Contrastingly, the IPCS argued that 'departmentalism should be abolished as a factor in class organisation' because it was 'wholly inconsistent with the concept of Civil Service employment which has great advantage in terms of flexibility and the organisation of government business and which enables the full use to be made of talent wherever it may be found in the Civil Service' (PRO: BA1/30).

The evidence submitted to the Committee generally tended to assume the continuance of formal and well developed grading structures in the Home Civil Service, and know and standardised pay scales, even if in the latter instance there were suggestions from the CSCA (PRO: BA1/20) and the IRSF (PRO: BA1/25) that those scales should be supplemented by special merit increases. To go beyond that, as the UK Atomic Energy Authority did, and to express opposition to automatic and uniform incremental salary scales and to advocate pay being based on performance (PRO: BA1/27) was out of keeping with the debate. When the General Secretary of the IRSF, Cyril Plant, told the Fulton Committee that shortening the length of incremental pay scales was 'the number one priority in the whole of the Civil Service movement today' (PRO: BA1/6), he gave the Committee another reminder about the difficulties of its task.

3. Structure of the Higher Civil Service

The proposals for a common management structure at and near the top of the Home Civil Service which were made in the Treasury's memorandum on 'The Future Structure of the Civil Service' of May 1966 became the main point of reference for such evidence as was submitted to the Fulton Committee about the prospective form which the structure of the Higher Civil Service should take.

In that memorandum, the Treasury suggested to the Committee that 'it would be practicable to produce a common structure broadly applicable to the Service as a whole extending from the Permanent Secretary level down to the maximum of the Assistant Secretary scale.' The Treasury envisaged a basic structure of numbered grades, recognising that there could not be complete uniformity in the pattern of pay or in the manner of inclusion of a considerable number of specialist posts, some of which would have to continue to have specific titles. The Treasury's primary aim in proposing the establishment of a common structure at or near the top of the Home Civil Service was

> to ensure that all suitable individuals are considered for the senior posts and that it is not necessary for them to cross Civil Service Class barriers, and recross them in the event of a return to a specialist discipline . . . In the long run, more scientists and professionals who have the potential

for top management might be attracted to the Civil Service if they knew that the highest posts in the general management field were open to them, and that training courses would be provided to equip them for management and to bring out their aptitudes for it (PRO: BA1/13).

In oral evidence, Louis Petch, representing the Treasury observed:

already there is the possibility of putting a professional man into what is at present an administrative post, and to some extent vice versa. This is not something which is unheard of now, in fact there is a great deal of this. When you come to the Higher Civil Service, there is a spectrum of jobs ranging from what you might call the purely administrative to the purely technical. There are many jobs which combine the two. In many cases you will find, for example, a scientist in charge of a research institute, he is in charge of the place, he is running the show, he is doing quite a lot of administrative and managerial work as well as his scientific work. So that there is not now a clear division between administrative and professional, there is every gradation between the two. And you will find professionals already in many cases doing quite a lot of managerial work. We are proposing simply to say that in future we are not going to put some of these posts on one side of the fence and some on the other, we are going to say they are all Higher Civil Service, and we will find the best man for the job whatever his origins, whichever way he has come up the ladder, and put him into it.

In reply to sceptical questioning from Sir James Dunnett, Petch later added that 'my expectation would certainly be that you would still tend to find the Permanent Secretary post occupied in the main by people who had come up the administrative way' (PRO: BA1/5).

Sir Burke Trend told the Committee that he

thought it very important to bring the Scientific and Professional Classes into closer relationship with the Administrative. The two were educated to think in different categories. Administration was a political art involving the judgment of men and situations. Scientists and professionals thought in different measurable categories. Many . . . did not want to be involved in decision making. But those who did could be no less good at it than those who came from arts disciplines, and he thought it very important to give them the opportunity. He would therefore like to see the Scientific and Professional Classes amalgamated with the Administrative, at the top at least this was more important than the Administrative/Executive merger. However it was achieved, the main object would be to be able to select and train at an early stage those Professional civil servants who were suited to and had an interest in the policy making activity (PRO: BA1/4).

Another Permanent Secretary, Sir Antony Part, stated in his written evidence that

the senior ranks of the Civil Service, particularly perhaps from Assistant

Secretary level upwards, need more initiators and potential change makers . . . We want the best people wherever we can find them and not necessarily only in their early twenties . . . We must get away from the traditional idea that experts of professional origin are essentially advisers to administrators and that if there is a mixed team the administrator must always be the head of it. Often he should be, but sometimes a joint arrangement is best, sometimes a professional should be the leader, and sometimes the post should be open to the most appropriately qualified man of any origin. Moves in the last direction are inhibited by salary differentials between the Classes . . . The aim should be to have a Higher Civil Service – from Assistant Secretary level upwards – in which there are as few salary differentials as possible between people of different origins (PRO: BA1/22).

In oral evidence, though, Part (not entirely consistently) also observed that 'on the policy making side . . . the professional who could go all the way with the administrator over the latter's very wide range was an extremely rare bird. This was not surprising; few men could master two professions' (PRO: BA1/4).

'There are about 6,000 officers in the Higher Civil Service in the grades above the Administrative Principal and over two-thirds are in the professional classes.' the IPCS informed the Fulton Committee in its written evidence. 'At Assistant Secretary level and above, there are over 2,200 officers, just under one half of them in the professional classes. Despite this, of the 36 posts at Permanent Secretary level, 33 are filled by members of the Administrative Class.' The IPCS proposed that 'above the level of Administrative Principal and the broadly equivalent professional grades, there should be a single hierarchical structure in which posts would be filled strictly on merit from all suitable people irrespective of their original profession.' The IPCS recognised that this proposal 'which amounts to a "one class" Higher Civil Service' would mean the provision of more positive career planning and training than were then available. Such a Higher Civil Service would give 'reality to the ideal of flexibility, for any post ceases to be considered the preserve of a particular Class. To quote only one absurdity that would disappear, posts in the vast field of general financial management and control are currently restricted to members of the Administrative/Executive Class. Professional accountants are not even allowed to apply for these posts – simply because they are members of the Professional Accountant Class.' The IPCS acknowledged that some posts in the Higher Civil Service would require 'what is traditionally the expertise of the Administrative Class', and that others would 'certainly require specific professional qualifications' such as the post of Treasury Medical Adviser (PRO: BA1/30). In between, though, there was what William McCall, the General Secretary of the IPCS called in his oral evidence 'a great grey area' which should be open to 'the best man for the job regardless of his original profession' (PRO: BA1/8).

The IPCS commissioned a comparative study of the role of specialists in the Civil Services of France, Germany, Sweden, Australia, and the USA, which was circulated to the Committee, prefaced by a succinct summary written by Professor F. F. Ridley of the University of Liverpool (PRO: BA1/33), and subsequently published as a book in 1968 by Allen and Unwin, with Ridley as editor, entitled *Specialists and Generalists*. In oral evidence, McCall described the contributions to the symposium as being 'a little uneven' in quality. The material on France, as Norman Hunt observed, represented 'a very good piece of work,' but, as McCall conceded, that on the USA was much less impressive, which was ironic, given that apart from the domestic example of the UK Atomic Energy Authority the IPCS's structural proposals for the Higher Civil Service were most influenced by American arrangements (PRO: BA1/8).

The evidence to the Fulton Committee about the future structure of the Higher Civil Service understandably tended to be mainly concerned with the desirability of the further integration of scientists and professionals into policy and management, and the practicality of such a development. No committee of inquiry into the Civil Service would have been complete without the familiar argument that the Service should be used as an example for others to copy, in this case to effect the general enhancement of the status of scientists and professionals as a matter of national policy. In advancing this view, the IPCS, refreshingly, made no attempt to disguise the reality that its proposals in relation to the Higher Civil Service were designed to benefit its membership (PRO: BA1/30). The Secretariat, striving to organise the mass of evidence for the Committee, thought that the arguments in favour of greater integration of scientists and professionals tended to rest on two main theses. The first was the needs of the work, meaning that scientists and professionals had special contributions to make to policy-making and management. The second was the needs of the Service, meaning that good scientists and professionals could only be attracted and developed to their full potential if they were given larger opportunities (PRO: BA1/38).

Both arguments were advanced in evidence by James Lighthill, Lucasian Professor of Mathematics at the University of Cambridge and a former Director of the Royal Aircraft Establishment at Farnborough. Lighthill thought that

> at the high levels scientists should be given more responsibility for policy. A senior scientist was very much an administrator. The difference between the Administrative Class and the scientists was not fundamental; both had very high intelligence in common, and he had found that they usually had a great respect for each other. Therefore senior scientists should be more thoroughly merged with the Administrative Class. This did not mean that they should become members of the Administrative Class (at lower levels it would clearly be better to have two hierarchies for purposes of pay, promotion and so forth), but in departments like

the Ministry of Aviation the best man irrespective of whether they belonged to the Administrative or Scientific Class should be chosen for the highest posts . . . It was particularly important that scientists should be given more financial responsibility. At present the situation encouraged the scientist to ask for more money and the administrator to oppose it, both as a matter of course; that was neither necessary nor desirable (PRO: BA1/3).

Sir Solly Zuckerman, the Chief Scientific Adviser to the government, emphasised in his evidence that 'at present scientists were not given enough responsibility for policy making. It was particularly important that scientists were not financially accountable for their work and did not have to appear before the Public Accounts Committee. This tended to breed the cynical attitude that it was someone else's business to worry about the financial and economic implications of their work' (PRO: BA1/4).

Sir Richard Way, Permanent Secretary at the Ministry of Aviation, told the Committee that 'generally speaking engineers took well to management, and were better at it than scientists' (PRO: BA1/3). Sir Arnold Hall, one of Lighthill's predecessors as Director at Farnborough, while not expressing the same view, thought that engineers could play a valuable part in Civil Service administration, while adding: 'Ideally, it needed the engineers with some training in costing and economics . . . but our educational system, unlike the *Ecole Polytechnique* in France, did not in general produce such persons.' That said though, he believed that 'the engineer could learn to take these factors into account if he were given more responsibility for doing so . . . A senior technical adviser should have the accounting responsibility for his advice' (PRO: BA1/2).

Sir Richard Way told the Committee that he was much in favour of getting more scientists on to administrative work. In this context, he was using the word 'administrative' in the rather specialized meaning which was attached to it in the Civil Service.

> A great deal of administration in the Civil Service, in the more usual sense of the term, was carried on otherwise than by "administrators" – for example, establishments like Farnborough were run by scientists. He would himself like to see scientists making a greater contribution towards administration in the Civil Service sense. The difficulty was to persuade good scientists to become interested in administration at a sufficiently early stage in their careers. If they were to go to the top they ought to have experience at Principal level, and very few good scientists wanted to move across at that stage. They preferred doing their scientific work, they were frightened by the political aspect of administrative work and they were not attracted by the thought of spending their time preparing drafts for Ministers and engaging in the exercise of financial control . . .
> The trouble was that most scientists, even the ones at the top who were administering big establishments, did not want to think of themselves as

administrators. The concept of a Scientific Class 'raring' to move over to administration was just not true.

Way was emphatic that 'it was no use looking for potential administrators among scientists who had ceased to be useful in their own field.' He was asked whether the scientists in the Ministry of Aviation had feelings of frustration and grievance because they were segregated from the Administrative Class and had in effect to take orders from people they regarded as amateurs. He replied that 'this in general was not the case in the Ministry of Aviation, although there were admittedly a few scientists, some of them rather vocal, who did express such sentiments' (PRO: BA1/2).

The IPCS recognised that 'it is frequently argued by the Treasury' – and also, in this case, by Sir Richard Way – 'that scientists and engineers have had opportunities to broaden out but they do not really want them. We think that is wrong. We think it is contrary to experience in the Atomic Energy Authority. It is certainly contrary to experience in other countries where they do not have this problem' (PRO: BA1/5).

The oral evidence submitted by the Council of Engineering Institutions was so disparate in content and tone that it took all the skills of the Secretariat to render it in summary. The CEI were fairly represented as being 'in favour of a common structure at the top of the Civil Service. Labels should disappear at this point, and the Permanent Secretary job should go to whoever was best qualified for it. The engineer was capable of becoming a general purpose manager in mid-career, and in large industrial firms many did so. Post graduate training was probably the key; the main aim was that the engineer should not be shut out because he was an engineer.' Of the parallel hierarchy arrangements involving administrators and engineers at the Ministry of Public Building and Works, much drawn to the Fulton Committee's attention, Sir Robert Wynne-Edwards of the CEI observed: 'I think it is complete nonsense. I do not see how an engineer can ever be trained to be the manager if he is always at someone else's apron strings.' The engineer had to have financial responsibility young. Responding to a question from Robert Neild that had the character of a statement in favour of the need to establish a British equivalent of the *Ecole Polytechnique*, Wynne-Edwards thought that such an idea was interesting, but 'it might mean fifty years before it meant anything, and we cannot wait that long.' Ewen M'Ewen said that 'there are snags as well as advantages in the French scheme . . . I have worked in France and have had engineers working for me in France, some of them from the *Polytechnique* . . . a closed shop, Masonic fraternity. They had a marvellous opinion of themselves and certainly scratched each others' backs. Other engineers that I had were not the products of the *Polytechnique* but of the despised university courses in Lille, and they were very good. It has grown up over the past 150 years, and developed this mystique, but not all of it is good' (PRO: BA1/7).

'Scientists and engineers . . . considered a Civil Service career unattractive

because they were not given their part in making policy and taking decisions',
Lord Kings Norton, formerly Harold Cox and at one time a senior member
of the Scientific Civil Service, told the Committee adding that:

> In part this criticism was justified and it showed a defect in the Service,
> but at the same time there were probably few scientists and engineers
> equipped for responsibility of that kind. There was a weakness in our
> scientific education; scientists and engineers were not educated to take
> account of non-scientific factors, in particular of financial and economic
> considerations. Industry too encountered a shortage of such people. In
> this respect, our educational system lacked the sort of training provided
> by the *Ecole Polytechnique* in France.

Asked if he thought that a Staff College should be set up for 'technocrats' in
the Public Service, including local government and nationalised industries,
as well as central government, Lord Kings Norton said that 'it would be very
valuable and suggested that Cranfield might serve as the nucleus for it' (PRO:
BA1/2).

Professor P. M. S. Blackett, while wanting to see more scientists in senior
administrative posts, and welcoming developments in the Ministry of Technology (where he had an advisory role) that had led to this, also observed
that 'in general . . . the department's scientists were still terribly naive in
financial and management matters' and there was a need for them to have
more opportunity for management training (PRO: BA1/7). Lord Franks told
the Committee that it was

> important for the professionals to have conspicuous and open oppor-
> tunities to move over to top administrative jobs. He suspected that not
> many would in practice do so, but the existence of the opportunity would
> be important in itself. The big problem here was that the dice were loaded
> against the professional who had spent his first 15–20 years buried in his
> expertise; he was unlikely to be good at the complex game which brought
> in other civil servants, Ministers, Parliament, and the public. It would
> be necessary to give him early experience as well as training in the
> administrative role (PRO: BA1/3).

The former minister, Aubrey Jones also said in his evidence that 'specialists
in the Civil Service, including scientists, should be eligible for promotion to
the most senior administrative posts' while adding that 'at present very few
of them had the qualities required; for instance, as Minister he had wanted
to have a scientist as Permanent Secretary of the Ministry of Supply but had
not been able to find a suitable man. This deficiency, which was encountered
in business too, sprang from a weakness in the educational system, that is,
from specialization too early at school. It should be made good by giving
scientists in the Civil Service training in and experience of management' (PRO:
BA1/3).

The FDA was opposed to the Treasury's proposals for what the Association
described as 'a Higher Management Class embracing all administrators and

specialists above a given rank (say the equivalent of Assistant Secretary).' This was because they believed that the creation of such a Class 'would obscure what we see as the essential difference between the specialist and the administrative contribution, while the flexibility it would provide could be achieved in other ways.' The FDA argued that 'the specialist who becomes fully able to perform the administrative role thereby ceases to be a specialist, and will in turn need other specialists to provide the element of expert knowledge that is essential to the dialogue. We see merit also in the preservation of separate grade structures running up to the highest levels both for the Management Group and for the specialist classes. This will offer the incentive of clearer promotion prospects and enhance the professional standing of those concerned' (PRO: BA1/21).

When it came to the presentation of oral evidence, the FDA's representatives stuck to their guns without discomfort in the face of hostile questioning from Robert Sheldon, Norman Hunt and Robert Neild in particular. R. B. M. King, replying to a lengthy question from Neild, said that the FDA was opposed to a unified Higher Civil Service for good reasons, one of which was 'because we think it would have an adverse effect on Administrative recruitment – if the potential recruit can see a career up to a middle level but beyond that only an amorphous mass of posts undefined and undesignated.' To the question 'Well it works in industry, why should it not work in the Civil Service?' which Norman Hunt was seen as asking by implication, J. A. Battersby told the Committee that the FDA's answer would be that 'industry does not have an ossified class structure with published salaries and grades and so on, and the Civil Service does, and the chap who is thinking of coming into the Civil Service wants to have a look at the sort of organization he is coming into.'

> In reply to a specific question from Hunt, Battersby said that
>
> there are, of course, very real problems of specialist/administrator relationships and I certainly do not pretend to have an answer to them . . . but I think one has to have regard to their size relative to other problems. There are thirty-three major departments of State that are headed by Permanent Secretaries and I think it is fair to say that the problem of administrator/specialist relationships is acute in six of those. The six will become five when the Ministry of Aviation functions are split between the Ministry of Defence and the Ministry of Technology. In the remaining twenty-eight departments the duties imposed upon Permanent Secretaries are of such a wide ranging nature that the services of an enormous range of specialists are called upon, and I think it is not unreasonable to suppose that in the normal run of things it is fairly unlikely that the corpus of specialist knowledge contained within one of these remaining twenty-eight departments could throw up people of the same calibre as the administrators. I am not saying it would not happen, just that it is less likely.

King drew attention to the fact that, besides the Administrative Class, the FDA also spoke on behalf of two specialist groups, the economists and the statisticians, and the panels representing them had 'independently reached the conclusion that they want to retain their separate identity all the way to the top. They do not want to be merged into a general Higher Management Class.' Taking up a point made by Neild, T. S. Pilling, the FDA's Chairman, said that it was accepted that administrators would have to become 'more specialized' than in the past, 'but they would also retain what one might call a substantial lay element from their working experience. I think it is this lay element that we see as rather strongly required in the work falling to many of the topmost posts.' Battersby told the Committee that 'we do not think in fact that the prospects of our members would suffer if a Higher Management Class were created, because we think on merit they would probably come out much as they do now' (PRO: BA1/5).

The FDA was not lacking in confidence or competence in defending the interest it represented, but it was short of support. Nevil Johnson wanted 'formal recognition that at the highest levels – above Assistant Secretary and its equivalent in other Classes – positions should be so defined and filled that the structure of parallel hierarchies gradually disappears.' He added, though, that

> it is rather too facile to say that posts should be filled by the best man, regardless of his Class and specialism. Nor does one get very far by treating the members of all Classes above a certain level as members of a Higher Management Class. The first need is to define realistically the functions of the directing posts in departments, taking care that at this level we overcome, whenever possible, the division between administrative and technical functions. It will then be a question of deciding which posts are best filled by people with administrative experience and which by the professional expert (PRO: BA1/24)

Sir Solly Zuckerman, while regretting that 'scientists were very seldom included among the policy makers' when they were needed to take 'a synoptic look at wide policy questions with a scientific content' and 'in such departments as the Ministry of Aviation and the Ministry of Technology where the greater part of policy was based on scientific factors,' recognised that 'it would always be necessary to have a vertical structure for those scientists who would be needed purely as scientists' (PRO: BA1/4). Sir Andrew Cohen was opposed to what he called 'a Senior Management Grade comprising both administrators and professionals,' expressing concern about the possible adverse effects such a structure would have on the recruitment of, for instance, economists, the professional group he knew best. Cohen, though, also wanted arrangements whereby 'mobility from the professional side to management posts' would be 'made easy without having to cross Class barriers' (PRO: BA1/22), which was, of course, one of the objectives of the Treasury's proposals for a unified Higher Civil Service.

There was some disagreement among those giving evidence about the point at which the common structure at or near the top of the Home Civil Service should start. Sir Laurence Helsby, on behalf of the Treasury, told the Committee that, at Under Secretary level and above, what that department wanted to see created was

> an open society with no artificial barriers . . . We would like to work towards a classless society – not that Classes have in fact, I think, inhibited movement so much as some people have suspected. The fact that the Administrative Class has been made up as to about 40 per cent by people taken in from other Classes illustrates that point. But the side pieces, you may say, of the Administrative ladder have been painted a different colour, and it looked as though the fact that they had been painted a different colour might inhibit movement. Possibly psychologically it did inhibit movement. At any rate, let us have none of this in the future – let them all be painted the same colour.

As to why the boundary was drawn where it was, another Treasury witness, Louis Petch later explained: 'What we are saying is that at the top we want a common structure because in this field there is a large number of posts which could be filled almost equally effectively by a man who has come up the scientific ladder, or sometimes up the engineering ladder, or a man who has come up the managerial ladder . . . but when you get below the Assistant Secretary maximum, then the number of posts in this category becomes a far smaller proportion.' There was also the point, Petch said, that 'the chap who comes into the Civil Service and who is quite keen to practise his own professional discipline, wants to see a career ahead of him in that discipline, which means that many of them like to see a hierarchy stretching up at least to the Assistant Secretary level in their own discipline. Now, if this thing faded out and became fuzzy, you might not get all the recruits that we have at the moment.' Petch also argued that unifying structures even at the minimum of the Assistant Secretary grade would necessitate that grade being divided into three (PRO: BA1/9).

The IPCS hoped that 'the Committee will not be deflected by transitional problems from a conclusion about the best form of long term organization,' which was one in which 'common entry to the Higher Civil Service' began 'above the level of the present Principal and other broadly equivalent grades.' The IPCS wanted the unified structure to begin there because it was 'above the level of Principal that senior managerial decisions begin to be made; for example, in Whitehall, Assistant Secretaries tend to head separate divisions,' but also because 'to make the Service common to all Classes above Assistant Secretary sets the level at too late a stage in an officer's career. This is particularly true for professional officers - although it should be noted that the painfully slow progress of those who reach the equivalent of Assistant Secretary reflects not the lack of capacity but the structure and career prospects as they now are' (PRO: BA1/30). With similar self-interest, the SCS opposed the establishment of a common structure at the Principal maximum because it would damage the prospects of the Executive Class (PRO: BA1/34), and, ironically, just at the time when there was a real possibility of the formal divide between that Class and the Administrative Class being removed.

4. *The structure of the general classes of the Home Civil Service*

As had been the case with the Higher Civil Service, the Treasury's memorandum of May 1966 on 'The Future Structure of the Civil Service' largely shaped discussion of the structure of the General Classes of the Home Civil Service. 'The proposal here is that a new management structure be created which would comprehend the present Administrative and Executive Classes,' the Treasury wrote, and, while recognising that there would be intermediate posts which would fill 'an essential and specific role, particularly in regional organizations', it envisaged a broad structure of eight grades.

Grades I, II and III would be equivalent to the existing Permanent Secretary, Deputy Secretary, and Under Secretary grades respectively, Grade IV would embrace the existing Assistant Secretary and Principal Executive Officer grades, and Grade V would amalgamate the current Principal and Chief Executive Officer grades. Grade VI corresponded to the existing Senior Executive Officer grade, being 'a senior managerial level with specific use in certain fields of office management and control.' Grade VII, 'the middle level of office management', was equivalent to the current Higher Executive Officer grade. Grade VIII, which was described as 'the basic working grade in the management field', was equivalent to Executive Officer in the existing structure, or, at least, the Treasury so described it.

Entrants to this 'new structure' were to come 'in the main from four sources.' Firstly, the promoted Clerical Officer would come into the basic Grade VIII, normally in the top half of the salary scale. Secondly, what the Treasury called 'the 18 year old A level entrant' was to 'come in on a short scale designed specifically for this type of officer but would proceed on to the main Grade VIII scale after, say, three years. His normal career expectation would be Grade VI – but facilities and opportunities would be there for him to go higher.' Thirdly, there would be 'the graduate entry' which 'would need to be much larger than the existing Assistant Principal entry, building up possibly to several hundred a year . . . Graduates would enter the Grade VIII scale at an appropriate point, and their training and development would be specially watched. The majority could expect promotion to Grade VII after about five years, and their normal career expectation would be Grade V. Some would pass straight from Grade VII to Grade V.' Fourthly, 'within this large graduate entry, a proportion, roughly equivalent in size to the present Assistant Principal entry might be "starred" or otherwise designated on the strength of their academic records and their performance at the selection stage. They would enter one or two increments higher up the scale and would have a career in their first years close to that of the present Assistant Principal.'

The Treasury believed that some arrangements on these lines would be necessary for two reasons. One was that 'it must be made clear to the most able young men and women that the Service wanted them and that they would have a career from the start no less attractive than is offered now.' The other was that

> departments can operate on only a limited scale the arrangements whereby the Assistant Principal is given special training and experience in the early years of his career, and would welcome some initial guidance of this kind in planning the first appointments of their graduate entry. Under the arrangements suggested, however, there would be movement, in both directions, both during and after the probationary period between these two levels of graduates. Those who maintained their performance at, or turned out to be outstanding enough to break into, the higher or "starred" level would normally have a period in a Private Office which could probably best be covered by promotion to Grade VII, and would then be promoted to Grade V (PRO: BA1/13).

In December 1966, the Treasury issued a further memorandum which stated that 'for the future we envisage the present pattern of the general Clerical Officer and the subordinate Clerical Assistant continuing as before. There is no suggestion that the creation of an integrated structure for the posts above them should erect any barrier to the access of the Clerical Officer to those posts. Indeed, the simplest recognitions of this would be to rename the present Clerical Officer grade as Grade IX, and the Clerical Assistant grade as Grade X in our suggested unified class structure' (PRO: BA1/27).

This begged the question of why the Treasury had not emphasised this in the first place instead of doing so in response to criticisms made in the CSCA's written evidence when submitted in August 1966 (PRO: BA1/20). Of the Treasury's proposals for a merged Executive-Administrative Class, L. A. Wines, General Secretary of the CSCA, said in oral evidence that 'the critical comment we made derived from the circumstance that the Treasury stopped at its Grade VIII, which created in our minds an assumption or a fear that the Treasury's thinking was that its Grade VIII would represent the lowest rung on a career ladder and that the work below its proposed Grade VIII would be relegated to some non-career type of general clerical agent.' What the CSCA feared was

> the Treasury seeing things as an "Officers and Other Ranks" conception, with the Grade VIII the Army Lieutenant or the Navy Sub-Lieutenant, and the rest of the Civil Service general work . . . being relegated to the "Other Ranks" without . . . even the leavening in the Forces of an "Other Ranks" class career. We feel very strongly . . . that there is no need for a class division as distinct from a grade division between the Treasury's proposed Grade VIII and the very large volume of work immediately below. And by extension, of course, we believe that the grading system proposed by the Treasury could and should be continued lower down.

That is, . . . although our advocacy does not derive from this, consistent with a fairly recent reorganization in the Diplomatic Service (PRO: BA1/4).

So, in addition to the Treasury's eight-grade structure, the CSCA wanted a Grade IX, members of which would be assigned 'the superior part of the work now falling to the Clerical Officer grade, plus the lesser work now falling to the Executive Officer grade'; and a Grade X which would perform the remainder of the work now attached to the Clerical Officer grade and the better part of the work of the present Clerical Assistant which does not get transferred to machines or computers.' The CSCA, which disapproved of the developing practice of recruiting to the Clerical Officer grade across the age range from sixteen to sixty, thought that 'if recruitment of older people continued, the Grade X level could form a suitable entry level' (PRO: BA1/20). In oral evidence, L. A. Wines emphasised the CSCA's belief in 'orthodox recruitment for good class clerking, that is the good GCE Ordinary Level person,' whose career aspirations were presently handicapped by slow promotion and the widespread resort to 'all age' recruitment and the use of part time and temporary staff which had 'produced this feeling that . . . the Clerical Officer, the superior clerking grade, has lost and is losing status in official eyes as the years go by' (PRO: BA1/4).

There was little sign of respect for either the CSCA or the Clerical Class in the oral evidence which Treasury witnesses presented to the Committee about the structure of the Service. For example, in responding to the staff association's complaint about the slowness of promotion for Clerical Officers, S. P. Osmond observed that 'it is not for the CSCA to look virtuous about this; they have felt very strongly about age limits because of their concern for protecting the average member at the expense of the bright one' (PRO: BA1/5). T. H. Caulcott said of Clerical Officers that 'our present Chief Executive Officers are people who came in before the War largely as Clerical Officers . . . but we are not getting the quality at Clerical Officer level which we were getting in those days' (PRO: BA1/4). Asked by Norman Hunt why this was so, Osmond replied:

> Because the development of education has already hit that level much harder than it has hit the 18 year old entry level. The really outstanding Clerical Officers of the Thirties who were jolly glad to get a decent job at the age of 16 in the Civil Service, people of that quality at least go on to get their A levels now, and quite a lot go on to University. Really bright people, broadly speaking, are not leaving school and going for office jobs at 16. And a tremendous number of the Clerical Class are older people who have come in from elsewhere, or married women coming back to work – almost a cross section of the population. We are still getting a proportion of reasonably bright young 16 year old entrants, but it is a small number for the Class as a whole (PRO: BA1/5).

Another Treasury official, Harry Pitchforth, described the broad mass of

Clerical Officers as having become 'not, by and large, promotable' (PRO: BA1/4). Whether this was so or not, it was still the case that, as Louis Petch informed the Committee, 'sixty per cent of the Executive Class posts at the moment are filled by promoted Clericals.' Pitchforth's view was that 'we have scraped the barrel for promoted COs to do this job, but we do not get the really good COs that we used to get who rose up to be CEO, and Permanent Secretaries in one or two cases. They just do not come in now' (PRO: BA1/5).

The importance of the role of the Executive Class was stressed not just, of course, by the SCS in its evidence, but more disinterestedly by Professor W. J. M. Mackenzie who observed that 'almost all public attention goes to problems of the Administrative, Scientific, Technological, and Professional Classes, and this is natural because these are very general problems about government, society, and the economy. My feeling now is that they cannot simply be treated as Civil Service problems; they are inclusive problems and not soluble by tinkering with Civil Service organization.' He told the Committee that 'unlike most of my academic colleagues, I feel that the central problem which is truly a Civil Service problem is that of maintaining the efficiency, honesty, prestige and morale of the great executive departments such as Inland Revenue, Customs and Excise, Pensions and National Insurance. Without such services a modern State cannot run at all' (PRO: BA1/29).

> Mackenzie said that
>> the country was fortunate in inheriting from Victorian times its good quality middle level Civil Service. For the foreseeable future there would be a need for that kind of civil servant for, for instance, taxation and contract work. He was not sure what was happening to the traditional grammar school entry which had manned those levels of the Service . . . Until recently, at least, the Civil Service had claimed, to his surprise, that the traditional grammar school entry was being maintained. His impression was that even if the numbers were holding up, the quality was going off, and recently the Civil Service itself had expressed concern about that. He agreed with there was therefore a need to recruit more run of the mill graduates. He hoped that it would be possible to recruit sufficient who would be content with the old fashioned career pattern (PRO: BA1/6).

The graduates that the Executive Officer currently attracted were 'pretty awful' according to the Treasury Under Secretary, Harry Pitchforth, who told the Committee that in the new structure 'what we would go for is something like the Cadet Officer Ministry of Labour type of scheme. You would bring a man in at the appropriate point of the scale, but after he has looked around on the Executive grade you would, by agreement with the associations, as is done in the Ministry of Labour, put him on higher grade work after a couple of years, he would get on to Higher Executive Officer type of work after a year or two' (PRO: BA1/5).

C. H. Sisson, as Principal Establishment Officer at the Ministry of Labour, submitted detailed material to the Committee about recruitment to the Cadet scheme there (PRO: BA1/31) as well as presenting oral evidence during which it was stated that the scheme had been revised in 1966 to make it no longer part of the Special Departmental Classes competition as in the past but as specific management recruitment to the Ministry of Labour in which there followed swift advancement instead of – as Sir James Dunnett put it in a question – 'five years soldiering away as an Executive Officer.' Sisson observed:

> We came to the conclusion . . . that one of the great weaknesses of our scheme in the past, and the reason for a good deal of the wastage, was that we could not give people sufficiently interesting work soon enough, and we resolved that we would alter this. The scheme we now have works like this: people come in, for six months they learn the down to earth work of an Employment Exchange, they do work equivalent to a Clerical Officer, then for a year they are again employed in an Employment Exchange, as our equivalent of an Executive Officer, on supervisory work. At the end of that period they are due to go on to what is in effect Higher Executive Officer work. They are not at this time promoted to HEO, but they do work which is in every way appropriate to that grade. After three years the plan is that they shall in fact be promoted, if they are fully competent, and they will be promoted by special promotion arrangements, which means they will not be in open competition with all the rest, but they will be considered as a group, and if they are up to standard they will go on to the HEO scale.

Sisson and his former Permanent Secretary, Sir James Dunnett, agreed that a weakness of the Treasury's structural proposals was calling the graduate entrants Executive Officer and giving many of them EO work instead of, as in the revised Ministry of Labour scheme, singling the graduate intake out for special attention (PRO: BA1/7).

The Treasury's structural proposals in general did not impress Norman Hunt who asked that department's representative: 'Is your scheme not open to the criticism that it is really no change, because you are just taking in the present Administrative Class and calling them stars and maintaining the exact position among the Administrative and Executive Classes because you are taking a lot of other graduates in who are not going to get privileged treatment?' S. P. Osmond replied that: 'It is not the same. I think this will fall into place when we produce our proposals for training, because this will emphasize that instead of going in at the bottom of a ladder which puts a great deal of emphasis on seniority we are looking at all these people individually and putting the best ones on training courses. So it will not be a matter of being the same as it is today' (PRO: BA1/4). This reply evaded the issue of starring which, understandably, Hunt would not leave alone; and Osmond, under later questioning, said that the Treasury would not 'start off without starring and introduce it if necessary' – as Hunt suggested – 'because you would be taking the plunge of almost deliberately not offering any incentive to the present Assistant Principal type and you would be putting your risk that way.' Osmond's fellow Treasury witness, Harry Pitchforth, said of the Assistant Principal intake was that what we are worried about was that without starring 'these chaps will walk out; they do not want to come into a big department where they might finish up in the Labour Exchange at Wigan, they want to advise Ministers.' Private Office experience was 'tremendously valuable', Louis Petch told the Committee, 'You really see the wheels go round in a Private Office'; and the number of Private Office places being limited was used as a means of trying to see off questions from Robert Sheldon in particular about preferment among the graduate intake being solely on the basis of performance of work (PRO: BA1/5).

Part of the advantage of merging the Administrative and Executive Classes as proposed by the Treasury was purely presentational, S. P. Osmond told the Committee:

> A certain amount has been said about the separation of the Administrative and Executive Class representing even to some extent outmoded social distinctions . . . and . . . you get rid of that source of criticism, but, more substantially, this would increase flexibility in the Service. As you know . . . there is in fact already a great deal of movement from the Executive to the Administrative Class . . . Nonetheless, it is inevitably, as long as we have got separate Classes, a fairly formal and almost solemn thing to move someone from one Class to the other, and great consideration is given to whether people are really up to being moved, and they go in front of the Civil Service Commission very often, or at any rate in front of a very strong departmental board. It is a very big step in a man's career and once he has taken it he cannot go back without wearing something of the badge of failure. Therefore there is a bit of inhibition against taking a chance on a man . . . If you merge the Classes you do away with these difficulties and give yourself a good deal more flexibility in moving people around (PRO: BA1/4).

The issue of starring certain graduates kept being returned to in the evidence, and when Lord Simey raised it once more, Harry Pitchforth, for the Treasury, said that

> it is a fact . . . that we do feel, unless we can offer to 40 or 50 people from university a kind of semi-assurance that if they come in they have a special run in this way and have a career prospect in the first few years, in fact we shall not get them. They will not come in because other people will offer them this kind of assurance – the Diplomatic Service and other people – and we shall lose them. That is a gap which we cannot afford. I sense in some of the comments which people make that there is a sort of feeling that the word "starring" is wrong. We are not particularly wedded to this word; it is something we cribbed from the Navy who use

it for their engineers, and indeed in the initial stages of writing this paper we did call them Cadets A and Cadets B (PRO: BA1/5).

Pitchforth had elsewhere stated that 'we started off on the basis of having two Cadet entries, Cadet A, which would be the Assistant Principal, and Cadet B, which would be a separate list' (PRO: BA1/4). Pitchforth interpreted the Treasury's proposals as meaning that all the graduate entrants would receive preferential treatment, saying that 'in fact you are starring, or sub-starring, you are asterisking 300 as against the rest,' which meant that 'you have still got a separate Executive Class' meaning the 18 year old entry (PRO: BA1/5).

The Treasury's proposals formally to merge the Executive and the Administrative Classes attracted widespread support from, among others, bodies as diverse as the Labour Party (PRO: BA1/27), the Liberal Party (PRO: BA1/25), the British Institute of Management (PRO: BA1/26), the Institute of Personnel Management (PRO: BA1/29), the Gas Council (PRO: BA1/33) and the County Councils Association (PRO: BA1/29). Academics such as Peter Self (PRO: BA1/25) in principle supported the merger too. Naturally, the SCS did the same while, understandably, wanting the increase in the graduate intake to be phased in slowly to protect the career expectations of the existing Executive Class (PRO: BA1/20). Under the current structure, 'there is no attraction at all for a graduate to come into the Executive Class', Leslie Williams told the Committee, observing that eventually an entry of 'two or three hundred mainstream graduates . . . would be a very lively addition to the Civil Service' (PRO: BA1/5).

There were some divisions of opinion among serving and former higher Civil Servants when giving evidence about the desirability of a merger between the Executive and Administrative Classes. Sir William Armstrong told the Committee that 'he agreed with the Treasury paper on structure but thought that a massive sorting out of jobs would be needed to articulate the future structure' (PRO: BA1/3). Lord Normanbrook said that the Treasury's proposals had the merit of addressing 'the change in the educational system', but 'it was necessary to be careful not to dilute the Class structure to the extent of repelling the first rate graduates' (PRO: BA1/3). Sir Edward Playfair opposed the merger of the Executive and Administrative Classes and, while 'avoiding the emotive names and associations of the present Classes' and not necessarily dividing the work up as at present, he wanted a structure 'designed to give separate treatment to the fliers instead of including them formally (with more or less special terms) in a single large management class with something between 70,000 and 80,000 members.' Playfair wrote that 'the main reason for keeping the fast running stream separate is to keep its members clear of the rules and pressures governing promotion in a large and highly organized class of civil servants' in which 'seniority will always play a fairly large party' with 'a tendency towards mediocrity, viscosity and Buggins' Turn. ' What were best were arrangements which enabled the exercise of 'that degree of arbitrary judgment which is needed if the best men are to get quickly to the top,' he observed, adding that 'to amalgamate the two types, with separate rules for fliers within the main class is likely to increase bureaucratic governance of the Civil Service and to tie it down by agreements with the trade unions' (PRO: BA1/27).

The Chairman of the Board of Inland Revenue, Sir Alexander Johnston, told the Committee that he disagreed on several counts with the proposals in the Treasury paper on the future structure of the Service. He said that

> he would be unhappy to see the abolition of the Administrative Class, although, since the word class was an emotive one, there should perhaps be a change of name. Whatever happened to the Civil Service there would continue to be a number of people who would be concerned with policy formation, advising Ministers and so forth, in other words, an Administrative stream. Something like the Assistant Principal grade would continue to be necessary as a training grade for that stream. Although the Treasury proposals envisaged a separate 'starred' graduate stream, there might well be pressures from staff associations in due course to treat all graduate entrants the same, which would be difficult to resist. The abolition of a separate and in its way privileged Administrative stream would be disastrous for recruitment.

Johnston thought that 'the overall number of graduate entrants envisaged in the Treasury proposals was too large.' For, 'if they were to be recruited on the scale proposed, a great many of them would have no prospect of ever doing anything but Executive Class type work; there was perhaps an unwitting dishonesty in the Treasury proposals in that they might give the impression that this would not be so.' Further, 'a large graduate entry would in effect close the door of promotion to school leaver entrants. This would be a bad thing . . . For all the expected expansion of higher education there would still be able men who wanted to start work at 18' (PRO: BA1/3).

The Treasury proposals on the structure of the General Classes overlaid the discussion, focusing attention on issues of recruitment and, disproportionately, on the graduate intake; and deflected attention away from the issues of career specialisation in the Classes concerned, and what some saw as the need for greater professionalisation. Sir Arnold Hall (PRO: BA1/3), Professor Peter Self (PRO: BA1/7), Nevil Johnson (PRO: BA1/24), the Royal Institute of Public Administration (PRO: BA1/28), the Labour Party (PRO: BA1/27), and the former Treasury Principal, Peter Jay (PRO: BA1/32) were among those who argued that administrators should specialise more; and Johnson and Jay were also present on the list of those submitting evidence, which included such diverse bodies as the British National Export Council (PRO: BA1/26), the Sheffield Regional Hospital Board (PRO: BA1/27), and British Railways (PRO: BA1/29), that were critical of the current level of mobility between jobs in the Administrative Class. Sir Laurence Helsby (PRO: BA1/3), Sir William Armstrong (PRO: BA1/3), F. A. Bishop (PRO: BA1/2), and, with reservations, W. S. Ryrie (PRO: BA1/31) were among the serving and former officials who conceded the case for greater specialisation; and Sir Douglas Allen (PRO: BA1/9), Sir Charles Cunningham (PRO: BA1/3), Sir Maurice Dean (PRO: BA1/2) and Sir Richard Way (PRO: BA1/2) all endorsed a mobile career pattern. If a note of individuality was needed to liven up discussion of a well rehearsed subject, if one that was not being fully addressed, as has been seen, Sir Alexander Johnston was the most likely to supply it. 'There were perhaps too many grades in the Administrative Class', Sir Alexander observed, 'Departments often seemed to work best in the holiday season when some layers in the hierarchy were removed. On the whole, the superfluous grade was perhaps most frequently that of Under Secretary; the grade was needed for career purposes but not always for organizational purposes' (PRO: BA1/3).

5. *The structure of the specialist classes of the Home Civil Service*

'It is difficult to see any consistent approach or set of principles in the present organization of Classes', the IPCS observed in that part of its written evidence submitted to the Fulton Committee which related to the structure of the Home Civil Service:

> General Treasury Classes are responsible for many specialist functions, but in some departments – notably the Inland Revenue, Ministry of Labour, and Customs and Excise – many staff are organized in Departmental Classes although their work is no more specialised than that undertaken by the General Treasury Classes. Some of the so-called 'specialist' Classes – for example, the Scientific Classes, the Works Group, the Technical and Drawing Office Classes – normally embrace a wide range of disciplines; yet there are also different Classes which cover the same discipline. For example, a separate Treasury Class was recently formed for economists, although the Research Officer Class includes a considerable number of posts for which the same basic qualifications are required. Again, the basic qualifications required for Valuation Officers in the Inland Revenue (a Works Group related Class) are similar to those required for Land Officers employed in the Defence Department who are organized in the Works Group (PRO: BA1/30).

As the structure of the Home Civil Service had to embrace a wide variety of groups such as, for instance, Medical and Veterinary Officer Classes, it was only to be expected that it would be complex; and, as that structure had a long history, that it had irregularities in its arrangements was unsurprising. That the Service made do with a small Professional Accountant Class could be explained, if not necessarily justified, by reference to its historical growth. The developed hierarchy that traditionally the lawyers had been accorded with the Civil Service (Fry, 1969a, pp. 221–4, 248f, 448) may well have been one reason why the evidence that the Civil Service Legal Society submitted to the Fulton Committee (PRO: BA1/6, 25) lacked the critical edge detectable in that presented by the Society of Technical Civil Servants representing the Drawing Office Classes (PRO: BA1/6, 24), and by the IPCS. As in its evidence to the Tomlin Royal Commission, the latter, understandably enough, wanted a rationalisation of the structure of the Service for the benefit of the specialist groups that it represented. At the higher end of the Service, as always, the IPCS was seeking at the very least comparability of status and prospects for specialists in relation to the Administrative Class; and the Statistician Class, formed in 1946, and the Economist Class, established in 1965, had a formal structural relationship with that Class (Fry, 1969a, pp. 230–6). Farther down the structure, naturally, the IPCS sought to maximise career opportunities for its members.

'The nucleus of a new Administration Group' could be discerned by the IPCS in the proposals of the Treasury, the SCS, and the CSCA for the Clerical, Executive and Administrative grades up to the level of the Administrative Principal, a view which in this instance chose to ignore that the lowest grade of the unified Higher Civil Service that the Treasury envisaged was than of Under Secretary. With proposals leading to an Administration Group as a cited example, the IPCS recommended to the Fulton Committee that a Technology Group and a Science Group should be created. The former was to embrace the Works Group of Professional Classes up to Senior Grade, the Technical Works Engineering and Allied Classes, and the Architectural and Engineering Draughtsman Classes. The latter was to be formed from the Scientific Officer, Experimental Officer and the Scientific Assistant Classes (PRO: BA1/30). In later evidence, the IPCS proposed that the Research Officer, Economist and Statistician Classes and social scientists elsewhere in the Service should be included in a Social Scientist Group (PRO: BA1/43).

The Treasury opposed the merger of the Economist and Statistician Classes either with each other or within a General Service group, chiefly on grounds of recruitment, and argued in favour of keeping the Research Officer Class as it was, mainly on the grounds that the disciplines involved differed and the nature of the work was non-hierarchial, and the Treasury advanced these arguments independently (PRO: BA1/32) and then specifically in response to the IPCS's proposals (PRO: BA1/47). The FDA, with membership in the Economist and Statistician Classes, opposed the IPCS's plans for a Social Scientist Group because they confused 'the functions which may be assigned to a group of people with the disciplines which members of such a group deploy, and because, in the context of recruitment difficulties, there was no advantage in departing from outside practice which was to treat the disciplines separately' (PRO: BA1/46). Sir Harry Campion, Director of the Central Statistical Office, said that the recruitment difficulties of the Statistician Class were easing but it tended not to attract outstanding talent (PRO: BA1/2).

His successor as Director, Claus Moser, was unimpressed with 'the rump' of staff he had inherited at the CSO. Overall, as regards the Statistician Class there was 'a big shortage of staff' and Professor Moser said that the real problem was the image of the Service. Young statisticians did not particularly want to get close to economic policy; this desire came later. They were technocrats, and wanted to do really expert statistical work with the newest methods and computing aids. The Civil Service image was of inexpert and unexciting work, and it was partly deserved. People were often used on work for which they were over-qualified. Too many Executives were promoted into statistical work; what was wanted was more first class young graduates. Another problem was that the senior posts in the C.S.O. were held by people who had been there too long and were not exciting to the young (PRO: BA1/7).

The evidence about the Economist Class was also concerned with recruitment difficulties and with the related question of whether all or only some professional economists employed in government departments should be career civil servants. P. D. Henderson thought that the Civil Service could provide a lifetime's career for an economist, provided there were generous arrangements for sabbatical leave (PRO: BA1/2). The Permanent Secretary at the DEA, Sir Douglas Allen, envisaged a structure within which 'a fair proportion' of the professional economists would spend 'a great deal' of their working lives in the Civil Service 'with only occasional expeditions outside for rest and professional refreshment'; and 'there should also be another category for those who came into the Service for shorter periods'. Allen observed that 'if all professional economists came in and out for short periods, it would be impossible to integrate them adequately with the work of the department – this was where the employment of economists in the Service had gone wrong after the War' (PRO: BA1/9). The Head of the Government Economic Service, A. K. Cairncross, thought that the existing pattern whereby economists tended to move in and out of the Civil Service was broadly the right one (PRO: BA1/13), while recognising the need 'to have some people who would always think of themselves as primarily members of the Government Economic Service even though they spent some of their careers outside.' Cairncross added that 'the people who wanted to come in on an established basis were usually the less good ones' (PRO: BA1/2).

When the opportunity came for the Fulton Committee to examine the IPCS leadership about the proposals for a Science Group, the Committee proved to be at its least impressive. Largely irrelevant matters such as the General Secretary's opinion that pay arrangements for scientists outside the Civil Service were 'a jungle' and should be changed were given attention (PRO: BA1/8). The IPCS had argued that the Scientific Officer Class and the Experimental Officer Class were both 'graduate Classes' and that there was 'a strong case for combining the two' (PRO: BA1/30). The Committee could have asked the IPCS what the strength of the 'case' actually amounted to, and it might also have observed that there were only some graduates in the Experimental Officer Class.

In its written evidence, the Treasury rehearsed various arguments against the creation of a Science Group (PRO: BA1/32). 'The three separate Classes fit the structure and the way we are organizing the work quite well', Louis Petch told the Committee; adding that: 'This would be the general view of government departments and of senior people in the scientific field. I know that the IPCS takes the opposite point of view, but they have naturally a strong prejudice in furthering the interests of the big battalions, the Experimental Officers and Scientific Assistants, not the Scientific Officers.' Petch said that 'there is in the management field, where we have gone for a merger, a steady transition. Right through the hierarchy you get more experience and wisdom and you progress.' With the Scientific Civil Service, 'there is this hurdle of the professional qualification. At that point you are dealing with a slightly different kind of animal. The first and second class degree scientist is a man of a different calibre from the Experimental Officer. He is capable of working on the frontiers of science. That is the point. There is a much more definite division than there could be in the management field.' S. P. Osmond, taking the same line, also added that the 'sheer cost' of amalgamating the Scientific Officer and Experimental Officer Classes would be 'considerably greater' than those resulting from merging the Executive and Administrative Classes. Petch conceded that the Treasury has not explored the division between the Scientific Assistant Class and the Experimental Officer Class in the same depth as it had the other division between the latter and the Scientific Officer Class (PRO: BA1/8).

There was some support for a merger between the Scientific Assistant Class and the Experimental Officer Class among the five senior members of the Scientific Civil Service who appeared before the Committee in a personal capacity. They were divided in their views about any merger between the Scientific Officer Class and the Experimental Officer Class. Three of them, E. C. Cornford, M. B. Morgan, and H. Davies were against the idea and I. Maddock and H. R. Barnell were in favour (PRO: BA1/8). The UK Atomic Energy Authority, which had inherited the Scientific Civil Service structure, found the divisions to be 'artificial' and needing to be changed (PRO: BA1/27).

'I think the IPCS are trying to ignore the existence of the professional associations,' Louis Petch observed as a Treasury witness in oral evidence about that staff association's proposals for the creation of Technology Group to replace the Works Group of Professional Classes and other related Classes. 'There is a structure of associations which gives corporate membership to certain people, and they have an entitlement to a kind of work. We are conforming with the national structure.' Dame Elsie Abbot added that 'after the Second World War all these professional people were looked at in the same way' as the Treasury Classes had been after the First World War, 'and put on the map. It was a great tidying up operation.' Even when 'Sir Laurence Helsby and the Treasury were creating the Works Group . . . other departments resisted coming into it, because they wanted different recruitment etc. The Works Group was a great simplification of hundreds of different rates of pay, and then these others got tagged on afterward.' The Works Group, Petch said, was an 'historical accident.' The very term 'Works Group' was 'very dreary in the extreme', Petch believed; 'We ought to call this something like the "Professional" Group. There will be professions outside it – lawyers, doctors, scientists – but the titles of the grades would then be Architect (1), (2), (3), Engineer (1), (2), (3).' When Sir William Cook said that the Works Group was 'a conglomeration of different professions' and that the advantages of having such a structure were 'illusory,' Petch replied that it did mean 'one pay negotiation instead of half a dozen,' and the Ministry of Public Building and Works believed that with engineers, surveyors and architects working in teams, paying them the same grade for grade encouraged harmony. S. P. Osmond gave one reason for retaining a structure which distinguished between the professionally qualified and the rest, and one 'which I would not dare to say publicly' and this was that 'internal staff associations' would be 'rather hard to resist . . . unless you have a distinction to hold on to' (PRO: BA1/8). This had to be a reference to the IPCS, since the Society of Technical Civil Servants had argued for an improved career hierarchy for its members and against merger proposals (PRO: BA1/6, BA1/24).

When the Committee saw five senior architects and planners from the Civil Service, L. J. F. Stone, the Superintending Quantity Surveyor at the Ministry of Public Building and Works, represented most of them when he said that 'we would want a technical structure separate entirely from the professional structure', for without it there would be over-promotion of the unqualified (PRO: BA1/9). When the Committee saw five senior engineers from the Civil Service there was some interest in merging all engineers with the Scientific Officer Class; but none in removing the distinction between the professionals and the rest, because the Civil Service could not insulate itself from outside practice as this had implications for the recruitment of the ablest engineers (PRO: BA1/9). Sir Robert Wynne-Edwards encapsulated the views of the Council of Engineering Institutions when he observed that the distinction between professional engineers and technicians had to be maintained: 'one is much more qualified than the other. You cannot mix them in a bag and pull out anyone, or you will not get the top people' (PRO: BA1/7).

The Home Civil Service, though, was not getting 'the top people' anyway when it came to the recruitment not just of engineers, but of architects, accountants, lawyers, and, according to Sir Solly Zuckerman, scientists too. Zuckerman observed that

> the quality of the Scientific Civil Service was not satisfactory. It was often said that the run of the mill Principal Scientific Officer was played out; in his opinion too many of them had never been played in; they were hacks. At present one found very few able and promising young scientists, men who had just completed a Doctorate or similar qualification, who were sufficiently interested in the political and social matters appertaining to science to want to do some work in the Government

Service. Instead, their next objective was to become an FRS and after that to carry on trying to go higher and higher in the same direction . . . It was necessary to consider how to attract able young scientists into Government Service and also how to inspire scientists already in the Service. If there were in the Government Service more men with prestige in the outside world, that would attract able young men to join. Giving scientists budgetary responsibilities and a voice in policy making would make the Government Service able to offer scientists something which scientific work outside could not offer (PRO: BA1/4).

The Principal Establishments Officer at the Ministry of Public Building and Works, L. T. Foster, said that 'it was extremely difficult to get first class recruits at the salaries the MPBW were able to pay,' and also observed that 'when the professional head of the department wanted a man with bright ideas, he usually looked outside' (PRO: BA1/7).

The Barlow Report on the Legal Departments of the Civil Service of 1944 was circulated to the Fulton Committee and that it was unpublished was unsurprising given the view expressed that 'the deficiency of capable men in the Legal Civil Service is at present so great as to create a very serious situation' and urged that this must be remedied (PRO: BA1/18) It was unclear from the evidence whether matters had improved subsequently, and the Treasury Solicitor, Sir Harvey Druitt, told the Fulton Committee that 'the greatest problem of the Legal Class was recruitment, especially in the higher quality people for advisory work' (PRO: BA1/3). The former President of the Institute of Chartered Accountants, Sir Henry Benson, said in his evidence that 'the Civil Service needed to improve its recruitment of professional accountants both in numbers and in quality' (PRO: BA1/7). When one adds in too the remarks recorded earlier about economists and statisticians, the picture of the specialist groups in the Home Civil Service that emerged from the evidence submitted to the Fulton Committee was a less flattering one that that commonly found in the literature.

The Fulton Committee's Deliberations

The Fulton Committee seemed to come close at times to being overwhelmed by the scale of the evidence submitted to it on the structure of the Home Civil Service. This is not surprising, given that, for instance, and in addition to other evidence, no less than a total of thirteen Civil Service staff associations presented oral evidence before Committee members at that body's fourth, fifth, and sixth meetings of 1967 (PRO: BA1/6, BA1/7). The exchanges between the Customs and Excise Launch Service Association and Sir Norman Kipping's sub-committee on 31 January 1967 were among the most unrewarding any official committee of inquiry has experienced (PRO: BA1/6). The Committee proved to be much in need of the overview which the Secretariat's digest of evidence (PRO: BA1/38) and Sir James Dunnett's memoranda provided, which is not to say that in the latter case the advice presented was heeded.

'The Committee agreed that the Civil Service should be a career Service in the sense that the majority would enter with the expectation but not the guarantee of a lifetime's employment' according to the record of the Fulton Committee's twenty-fifth meeting of 1967 (PRO: BA1/9); and a similar phrase was to be found in the Fulton Report, prefaced by a recommendation favouring 'a much greater flexibility of movement between the Civil Service and other employments,' and followed by another stating that 'the great majority of those who come to occupy top jobs will in practice be career civil servants' (Cmnd. 3638, 1968, para.134).

The supporting arguments used in the Fulton Report were similar too, even though at the Committee's thirtieth meeting of 1967 'some members wondered whether there was any reason why a career in the Service should be regarded as essentially different from a career elsewhere' (PRO: BA1/10). In fact, two such reasons has been advanced in discussion at the Committee's twenty-fifth meeting of the year. The first had been that 'it was important that the civil servant should not come to regard every outside body with which he did business as a prospective employer.' The second was that 'the civil servant should not come to feel that he could only keep his job by pleasing his Minister or his official superiors' (PRO: BA1/9). Both these arguments found a place in the Fulton Report (Cmnd. 3638, 1968, para.134).

Given its preference for a career Civil Service subject to more mobility into and out of its ranks than in the past, the Committee also had to decide what its position was to be about established civil servant status and pension provisions. In a subsequently circulated letter, Sir John Wall had written to Richard Wilding on 27 February 1967 saying that he felt quite sure that 'a contributory pension is right' and that provision should be extended to temporary civil servants (PRO: BA1/32). A year later, the Committee was informed by that department that 'the Treasury has long been unhappy about the link between establishment and pensionability.' Though it was a matter to be dealt with through the National Whitley Council machinery, the Treasury took the opportunity to emphasise that 'if all service after an initial qualifying period were to be made pensionable, this would add considerably to the cost of Civil Service superannuation', and the Treasury's view was that 'the distinction . . . between established and unestablished staff should be retained' (PRO: BA1/49). At its thirtieth meeting of 1967, though, the Committee had already made up its mind that 'the concept of establishment served no useful purpose.' The Committee had also agreed that 'there should be no impediments to a man's leaving' the Service 'voluntarily' with the corollary that it should be made easier for 'management to get rid of a man known to be inefficient.' The Committee agreed too that 'there should be regulated late entry' into the Service 'up to the level of Assistant Secretary,' and that the pension arrangements of the Service should be brought into line with outside practice. This meant that 'pensions should be contributory'; but, above all, members 'disliked the use of pensions as an impediment to mobility' and their view was that 'pension rights should be freely transferable' (PRO: BA1/10). Similar sentiments and related recommendations found their place in the Fulton Report (Cmnd. 3638, 1968, paras 123–44, Appendices G and H).

Given its wish to retain a career Civil Service, the Fulton Committee had also to decide whether the structure of that Service should be organised on a unified or departmentalised basis or as some combination of the two. In its deliberations, the Committee found difficulty in divorcing the issue of separate departmental organisation in principle from the facts of the existing Departmental Classes. At its meeting on 18 May 1967 the Committee instructed the Secretariat to prepare and circulate a memorandum on the subject (PRO: BA1/8) which was done (PRO: BA1/38). On 1 August 1967 the Committee instructed the Secretary to consider 'how far it was possible to arrive at an estimate of the residual number of Departmental Classes on the assumption that only the larger and more specialized should remain' (PRO: BA1/10) and a second memorandum was produced with four attached folders (PRO: BA1/45). On 14 November 1967 the Committee considered all this material and thought that 'there might be four fundamental criteria by which to test the case for preserving an existing Departmental Class as a separate branch of the Service: specialization as measured by the practicability of inter-changing staff, separate recruitment, size, *esprit de corps*.' The Secretariat were instructed to carry out an exercise which applied these criteria to particular Departmental Classes listed in the folders (PRO: BA1/10). None of the Departmental Classes in the Home Office and the Army Department of the Ministry of Defence which were examined met these criteria.

Michael Simons concluded that the solution to the problem of assimilating Departmental Classes depended to some extent on the model adopted for the rest of the Service.

> If we went all the way and recommended a single grading structure with common pay scales, logic surely demands that Departmental Classes generally should be included. This would be possible, though there would obviously be complicated negotiations to determine all their places in the grid. It might be appropriate on purely managerial grounds to leave out a few large and distinct services like the Prison and Coastguard Services . . . but in general if it is right to merge all the widely varying trades and disciplines of the General Service Classes into a unified grading system, it is hard to see any convincing reasons for excluding the departmentals. If, on the other hand, the general model adopted is one in which there remains occupational groups with their own pay and perhaps grading structures (below the Senior Policy and Management Group, however defined), some of the groups must probably remain departmental.

Then, Simons wrote, the problem arose as to 'which of the present Classes should be recognized as being in this position, and which should not', and, given that 'we can find no automatic formula', it followed that 'the approach must be pragmatic', which would mean, for instance, that 'some large and/or highly specialized groups should remain distinct', notably the Tax Inspectorate (PRO: BA1/48).

'The problems of structure would in some ways be much simpler if each department employed its own staff independently, and constructed its own grading system to fit the precise needs of its work and staff,' the Fulton Committee observed in its Report; 'But the Civil Service cannot be run in this way . . . the Service must be a flexible, integrated whole; it must continue to be a unified Service' with 'a structure that is common throughout' (Cmnd. 3638, 1968, para.196).

Having rejected one form of radicalism, the Fulton Committee proceeded to take up another when it recommended 'the creation of a classless, uniformly graded structure' for the Home Civil Service 'of the type that is now being adopted in many large business firms and similar to the system used by the Civil Service in the United States'; and 'on the basis of the advice we have received,' the Committee thought that 'some twenty grades could contain all the jobs from top to bottom in the non-industrial part of the Service.' Each grade was to carry 'a range of pay' which ought to be 'relatively broad', and 'there should be overlapping of salaries between grades.' By means of 'careful job evaluation' the Committee envisaged that 'all the jobs now performed by the many different Classes should be fitted into the appropriate grade.' What the Committee saw itself as proposing was

> essentially a pay structure; it is not designed to determine the actual organization of work. The precise organization of each block of work, and the number of working levels in it, should be determined solely by what is required for the most efficient achievement of its objectives. Thus, in any division, job evaluation would show that only a selection of the twenty or so grades should be used – the smallest number needed. There should be no set pattern. Within this overall structure, there will, of course, continue to be a great variety of groups of staff (ibid., paras 218–22).

'Some members argued that the Service should adopt a single unified structure' at the Fulton Committee's meeting on 2 May 1967, though the minutes did not record which members took this line. There was opposition on the grounds that 'a unified structure was difficult to reconcile with a clear and unmistakable call for greater professionalism' which, not least for reasons of recruitment, necessitated the retention of occupational groups, certainly below the level of the Higher Civil Service, and reserved positions for the general service group which would otherwise be too exposed in a structure in which sideways movement would be in one direction only. A note in the minutes suggested that 'in substance there was not much between the two points of view' (PRO: BA1/8) but, at the following meeting a week later, Robert Sheldon reserved his position on the conclusion drawn (PRO: BA1/8).

In response to reflections on structure from the Chairman (PRO: BA1/37) and other material from the Secretary (PRO: BA1/37), at the Committee's meeting on 20 June 1967, Sheldon emerged as a proponent of a unified grading structure on the Committee, opposing the retention of occupational groups in all but the most exceptional cases, such as doctors and lawyers, even below the Higher Civil Service (PRO: BA1/9). At the meeting at the Isle of Thorns on 22 and 23 July 1967, the Committee agreed 'to adopt a common grading structure (below the higher management structure), within which the various categories of staff would be paid, recruited, trained and managed separately, as a provisional working hypothesis, and to examine it further in the light of the report of the Management Consultancy team and other evidence' (PRO: BA1/10). In response to the relevant draft chapter of its Report from Norman Hunt and the Secretary (PRO: BA1/46), at the Committee's meeting on 5 December 1967 'most members were inclined to prefer on balance . . . going the whole way to a single unified grading structure . . . However, members would reserve their final positions until the Committee had discussed the problem with experts from industry and with the Treasury' (PRO: BA1/10).

Hunt and Wilding had informal talks with the Treasury immediately before Christmas 1967 on the subject of a common grading structure, and prior to the Committee's meeting on 9 January 1968 the Treasury presented a paper (which was not subsequently published) about the structure of the Civil Service. The Treasury wrote that

> the nature and needs of the work are now the primary factor determining the grading system; there would be a danger that they would be subordinated to the demands of uniformity imposed by a common structure. The different grading structures of the various Classes in the Service also take into account a number of other factors as well as the primary one of the customs and needs of the different types of work. For example, they reflect the different levels of entry, the need to provide an adequate career for those who are not going to progress even to the top of their own hierarchy which may itself end short of the Higher Civil Service, and the need to provide an appropriate pyramid of top posts, both to control the work and to provide opportunities and incentives for new entrants. The force and effect of these factors differ in various occupations and a common hierarchy which had as few levels as say the present Clerical/Executive/Administrative Classes could not possibly cater for the wide variety of needs.

The Treasury emphasised that 'this is far from saying that the existing grading structure is satisfactory in all cases nor that the number of Classes is necessarily right (in some cases, particularly in the Departmental field, the Treasury view would be that it is not) but desirable improvements can be achieved without a common structure.' The Treasury, of course, had made its own structural proposals, but whatever the structure adopted 'what is required is a deliberate policy of fostering movement between disciplines where this is profitable to the Service and a regular practice of regarding suitable posts as open to all appropriately qualified people in the relevant Classes or streams: this would involve examining more closely the total pool of talent available in all departments – i.e. a continuous policy of closer staff management for the Service as a whole' (PRO: BA1/48).

'It would be possible to devise a common grading structure for the Civil Service based on job evaluation methods', the Treasury wrote, adding that 'this would . . . involve an operation on a very large scale and would be vastly complicated given the wide range of Civil Service work . . . By comparison, the creation of a single salary structure for the Higher Civil Service above the maximum of the Assistant Secretary's scale would be easy. The numbers of staff, the variety of occupations and the complexity of the existing structures are far less at the higher level and the staff associations are here much less of a force particularly as they have no right of arbitration.'

The Treasury also observed that

> it is generally accepted that within a common structure there would have to be separate occupational groupings, whether professional disciplines, functional streams, or probably both. In theory it would be possible to pay the members of one profession in any particular grade on a scale which differed from that applying to members of another profession in the same grade, so that in accordance with the principle of fair comparisons the differing salary levels of professions in comparable jobs outside the Service were reflected. In practice, however, we do not believe that this could be made to work. In the first place the whole concept of a common structure would encourage a much greater consciousness of relative status throughout the Service. But, even more important, if it had been established by a process of job evaluation that Job A ought to be in the same grade as Job B, it would not be possible to maintain that their responsibilities were not so similar as to make salary differentiation unjustifiable. Moreover, the difficulty would be aggrevated by the fact that the individual salaries of Civil Servants are public knowledge.

The Treasury added that 'since a common structure could hardly be introduced on any basis other than a rounding up of existing pay levels, where these did not fit precisely into the new structure, the additional expenditure involved could be very considerable.' Further, 'it would also be impossible to continue to determine pay on the basis of fair comparison with outside rates of pay in the manner recommended by the Royal Commission on the Civil Service 1953–55' (PRO: BA1/48).

Contemporary incomes policy had already interfered with the application of the Priestley formula anyway. On 28 November 1967, the Fulton Committee's Drafting Sub-Committee had instructed the Secretary 'to consult the Treasury about the principle of fair comparison in relation to present Government policy' (PRO: BA1/55). Earlier, on 27 June, at a meeting of the main Fulton Committee, Sir Philip Allen had wondered whether 'some of the previous discussion of an open structure did not approach the margin of the Committee's terms of reference, since, in his view, an open structure without any identified groups was scarcely compatible with the Priestley principle of pay research which had been excluded from the terms of reference' (PRO: BA1/9). This exclusion did not stop the Committee from endorsing the Priestley formula in its Report, while expecting 'the outside comparison to be made as part of the process of job evaluation' in a unified grading structure (Cmnd. 3638, 1968, para.226). The Committee did show a spark of radicalism in expressing a preference for performance pay instead of automatic progress through a salary scale by means of annual increments, and especially so in the case of the Higher Civil Service (ibid., para.229). Except at or very near the top of the Service, the majority of the Committee thought that 'each grade should carry a range of pay' (ibid., para.228) but, in a published note of reservation, Sir William Cook, Sir Norman Kipping, and Sir John Wall stated that 'we see no reason why the principles of job evaluation and outside comparison should not extend to the most senior posts in the Civil Service' (ibid., p.73). Lord Franks, when giving evidence as Chairman of the advisory committee on Higher Civil Service pay on 5 March 1968, said of the Priestley principle of fair comparison that 'it had a ratchet effect on the level of wages and salaries which was undoubtedly inflationary' (PRO: BA1/11). The Committee, and particularly the members named immediately above, effectively elected to take no notice. The same treatment was meted out to the Treasury's evidence about unified grading. 'We have tried to be constructive', Philip Rogers told the Committee, but, to judge from the exchanges of view, the list of 'difficulties' that the Treasury presented to the Committee at the meeting held on 9 January 1968 was too long for those who advocated unified grading throughout the Service, and the discussions were enlivened only by sparring between Dunnett and Hunt about the obvious effects of such a structure on the prospects of the Executive Class which the latter chose to deny (PRO: BA1/11).

The taking of evidence from a big firm operating a unified grading structure had been suggested to the Committee by Hunt at its meeting on 14 November 1967 (PRO: BA1/10) and taken up by the Committee at its first meeting of 1968, when it was decided to invite representatives of British Petroleum to talk to the Committee and also a representative of McKinsey's to discuss American practice (PRO: BA1/11).

Hunt and the Secretariat had discussions with BP before the relevant meeting, and material was circulated to the Committee which informed it that BP operated 'a unified/single grading structure of the type recommended in our Management Consultancy Investigation.' This structure had been introduced between 1961 and 1963. The most highly paid staff had *ad hoc* salaries outside the structure, which comprised twelve grades. Jobs were placed into grades as a result of job evaluation. Each grade represented a level of responsibility and skill and carried an authorised salary range. The salary scale for each grade was long (each maximum was 50 per cent above the minimum for the grade) and there was overlapping between grades (the minimum for each grade was 20 per cent above the minimum of the grade below). The grades did not automatically confer rank or status in a chain of command. The BP grading system applied to at most 7,500 staff, but 'it was the view of BP that numbers made no difference to the practicability of the system. Indeed, the larger the organization, the greater the need for such a system. A small company in which all the jobs and individuals were familiar to top management might not need it. It enabled the large company to do in a systematic way what it would be trying to do anyway. Almost all the international oil industry operates a similar system, and also many big firms in other industries' (PRO: BA1/48). When P. D. Ince and B. W. R. Mooring gave oral evidence to the Committee on February 6th 1968 on behalf of BP, the view that unified grading was even more suitable for a larger organisation than their company was not closely examined (PRO: BA1/11).

Although Lord Fulton found material circulated by Roger Morrison of McKinsey's prior to his appearance before the Committee on 13 February 1968 to have been 'beautifully prepared', Morrison proved to be unsure about facts concerning the structure of the US Federal Civil Service which the Committee asked about and at that stage needed to know. What Morrison was clear about was his opinion that it would be wrong to limit unified grading to the Higher Civil Service because, even if it was postulated that the main objective was to achieve mobility at the higher levels, integration at the lower levels was needed to develop people capable of doing the top jobs (PRO: BA1/11).

'I think there are people still making up their minds, so we are not asking you to come and talk to us today as if we are in fact in front of you with a solid viewpoint,' Fulton told the Treasury witnesses who appeared before the Committee on February 20th 1968 to discuss unified grading once more. In private business afterwards, the Committee agreed that Hunt and the Secretary should prepare the relevant chapter in the form of two drafts, one of which to be 'written throughout from the point of view of those members who preferred a single unified structure', and the other 'setting out the area of agreement as far as it went' (PRO: BA1/11). Hunt eventually produced a draft chapter (PRO: BA1/50) which, subject to minor amendment, Simey and Allen were prepared to agree to at the Committee's meeting on 23 April 1968 (PRO: BA1/11), and only then did unified grading throughout the Service become a formally agreed recommendation.

In his own opinion and in that of some others on and connected with the Fulton Committee, Robert Sheldon was particularly influential in the eventual adoption of this recommendation.

> My major contribution to the work of the Fulton Committee was my advocacy of unified grading, Sheldon recalled; I came to the view very early on what a load of rubbish the present structure was with its

Messenger Class and the like, all supposed to be offering people careers. It was a toy that I'd had as a child, Jungle Jim, like a cat's cradle. I remember that at a dinner that the Fulton Committee had at the United Oxford and Cambridge University Club in December 1966 my frustration led to an outburst in which I said that we'd had five months to deal with this nonsense and nothing seemed to be happening. What we needed was a unified grading structure. I seemed to get no support and it looked like I would have to draft a Minority Report on structure, with all the extra effort that such a move would involve. Then, a month or so later, in conversation, Norman Hunt told me that he agreed with me on unified grading. It was a wonderful day for me. John Fulton called unified grading 'the core of the Fulton Report' (Interview, 1988).

Richard Wilding's recollection was that

Robert Sheldon was enormously assertive in pressing for the Civil Service to have a unified grading structure. It was an interesting example of how a determined committee man can have a disproportionately strong influence on the outcome when many of his colleagues were less certain. What everybody was agreed upon was that there should be a common structure down to Under Secretary. Even the troika of Dunnett, Neild and Hunt did not want unified grading to go beyond Principal. Robert Sheldon wanted the Committee to go from the top to the bottom of the Service and by pressing and pressing on the matter he got his way.

Wilding recalled Sheldon using the analogy of Jungle Jim (Interview, 1988), as did Walter Anderson, who said that 'Sheldon really pressed on the structure question' and 'I backed Robert's ideas' (Interview, 1988).

Judging by their interventions at the Committee's meeting on 20 February 1968, Sir Norman Kipping and Sir John Wall were advocates of unified grading too, though the latter wanted the arrangement to be taken only down to and including the Executive Officer grade (PRO: BA1/11), a view which he confirmed in a letter to Dunnett on 15 March 1968 (Crowther-Hunt Papers: Box 3). Sheldon established a position on unified grading at, for example, the Committee's meetings on 9 May (PRO: BA1/8), 23 May, and 20 June 1967 (PRO: BA1/9), but whether it was the decisive one in the overall discussions was a matter of view. Dunnett, for one, had no recollection that this was so, and stressed the influence of Hunt and the Management Consultancy Group (Interview, 1988); and it was the case that within the form of unified structure that the Committee actually recommended, Sheldon's position on groups was not followed.

Of the various members of the Committee, it was chiefly Dunnett who produced memoranda representing systematic thinking on the future structure of the Service. In a letter to the Secretary dated 15 January 1968, which was also circulated, he argued against 'a classless uniformly graded Service' both as a concept and as a practical proposition. Besides there being 'a real danger of salary inflation' following any attempt to introduce such arrangements, Dunnett added:

> I think it vitally important the under our new system people of ability should advance to the level of Principal and Assistant Secretary at least as quickly as happens now. Given the nature of Civil Service unions, I think a unified structure of the kind proposed would make this substantially more difficult than it is already. We are going to have enough trouble with this point when we amalgamate the Administrative and Executive grades and the Scientific Officer and Experimental Officer Classes as a number of our witnesses have pointed out. If we go even further, the difficulties of pushing really bright people ahead fast are . . . going to become greater (PRO: BA1/48).

In earlier memoranda, circulated on 5 May 1967, Dunnett had envisaged a Senior Management Class comprising 'a merged structure' for 'the top posts in the Civil Service' with posts up to Assistant Secretary and its equivalent requiring the 'different treatment' of being organised into 'broad groups' with three or four grades within them which he preferred to be numbered ones. As for the graduate entry to the general service area, he was sceptical about the Treasury's structural proposals, believing that all graduates should enter as Cadets and not as Executive Officers. 'There should be some specific distinction at this stage if the first class entry is to be encouraged to come in,' Dunnett wrote; also observing that 'I do not think that in practice it would be possible, even if one has no starring system or any kind of difference as between Class A and Class B cadets, not to apply some measure of distinction in practice. For example, if in a particular year a particular department required eight or nine cadets, they would, inevitably, as good managers give preferential treatment to the real flyers as opposed to the more pedestrian entry.'

Dunnett repeated the concern that he had expressed elsewhere about the future of the Executive Class entry (PRO: BA1/3) and in a memorandum circulated in March 1967 he wrote: 'I think it is fair to say that we probably have the best Executive Class Civil Service in the world . . . Certainly in my experience the Executive Class as a whole, which is moving towards increasing specialization the whole time, compares extremely favourably with similar people in the American Civil Service, the Commonwealth Civil Services and, I think, the European Civil Services as well' (PRO: BA1/33). He also circulated material about the Clerical Classes which proposed changes designed to distinguish between the career entrants and the rest (PRO: BA1/37).

For all its intellectual clarity, there was no evidence that Dunnett's memoranda had much direct influence on the way in which the Fulton Committee's conclusions about the future structure of the Home Civil Service emerged, especially as the relevant discussions crossed and re-crossed the subject area without benefit. It was clear from the balance of argument in the private discussion that followed the Treasury's evidence on 18 July 1967 (PRO: BA1/9) that the Committee would eventually recommend the creation of a Senior Policy and Management Group 'comprising all posts in all grades from the Head of the Civil Service down to, and including, grades that are today equivalent to Under Secretary' (Cmnd. 3638, 1968, para.222). Below this level, the Committee recommended the retention of occupational groups (ibid., para.223), as it was almost bound to do after the meeting on 20 June 1967 when, with Robert Sheldon on that occasion reserving his position, the Committee agreed that groups were needed, if only general service and non-general service, and in discussion separate treatment for doctors, accountants and lawyers at least was envisaged; and it was said that 'there was a good case for retaining the large departmental groups in Inland Revenue and Customs' (PRO: BA1/9).

Though at the Committee's meeting on 1 August 1967, Sir John Wall suggested that the Clerical Classes should not even be included in the common grading structure (PRO: BA1/10), a view which, as we have seen, he continued to adhere to, he did not press the matter, and all that was surprising about the Fulton Committee proposing 'the merger of the Administrative, Executive and Clerical Classes' in its Report was the accompanying phrase 'as recommended to us by the Treasury' (Cmnd. 3638, 1968, para.215). This overstated the dependence on the Treasury's evidence. As first advanced, of course, the Treasury's proposals had been for an amalgamation of the Administrative and Executive Classes, with the Clerical Classes only being added later, almost as if, like Sir John Wall, the Treasury officials had wished to draw the line at Executive Officer level, and without Wall's restoration of 'the old Higher Clerical Officer ganger job' (Crowther-Hunt Papers: Box 3) as a career outlet of the kind that it will be recalled L. A. Wines of the CSCA pointed out was absent from the Treasury's original plans. Then again, in its Report, the Committee actually recommended that 'for the graduate entry, and for those who have shown the highest ability among non-graduate entrants, we propose the introduction of a training grade' (Cmnd. 3638, 1968, para.95), an implicit rejection of the Treasury's ideas for 'starring' some graduate entrants which the Committee only made fully explicit later (ibid., Appendix F, pp.163ff).

Within the Fulton Committee, it was Robert Neild, in a paper dated 29 March 1967, who pressed the case for greater specialisation among administrators in the future (PRO: BA1/32). At the meeting on 3 and 4 July it was agreed that though 'the question of a general service group and its streaming was for further discussion . . . the professionalism of general service staff should be thought of as lying primarily in not administration itself but in a knowledge in depth of some field of activity' (PRO: BA1/9). When the Committee met at the Isle of Thorns on 22 and 23 July 1967 it was recognised that 'especially when the Administrative and Executive Classes had been merged, the concept of a broad pool channelled into specialist streams would be the right one', and that 'it was unsatisfactory to regard the general service simply as a residual category . . . It was common ground that this function was closely related to the direct service of the Minister, that it required the high development of a particular kind of judgment, but that this judgment, no longer sufficient by itself, must be based upon definite knowledge and experience of subject matter.' The 'new professionalism' which the Committee sought was 'that of the man who could conduct a dialogue with the expert, who could produce major thinking of his own after living with the evidence, who could, so to speak, review the book and not merely quote from it' (PRO: BA1/10). After considerable previous indecision and drafting activity, it was decided at the meeting on 5 December 1967 that 'it was not for the Committee to identify all the streams' of administrators that would be needed in future. What the Committee needed to do was to 'enunciate the principle' and to give examples (PRO: BA1/10). In the Fulton Report, the Committee identified two streams of administrators, economic and financial, and also social administrators, and assigned the Civil Service Department the task of finding more (Cmnd. 3638, 1968, paras 45–7).

'The Civil Service . . . has been slow to recognize the benefits that would flow from a much larger recruitment of particular categories such as accountants, statisticians, economists and Research Officers and their employment in positions of greater responsibility,' the Fulton Committee observed in its Report, drawing special attention to 'present practice in the Civil Service' which 'severely restricts the role of the Accountant Class and excludes its members from responsibility for financial control' (ibid., paras. 36–7). The Committee's Management Consultancy Group had made much the same observation about the use of professional accountants, and as late as 1 December 1967, under the chairmanship of Sir Norman Kipping, Sir James Dunnett, Norman Hunt, and Sir John Wall discussed the issue with, first, the Accountants Joint Parliamentary Committee, and then with Treasury witnesses. Dunnett stated:

> I am bound to say, from my experience in the Ministry of Supply and the Ministry of Defence, that the quality of the accountants we have is very poor. I had an occasion recently where there was a question of a lot of departments involved in placing a contract with a firm, and it was very dubious whether the firm was solvent or not. Who are you advised by? Normal administrators who cannot read a balance sheet, and an accountant who, if he was outside, I would not employ for five minutes. This does not seem to me a very efficient way of proceeding. But we go on with this, and at present rates of pay all that we will get is another accountant who will be the same sort of chap that we have already got. I am not saying we want the place flooded out with accountants, but I do find something in the problem put to us by the profession, that you really do need some accountants who are better qualified, and that you will not get them without a better career prospect (PRO: BA1/10).

The Committee gave most attention to the use of accountants in the Home Civil Service in Appendix D of its Report, in which it also considered the role of lawyers and Research Officers too. The Committee seemed to think that the introduction of a unified grading structure would solve the problems of the Research Officer Class and it never really took up the IPCS's idea of a Social Scientist Group (Cmnd. 3638, 1968, pp.150–6).

Though on the surface it was to seem otherwise, the Fulton Committee did not simply endorse the other ideas on structure in relation to specialist groups that the IPCS advanced. At the meeting on 23 May 1967, for example, Sir William Cook suggested that 'the Committee should consider whether the Scientific and Works Group Classes should be brought together in a single Science and Technology Group . . . The distinction between the work of the Scientific Classes and the Works Group was, in practice, blurred. The distinction did not sort men out according to the professional disciplines since there were, for instance, engineers in both Groups' (PRO: BA1/9). On 27 June 1967 Fulton observed that besides the General Service Group, it might be possible to have a structure comprising the Scientific Civil Service, the Professional Civil Service, which would include 'the nationwide professions – medicine, law, accountancy etc.,' and 'another group for specialisms, mainly departmental, which were peculiar to the Service, such as the Inland Revenue.' The Committee agreed 'to treat the groupings suggested by the Chairman as a provisional working hypothesis' for drafting purposes (PRO: BA1/9). In its Report, of course, the Committee's view was expressed as being that 'within a unified grading structure . . . the whole problem of the separate Departmental Classes can be dealt with' (Cmnd. 3638, 1968, para.239). At its meeting at the Isle of Thorns on 22 and 23 July 1967 the Committee seemed unenthusiastic about any form of grouping (PRO: BA1/10), whereas at its meeting on 3 and 4 July 1967, it had, with reservations, envisaged mergers covering the Scientific Civil Service, and the establishment of a Construction Group covering the existing Works Group and supporting Classes (PRO: BA1/9).

It may be that with regard to these specialists the Committee's difficulties were encapsulated by Sir James Dunnett when he wrote in March 1967: 'I am quite clear myself that while I think many of the claims of the scientists and the engineers as put in by e.g. the IPCS are exaggerated and activated at any rate to some extent by considerations of material benefit, the scientists and engineers have not yet been accorded the position that they will have to have in the Civil Service of the future' (PRO: BA1/33). So, when it came to decisions the Committee seemed to put to one side, for instance, evidence that it received from Sir Arnold Lindley in early 1968 that 'there had been over-promotion of engineers' even under the existing structure (PRO: BA1/48, BA1/56) and recommended the merger of the Works Group of Professional Classes, the Technical Works, Engineering and Allied Classes, and the Architectural and Engineering Draughtsman Classes', and also the merger of the Scientific Officer, Experimental Officer, and Scientific Assistant Classes (Cmnd. 3638, 1968, para.215). Then, after adding to its Report a slender appendix on the Supporting grades throughout the Service, for whose problems, it will now be guessed, the unified grading structure provided the answers (ibid., p.177f), the Committee was free of the subject of structure which had threatened to submerge it.

Chapter 7

Recruitment and Training in the Civil Service

The Context for Change

'The Administrative Class, which occupies all the controlling positions in the Home Civil Service, consists to an overwhelming extent of the fortunate few who can manage to get to Oxford and Cambridge; and the entrance examination has always been expressly designed for that purpose.' This observation by W. A. Robson, the Fabian academic, some thirty years before the appointment of the Fulton Committee (Robson, 1937, p.16) exemplified the controversy which accompanied most discussion of the subject of direct entry recruitment to the Administrative Class of the Home Civil Service. 'It is intolerable that the Universities of London and of the provincial towns should find their students (who are drawn largely from lower social strata) virtually debarred, or at least seriously handicapped, from entry into the highest grades of the Service, especially when one considers the relative importance of the work these Universities are doing in the social sciences.' Robson, connected with London University and a social scientist himself, went on: 'There is a manifest anomaly between the widened political opportunity which enables men and women of working class origin and experience to secure the highest positions of political power . . . and the arrangements which require the leading officials to be drawn from narrow strata in the upper levels of society' (ibid., p.17).

Whether, even at or near the top, the Civil Service, outside the Diplomatic Service, ever really was particularly socially exclusive once open competition displaced patronage seems as doubtful as the possibility that the student populations outside Oxford and Cambridge were dominated by those of modest origins. Sole reliance on promotion from below, practicable in the inter-war era at least, given the talent attracted by the open competitions to the Executive and Clerical Classes, might well have provided an Administrative Class of a more socially democratic composition. Naturally enough, interested parties such as the CSCA and its leaders made proposals for 'ground level entry' (Fry, 1969a, pp.191–4), but only rarely did an outside reformer (e.g. Monck, 1952, p.5f) follow suit. Maximum efficiency in public administration was more widely taken by reformers to mean the direct entry recruitment to the Administrative Class of the brightest and the best of the university graduates, and the democratisation of the intake into higher education was one favoured means of changing its composition and outlook. The other was to 'professionalise' the Administrative Class away from the view commonly attributed to it that the Greats man from Oxford was the ideal administrator. When the Fabian authors of *The Administrators* wrote in 1964 about its proposals for post-entry training that 'we have been influenced a good deal by the success of the French *Ecole Nationale d'Administration*' (Fabian Group, 1964, p.29) they were not alone, and few reformers failed to note too that 'preference for relevance' was practised in the recruitment process.

One hundred years after the publication of the Northcote-Trevelyan Report, the Civil Service Commission described its task accurately when it said that in recruiting to a Service-wide Administrative Class it was seeking 'general purpose all rounders' (Priestley evidence, p.53). The simple and swift triumph of the Macaulay principle of 'preference for irrelevance' in direct entry recruitment favouring the humanities, though, did not necessarily characterise all the period in between. Of course, nothing came of Benjamin Jowett's proposals appended to the Northcote-Trevelyan Report that the open competitive examination should recognise 'the special requirements of the higher departments of the public officers', meaning, for instance, 'a knowledge of the principles of commerce, taxation, and political economy' in the case of recruitment to the Treasury and the Board of Trade (C. 1713, 1854, p.27). Similarly, though Macaulay famously recommended that entry to the Indian Civil Service should be on the basis of 'an excellent general education' and the Home Civil Service eventually followed the example, Macaulay's further recommendation that entrants should be subsequently given 'a special education' to enable them 'to despatch the business' (Cmnd. 3638, 1968, p.121) did not foster a similar emulative tradition in formal post-entry training. This mattered less, of course, in the period before Warren Fisher, not just because, generally, the work must have been less demanding or at least less complex, but also because administrators given a less mobile career pattern had more opportunity of learning 'the business' in departments for the subject matters of which their university studies had not often prepared them to deal.

As a matter of fact, the Greats man did not always have things all his own way in the Administrative Class competition, even if some thought that the Civil Service Commissioners desired this. In 1912, Graham Wallas, as a member of the MacDonnell Royal Commission, elicited the information that in the Class I examination of the time only the Greats man did not have to get up subjects additional to those of his original university studies to find the necessary marks in the competition (MacDonnell evidence, q.20,784-20,786). Nevertheless, graduates in mathematics and the natural sciences were prominent in the order of merit in the Class I competitions of the time. The future Permanent Secretary, Sir John Anderson, who headed the Class I list in 1905, was an example, additionally getting up economics and political science specially for the competition (Wheeler-Bennett, 1962, pp.9–19). After 1905, the Civil Service Commission diminished the weighting given to mathematics and the natural sciences, in the opinion of one observer with the aim of lowering the success rate of such graduates in the Class I competition (Kelsall, 1955, p.61). If so, it was not entirely effective, since in 1912, 1913 and 1914 as the MacDonnell Royal Commission reviewed the Service, the Class I list was headed each time by a Cambridge graduate with such a background (Cd. 6913, 1913, p.iii; Cd. 7497, 1914, p.iii; Cd. 7983, 1915, p.iii). An example was the future Permanent Secretary, Sir James Grigg, who was top of the list in 1913, having, among other studies, additionally read economics when preparing for the competition (Grigg, 1948, p.33f). Half a century later, the Fabian pamphleteers in *The Administrators*, citing the Macaulay principle of recruitment, recorded what had become by then a familiar complaint about the domination of the Administrative Class entry by liberal arts graduates from Oxford and Cambridge to the exclusion of those from all universities with degrees in science or mathematics (Fabian Group, 1964, pp.3, 17, 26, 41). The likeliest explanation of why there eventually came to be relatively fewer entrants to the Administrative Class with the Anderson or Grigg type of background was not prejudice against them on the part of the Civil Service Commission, actual or ascribed, but the professionalisation of science and the expansion of careers in it both inside and outside the Civil Service (Cardwell, 1972, pp.228–56).

No comparable growth in alternative opportunities took place for graduates in the humanities even from Oxford and Cambridge, and, always prominent in the Class I list, such graduates dominated the open competitive entry to the Administrative Class of the Home Civil Service in the inter-war years, and, indeed, all the way down to the period when the Fulton Committee began its investigations. Changes in the methods of direct entry recruitment made no difference. Whether entry was by Method I, as the traditional literary competition came to be known, or, from 1948 onwards, by Method II, which was essentially an extended interview system, the ideal sought first became and then remained the Warren Fisher mobile administrator, even if authorship was disguised for some by the elegance of the public exposition of the virtues of the all-rounder mounted by Fisher's eventual successor as Head of the Service, Sir Edward Bridges. In his pronouncements in the 1950s, Bridges made no secret of his approval of the sentiments in the main body of the Northcote-Trevelyan Report that recruitment of administrators should be on the basis of 'general ability' rather than 'special requirements' (Bridges, 1954, p.321). In the Bridges era, little or no progress was made for years in central provision for post-entry training, despite the proposals of the Assheton Report of 1944 (Cmd. 6525, 1944), for example, being modest in scope. Similarly, it was unsurprising that when some Treasury officials came across management techniques and related theorising in the later 1940s, they treated them with an amused contempt which seems to have been as genuine as their department's distaste for the Institute of Public Administration (Chapman, 1988, p.248).

In its early form, the IPA had been a body which had pressed for the professionalisation of public administration. That the SCS, representing the interests of the Executive Class, played a major role in the foundation of the Institute (Nottage and Stack, 1972, pp.281–304) was a fact unlikely to disarm its opponents. The view that promotion within the Service at all levels should be dependent on success in the formal study of public administration continued to be pressed for by E. N. Gladden from the Executive Class in various writings (Gladden, 1956, pp.189ff; Gladden, 1958, pp.235ff). Only the consciously virtuous in the Administrative Class would seem likely to seek or approve of such training if they could get to or near the top without it. In the late 1950s, C. H. Sisson, returning to the Administrative Class after a brief foray into academic life, and versed in what he called 'administrative science fiction', was as dismissive of Gladden's ideas as he was of continental European and other foreign notions of 'preference for relevance' in recruitment to the Civil Service, and of their insistence on extensive formal post-entry training (Sisson, 1959, pp.33ff, 132–8).

Complacency on the Sisson scale did not survive the Plowden Report on the Control of Public Expenditure, the managerialism envisaged in which changed the officially perceived role of the Administrative Class. Even if working practice did not change that much, there could not be managerialism without management training, and the establishment of the Centre for Administrative Studies in 1963 by the Treasury was followed by the appointment two years later of a Treasury Working Party, chaired by S. P. Osmond, which was certain to recommend an expansion in provision for post-entry training. The Fulton Committee had to deal with this prospect and with the Civil Service's problems of direct entry recruitment, not the least of which was the future of methods of recruitment devised for an Administrative Class elite now that there was to be a wider graduate entry, and the issue of 'preference for relevance'.

Review of the Main Evidence

1. Centralized direct entry recruitment to the home civil service, methods and procedures

'I do not think we have heard enough about the Executive Class and the problems connected with that', Lord Fulton remarked to Sir George Abell, the First Civil Service Commissioner at the outset of the afternoon session of the Fulton Committee's meeting on 6 December 1966. The Chairman was referring to the morning session, also attended by the Civil Service Commissioners, which had been largely devoted to discussion about methods of recruiting general graduates to the Administrative Class and the 'starring' question (PRO: BA1/5); as had that when Abell had appeared previously on

7 June 1966 (PRO: BA1/3). If one adds in the 'preference for relevance' issue too, the Administrative Class and successor arrangements dominated the evidence submitted to the Fulton Committee about direct entry recruitment to the Home Civil Service, including the main written evidence submitted by the Civil Service Commission (PRO: BA1/23). The recruitment of scientists and engineers to the Service was discussed at length when Abell and Sir Frederick Brundrett, a fellow Civil Service Commissioner, appeared before the Committee on June 20 1967, when those matters were specifically on the agenda (PRO: BA1/9), but general discussion on recruitment did not leave the Administrative Class to one side for long and that on the afternoon of 6 December 1966 was no exception.

'The Civil Service Commission behaved as if the Service was already attractive and they only had to select. This was not true', Sir Philip Morris, the Vice-Chancellor of Bristol University, observed in his evidence to the Committee, believing that 'people who would be capable of handling human situations and getting the right answers to problems would not be found by Burlington Gardens methods. It was impossible for examiners to assess the potential of people with backgrounds quite different from their own.' Morris suggested that there should be 'a close look at dispersing the recruitment function and giving the greatest possible freedom to departments and establishments' (PRO: BA1/4). This was already the case with the Scientific Civil Service, of course, and Professor James Lighthill was clear in his evidence that 'Farnborough enjoyed advantages in its system of direct recruitment. University Professors were visited and asked to suggest potential recruits' (PRO: BA1/3). Citing the past experience of the Admiralty, W. G. Harris, the Director General, Highways, at the Ministry of Transport, thought that greater resort to the departmental recruitment of engineers would have similar benefits (PRO: BA1/2). Of the recruitment of architects, Sir Donald Gibson, Director General of Research and Development at the Ministry of Public Building and Works, observed that 'the Civil Service Commission seems too ponderous and slow to compete with the outside world' (PRO: BA1/22); and other evidence about that Ministry stated that 'in a competitive situation only the less able candidates have time to wait for the mills to grind' (PRO: BA1/36). Consultations with Youth Employment Officers in the Ministry of Labour revealed 'the time lag in making appointments and the complexities of the application forms' to be 'deterrents to recruitment', and 'the introduction of departmental recruiting at Clerical level' was thought to be 'an improvement which might be extended to the Executive level' (PRO: BA1/29).

The candid C. H. Sisson observed in his evidence that

> the Civil Service Commission . . . really still operates on the mythology that thousands of people are scrambling to get a job in the Civil Service, as indeed they were when I was getting in. They find it very difficult to adjust themselves to conditions where they are the personnel department of a vast concern trying to go out and get people. I would like to see . . .

recruitment in the hands of a body which was staffed by people joining in and out on loan from user departments and not staying too long, most of them on a three year loan. I think you would get a different sense of urgency about the matter.

Sisson noted the departmental recruitment of Clerical Officers, and, thinking of arrangements in terms of temporary initial appointments later to be centrally confirmed or otherwise, envisaged introducing this 'a bit higher up' (PRO: BA1/7).

'The General Service Classes should still be recruited centrally, even though scientists and engineers were often recruited departmentally or even locally,' Sir George Abell stated in his evidence to the Committee on June 7th 1966;

Centrally imposed standards for establishment were necessary if large inequalities and scandals were to be avoided; and while temporary appointments were often attractive to scientists, he thought this was generally not true of the General Classes, who had no recognized expertise and for whom a permanent job was very important. Government administration was in his view a professional skill, but not one which was readily marketable outside the Service (PRO: BA1/3).

At the Committee's meeting on December 6th 1966, K. M. Reader, a Civil Service Commissioner, said that

we have delegated Clerical Class recruitment to departments, although we continue to have centralized recruitment in addition to departmental recruitment for London posts. Everything possible is done to recruit in the regions by means of regional advertising by departments, and sometimes, in areas like Edinburgh and Cardiff, there is a certain amount of competition. The regions recruit much as we ourselves would recruit, and the local people do have a number of rules laid down by us.

Reader confirmed that this local clerical recruitment was to established posts and said that the variety of qualifications cited by candidates was such that the Commissioners had issued a 'Bible' of them for the guidance of departments. Sir George Abell observed that, though he was 'very much in favour of delegation of Clerical recruitment', he felt that 'we must await the outcome of the Committee's deliberations' before the possible future delegation of Executive Class recruitment was fully considered (PRO: BA1/5).

'Public attention was concentrated on the Administrative Class' even though 'this was a very small proportion of the Civil Service: 0.4 per cent,' Sir George Abell stated when giving evidence to the Committee on 7 June 1966. The First Civil Service Commissioner thought that 'the Service got a reasonable share of the ablest graduates . . . The first half to two-thirds of the entry to the Administrative Class were of very high quality. It was very hard to be sure about the remaining one-third, especially as departments had had to be lenient over probation at a time of severe shortage.'

Abell considered that

many unsuccessful candidates might . . . be capable of useful work in the Service and he agreed with the Treasury proposals on structure in principle. In practice, however, he foresaw very considerable problems. The Bank of England had operated a common entry linked to school leaving age, and this had been very unattractive to graduates faced with the prospect of several years of dull work without much responsibility. In order to attract the best graduate entry, the fliers would have to be assured of being labelled with a star for accelerated promotion; if all started equal, they would diverge sharply and quickly thereafter.

When he was asked whether it would not be better to select the best people by means of a two year training course, which might be less risky than a system of 'starring' at the outset, Abell said that 'this was possible; training courses did supply evidence of people's capacities. But extending the "school" period might discourage recruitment, and he thought that it would be difficult to persuade the rest of the staff under a new system that the future elite should be picked otherwise than on the basis of their performance on the job' (PRO: BA1/3).

The arrangement for selecting the elite both presently and prospectively was actually by means of performance in the entry competition and not 'performance on the job', and the Treasury's structural proposals involving a wider but differentiated graduate entry to the General Classes of the Service provided the opportunity for a more broadly based discussion than the familiar debate about recruitment to the Administrative Class. Few took the opportunity, and it was difficult to believe that many of those giving evidence from outside the Service had ever heard of the Special Departmental Classes competition or of the Ministry of Labour Cadet scheme that until recently had been part of it. One advocate from within the Service of 'starring' graduate entrants, C. H. Sisson, made the point that a department like the Ministry of Labour, with a great number of out-stations, would find it impossible to sort out the headquarters type, that is Assistant Principal, from the field type, that is the Cadet, in a reasonably short time from among a large undifferentiated entry (PRO: BA1/7).

As we have noted elsewhere, 'starring' was an issue relating to structure as well as to recruitment, and that the Treasury (PRO: BA/14, BA1/5), the Civil Service Commission (PRO: BA1/3, BA1/5), and serving and former higher civil servants like Sir Charles Cunningham (PRO: BA1/2) and Sir John Maud (PRO: BA1/5), and Assistant Principals already in post (PRO: BA1/18), would be in favour of 'starring' certain graduate entrants, and that the SCS (PRO: BA1/5, 20) would lead the opposition, did lend an air of predictability to the arguments about this matter which only the exceptional piece of evidence escaped from. The former higher civil servant, F. A. Bishop, for instance, told the Committee that the examination system was a very hit and miss one.

It might attract the candidates whom the examiners thought the most able people but they were not necessarily the ones the Service needed. Academic training was not always the best equipment for the top jobs;

for managerial and financial work the type of man now found in the Executive Class was as good as any other. It would be better if the potential members of the Higher Civil Service could be picked out after they entered the Service by careful scrutiny of people over the whole field (PRO: BA 1/2).

Professor Nicholas Kaldor of Cambridge University argued that

the present system of selection for the Administrative Class was not infallible and it should be deferred until men had proved themselves on the job. This meant taking in more people in a general graduate entry combining the present Administrative and Executive Classes. There should be a longer and more genuine probationary period of about five years. However, there was still a need for an elite which should be even smaller and of higher quality than the present Administrative Class. Candidates for this elite should be chosen after five years in the Service. They should then go a Staff College on the lines of ENA in France for a two year course in public administration and the disciplines related to it. The course should be in the nature of a post-graduate degree course and perhaps those who were successful ought then to be entitled to put some letters after their names. There could be some variation in the courses depending on the kind of department from which people came to the Staff College (PRO: BA1/3).

'What is the difference between having a two Class entry as at present and having a one Class entry with a starring system? Are the two things the same?' Walter Anderson asked the First Civil Service Commissioner, when he gave evidence on 6 December 1966, to receive the reply that 'there is a fundamental difference here. For myself, I think that if you give your 100 stars on selection your point would be valid. It would be the old system by a new name, and you would not get your graduates below the line in the numbers that you want or in the quality that you want. But if you give only a small number of stars and you leave the rest to be competed for, and especially if you start them all on the same salary, I think this really does make it one class.' Given that 'some members of the Committee said "No" and one of the Civil Service Commissioners, K. A. G. Murray was indicating agreement with him, Anderson persisted, saying that 'if we are going to merge, then we must not make it, if you like, a rose by another name.' Sir George Abell eventually replied, overruled his colleague and observed that 'from a purely selection view, it is quite clear. If these people could be prisoners and you could be sure of having them all, then why star them? Let them prove themselves on the job. But since we have got to recruit around the place we simply must get people who are prepared to come on our terms, and our terms, in my judgement, must include some stars for the best of them; otherwise, you would go without these people, which could be disastrous.'

Earlier, Abell had observed that 'one has to face the fact that 66 to 80 per cent of our people come from Oxford and Cambridge,' and stated 'I am convinced that we should destroy the top quality of the Civil Service if we do not have any starring.' He envisaged a smaller starred entry of general graduates to the Service than the Treasury's initial structural proposals had seemed to suggest, with the other stars being left open to competition among the remainder of the wider graduate entry. Simey thought that the Civil Service Commission's approach represented 'a good British compromise', and Dunnett said that 'we are only talking about what you do in the first five years of their service. Once they come into the general management grades, they are all the same; the starring has disappeared.' Nobody on the Committee chose to take up Murray's line on the favoured graduates, which was that 'they are only "starlets" who are being groomed for stardom' (PRO: BA1/5). At least in evidence presented on 20 December 1966, Treasury witnesses talked of the general graduate entry in much the same terms as Abell had done, while not seeing themselves as having departed from the department's original proposals (PRO: BA1/5).

Evidence about the means of selection for an expanded graduate entry inevitably got mixed up with discussion about the existing Method I and Method II forms of entry into the Administrative Class. Sir Douglas Haddow, the Permanent Under Secretary of State for Scotland, said that 'he would be sorry to see Method I go; he thought that both Methods were needed' (PRO: BA1/4). Thomas Balogh told the Committee that 'there is hardly any doubt in my mind after my own experience as a civil servant that the competitive system based on a written examination should not merely be preserved but that the weight assigned to the interview as against the examination should be reduced to the pre-war level. The interview system, even as strengthened with the so-called country house test, has not been a success. It is subject to the fallible preferences of the interviewing boards; and these seem very fallible indeed' (PRO: BA1/12).

Method I had few other defenders. The Permanent Secretary at the Ministry of Technology, Sir Maurice Dean, said that

> Method I was probably on the way out anyway, but Method II still placed great emphasis on the English paper which was extremely stiff and probably frightened off some good potential candidates. The theory was that the English paper tested whether a candidate was likely to be good at the paper work of the Administrative Class: marshalling facts and setting out a problem clearly and concisely so that senior officials and Ministers could get the essential information and advice they needed by a quick reading. This was an important part of the work of many administrators but there were also jobs which could be done by people whose strength lay in other directions, and the Civil Service could not afford to do without such people.

Dean stated that he would be 'in favour of providing for entry by interview only, in the same way as business firms recruited promising young graduates' (PRO: BA1/2). The former Treasury official, Sir Henry Wilson Smith said that 'he would like to see the Civil Service depart from the written examination and rely more on the Method II type of entry and the candidate's past record' (PRO: BA1/2). Two academics from Sheffield University, Bernard Crick and William Thornhill, were not alone in advancing the opinion that the recruitment of general graduates 'should in future be confined to the Selection Board procedure (the present Method II)' even if their description of Method I as having 'a class bias of its own' had more novelty (PRO: BA1/27). While not ruling out cultural bias being present in a primarily written examination like Method I, there would be more opportunity for 'class bias' in the extended interview arrangements for Method II, and, as the academics concerned had criticised Oxford's dominance in Administrative Class recruitment, it was at least possible that Dean was right when he told the Committee that 'Method II was undoubtedly easier for people who were used to the tutorial system at the older universities' (PRO: BA1/2). Against that, and given that diminishing the dominance of Oxford and Cambridge in the direct entry was close to being an obsession with some reformers, account had to be taken of the evidence of the Civil Service Commissioner, K. M. Reader, who informed that Committee that 'in the 1957–1960 period, 78 per cent of the Method I successes were Oxbridge, and now it is running at about 90 per cent . . . With Method II, of course, the position has gone the other way' (PRO: BA1/5).

The fate of Method I was effectively settled by the evidence which the Civil Service Commission presented to the Committee on 6 December 1966. In response to a question from Sir James Dunnett, K. M. Reader said that there were 66 candidates for 155 papers in the Method I examination held in July 1966, adding, in answering Lord Simey, that this was in contrast to something like 500 candidates sitting the qualifying exam as Method II or dual candidates in January. 'Method I has so many disadvantages', Reader said, not least 'to have to take another academic examination so soon after finals. No other employer insists on that.' Method I was 'long drawn out' compared with Method II. Reader told the Committee that 'going round the universities, I have not discovered anyone in "Redbrick" universities putting in an appeal for the continuance of Method I at all.' Indeed, the prevailing view seemed to be that 'Method I as it stands gives an advantage to Oxford and Cambridge' because 'the present Method I syllabus does tend to reflect more satisfactorily those university courses that are rather tightly knit.' Another Commissioner, K. A. G. Murray, emphasised that, though 'it used to do', Method I no longer offered 'a more democratic entry into the Service . . . in the sense of a more grammar school, fewer public school, fewer Oxbridge.' Compared with Method II, its record was 'much worse.' Sir George Abell told the Committee that he was in the Indian Civil Service 'when they started introducing something of the Method II way of selecting people there. It was quite noticeable, the change in the number of "problem children" that you had around. They dropped to almost nothing, whereas we had always got a certain number of amiably dotty people around whom we fitted in where we could. One longed to have jobs of librarian, or something, where they would be thoroughly interested, but not in the way of administration of management.' So, not surprisingly, the First Civil Service Commissioner sounded out the Committee about the possibility of ending Method I in 1968 (PRO: BA1/5).

The qualifying examination for Method II, which comprised an essay, English, and a general paper, served two purposes, K. M. Reader told the Committee, 'The first one is to serve as a sieve, to keep the numbers coming to the Selection Board to reasonable proportions; and, secondly, through the script readers' comments, they do give the members of the Civil Service Selection Board an overall impression of the candidates' intellectual qualities, which CSSB find extremely valuable.' Sir George Abell said that 'what we want is brains in an all rounder.' He was unapologetic about the fact that 'we turn down a surprising number of Firsts in Method II . . . something of the order of one-third to one-half of the Firsts who apply.' The Civil Service was looking for 'the man who has got personality as well as brains,' and Sir George thought that 'managerial qualities are very well spotted on the two days extended interview by CSSB.'

Norman Hunt observed that he found that these CSSB reports

> help enormously when one is on a Final Selection Board, because they do focus you on a range of marks which otherwise you would not necessarily get. On the other hand, I wondered whether there was not a certain amount of artificiality about that, because what appears as a final scientific mark from CSSB is not in fact quite as scientific as I would have expected it to be. You have in front of you a scientific mark from a CSSB which says, 'The Chairman's view in the end is that this man is 220,' or, 'that this man is 240.' This inevitably produces the situation on the Final Selection Board in which the members, particularly if they have been told not to disagree too much with the CSSB, are not going to get too wide of that. The curious thing, I think, is that the mark from the CSSB, which I would have thought was a very scientific mark, really is not in fact any more than a collation of a whole series of interviews – longer interviews, it is quite true – and is not, in the last analysis, a much more scientific mark than any two or three people would themselves produce.

The best that Abell could reply was to say that 'I do not believe we should make so many good selections if we had no Civil Service Selection Board.' Hunt also stated that when he had been one of the seven members of the Final Selection Board the 'user' element had not been strongly represented, to which Abell replied: 'On a typical Board we may have either two or three civil servants, apart from the First Commissioner. There is far more representation, both of the departments and of the universities on the Board than there used to be.' When Hunt pointed out that this could produce a situation in which the 'user' element was in a minority, Abell saw 'no harm' in this, though he did add that 'experience makes Mr Murray think the Final Board rather a lottery, and one has to be humble about the half hour interview and agree it is not enough, but where we find the Final Board makes a great contribution is in taking the borderline cases and deciding which of those should be given the benefit of the doubt and which should not.' In the case of Method II, in contrast with Method I where the interview marks were simply aggregated with others, the Final Selection Board's opinion was decisive, even if the CSSB's most favourable recommendations were unlikely to be overruled (PRO: BA1/5).

The Civil Service Commission's plans for recruiting a much larger intake of general graduates involved adapting the existing Method II procedure. Firstly, there would be

> a one day qualifying examination consisting of elements of the present qualifying examination combined with objective tests of the type now given to candidates at the CSSB and others specially devised by the Commission's Research Unit. Those with First Class Honours degrees and those with Second Class degrees together with post-graduate degrees would be exempted from this examination as at present.

Secondly,

> those with high marks in this examination and those exempted from it by virtue of degrees with First Class Honours would go direct to the CSSB for tests and interviews substantially on present lines. Amongst these (a) candidates assessed by the CSSB as likely to be suitable for the 'starred' entry would go to the Final Selection Board with whom the decision would rest. Those not considered by the Final Board to be up to the standard required of the 'starred' entry would be offered general Grade VIII appointments; (b) others thought by the CSSB to be suitable for the general though not for the 'starred' entry would be offered Grade VIII appointments without further interview.

Thirdly,

> the remainder of those who qualified at the initial examination and those exempted from it . . . would be seen by Interview Boards consisting of a Chairman and two members. These Boards would recommend for consideration by the CSSB all candidates who might conceivably be suitable for the 'starred' entry, could recommend others for appointment to the general graduate entry to Grade VIII or could recommend others for appointment to the general graduate entry to Grade VIII or could recommend rejection. To ensure, so far as possible, a uniform standard of assessment the Board's recommendations would be considered by the Commissioners in the light of candidates' records and reports from universities. Normally those recommended by the Interview Boards for the 'starred' entry would go to the CSSB and, save in doubtful cases, would not be asked to appear before the Final Board. Those not considered up to the standard for the 'starred' entry could be recommended by the CSSB Selection Board for the general Grade VIII entry without further interview. Candidates recommended by Preliminary Boards for the

'unstarred' entry would not go to the CSSB unless the Commissioners thought that in the light of university reports and records the verdict of the Preliminary Board should be retested. In practice, this would mean that in most cases appointment to the 'unstarred' Grade VIII entry would be made on the recommendation of the Preliminary Board' (PRO: BA1/23).

This was plainly a viable scheme, given adequate staffing; and, subject to the same condition, so was the alternative outlined in separate evidence presented to the Committee by J. H. T. Goldsmith, a former Civil Service Commissioner and Chairman of the CSSB between 1951 and 1963. Goldsmith proposed dispensing with the qualifying examination, which he saw as an unreliable test, and his preferred scheme was for all candidates for general graduate posts to be put through a shorter CSSB procedure. There would be provincial CSSB centres, and the decision on appointments would be that of the Final Selection Board. Separate arrangements would made for post-graduates, possibly taking the form of a written test and interview (PRO: BA1/22). In correspondence with the Committee, Goldsmith emphasised that 'the decentralization of CSSB in the way I have suggested is essential' (PRO: BA1/39).

'It is questionable whether any system of selection can achieve the kind of accuracy we have aimed at, particularly with young and inexperienced candidates in their final year at a university,' Goldsmith stated in his evidence to the Committee;

> Both Method I and Method II have achieved, in the main, what they set out to do and provided the Service with recruits who with very few exceptions are expected to reach the upper middle ranks in their Class where in the Administrative Class, the Diplomatic Service, or the Tax Inspectorate. But follow up operations show that a disconcerting number of officers who have served long enough to be recognized as fliers were not so assessed at the time of selection, and statistical treatment of the follow-up material suggests that at least 50 per cent of those rejected might also have reached the upper middle ranks, although at the cost of a much higher proportion of failures than at present. But one would need to be more confident about the validity and reliability of departmental recording for such statistical treatment to be accepted as accurate evidence (PRO: BA1/22).

It was at least interesting evidence that emphasised the complexities of the issues relating to direct entry recruitment that the Committee faced, and to which we will return after considering the main evidence that it received about post-entry training.

2. Centralised post-entry training in the home civil service

When a Treasury memorandum submitted to the Fulton Committee on 6 April 1966 stated that 'most Civil Service training is provided by individual departments for their own staff' (PRO: BA1/12) the intention must have been to emphasise the obvious. Then again, when the FDA (PRO: BA1/21), the CSCA (PRO: BA1/24), and the Civil Service Union (PRO: BA1/22) noted the need for adequate staff margins to facilitate greater provision for training, those staff associations naturally did not make much of this because they were only emphasising practicalities. Further, when the IPCS told the Committee how much it welcomed the Osmond review of training and then made clear its belief that 'for all Classes and groups management training should be an integral part of career development' (PRO: BA1/30), the staff association was underlining the expectations present within the Service. It was only the exceptional piece of evidence that was submitted to the Fulton Committee which considered post-entry training in general terms at all, let alone the practicalities. This was particularly true of the evidence from outside the Service. Overwhelmingly, such evidence concentrated on the future central provision of formal post-entry training for entrants to whatever was to succeed the Assistant Principal grade of the Administrative Class. 'The setting up of the Centre for Administrative Studies in 1963, and the decision to send all Assistant Principals on a twenty week course there represents a significant advance on the thinking of the years following the publication of the Assheton Report,' wrote Nevil Johnson, who went on to add that 'there is little of the spirit of professionalism to which the *Ecole Nationale d'Administration* is unashamedly committed' (PRO: BA1/24). These sentiments were shared by others, though few took the trouble, unlike the former official, to present the Committee with a preferred and developed training programme of their own.

That the CAS should be expanded into a Civil Service College was a proposal that was advanced by several of those who gave evidence. The economist, Ralph Turvey, for instance, suggested that 'the Centre should be given extended functions' and translated into 'an institution of higher learning' which would conduct research including 'examinations of policy questions' (PRO: BA1/29). The academic, Trevor Smith, wrote that 'there is a strong case for the creation of a Civil Service Staff College operating within the Civil Service framework.' This College would provide 'a variety of courses in specialist administration for members of the management grade to be attended after two or three years service', 'more general executive development courses for those mid-career civil servants selected as potential policy makers from the management grade and from the Professional and Scientific Classes', and 'extended advanced seminars for senior policy makers.' Smith believed that 'a prestigious College would foster a sense of *esprit de corps* and would help in developing a code of ethics for civil servants' (PRO: BA1/27).

Professor Peter Self told the Committee that

> at present training for Assistant Principals concentrated very much on economics and statistics. Those subjects were very important parts of the administrator's training and something like the present course at the CAS should continue to be given to all recruits who were not already

educated in economics and statistics. However, economics and statistics alone were not a sufficient training for the job of the modern administrator and needed to be put into a wider context ... A general training in the social sciences should be provided by a year's course for all administrative recruits. Preferably it should take place immediately after entry but if for practical reasons the Civil Service found it better to give it after, say, two years then he would see no objection. Performance on the course should be taken into account in assessing recruits' potential and sorting them out.

In addition to this training of recruits, Self said that 'administrators should go on specialized courses according to the work they were doing later in their careers from the thirties onwards.' He thought that 'the Civil Service should run its own administrative training centre or Staff College which would undertake the greater part of the year's course for recruits. Graduate schools of government administration should be set up in one or two universities to take part in the training of administrators. Civil servants would normally attend these schools for specialized courses later in their careers, and also part of the training of recruits should take place there' (PRO: BA1/7).

Thomas Balogh told the Committee that

he would like to see a Civil Service College which would give post graduate training like a university. The course should be for a year or longer, with some practical administration sandwiched in on the lines of the French method. The first half of the course might consist of social sciences and mathematics and the second half, after the practical experience, would deal with administrative problems. The students would be re-examined at the end of the course and the successful ones would get a diploma. There would be wastage of about 30 to 40 per cent who might go into industry, which should then pay for their training. The College should be headed by a Vice Chancellor and should have one or two Deans but the Professors and teaching staff should be part-timers brought in from various universities. If alternatively it was thought better to attach the College to an existing university, then Oxford and Cambridge would be better than the others because they were big enough to have constant rows going on and this was stimulating (PRO: BA1/2).

The idea of a Civil Service College naturally appealed to, say, the IPCS (PRO: BA1/30), and the Labour Party matched the academics with its proposal for 'a greatly expanded CAS which should have the size and status of a graduate school of government' (PRO: BA1/27). Some other evidence favoured less exclusive forms of training. International Computers and Tabulators thought rather grandly in terms of 'a civilian version of the Imperial Defence College' drawing students in late career from 'the Civil Service, industry, the nationalized industries, local government, and the universities.' Mid-career training was to be conducted at a business school, and initial training within the Civil Service itself (PRO: BA1/24).

In his evidence, Sir George Mallaby drew attention to the work of the Committee on the Staffing of Local Government that he was chairing, which he said was going to recommend that 'at about age 40, there should be a Civil Staff College course for those senior officers at Brigadier level in local government, the Civil Service, and industry who were likely to rise to the very top posts.' Mallaby indicated other proposals, including management training at 30, and arrangements involving earlier formal qualifications being obtained following training (PRO: BA1/5). The Mallaby Committee's findings were later circulated to the Fulton Committee (PRO: BA1/35), and the Mallaby Report itself specifically mentioned the Imperial Defence College as an example to be followed (Mallaby Report, 1966, paras.381–5).

The TUC proposed a National Planning College which, together with others, civil servants would attend (PRO: BA1/29), but when its representatives appeared before the Committee this idea was not developed (PRO: BA1/8), and the same was the case with the CBI's suggestions for more common training arrangements for those in private industry and in the Civil Service (PRO: BA1/5, BA1/25). Professor Self was one witness who opposed such common training on the grounds that the tasks involved were so different (PRO: BA1/7).

Two things marked out Nevil Johnson's memorandum from the general run of evidence submitted to the Committee about post-entry training. The first was that, in contrast to Self's view that effectively the Service could decide the timing of formal training, Johnson argued that appropriate training should begin before the allocation of new general graduate entry entrants to departments. Secondly, Johnson, following the French example to some extent, actually had an articulated scheme for management training which involved 'one year of formal instruction, one year of secondment outside central government, and up to four years of practical experience in departments.' Unlike some others, Johnson emphasised the need for the 'further development' of 'induction courses and management training for the Specialist Classes' (PRO: BA1/24).

What overshadowed the other evidence submitted to the Committee on post-entry training was the Report of the Treasury Working party on Management Training in the Civil Service, a summary of the findings of which was made available to the Committee by its Chairman, S. P. Osmond, as early as 12 September 1966 (PRO: BA1/20) with the Report itself being circulated on 6 February 1967. The terms of reference given to the Working Party required it 'to consider the training needs for middle and higher management in the Civil Service and to submit recommendations on the length, content and organization of such training, taking account of the long term future of the CAS and the desirability, or otherwise of setting up a Civil Service Staff College.' Besides Osmond himself, for most of its existence the Working Party comprised four serving officials (M. E. Allen of the Diplomatic Service Administration Office, R. Haynes of the Ministry of Defence, C. D. E.

Keeling of the Treasury, and C. H. Sisson of the Ministry of Labour), four representatives of the Civil Service staff associations (R. A. Hayward, R. B. M. King, William McCall, and Leslie Williams), three academics (Professors Jean Blondel, D. C. Hague and E. A. G. Robinson), and one representative of private industry (J. Parsons of Guest Keen and Nettlefolds).

The Working Party recommended that 'up to the age of about thirty, training for management should be based on two pairs of courses – a 4 week and an 8 week course for a substantial number of staff and two 20 week courses for a smaller number of selected staff.' In its view,

> all graduate entrants and the eighteen year old intake to the General Management Class should take a 4 week Introduction to Management Course at about the age of twenty-five. On the strength of departmental reports and performance on this course, the most outstanding would be selected to take the two 20 week courses. The first would have much the same content as the present 20 week course at the Centre for Administrative Studies and would be taken at about the age of twenty five. The second course would cover further subjects and would be taken at about the age of twenty-eight.

The Working Party also recommended that 'graduate and eighteen year old entrants expected by the age of thirty to reach eventually Chief Executive Officer or higher, but who had not been selected for the 20 week course at the age of twenty-five, would take an 8 week Middle Management course. On the basis of departmental reports and performance on the course, the most outstanding would be selected to take the second of the 20 week courses.' The Working Party said that 'Professional and Scientific civil servants would be eligible, if their training needs and potential future advancement justified it, to attend either or both the 20 week courses. For some wishing to move into general management at the age of thirty attendance at the 8 week course might be followed by the second of the 20 week courses.' They anticipated that

> for staff in mid-career and later, management training would be flexible, related to the needs of the department, and the development of the individual and should as far as possible provide opportunities for the civil servants to study in the company of businessmen and staff from other occupations. Some would attend courses at the new Business Schools, or at the Administrative Staff College, and others might take courses of similar length at other institutions. Periods of release to become familiar with the background to new posts – sabbatical and study leave would also be important. Seminars, some organized by the Civil Service and others by outside organizations, would keep older civil servants informed of developments in management.

The Working Party said that 'any development of management training in the Civil Service should be based on a far more extensive research programme than at present', and they envisaged that 'the training recommended . . .

would be planned and directed by a single Civil Service organization. Courses would be run in a Civil Service management training establishment in two parts – a non-residential London centre developed out of the present Centre for Administrative Studies, and a residential centre out of, but with good communications to, London.'

A possible division of work between the residential and non residential centres would be 'on a functional basis with the London centre specializing in the particular fields in which the Centre for Administrative Studies has acquired experience – economics, economic statistics, decision theory, and industry – while the residential centre specialized in the study of government, social administration and statistics, organization and staff management.' The Working Party recommended that 'staff already in mid-career when the new plan was introduced would receive a modified plan of management training,' and it recognised that 'the success of the new plan will depend on effective career development, job rotation, and appraisal procedures being applied to more staff than at present.' They emphasised that they had

> thought it right to build on the best features of the present system rather than abandon it for some completely new concept. This is why we propose to develop the new organization from the CAS and to combine training with practical experience and job rotation rather than to have a lengthy period of formal training with little or no practical background. It is for this reason too that we advocate the development of the existing central management of Treasury training courses in the form of an organization which, even though perhaps under another name, will give the Civil Service a Staff College, which many have advocated over the last twenty or twenty five years (PRO: BA1/30).

When S. P. Osmond and C. D. E. Keeling appeared before the Fulton Committee on 14 March 1967 as representatives of the Treasury Working Party, the former observed about that body's activities that

> we were almost bound to do our work on the assumption that in some form or other the Civil Service takes in people with general qualifications or general education rather than recruits . . . a series of specialists, partly because this is not only the kind of Service we have today but, with certain variations, is the kind of Service, at any rate as far as the General Management Classes are concerned, that has been recommended to you from various sources including the Treasury and the Society of Civil Servants.

As Keeling was Director of Training and Education at the Treasury, naturally enough the exchanges with the Committee involved a defence of the particular manner in which the CAS had developed, as well as consideration of the Osmond Working Party's proposals. At one point in the evidence, when Osmond observed about the need for management training in the Scientific Civil Service that 'I would accept that there is a need for more of that than we have done in the past,' Sir William Cook commented that 'you have done damn all in the past.' More commonly, though, the exchanges tended to be bland.

Osmond told the Committee that 'we have not found . . . that people with economics degrees have been wasting their time or being bored or failing to learn anything in the economics part of the Centre for Administrative Studies because part of that work at any rate is concerned with applying a measure of economic knowledge to the problems of government.' He emphasised that 'we have not been trying to produce professional economists' only 'administrators with more understanding of basic economic concepts.' Robert Neild observed that

> if you want everyone to have some grasp of economics, this, that and the other, an all rounder, then you are content with a fairly thin layer of economics, with ten mornings or whatever it is, it may be sufficient, but where I have difficulty with this Report is in trying to decide what you were trying to give these people. It is all under this portfolio term "Management Training" – one of those ghastly portfolio words that can mean many things to different people – and when you come down to it . . . I can see it contains economics and statistics combined with ADP as a particular form of statistical analysis, but what really does it contain beyond that?

This was as much a statement as a question, which invited, as it received, a factual reply about organisation theory and other subject matters. When Sir James Dunnett said that 'I think it would be very odd if the Civil Service were the one large organization in the country which had no residential training', Osmond agreed, having earlier stated that 'the thing to avoid, it seemed to us, was first of all any arrangement which could be basically very unpopular.' This might be thought to have been a curious priority, but the issue was not going to be pressed in questioning which the Treasury officials were able to field with comfort.

Oddly, only Sir William Cook on the Committee raised the matter of the ENA and the contrast that this approach represented compared with that of the CAS and the Working Party's proposals. Cook asked, 'Rather than this method of training or education, whatever word you like to use, taking people from any sort of background and twisting them round in this way, would you not be better to adopt the French system?' Understandably, S. P. Osmond preferred the Working Party's scheme, though it was interesting that one of his main reasons was that 'I think there is very little opportunity for a man in the French system to come up from below.' When Cook suggested that this was 'a detail', Osmond replied that it was 'a very important detail.' The Treasury official also commented that 'we had a French member of the Working Party who is something of an expert on the French system and it seems no part of his thesis that we should adopt the French system' (PRO: BA1/7). Professor Blondel's views, though well worth noting, did not settle the matter even in relation specifically to post-entry training, let alone the issue of 'preference for relevance' in the direct entry recruitment of administrators that was inherent in Cook's question.

3. 'Preference for relevance' in direct entry recruitment of administrators

'It appeared to be becoming generally agreed that the old idea of a Platonic Guardian class, that is, of an Administrative Class of able men recruited irrespective of their educational discipline and expected to apply common sense and intelligence to the problems of government as they arose, was extinct,' W. J. M. Mackenzie, at that time the doyen of British political science told the Fulton Committee (PRO: BA1/6).

To judge from their evidence to that Committee, as we shall see, some leading contemporary politicians still saw a place for this sort of 'Guardian class' and expressed opposition towards 'preference for relevance' in the direct entry recruitment of administrators, as did several other witnesses. The 'greater number of witnesses either dislike or see no need for such preference,' the Committee's Secretariat recorded in its digest of evidence. Others 'took up a mid-way position' and, correctly, few were cited as advocating 'preference for relevance' (PRO: BA1/38). However, a different classification emerges if one categorises the evidence in terms of those who still wanted 'irrelevant' direct entry recruitment of administrators without 'relevant' post-entry training, and those who did not. After all, the former arrangements had been those which had characterised the Administrative Class when Sir Edward Bridges and Sir Norman Brook had held the post of Head of the Home Civil Service only a few years before. Using this classification, conservatives in this sense, like the radicals, were outnumbered. When he gave evidence it was clear that Lord Bridges had come to hold 'a mid-way position' in those terms, even if Lord Normanbrook had not. Various forms of pragmatic or moderate reformist positions in fact typified much of the evidence, often being rendered conservative in effect because of an inability to look beyond the framework of reference that the existing Civil Service represented. The CAS, even an expanded successor institution, was not the only line of development in post-entry training that could be proposed for the Service. Those witnesses who relied on 'relevant' post-entry training to offset 'irrelevant' direct entry recruitment of administrators rarely envisaged anything as formidable as a form of the French system, and failed to see the overriding necessity to make performance in such training a decisive element in careers if it was to change the administrative culture.

To one side of the main debate were those who advocated 'preference for relevance' for applicants with scientific degrees. The Royal Society (PRO: BA1/25), the Royal Institute of Chemistry (PRO: BA1/29), and Sir Arnold Hall, an industrialist and a former Principal Scientific Officer in the Civil Service (PRO: BA1/2) all proposed this. They got a predictable response from Sir George Mallaby, a former First Civil Service Commissioner, who thought that 'the argument that more scientists should be attracted into the Administrative Class was misguided. They should join the Scientific Civil Service and start by doing the scientific job they wanted to do. Those who were suited should move into management jobs at a later stage. It was a waste of a good scientists to put him into the Administrative Class from the start' (PRO: BA1/10). Lord Normanbrook took a similar line (PRO: BA1/3). By implication, the professionalisation of science cast doubt upon the abilities of those who did not wish to persist with it.

The main debate, of course, was about whether or not 'preference for relevance' should be given to those with degrees in economics and related subjects, and among the politicians who gave evidence radical attitudes were in short supply. Enoch Powell, a former Minister of Health, forthrightly asserted his preference for the lay administrator over the professional, being prepared to exclude the latter from leading administrative posts even if he or she had the necessary personal qualities. Powell believed that 'those with an education in the humanities, notably Classics, English, and (to a lower extent) modern languages, who had been trained in the precise use of words, had a great advantage' (PRO: BA1/4).

Denis Healey, the then Secretary of State for Defence, thought that numeracy was less important than literacy, adding that

> members of the Administrative Class with a background of, say, Greats, were in general quite good at counting when necessary; nor was the orientation of the arts man to science an insurmountable problem, provided that he had a good brain. It was not therefore necessary to recruit to the Administrative Class more men with a background in economics (a bastard branch of the bastard science of psychology) merely in order to improve the level of numeracy. A knowledge of advanced economics was not necessary at the level of the Administrative Class. Moreover, a man who had read economics years ago and still considered himself an expert in the subject might be positively harmful (PRO: BA1/3).

Reginald Maudling considered that 'the suggestion that administrators in the economics departments should have a university education in economics was nonsense. If it were true that administrators needed such an education, then it would be equally true that Ministers needed it.' That prior knowledge of economics might well be an advantage to the holder of the post of Chancellor of the Exchequer, as Maudling had once been, does not seem to be that outrageous a notion, but Maudling plainly thought otherwise, going on to say that 'civil servants in the Treasury needed a fair degree of understanding of economics but not necessarily an academic background in the subject, which, indeed, might often be a drawback' because 'a vestigial tail of expert knowledge was often accompanied by a vestigial tail of expert prejudices.' Maudling was prepared to envisage post-entry training for administrators, although this would be to enable them 'to understand the language of, say, economics, but not necessarily to speak it' (PRO: BA1/6).

Aubrey Jones, another former Conservative minister, 'would not advocate the recruitment of a different type of man to the Administrative Class,' but 'a wider training' in the form of secondments outside the Service (PRO: BA1/3). Roy Jenkins, the then Home Secretary, was 'a strong supporter of retaining the role of the administrator pretty well in its traditional form.' He was 'against the grouping of departments for the purposes of recruitment and movement of staff,' and while he envisaged recruits then having 'an academic training more directly related to government activities' he was 'reluctant to accept that it was essential' (PRO: BA1/30).

Anthony Crosland, the then Secretary of State for Education and Science, said that 'he did not think that the educational background, which was usually non-specialized, of the average administrator, was a disadvantage. As far as his Department was concerned he would be content to continue to get a reasonable cross-section of graduates. The matter might be different in the Treasury and the DEA' (PRO: BA1/4). Of the politicians who gave evidence, Richard Crossman, the then Leader of the House of Commons, was the one who came closest to a radical position when he told the Committee that 'personally he would take what he could get but other things being equal he would prefer the Civil Service to recruit to the Administrative Class some men – not necessarily all but more perhaps than at present – with an education in relevant subjects' (PRO: BA1/7).

Radicalism did not characterise the evidence that those connected with academic life gave to the Committee on this matter, since only Professors Nicholas Kaldor and Claus Moser advocated 'preference for relevance.' Moser said that 'this would have a great and excellent effect on the universities. The typical school leaver was now much more technocratically minded – a change visible over the last ten years. Nothing was more damaging to Civil Service recruitment than its image as an occupation essentially for arts graduates with a wide background . . . the Civil Service needed to offer jobs in all its branches in which one could become an expert' (PRO: BA1/7). Kaldor said that the main problem was the need to introduce more professionalism into the Civil Service. He was sceptical about 'the intellectual brilliance and adaptability of the Greats man' as the ideal administrator, and 'taking the Treasury as an example, it was a policy making department in the financial and economic field and therefore its recruits should have a degree in economics' (PRO: BA1/3). At the other end of the spectrum, Elizabeth Chilver, a university administrator and a former civil servant, was against 'preference for relevance', believing that 'the Civil Service should recruit on general ability, irrespective of the subjects which a candidate has read.' She thought that administration was too diverse for there to be 'relevant' university courses, and she expressed pessimism about the personal qualities of those who would be attracted to such courses should they be devised (PRO: BA1/4).

This was at least a straightforward position in some contrast with the complex evidence of Professor W. J. M. Mackenzie, whose views taken as a whole did not entirely justify the conservatism ascribed to him in the official digest of evidence (PRO: BA1/38). Some of his evidence was conservative because he followed up the remark which was cited earlier, that the conventional Administrative Class was widely seen as being obsolete, with further observations that there were 'no easy criteria to determine the background and the personal characteristics required for the policy making element of the Civil Service in a technological age,' and 'it would be wrong for the Committee to recommend proposals for the Civil Service which would only be valid on the assumption of one kind of environment in the future.' So, 'bearing in mind . . . the need to hold open the options,' Professor Mackenzie, a Greats man himself, thought that 'the Civil Service should continue entry of the traditional kind, that is very able men irrespective of their discipline, out of which flyers should be selected.' Though he recognised the need 'to bring in professionalism from the relevant disciplines,' Mackenzie emphasised the difficulties in grouping departments for any form of specialised recruitment from the social sciences (PRO: BA1/6). Those conservative sentiments, however, conflicted with the other views that the distinguished political scientist expressed about the future structure of the Civil Service which were undermining of the career service and, hence, a radical departure from existing arrangements.

Most witnesses connected with academic life preferred to rely on post-entry training rather than on direct entry recruitment to ensure that administrators possessed 'relevant' knowledge. Given his earlier polemic lauding economists, it was surprising that Thomas Balogh took this line. Possibly through subsequent experience within the machinery of government, Balogh had come 'to believe that it was a good thing to recruit people educated in different disciplines, including Classics. One could train them after entry . . . on the lines of the French method' (PRO: BA1/2). Balogh's position as it had developed was perhaps more fully expressed in a letter to Robert Neild dated 25 July 1967, sent after Balogh had talked with Sir Edward Boyle. Balogh wrote that

> one thing he said rather worried me . . . It seems that there is an opinion which holds that the recruitment of young men should be biased in favour of social studies, especially economics. I myself would feel that this would be an acute – albeit rather more sophisticated – form of our inveterate tendency to amateurism. I do not believe that a young man with a BA, even it it is in economics, needs no further training or that his university curriculum would so decisively influence his further career as to make compensatory increases in training impossible. Given the disastrous shortcomings of the British educational system which seems determined to enforce specialization at the ripe age of fourteen or fifteen, it seems to me that we should revert to the Trevelyan system of recruitment through written examinations with rather less, possibly 25 per cent, emphasis on interview. We should then put the young men through a

training course which might be more elaborate in those cases where the man is obviously fitted for an economic development by his general quantifying capacity (though not necessarily mathematical). In this way, one would be able to get the best people who have been badly advised still within the Service without having the disasters of Bridgerism. Moreover, there are a number of departments where sociological and historical inclinations are far better than economic ones and where the training course should be accordingly modified. I feel that we have gone far too far in the direction of economics. The syllabus of the Administrative University, as I should like it to be called, should be elaborated by a separate commission on which all social sciences should be represented (Crowther-Hunt Papers: Box 9).

Among other academics, Peter Self said in his evidence that 'the British system . . . of recruiting administrators among the ablest products of higher education regardless of discipline should be continued because it provided a less inbred Service and a lively mixture of backgrounds. However, for his job in modern government the administrator should have a general social science training in economics, some sociology (with particular emphasis on social structure), comparative government and administration, organization theory etc.' As noted earlier, Professor Self looked to post-entry training to provide this background (PRO: BA1/7). An academic authority on social administration, Richard Titmuss was 'sceptical about the value of a specialized degree,' and he praised the 'good material' that Oxford and Cambridge provided for the Service, while envisaging 'the right specialized training' being given to them in a university in later career (PRO: BA1/4). Lord Redcliffe-Maud told the Committee that in the direct entry recruitment of administrators, 'the need was for men trained in a robust and exacting intellectual discipline irrespective of the subject. However, it followed that the responsibility for training in relevant subjects lay with the Service itself' (PRO: BA1/5).

Not surprisingly, the FDA believed that 'it is right to continue to recruit administrators, regardless of the subject of their degree, according to their ability and personal qualities' (PRO: BA1/21), and most serving and former administrators agreed, even if outright conservatives were in a minority. Citing Enoch Powell's views on the virtues of the lay administrator with approval, Lord Normanbrook said that 'members of the Administrative Class who read economics years ago were no good as economists; they were the real amateurs. There was a need for members of the Administrative Class who were able to communicate with economists but they should not be treated as experts' (PRO: BA1/3). Nobody was suggesting though, that, should the Civil Service introduce 'relevant' recruitment of administrators, it would cease to employ economists, and for communication with them it was difficult to see how having no knowledge was preferable to possessing some knowledge. Sir George Abell, the First Civil Service Commissioner, saw 'positive advantage in a variety of educational backgrounds in the Administrative

Class, and would think it a bad thing if the pendulum swing so far that it was manned only be economists and social scientists' (PRO: BA1/3). C. H. Sisson, of the Ministry of Labour, doubted whether there was more than a marginal advantage in having read a relevant subject. He said that 'the benefits . . . would be quite real, but they would wear off in time' (PRO: BA1/7). Nevertheless, 'a marginal advantage' might be worth having. S. P. Osmond and Desmond Keeling, giving evidence on behalf of the Treasury Working Party on Management Training said that experience at the CAS was that 'a man with a good Classics degree was better than a man with a bad economics degree.' However, they conceded that 'those with a degree in a relevant subject absorbed the . . . training more quickly and more thoroughly'(PRO: BA1/2).

'It was no longer sufficient to recruit an administrator who could "use" experts while remaining quite innocent of their ways of thought,' Lord Franks told the Committee; observing that 'the great problem was the split between quantitative and literary education', for which a short term solution might be 'to run one year courses at three of four universities for new graduate entrants to the Civil Service in which those who were under-educated either in quantitative or in analytical (i.e. generalist) ways of thought could be taught to "navigate in both languages" ' (PRO: BA1/3).

Most of the other serving or former officials who gave evidence did not favour 'preference for relevance' in recruitment, but they were not normally wholly dismissive about post-entry training. Sir Maurice Dean, formerly Permanent Secretary of the Ministry of Technology, did say that 'it was possible to have too much training,' but he did favour there being 'a fourth year at university studying relevant subjects such as economics' (PRO: BA1/2). Sir Richard Powell, Permanent Secretary of the Board of Trade, said that 'the flyer could cope with any problems whatever his education' and prior knowledge of economics did get out of date, but he did concede that administrators of 'only average ability might do better than now if they had formal training in the social sciences' (PRO: BA1/3). Sir Richard Way, Permanent Secretary of the Ministry of Aviation, was 'not in favour of restricting recruitment to graduates who had done some relevant course, since that would simply mean losing good potential civil servants. If anything was to be done before entry it would have to be a fourth year in public administration, but in his view it would be better to have the course of formal training after the recruit had been in the Civil Service two or three years' (PRO: BA1/2).

Dame Evelyn Sharp, formerly Permanent Secretary at the Ministry of Housing and Local Government, said that there was no need for recruits to the Administrative Class to have a highly specialised education

> It was not necessary to recruit hordes of economists and other specialists, but more a just proportion. Administrators should be equipped with an understanding of the quantitative approach to problems and she herself had felt a personal lack of that in her background. Post entry training

should give administrators a sufficient knowledge of the language of economics, statistics and so forth to know when a problem required specialist advice and to understand that advice. It was not necessary to go beyond that because the higher civil servant's job was politics. There was no department in which the general administrator was not needed; even in such departments as the Ministry of Aviation and the Ministry of Technology civil servants were still under a political master who needed political advice. That, rather than some other professional speciality, must be the background of senior civil servants (PRO: BA1/4).

In view of his past opinions, the most interesting evidence that the Committee received was that of Lord Bridges, who had come to believe that

the Civil Service ought to recruit many more men part at least of whose education had been in relevant subjects. Some progress had been made, for instance, in building up the economical and statistical sides of the Service, but the process should go a lot further. The Civil Service had been rather slow in bringing in men trained in the social sciences, and should make more use of university courses in management and public administration. It would be a good thing to have more recruits to the Administrative Class educated in the natural and applied sciences. However, while trying to get more recruits with an education in these and other relevant subjects, the Service should do nothing to rule out men with a good general background, that is to say a good degree irrespective of its subject. To do so would be to lose some of the very best potential talent. A highly intellectual man with a trained mind could readily acquire the necessary background in relevant subjects on courses after recruitment to the Service (PRO: BA1/8).

Sir Douglas Allen, then the leading administrator at the DEA, was widely believed to be the only Permanent Secretary who advocated 'preference for relevance' in evidence to the Committee (e.g. Hennessey et al., 1988, p.48; Hennessey, 1989, p.204) but, in fact, the then Head of the Home Civil Service, Sir Laurence Helsby, did so too. He was against dividing the Civil Service into groups of departments to obtain specialisation. The Civil Service manager of the future over the whole field would need to be a 'professional in management with a greater knowledge of the special skills and techniques relevant to his job, including statistics, economics and some of the techniques of social studies.' While he looked to post-entry training 'perhaps more intensive than that recommended in the Osmond Working Party Report,' and while retaining the Method II means of entry as a general test of administrative potential, he suggested a remodelled Method I, instituting 'a written examination in those subjects only which were relevant to the work of Government; to say that this indicated the special interest of the Civil Service in these subjects and that it offered a special method of entry to those who had qualified in them.' Sir Laurence recognised the possibility that 'a new Method I on these lines would lead to some universities specializing in preparing for it and to some students choosing their university on this basis,' but he saw 'no harm in that.' Helsby linked 'relevance' and the starring of some graduate entrants (PRO: BA1/8); and, in his evidence, Allen was clear that the Civil Service should introduce a bias in its recruitment processes to 'favour the study of subjects which were useful to government, which meant economics and related subjects and qualifications in them should enhance career prospects' (PRO: BA1/9).

So, with important exceptions, the main evidence that the Fulton Committee received was antipathetic to 'preference for relevance' in the direct entry recruitment of administrators. Of course, the Committee had no need to reflect the balance of this evidence in its recommendations, and, in fact, a majority of the Committee took a radical line.

The Fulton Committee's Deliberations

The 'sketch of the task' that its Chairman presented to the Fulton Committee on 20 June 1966 prior to its Sunningdale Conference inevitably gave prominence to '(a) the Civil Servant's education, (b) recruitment, (c) training – immediate post-entry training and through-career' as major issues (PRO: BA1/17). The expansion of the general graduate entry to the Service and the question of 'starring' certain graduates within that intake, which were, of course, matters of structure as well as of recruitment, did attract a substantial amount of attention from the Committee in its deliberations; and this was the case too, as will be seen, with the issue of 'preference for relevance' in the recruitment of administrators. The Committee, though, gave less time in its deliberations to the methods and procedures of direct entry recruitment and questions of post-entry training than might have been anticipated in principle, and among the reasons for this were developments actual and proposed within the Civil Service that impinged on its work. Two items from the minutes of the Committee's meeting held on 17 January 1967 illustrate this.

In the first of them, it was recorded that the Chairman said that Sir George Abell (First Civil Service Commissioner) had written to him to ask for a talk about the possibility of abolishing the Method I competition while the Committee was still sitting. 'It was agreed that the Chairman should tell Sir George that the Committee were not at present able to bless this step and must reserve their right to grumble if Method I had been abolished in advance of their Report.' The next item was about the Treasury's Working Party on Management Training, and the minutes record that the Secretary said that Mr Osmond had consulted him about the publication of the Working Party's Report: 'It would be submitted simultaneously to the Chancellor, by whom the Working Party had been set up, and to the Committee. Since the staff associations were represented on the Working Party and very keenly interested, the Report must be expected to leak, and for this and other reasons the Treasury would like to publish it. The Committee instructed the Secretary to tell Mr Osmond that they would like to see the Report before taking a decision on this' (PRO: BA1/6).

Following the circulation of the Report (PRO: BA1/30), at its meeting on 14 February 1967 the Committee stated that it wanted more time to consider the material before agreeing to its publication, and it also insisted on seeing 'a draft of any covering statement that would be made about its status' (PRO: BA1/7). This draft was circulated (PRO: BA1/31), and at its meeting on 21 February the Committee 'agreed that they would not wish to object to the publication of the Working Party's Report if their wishes could be met on two points.' The first of these was that

> the draft Parliamentary Answer and Press hand-out should be amended to make clear that in spite of the fact that the Working Party had been set up independently and had reported to the Chancellor, its Report was now being referred to the Committee as a piece of evidence to be considered in the same way as the rest of the evidence. It would meet the case if the words "and will be considered by the Committee as part of the evidence submitted to them" could be added at the end of the second sentence of the Parliamentary Answer and appropriately in the Press hand-out.

The second point was that 'there should be a private exchange of letters between the Chairman and Sir Laurence Helsby making clear that the Committee agreed to the publication of the Report on the understanding that this would in no way inhibit their freedom to express other views or put forward different recommendations on the subject of management training in their own Report in due course' (PRO: BA1/7).

The statement that the Chancellor of the Exchequer, James Callaghan, made to the House of Commons on 7 March 1967 about the Osmond Working Party's Report (742 HC Deb. 5s. Written Answers. c.239) took the form that the Fulton Committee insisted on, as did the Press statement. The Committee's insistence on its right to have an independent position, however, did not mean that it had one. The Committee visited the CAS on 7 June 1966 and, to judge from the record, the reaction of some members was critical. Robert Neild, for instance, said that

> having looked at the syllabus of the twenty weeks course and at some of the lecture notes supplied by the Centre, he thought that so much ground was covered in the time that it was inevitable that the knowledge would be spread wide and thin. He wondered therefore whether the course was really meeting its objective of enabling members of the Administrative Class to communicate with specialists in economics and statistics. The course was unlikely to be related to the work an Assistant Principal had been doing in his department beforehand or to that he would be doing afterwards, since he would usually find himself in a Private Office job fairly soon. He thought that the course for Assistant Principals from the economic departments should be longer and more

profound, and that for the others there should be shorter periods of formal training alternating with and relating to the work of their departments (PRO: BA1/3).

As his questioning of witnesses and other interventions indicate, Neild admired the French system of training higher civil servants and wanted something similar for Britain. Not all his colleagues shared his views. For the model of the Civil Service College to follow, Sir Philip Allen later observed, 'What I had in mind was something like the Police Staff College at Bramshill' (Interview, 1988). Though the example would be one that was familiar to a civil servant with experience in the Home Office, it was not surprising that other members of the Committee had a different view. Even without dwelling on the past controversies associated with the former Metropolitan Police College at Hendon, the history of central training in the Police Service did not suggest that it was necessarily an example that the Civil Service needed to follow (Cmd. 7070, 1947; 1450, 1961; 1728, 1962, paras 308–16; Police Council 1962; Police Council 1963a–e; Parker, 1980, pp.219–32; Parker, 1990, pp.453–75), and a critical review of higher training courses at Bramshill prepared for the Home Office by the Department of Education and Science in 1969 (Home Office 1969) tended to confirm this.

If the Fulton Committee was going to depart markedly from the Osmond Report's scheme, it had to devise plans of its own, possibly by means of a special sub-committee, and commission supporting research activity. No such plans were made. The Committee decided at its meeting on 11 July 1967 that 'the Report should be ambitious about scale and numbers. There should be both a residential college and a centre for non-residential training . . . The residential college might be at Greenwich, as the Prime Minister had suggested' and 'the non-residential centre should probably be separate and in Central London.' The Committee thought that 'it would be desirable to make courses, both at Greenwich and elsewhere, open to participants from private industry and commerce, nationalized industries, local government etc. This applied both to the early courses in the general service training grade and to later management courses.' Further, 'in addition to internal training courses, there should be a big expansion of external training. In particular, selected 18 year old entrants to the general service should be sent outside to get degrees . . . and entrants to the scientific and technological services should be sent to get degrees in engineering etc. Use should also be made of business schools; the Service should not attempt to be self sufficient in training.' The Committee thought that links with universities should be as wide as possible, 'and Greenwich should itself carry out research into administration and government problems. Some members thought that the idea of a link with a single graduate school attached to one university was not therefore attractive; it would be apt to restrict contact with, and the recruitment both of teaching staff and of entrants to the Service from, other universities; and would discourage the Civil Service from doing its own research. Others nevertheless saw some advantage in a university link.' The Committee recognised that 'there should be a distinction between central and departmental training. Many departments would still need to train their own staff, e.g. the Inland Revenue Tax Inspectorate . . . but some departmental training might be taken over by the centre' (PRO BA1/9).

At the Committee's meeting on 1 August 1967, the Secretary reported that the Prime Minister had now gone on record to the effect that the Royal Naval College at Greenwich should be considered as a possible site for a Civil Service College and related administrative arrangements were indicated (PRO: BA1/10). As far as the general graduate entry was concerned, the Committee had decided at its meeting on 3 and 4 July that 'recruits to the management training grade should spend a year or two years in departments before going to training courses in order, first, to get the feel of things, and, secondly, to determine whether they should be kept in the Service and what level of training and career they should be given.' The Committee added that 'performance on training courses should be taken into account in determining the level at which trainees passed out of the training grade' (PRO: BA1/9). The importance which the reformers on the Committee placed on formal post-entry training for administrators ought to have led them to recognise that if the relevant courses were to be seen as having the desired status they needed to be located at the outset of the administrators' careers, and performance on those courses needed to be a decisive element in the careers of the civil servants concerned and not just 'taken into account.'

The Management Consultancy Group's observations that the 'total training effort' in the Civil Service was 'very impressive by any standards' and that 'in our experience it was on a scale rarely matched by industry' (PRO: BA1/74) was in some contrast with the criticisms made by academics over the years; and the Fulton Committee's own treatment of the subject in its Report was surprisingly brief, and certainly lacked not only a cutting edge but, after agreement at the Committee's meeting on 2 April 1968 not to include an appendix on training at the Civil Service College (PRO: BA1/11), it lacked detail too. The Fulton Report, naturally enough, recommended the establishment of a Civil Service College with a training and research role (Cmnd. 3638, 1968, paras 99–103). The College was to have its own governing body 'consisting not only of civil servants but also of men and women drawn from a wide range of interests outside the Service,' while also being 'under the general direction of the Civil Service Department which will be responsible for the training policy of the Service as a whole' (ibid., para.114). The Committee stressed the need for residential as well as non-residential provision for training and discussed location (ibid., para.104). On the crucial matter of the formal post-entry courses for administrators in early career the Committee stated that those were to be attended after the entrants had completed their probation (ibid., para.106). This was to take the same position as the Osmond Working Party, and indeed the Fulton Committee's observations about post-entry training generally departed little from the Working Party's scheme, a reality that was not disguised by omitting to acknowledge this.

The Fulton Committee recommended that 'the Civil Service Commission should cease to be a separate and independent organization' becoming 'part of the new Civil Service Department' (ibid., para.63) which was an important change; but the limits of the Committee's radicalism were exemplified by its observation that 'we considered the case for handing all recruitment over to the departments; but we rejected this on the grounds that it would encourage wasteful competition, place the less glamourous departments at too great a disadvantage, and break up a Service which, in our view, should remain unified' (ibid., para.67). The Committee considered that 'in general . . . all non-specialist graduates and their equivalents should be recruited centrally by the appropriate section of the new Civil Service Department.' A majority of the Committee (Fulton, Allen, Anderson, Boyle, Dunnett, Hunt and Simey) wanted there to continue to be two main methods of entry for administrators (ibid., para.82) it being said that

> though Method I is clearly unsatisfactory and unfair in its present form, the majority of us consider that it should be retained in a modified form. It should remain primarily as a written examination. The papers set, however, should be limited to those that have an obvious vocational link with the work of one or other of the administrative groups or the further specialisms that may develop within them . . . It will be for the Civil Service Department to settle the precise subject a candidate may offer in the examination and also the number of papers a candidate will be required to take. We would expect the papers to offer candidates the opportunity of answering questions related to the problems of modern government in one or other of the following main fields – economics and business studies, social and administrative studies, science and technology (ibid., p.159)

The majority seemed to have been influenced by the ideas of Sir Laurence Helsby. A minority of the Committee (Cook, Kipping, Neild, Sheldon, Wall) wanted Method I to cease to exist altogether (ibid., para.84) as had been made evident at the Committee's meeting on 23 April 1968 (PRO: BA1/11).

Method II attracted criticism from the Committee, if insufficient of it initially for Robert Neild. In response to the record of the Committee's discussion of recruitment methods at its meeting on 11 July 1967 from which he was absent (PRO: BA1/9), Neild wrote to his fellow members, on 21 July 1967, saying,

> I am concerned to see . . . that the Committee has endorsed the view that the selection procedure should include a Final Interview Board in addition to the CSSB. When we were in France, the French told us that they regarded an individual interview of this kind as 'a dishonest method of selection.' I think their view is right. If a candidate has done his University examinations and has been through the CSSB, his academic

attainments, his administrative ability and his qualities of character will already have been assessed. What reason is there why a further interview should take place? I can see one possible reason. That is to see whether the candidate is congenial to his future boss and suited to the kind of work that he is going to do. But that would mean sending candidates to be interviewed in departments by those to whom they were going to work.

Neild thought that 'the personal interview' was a hangover from the period when the CSSB and proper training did not exist.

> It now entails duplication . . . Apart from adding up marks the Final Board can only act as an amateur psychological panel, eliminating unstable characters, or as a judge of 'character' and 'personality.' The first is better done at CSSB. The second is an expression of personal prejudice. But the personal prejudices of a board of people for whom the candidate is not going to work are irrelevant. They are likely to be capricious or unconsciously narcissistic (leading to a perpetuation of a species). In fact, I have been told that with this kind of interview there is little or no correlation between the marks awarded to the same candidate put before successive boards of different composition (PRO: BA1/43).

'No one starting from scratch would devise a three stage system today,' the Fulton Committee observed about Method II, in remarks plainly influenced by Neild's views; and the Committee also expressed 'serious doubts about the staffing and methods of work of the Civil Service Selection Board' as well as about 'the role, composition and method of work of the Final Selection Board' (Cmnd. 3638, 1968, p. 16f). These were matters which the Committee needed to follow up itself, but having earlier recommended that a further inquiry was needed to seek means of speeding up recruitment procedures (ibid., para.70), the Committee decided that the same body should be asked to make recommendations, within the framework of the Fulton Report, about 'reducing the subjective element in Method II' (ibid., p.16f).

At the meeting of the Fulton Committee on 30 January 1968, 'most members expressed support for giving preference for relevance to candidates who had studied relevant subjects' in the direct entry recruitment of administrators (PRO: BA1/11), and this majority comprised Fulton, Anderson, Boyle, Cook, Hunt, Neild, Sheldon and Wall. Hence, the minority consisted of Allen, Dunnett, Kipping and Simey. As we have seen, the Committee divided differently when it came to methods of open competitive direct entry of administrators. When it came to the structure that the administrators would be recruited to, the Committee's recommendation of a division between economic and financial administrators on the one hand and social administrators on the other was published without explicit dissent. Those not favouring 'preference for relevance' seemed to rely on post-entry training to provide the necessary background. The Committee's Management Consultancy

Group was critical of the effects on the work of the Civil Service of 'irrelevant' recruitment of administrators.

'The divisions in the Fulton Committee over "preference for relevance" were not obvious from the beginning,' Sir James Dunnett has said subsequently, 'although everybody knew about Norman Hunt's dislike of Classicists. It was the kind of issue that comes up after discussions. Much depended on what the "preference" was for. One could see that a knowledge of economics was valuable at the Treasury, but somebody like Douglas Allen, who advocated "preference for relevance", would not count PPE at Oxford, for instance, as necessarily relevant' (Interview, 1988).

'The divisions on the Committee about "preference for relevance" were there from the start' in the opinion of Robert Neild (Interview, 1988). 'That there were divisions among the members of the Committee on "preference for relevance" was obvious from the outset,' Robert Sheldon recalled; 'Norman Hunt, Robert Neild and myself were always prepared to take the matter to a vote if necessary. I had an entrenched position on "preference for relevance" and so did Hunt and Neild. What we could not be entirely sure of was who would support us and who would be our opponents.' Sheldon added: ' "Preference for relevance" always had my complete support. I remember early on that we visited the CAS and found bright Arts people being taught economics. I exploded. Why not pick bright economists in the first place? The arguments on the Committee went on and on when it came to "preference for relevance" ' (Interview, 1988).

'Though the idea was never really crystallized out,' Sir Philip Allen's recollection was that 'the Fulton Committee was divided about "preference for relevance" from the beginning' (Interview, 1988). Lord Simey was clear about his sceptical attitude towards 'preference for relevance' in material circulated to his fellow members in March 1968 (PRO: BA1/50).

The Assistant Secretary to the Fulton Committee, Michael Simons, said that it was obvious that Allen was against 'preference for relevance' all along. The rest of the Committee appeared to be in favour at first, but Dunnett, Kipping, and Simey eventually lining up with Allen on the basis of the balance of the argument and concern about the effect on Civil Service morale of a radical change in recruitment practice (Interview, 1989). The Secretary to the Committee, Richard Wilding, recalled that discussion about ' "preference for relevance" went round and round interminably. The debate was there all the time. If one had been asked to predict at the end of the first six meetings how the Committee would have divided on the matter, the only surprise would have been that Sir Edward Boyle came down in favour of "preference for relevance" ' (Interview, 1988).

Though the Boyle papers contain no material on this issue, in discussions with the author about the Fulton Committee's work, Sir Edward Boyle never seemed to me to have any doubts about the virtues of 'preference for relevance'; and Walter Anderson, sometimes seen as a possible waverer on this matter, had a consistent position too. Anderson recalled: 'I was very much in favour of preference for relevance. I couldn't see why somebody with a First in Medieval French should go to the top of the Civil Service, just like that. Moreover, preference for relevance would encourage undergraduates to study subjects which would be most appropriate in the sort of department that would be their metier. In most areas of work, obviously, the study of economics was the most useful' (Interview, 1988).

Robert Neild pressed the same point in leading the discussion on 'preference for relevance' in a meeting of the Fulton Committee on 3 January 1967. 'Knowledge of economics was essential for administrators in the economic departments: the Treasury, the DEA, and the Board of Trade,' Neild said;

> The teaspoonful of economics provided by the CAS was not enough. Administrative recruits to these departments should have a thorough training in the subject, and he thought that they should have it before they entered the department, and preferably even before they entered the Service. He would not necessarily restrict entry to those whose first degree had been in economics or statistics. But those who had taken other subjects should be sent back to university, where the subject was best taught, at public expense before admission. He would not confine those with training in economics to the economic departments; they should spill over to other departments. But he would man the economic departments exclusively in this way, ignoring the Treasury's management function for this purpose. Professional economists who were up to date in their disciplines would still be needed as well. He would also be in favour of developing a *polytechnicien* type of training for applied scientists and engineers for recruitment into the technological departments. As regards the rest, he wondered whether a rigorous training in the social sciences should be developed for recruits to social departments, but was inclined to think the training in this field could take place after entry. A transitional problem would arise in the economic departments: those already there would be less well qualified to do their jobs than their juniors who would come in under the new system (PRO: BA1/6).

Intelligent men at risk of being declared intellectually redundant on grounds that they might well regard as specious, on the basis of, for instance, Dame Evelyn Sharp's view that the role of higher civil servants was essentially political, were not without their defenders on the Fulton Committee. The question of the *polytechnicien*-type engineer was treated as a separate matter (PRO: BA1/6), and discussions about 'preference for relevance' favouring economics and related subjects took place at seven meetings of the Committee in 1967, with those opposed associating themselves with positions already identified in the evidence, notably the pragmatic argument about first-rate talent always being in short supply and that the Civil Service could not afford to cut off any source. When the Secretariat listed outstanding questions for decision in June 1967 'preference for relevance' was still one of them (PRO:

BA1/37), and attempts designed to find a form of words that all the Committee could assent to led Robert Neild and Norman Hunt to reserve their position, later supported by Robert Sheldon (PRO: BA1/9). The drafting subcommittee was given the remit of finding an acceptable alternative (PRO: BA1/10) but, as we have seen, eventually the Committee chose the route of publicly expressed division.

Chapter 8

The Fulton Report and Reform of the Civil Service

The Fashioning of the Report

'The Home Civil Service is still fundamentally a product of the second half of the nineteenth century. The tasks it faces are those of the second half of the twentieth century. That, briefly, is the problem we have found and have sought to remedy.' Thus ran the opening paragraph of Robert Neild's contribution to the drafting of the first chapter of the projected first volume to be published by the Fulton Committee contained in material which was circulated to the Committee's Drafting Sub-Committee on 18 October 1967 (PRO: BA1/57).

The tone seems to have been deliberately provocative. Neild recalled:

> I was a strong advocate of a brief, forceful Report. I circulated copies of the Trevelyan-Northcote Report and the Macaulay Report. It seemed to me that our Victorian ancestors had set us a fine example of being outspoken, brief and robust. I wanted the Fulton Report to be a challenging Report, not one that was two-handed with weak conclusions. I was also keen to ensure that criticism of the Civil Service should be explicit and honest. We should say what we thought. I did not believe that change would come about otherwise. In retrospect, I believe that our directness was a good thing. The argument that if we had been more Panglossian there would have been more change does not bear scrutiny. The idea that politeness induces implementation is absurd. In matters of this kind, politeness, in the form of understatement and an excess of qualification, means you can be forgotten. The fact that our criticisms were bluntly expressed has meant that they have lived on. The tone of the objections to our criticisms of the Civil Service was not that so much that they were wrong as that they were rude (Interview, 1988).

'Any body of this sort reaches a point after a year or so when it ought to cut the cackle and get at the conclusions,' Richard Wilding, its Secretary, said of the Fulton Committee; 'You have to apply the spur of a possible but tight timetable' (Interview, 1988). Several efforts on Wilding's part to concentrate the Committee's attention on the form that its Report should take got little response until, on 11 April 1967, 'the Secretariat were instructed to prepare two outline draft chapters on assumptions and functions and men in the light of the discussion and to circulate them for the meeting on April 25th' (PRO: BA1/8). The proposed first chapter was criticised at the latter meeting on the grounds that 'the draft did not sound a clear call for radical reform, and references to the need for change were muffled by tributes to the Civil Service for having changed quite a lot already. Especially if the Committee's Report was to be a relatively short statement of principles (as opposed to a lengthy statement of how present practices could be assimilated to a new start), it would be important to say crisply what was wrong and what needed to be done' (PRO: BA1/8).

It was on 22 and 23 July 1967 , that

> the Committee agreed that they should aim to produce a first volume which was pithy, readable and as short as possible (preferably not more than 25–30 pages). If they tried fully to argue and illustrate each point in turn, the message would be lost in a mass of detail and the Report would not be read. The first volume should say, shortly and pungently, what was wrong and needed putting right; what sort of Service was needed and what should be done to get it. It would be necessary to produce a separate volume containing statistical material, the results of research and whatever other evidence the Committee decided to publish; and, probably, a further volume expounding and clarifying the recommended methods of achieving the objectives set out in the first volume.

The Committee decided that the shape might therefore be 'Volume I – the main Report, for general consumption; Volume II – detailed arguments and recommendations, mainly for Ministers, the Service itself, and students of the subject; Volume III – statistics, research and other evidence.' The Committee discussed 'the main headings of a first volume on this pattern,' and it agreed that 'a Drafting Sub-Committee should be set up. The Sub-Committee should consist of the Chairman, Sir Norman Kipping, Sir Philip Allen, Sir James Dunnett, and Dr Hunt, and should be served by the Secretary . . . Its first task would be to prepare drafts of the first volume' (PRO: BA1/10).

'Our conception of a short first volume is a practical and worthwhile proposition,' Hunt wrote in a note dated 27 September 1967 which accompanied a preliminary draft of the first volume that was forty-nine pages long. Hunt added: 'Subsequent drafts of about this length will achieve what we have in mind' (PRO: BA1/44). In material also circulated to the Committee on the same date, Richard Wilding drew attention to the Drafting Sub-Committee's view that Volume I in its final form would probably be 'a little longer' than Hunt's draft, possibly 'some 50 or more pages of print' (PRO: BA1/44). Hunt's draft and the other material were considered at the Fulton Committee's meeting on 3 October at which the Chairman observed that he thought that the first two chapters should provide an introduction with a bigger sweep, and discuss the functions of the Civil Service in policy making, higher management and man-management before going on to discuss the men, structure etc. that these functions would require:

> The conduct of this country's affairs over the last thirty years presented a difficult problem: the right course might be to say that it appeared to have been not very good, and that the duty of the Committee was not to seek to apportion blame for this between the Civil Service and other parts of government but to concentrate on what change the Civil Service would need in order to make its full contribution to the future. He was sure that it would be important for the Committee to live up to the legitimately large expectations that people had of it, and not to put in a Report which simply said all was well subject to a few changes in relative detail.

Robert Neild agreed that it would be wrong to apportion blame, but the Report should set out the obsolescence of the old Northcote-Trevelyan/Macaulay philosophy and formulate a new one.

> It would be useful to quote Northcote-Trevelyan and Macaulay and remind the reader that they set an ideal which had not yet been replaced, with the results that the civil servants now had not satisfactory framework in which to operate. The new philosophy should be one of 'dynamic professionalism' – that a better phrase was needed. Its core should be the need constantly to review the changing nature of the job and to adapt recruitment, training etc. to these changes. It would be a mistake to replace the static philosophy of the general administrator with a new but equally static philosophy of an economic administrator. What was needed was continuous adaptation. He thought that the Report should criticize the system (not individuals) quite harshly for the consequences of an obsolete and static philosophy. Unless it made clear that this had led to bad results, the case would not be fully made and the message would fail to get across. Provided however that the new philosophy was convincingly and forcefully expressed, people would come back to the Report in future even if not all the following detail was right.

The Committee 'endorsed the view of the Drafting Sub-Committee that Dr Hunt's draft confirmed the feasibility of a short first volume followed by a second volume which would deal with selected topics in detail. Some members thought that the present draft could be shortened and made more positive. But it was agreed that Volume I would have to stand on its own feet as a reasoned statement of the Committee's whole approach and should contain enough material to make clear that the major problems had been properly thought through.' It was also provisionally agreed that Wilding's draft offered the right basis for the drafting of Volume II (PRO: BA1/10).

In his draft Volume I, Hunt did write that 'the present Civil Service is essentially the product of the last half of the nineteenth century,' and that 'it is clear that the British Civil Service is in need of fundamental reform,' and he did list the six defects of the Service which were to find their place in the opening chapter of the published Report, including the supposed philosophy of 'amateurism' in the Administrative Class. The opening paragraph of the draft, though, read:

> Attitudes towards any Civil Service are ambivalent. On the one hand there's the healthy distrust of bureaucracy. It stifles individual initiative; it's a threat to liberty; it's soulless and unimaginative; it's restrictive and not creative; it's a brake on democracy; whatever its size it's always too big. On the other hand we continue to load our Governments with new tasks – some simple, but most increasingly complex. We expect them to maintain full employment and promote economic growth; we demand Government protection against unsound car insurance companies; we call on the Government to clear up the Torrey Canyon mess and ensure it doesn't happen again; whether it's exploration in space or the problems of the Common Market we expect the Government to take the right decisions – and in good time. This inevitably places bigger and more complicated/sophisticated demands on the Civil Service. Ideally therefore we need a Civil Service equipped to handle the new demands we make on Government without being open to any of the criticisms normally levelled at bureaucracy; this was the challenge which as a Committee we have tried to meet (PRO: BA1/44).

Wilding's circulated draft began as follows: 'It is our duty to consider how the Civil Service should be equipped and organized for its role in the modern State. In this first chapter, we review the tasks of Government as they are today, consider the role of the Civil Service in the discharge of those tasks, and set out what we believe to be the main defects which we think need to be remedied' (PRO: BA1/44). Neild's draft was also circulated to the main Committee (PRO: BA1/44). On 31 October 1967 the Committee discussed the draft opening chapter of the projected Volume I, and

> members thought that the chapter should be brief and direct in its language and preferred Mr Neild's draft . . . Dr Hunt and Mr Neild were invited to write a revised version of the chapter, consisting of Mr. Neild's draft . . . amended to take account of views expressed in discussion, and a new section on the six main defects, prepared in consultation with other members . . . Dr Hunt was invited to draft a further version of Chapters 2 and 3, and subsequently of the later parts of Volume I, in consultation with the Chairman and Sir James Dunnett . . . The Committee thought that it might finish Volume I by the end of the year (PRO: BA1/10).

Lord Simey's absence from the meeting on 31 October 1967 seems to have prompted Lord Fulton to write to him about developments on the Committee. Simey wrote back on 8 November to say that the Chairman's letter had eased his mind a good deal while also making it clear that 'I don't propose to come to London for the next meeting, as I cannot think that anything useful will be served by ploughing through drafts produced by Norman Hunt.' He observed:

The drafting of reports for consideration by the Committee is, of course, a substantial responsibility, and I have been very sorry to learn that Wilding's contributions have not been found acceptable. Frankly, my own view is that what is missing from our work is not so much skill in drafting, as agreement about the substance of the reports themselves. It is virtually impossible to draft a report without really clear agreement as to what is to go into it, and there has never been any common agreement about this. Wilding is now, I fear, a defeated and much disappointed man (Fulton Papers).

Wilding had simply been performing his duties as Secretary and playing a part in trying to push the business along. Simey was right about the divisions on the Committee. Indeed, as we shall see, he was to provide the most prominent example of them.

Fulton's own efforts at drafting the opening two chapters (PRO: BA1/57) had not been well received by his fellow members of the Drafting Sub-Committee (PRO: BA1/55), and the Chairman thought at one stage of the Committee employing a professional writer to prepare the final version of the Report. John Rosselli, an academic historian at Sussex University and former journalist, was asked to produce a sample rewrite of drafts of the early chapters, but these proved unacceptable (although some of his changes survived in the final version). Rosselli in fact pinpointed with admirable succinctness the Fulton Committee's difficulties in relation to publication, when writing to Lord Fulton on 5 December 1967: 'You cannot really have a latter-day Macaulay or Trevelyan-Northcote statement; the issues and the organization your Committee has to deal with are much more complex than anything the investigations of the 1850s looked into; nor are people today as sure of having found the key as those men were' (Fulton Papers). Not surprisingly it proved to be one thing for the Drafting Sub-Committee to circulate the Macaulay Report on the Indian Civil Service on 8 November 1967 (PRO: BA1/57), but quite another to emulate it.

After several months of drafting work, the Secretariat was able to circulate material on 22 February 1968 which abandoned the idea of a Northcote-Trevelyan type of main Report followed by a second volume giving details of proposals and supporting argumentation. On 27 February it was agreed that 'for the convenience of the reader most of the evidence should be published in a few large volumes, arranged in parts as appropriate,' although the Committee reserved its position about the shape of Volume 1. The arrangement decided upon was broadly that which became the published version (PRO: BA1/11), in five volumes, two of which (3 and 5) were in two parts.

The form which Volume 1, the Fulton Report itself, was to take seems to have been decided as late as the meeting on 30 April 1968, though there is no formal record of this (PRO: BA1/11). On 7 May Wilding circulated draft material accompanied by a note which stated that 'the order of the chapters has been revised on the lines discussed in Committee' – presumably a reference to the meeting of the Committee on 30 April.

Throughout the drafting stage, the Fulton Committee was divided about the form which the opening chapter of its Report should take, with the main critics of its intended style and content being Simey, Allen, and Dunnett. In a letter to Richard Wilding on 27 September 1967, Dunnett wrote that 'the more I think about Norman Hunt's draft . . . the less I think it will do in its present form.' He went on to observe:

> It is now becoming fashionable, e.g. the Nicholson book, to suggest that the Civil Service, and particularly the Higher Civil Service, has been inadequate for its tasks for a long time. This is not a view that, as a Committee, we would endorse. The preparations for mobilization in the years immediately before the War and the extent to which the resources of the country were mobilized during the War, e.g. to a far greater extent that in Germany, is a tribute by itself to the efficiency of the Civil Service. How well the country has been served since the War and how far some, at least, of our current ills could have been avoided by earlier reorganization of the Civil Service, are not subjects which the Committee feels it necessary to pursue. The Committee has regarded its task as being that of looking to the future. Much of what the Committee will wish to say will appear critical. It is therefore right at the outset to put these criticisms into perspective and to pay tribute to the loyal and devoted service which has been rendered to the country (Fulton Papers).

This sort of even-handedness, though, was always unlikely to be acceptable to Neild and other radicals on the Committee, whose views had much in common with those of Max Nicholson (Nicholson, 1967); and similarly when Dunnett, with some justification, commended the drafting skills of his Principal Private Secretary, John Bourn, to Wilding (Fulton Papers) this was to display a lack of realism about the prospect of what Bourn produced being widely adopted by the Committee. Dunnett's discontent persisted, and on 21 March 1968 a note from him was circulated to the Committee which stated that 'Chapter 1 of our Report is clearly of crucial importance. There are a few paragraphs in the present draft about which I remain basically unhappy . . . I dislike the first paragraph of the Chapter. It seems to me to be too bald and didactic as drafted. It may please some people. There are others, however, who would, I think, be put off the whole Report by the style of the first paragraph.' His own suggested 'less tendentious' opening paragraph ran: 'The foundations of the present Civil Service were laid in the nineteenth century. The tasks it now faces are those of the second half of the twentieth century. Our duty is to propose those changes that will enable the Service to discharge these tasks with the efficiency which the national interest requires and which modern knowledge and techniques make possible.' He produced re-drafts of four other paragraphs as well (PRO: BA1/50), but in all cases to little effect.

Shortly after this, Sir Philip Allen circulated a note entitled 'Comment on Chapter 1' which stated that

> I am bothered that the draft does not pay sufficient regard to the fact that the British civil servant must be seen in the context of a Parliamentary democracy. He is not operating a benevolent despotism. He is part of a machine which is entirely subordinate to political Ministers, and through them to Parliament and public. This political direction of the Government machine interacts with the operations of the machine and thus forms an 'integral part of the daily life of many civil servants' (para.23 of the Management Consultancy Group's Report). Civil servants are working ultimately for generalist Ministers who have to win Parliament's approval for what they propose and avoid Parliament's criticism for what they do and what is done in their name. The Administrative civil servant has therefore to have a lively sense of all aspects of politics so that he can discern what is politically possible, what is politically acceptable with an adjustment here or a difference of emphasis there. The intermingling of policy and politics is fundamental, and it has perhaps been obscured by the Civil Service's own tendency to describe his job as advising Ministers on policy. The administrator's job is to help Ministers with all the policy, practical and presentational aspects of their departmental work. For this he needs qualities of character, ability and judgement which cannot be neatly categorized into some professional specialism. And above all the work calls for a breadth of experience of government administration which enables the administrator to see not only what is required from his own narrow subject point of view but also to see what is in the broader public interest and is likely to be acceptable to a generalist Parliament and a generalist public. This does not mean there is not a great need for increased professionalism not only in the administrator's knowledge of the subjects he deals with but also in the techniques of administration and the operation of the machine. But the Report should not emphasize this to the exclusion of other qualities and skills.

Though Allen did not offer the Committee a revised opening paragraph, he did make other specific drafting suggestions, notably the removal of 'cult of the generalist' and of that 'cult' being 'obsolete at all levels' (PRO: BA1/50) without effect.

When Dunnett was later asked whether, together with Allen, he had considered publishing a Minority Report, he replied: 'If there had been a major cleavage in the Committee, there was the risk that a Majority Report more extreme than the Fulton Report turned out to be would have been published with more extreme action afterwards. A Minority Report would have given the impression that Philip Allen and myself were against change in the Civil Service, which was not the case' (Interview, 1988). Allen later observed about the situation in which he and Dunnett found themselves that 'it is very

difficult for a serving civil servant to defend the position,' and both Permanent
Secretaries agreed that 'we couldn't resign and hand in a Minority Report.
It would have looked terrible.' They had no recollection of acting in relation to
the Minority Report question on the calculation that the Labour Government
would be re-elected, and that what could be treated as Civil Service opposition
to reform could be used to justify more radical changes (Hennessy et al.,
1988, p.46). In writing about the Minority Report matter, Dunnett had
chosen to emphasise that 'it should be remembered that we were reporting
in 1968 when most people thought that Labour was bound to win the 1970
Election' (Dunnett, 1976, p.373). Richard Wilding observed about the Permanent Secretaries that 'they were in a weak negotiating position (or at least
thought they were) and won little by way of concessions' (letter to author,
5.7.89). The Committee's Assistant Secretary, Michael Simons, recalled that
Robert Neild and Robert Sheldon were particularly forceful in dealing with
the Permanent Secretaries' objections to Chapter 1 (Interview, 1989). Sheldon
stated: 'I did vehemently oppose any toning down of Chapter 1 of the Fulton
Report. Certainly, I would have divided the Committee if necessary' (letter
to author, 1.8.89). Neild's recollection was that the dissension over Chapter
1 did not have much to do with the content of the Report and its recommendations. 'Rather it was a question whether we should say that the
Civil Service was wonderful but needed changing along the lines we recommended, or should say that it had serious defects. Almost everyone admitted the existence of defects we listed. The hesitation was principally one of
tact, not hurting anyone's feelings and so on. So far as I can remember
what happened, the argument did not last very long; the criticisms were not
significantly toned down; and Simey produced his Minority Report' (letter
to author, 5.7.89).

If the Permanent Secretaries felt or actually were under pressure to conform
with the rest of the Committee's views, especially as regards Chapter 1, Lord
Simey had no such constraints upon him. The agenda for the Committee's
meeting on 1 and 2 April, 1968, issued on 27 March, included, among the
'relevant papers' about Chapter 1 that were to be considered not only the
memoranda written by Allen and Dunnett referred to already but material
from 'Lord Simey (circulated by hand at last meeting)' (PRO: BA1/11). The
minutes of that meeting, which was held on 25 and 26 March, do not record
this (PRO: BA1/11). Simey's note of reservation to Chapter 1 was formally
circulated to the Committee on 8 May (PRO: BA1/52). 'Out of the blue, as
far as I was concerned, he produced a kind of Minority Report,' Robert
Sheldon said of Lord Simey (Interview, 1988). Simey's behaviour did not
surprise Neild (Interview, 1988) nor Anderson, who saw Simey as being
'forthright. He wouldn't just fall in with the majority.' On re-reading it,
Anderson thought that Simey's note of reservation to Chapter 1 was 'a good
point of view' (Interview, 1988). Wilding observed that 'Simey made no secret
of his belief that a lot of what was being said around the Committee table

about the Civil Service was unjust and unsupported by the evidence' (Interview, 1988), and in Simon's opinion 'that Lord Simey issued a note of reservation to the opening chapter of the Fulton Report should have surprised nobody. Tom Simey told me that Neild's draft opening chapter at least had bite but the one that was destined to be published had no merit. Simey had informed Sir William Armstrong about this, and he had said that publication without some record of opposition from within the Committee would be disastrous for Civil Service morale. Simey himself made no efforts to associate the higher civil servants on the Committee with his note' (Interview, 1989). Simey's published note actually stated this (Cmnd. 3638, 1968, p.103). Dunnett later went so far as to say that 'although I spent a lot of time with him, I had no knowledge of Simey's link with the Treasury or about his intention to issue a form of Minority Report. I found this odd' (Interview, 1988). Allen's recollection about Simey's behaviour over the note of reservation was different: 'He told Ned Dunnett and myself about it, and that William Armstrong and the Treasury were helping him out, but there was no question of us putting him up to it. Some sort of Minority Report was his idea' (Interview, 1988). Whether or not both Permanent Secretaries who were members of the Committee had foreknowledge of Simey's intentions has to remain unclear, but what is evident is that Simey was not encouraged by them to act in the way that he did.

That Simey acted at all may have surprised some of his colleagues on the Fulton Committee, but the general content of his dissenting note should not have done so. Those colleagues were not to know that on his personal copy of Wilding's draft Chapter 1, which stated in paragraph 28 that 'the Service is still fundamentally a product of the second half of the nineteenth century,' Simey wrote in the margin 'first half of C20?'. They were not to know either that on the back of p.12, which dealt with 'the cult of the all rounder,' Simey had written 'Is the will of the specialist compatible with Parliamentary democracy?' (Simey Papers: MS16.8). In a memorandum circulated to the Committee in July 1967 about an 'Historical Introduction to the Report,' though, Simey had emphasised that 'any suggestions we have to make should be seen to be made on the basis of a full understanding of past history, and the possibilities of making use of past traditions and experience in planning for the future.' Further, Simey had appended a copy of an article from *The Economist* of 15 July 1967, which expressed scepticism about what is perceived as the current emphasis in the Civil Service on management skills and knowledge of economics and which, Simey wrote, made 'some relevant points on the importance which will continue to attach to good judgement' (PRO: BA1/40). Plainly, this was Simey's opinion too, and when his views were disregarded with the result, as he saw it, that Chapter 1 of the Fulton Report was 'unfair to the Civil Service', Simey used his position of academic freedom to say so; and also, it seems, his contacts with the Treasury. The core of Simey's argument was that 'whilst it is no doubt true to say that the foundations of the Civil Service were laid in the second half of the nineteenth century, it is surely also true that the main characteristics it displays today are mid-twentieth century developments' (Cmnd. 3638, 1968, p.101). Simey also wrote that 'so far as generalist knowledge and experience are concerned, I am sure that Macaulay's argument was right' (ibid., p.102). The practice of the generalist, though, was first fully developed in the Warren Fisher era, and it did not seem to suit either Simey or those from whom he differed on the Committee to recognise this.

Though Simey made clear to Norman Hunt his unhappiness with Chapter 1, for instance in a handwritten letter dated 10 March 1968 (Crowther-Hunt Papers: Box 3), his views were not seen as being sufficiently important by Hunt to be specifically referred to when, prior to discussions with the Prime Minister, in anticipation of the Fulton Committee's meeting on 25 and 26 March, Hunt set out in undated handwritten form the difficulties of getting agreement on the Committee. 'F's Chairmanship' headed the list of difficulties. 'If you want radical Report by June,' Hunt scribbled, then 'pressure on Fulton' needed to be applied. The 'civil servants [were] now delaying.' Hunt believed that 'Dunnett [was] looking to autumn.' The only 'firm major points' that had been agreed were 'move location of central management (but don't be beastly to Treasury)' and the establishment of the 'Civil Service College – (but even there Kipping and Ned, not too much training – and a lot can take place outside).' The Permanent Secretaries were 'only O.K.' on these subjects, otherwise being for 'toning down criticism Chap. 1,' as well as being out to 'demote planning units' and 'to weaken [the] concept' of such units and to question the need for units in every department. The Permanent Secretaries 'don't like streaming', the Prime Minister was to be informed, and they were opposed to 'Classlessness.' Hunt considered 'Fulton not sound' either on the 'abolition of Classes', an issue on which the Committee was 'split' partly it seemed about whether to draw the line at Principal level or that of Under Secretary. Hunt thought that there was a 'danger' of Fulton and Kipping 'compromising' on 'Principal and above' which would mean 'abolish class . . . for Officer Class and not for NCOs.' The manner in which the new Civil Service Department was going to be staffed also worried Hunt and he wrote in terms of there being a 'danger' of the Committee accepting the Treasury's proposals for a 'starred' graduate entry (Crowther-Hunt Papers: Box 3).

As things turned out, Hunt exaggerated the likely effectiveness of the opposition to the ideas that he and his allies favoured. Besides Simey's note of reservation, the only differences of opinion that survived to find a place in the Fulton Report itself were those over 'preference for relevance' in the direct entry recruitment of administrators (Cmnd. 3638, 1968, pp.28ff), over the retention of the Method I means of recruiting administrators (ibid., pp.30ff), over extending job evaluation and salary banding to the most senior posts in the Civil Service (ibid., pp.73, 83); and there were also two reservations by Hunt himself relating to the role of junior ministers, urging their involvement in promotions in the Civil Service (ibid., p.41) and in official departmental committees (ibid., p.94). In addition, five members of the Committee (Allen, Anderson, Dunnett, Kipping and Simey) recorded their disagreement with a suggestion from a majority of their colleagues that in five years' time a further committee should review progress in the Civil Service and report to Parliament. The dissentients thought that such a committee would be too disruptive and that it would be unlikely to limit itself to considering the implementation of the Fulton programme (ibid., p.99).

In the Fulton Report it was stated that the Committee held 89 meetings (ibid., p.184), but in fact only 85 meetings were officially listed as such. At the last of them, on 19 June 1968, the Committee agreed the form that the Press Notice should take, and signed the Report (PRO: BA1/11). The Fulton Report was published on 26 June 1968.

Reaction to the Report

The Fulton Committee's Report was to have the initial advantage of the support of the Prime Minister, Harold Wilson, which proved to be particularly valuable, given divisions within the Labour Government at the time. The Secretary of State for Social Services, Richard Crossman, learnt from the Chancellor of the Exchequer, Roy Jenkins, on 17 June 1968, that

> while I was away Harold had apparently circulated a paper recommending that we immediately accept the main recommendations of the Fulton Committee. This included making a considerable section of the Treasury into an independent Department to deal with the Civil Service, something which obviously affected the Chancellor, but Harold had come to his decision without saying a word to Roy . . . Clearly a thoroughly bad mood had grown up between these men . . . I was just leaving the room when Roy said, 'Now, Dick, let's be practical. If I agree with you about postponing the decision on Social Service cuts for a week will you give me your full support on Fulton?' 'Yes,' I said, 'if you will support me on Lords' reform as well.' And that, roughly speaking, was the deal we came to (Crossman, 1977, p.98).

Of 19 June, the Minister of Technology, Tony Benn recorded:

> I had a message that Harold wanted to see me and I went across at about 7.45pm. and stayed for an hour. He had Fulton with him. He was tremendously keen to get the Cabinet to agree tomorrow that we would accept, in principle, the three major recommendations of the Fulton Committee and he wanted to be sure I was on the right side. Well, this is damned silly because I had made more references to Fulton in every speech since the Election than anybody else. But he said that the 'Junta' led by Roy [Jenkins] and Denis [Healey] and others had been opposed to it and that there would be a big battle and this would be like the

> African arms deal all over again, and so on. He really has such a
> conspiratorial mind (Benn, 1988, pp.83, 85).

Also on 19 June, Barbara Castle, the Secretary of State for Employment and
Productivity, recorded:

> Tommy [Balogh] phoned to say Harold wanted me to know there was
> likely to be a row over Fulton at Cabinet tomorrow and he wanted me
> to back him up. Roy, though he liked the Report, was expected to argue
> the need for delay while we considered it. This would give the appearance
> of indecision and would give time for the Civil Service to get round us.
> Harold was keen to go ahead, as was Tommy. There were some points
> on which Tommy thought we should go further but 'this is the minimum'
> (Castle, 1984, p.464).

The Government's legislative programme and the proposed reform of the
House of Lords took up the early part of the Cabinet meeting of 20 June,
and 'after that we got on to Fulton,' Benn recorded, 'Harold opened and said
this would take a lot of consideration; that he thought the Government would
need to respond quite quickly and he favoured this. Then Roy, who tended
to agree with him, pointed out all the difficulties. It would mean extra public
expenditure for which there was no accommodation. It would upset the
Treasury. He thought we should respond cautiously, perhaps move slowly
into it towards the end of the year. This was really his way of trying to finish
it' (Benn, 1988, p.85). Barbara Castle wrote of this Cabinet meeting that 'it
was late when we got to the Fulton Report and I had only time to hear the
opening shots of doubt by Roy, Healey and Crosland.' She informed Michael
Halls, the Prime Minister's Private Secretary, that 'my only concern about
the Report (which, of course, none of us had been given time to read properly)
was . . . the suggestion that Harold should say that the increased expenditure
should be phased in. If there was to be any phasing in of new expenditure,
equal pay must have priority' (Castle, 1984, p.464f). Of the discussion which
took place in the Cabinet on 20 June and of the Prime Minister's interest in
the Fulton Report, Crossman wrote:

> I haven't asked him but I'm pretty sure that the reason he has committed
> himself to this Report so early and so personally is partly because he has
> a strong liking for Fulton and even more for Norman Hunt and partly
> because he thinks this way he can improve his image as a great moder-
> nizer. He put his case for immediately accepting the main rec-
> ommendations of the Report, including the creation of a Civil Service
> Department. Then the Chancellor put his case against what he described
> as precipitate action. Denis Healey, Michael Stewart and I supported
> Roy and all the support Harold got was from Wedgy Benn and Peter
> Shore, his two hirelings. He was so upset that at this point he stopped
> the meeting and asked that it should be resumed later (Crossman, 1977,
> p.103).

The critical Cabinet meeting was arranged for 25 June 1968. The Prime

Minister took the trouble to ensure support for the Fulton Report from Barbara Castle with a promise of a kind about equal pay. She observed: 'Just what his passion for Fulton springs from I'm not clear, except that he said the classics boys have always been against him and that he prefers the earthy, elementary school types like Michael Halls.' The Cabinet meeting itself began with the Prime Minister expressing anger about leaks to the Press about matters discussed at the previous meeting, and Castle recorded, 'we passed on to the rest of the agenda in a kind of daze' (Castle, 1984, p.468f). Benn's recollection was that 'we spent a long time on the Fulton Report and it was agreed that it should be published' (Benn, 1988, p.86). Once the leaks had been discussed, Crossman recorded, 'Harold started on the Fulton Report, where we gave him a very easy time. It's a second rate Report written in a very poor style by Norman Hunt. He and Harold are tremendous buddies who live in the same world of uninspired commonsense. The Report is perfectly sensible but, oh dear, it lacks distinction. However, it's been a success with the Press and the public. Harold needed a success for himself and Cabinet consented to his getting it with a Statement tomorrow' (Crossman, 1977, p.107).

Tony Benn later wrote that the Fulton Report was opposed by those Ministers who were 'in the pockets of their senior civil servants' (Benn, 1988, p.138). This was unlikely to be the case with, for instance, Denis Healey and Roy Jenkins. The latter wrote:

> The truth is that I never engaged very closely with the Fulton Report. I did not find it a good document even though Fulton had briefly taught me at Balliol. But I was somewhat torn on the recommendations. On the one hand I was sceptical about the setting up of the heavy machinery of the Civil Service Department (which scepticism I think has proved well founded). On the other hand I was uneasily aware that as Chancellor I had practically no time to deal with Civil Service problems. I think I saw Helsby, my Permanent Secretary on that side until April, no more than two or three times. So I was hesitant about taking a straight Treasury "what we have we hold" position. In addition . . . I had enough central responsibilities on my hands and also other disputes running with Wilson. So it was not to me a major issue' (letter to author, 20.1.92).

Denis Healey later wrote, after expressing admiration for the French Higher Civil Service and especially the ENA, that 'I have always regretted that I did not take advantage of the Report of the Fulton Commission to press for similar training of British civil servants; but as Defence Secretary I had more urgent problems at the time' (Healey, 1989, p.405). Though Ministerial responsibilities would not explain why Healey's oral evidence was among the most conservative that the Fulton Committee received, the weight of departmental duties would be one explanation why the reform of the Civil Service did not seem to be at the time as important a matter for Healey and some other Ministers as it became for Harold Wilson. Once the Prime

Minister's commitment became known, the discussions in and around the Cabinet about the Fulton Report seemed to become an opportunity for horse trading and, for Crossman at least, actions motivated by personal malice (Crossman, 1988, pp.98, 103), though not sustained and coherent opposition.

'I am confident that the Report will stand comparison with the historic Northcote-Trevelyan Report of more than a century ago,' the Prime Minister stated in presenting the Fulton Report to the House of Commons on June 26th 1968. Wilson continued: 'Just as the Northcote-Trevelyan Report called for a replacement of patronage by a system of independent selection based on intellectual attainment, the Fulton Report, while reaffirming the continuation of independence in recruitment, finds that insufficient attention has been paid to management in the Service, and calls for a new system of training, organization, and career management.' He described the Fulton Report as being 'an essential contribution to the modernization of the basic institutions of this country,' and said that the Government have decided to embark on the process of reform outlined by the Committee.

> First, we accept the proposal to establish a new Civil Service Department on the lines advocated by the Committee and the steps to bring this about will be taken at the appropriate time. Specific and formal arrangements will be made to ensure the continued independence and political impartiality, within the new Civil Service Department, of the Civil Service Commission in the selecting of individuals for appointment to the Civil Service. Secondly, the Government have accepted the recommendation to set up a Civil Service College to develop the training of civil servants broadly on the lines recommended in the Report. The timing of this will, of course, have to be fitted into a programme which takes full account of public expenditure control. Thirdly, the Government accept the abolition of Classes within the Civil Service and will enter immediately into consultations with the staff associations with a view to carrying out the thorough-going study proposed by the Committee, so that a practicable system can be prepared for the implementation of the unified grading structure in accordance with the timetable proposed by the Committee. This does not mean that the professions as such will disappear from the Civil Service, but it does mean that movement throughout the Service for them and for all civil servants at all levels will be unimpeded. This will mean that for everyone in the Civil Service, whether from school, whether from a college of technology, or from a university, whether he or she comes in from industry or from a profession – all in future, the school leaver, the graduate, the accountant, the engineer, the scientist, the lawyer – for all of them there will be an open road to the top which, up to now, has been, in the main, through the Administrative Class.

The Prime Minister added that 'decisions on the remaining recommendations of the Committee will be announced in due course following the necessary full discussion with those concerned, including particularly, as I have said, the Civil Service staff associations,' and announced that the Paymaster General, Lord Shackleton would assist him in setting up the Civil Service Department and in controlling its day-to-day operations when established. Then, having earlier expressed appreciation of the Fulton Committee's achievement in producing recommendations 'designed to produce a Civil Service . . . which, while preserving the best of the old, is adequate in every way to deal with the problems of the fourth quarter of the twentieth century,' the Prime Minister, noting the criticisms of the Civil Service made in the Fulton Report, concluded by paying tribute to 'the very able men and women at all levels in the Service who, with the highest standards of integrity and impartiality, have served the nation's interest under successive Governments for so long' (767 HC Deb. 5s c.454–59).

In the brief exchanges which followed, Edward Heath, the Conservative Leader of the Opposition, welcomed the Fulton Report and related it to the need for wider changes in the machinery of government (ibid., c.459), and the Prime Minister responded favourably, taking the opportunity to refer to 'the very important volume of the Management Consultancy Group's Report' (ibid., c.460).

The Fulton Report was debated in the House of Lords on 24 July 1968. No such debate, of course, would have been complete without the sentiment being expressed that 'we possess the best Civil Service in the world,' and Lord Brooke of Cumnor, a former Conservative minister, duly obliged (295 HL Deb. 5s. c.1194). Lord Annan, a former wartime civil servant, contrived to agree with the views presented in Chapter 1 of the Fulton Report and those in Lord Simey's note of reservation (ibid., c.1182); but for most who contributed to the debate the tone of Chapter 1, and the charge of amateurism against the Administrative Class that it contained, was only one basis for adverse criticism of the Report. The Minister responsible, Lord Shackleton, said that 'my position is not one which might be described as the defence counsel for Fulton' (ibid., c.1186), though it was a role that he actually played with teasing skill in response to what he recognised as 'the general weight of the contribution of our . . . civil servant Peers.' Shackleton observed that 'we are beginning to get very near to those passionate discussions which reach their maximum heights of violence only in academic circles' (ibid., c.1185). Lord Bridges stated that 'I came here determined to say something about Chapter 1' which had 'certainly caused a great deal of resentment and ill feeling in the Civil Service.' He was clear that if he had been a member of the Fulton Committee, he would certainly have joined Lord Simey in signing his Minority Report (c.1173).

Lord Sherfield, who, as Sir Roger Makins, had succeeded Bridges as a Permanent Secretary to the Treasury, said of Simey's note of reservation that 'I think I agree with almost every word of it, and also with the substance of the reservations which he has made, with some of his other colleagues on other points in the Report.' Sherfield observed that the Fulton Report did not make very good reading for people who had spent most of their lives in the service of the State: –

> 'not so much for its recommendations, some of which are perfectly sound, but for its general approach and tone and for its immoderate attack on the performance of the existing Service, particularly the Administrative Class. It seems to me that the Commission have tried to keep up with the times but have succeeded only in keeping up with the slogans of the times. One expects, of course, the pendulum to swing, but it is a very long swing from the advocacy of a First in Greats to a diploma in social psychology as the ideal training for a Government servant . . . I am tempted to describe the notion that a man with a degree in economics and sociology is likely to make a better manager or administrator . . . than a graduate in philosophy or history as . . . poppycock' (ibid., c.1120–21).

Another former Permanent Secretary to the Treasury, Lord Helsby, as Sir Laurence Helsby had become, chose the path of faint praise: 'This is a Report that contains many admirable recommendations which . . . will enable the Service to develop usefully in coming years, but it is not a radical or a revolutionary Report' (ibid., c.1100).

When Lady Sharp, the former Dame Evelyn Sharp, said that 'there is great indignation in the Service that the Committee wholly failed to acknowledge the great efforts that have been made by the Service to adapt to the changing scope of Government and to improve their methods and their management' but was sure that 'no civil servant, past or present, wants to spend time on that' (ibid., c.1085–86), she was wrong. Nevertheless, in tone, Lords Robbins and Plowden, who had primarily made their careers outside the Civil Service, were among the most severe critics of the Fulton Report. 'To one who for nearly thirty years has had close contact with the Civil Service, as a temporary civil servant in war and in peace, as a Chairman of a public corporation and as an industrialist, the Service described in Chapter 1 is unrecognisable,' Plowden observed; 'The picture is untrue and unfair. It seemed so to . . . Lord Simey, with whose reservation I fully agree. The Chapter is unworthy of a document of such importance and of the distinguished men who constituted the Committee' (ibid., c.1158). Plowden added:

> I have been critical of the Report because I believe that the Committee have missed a great opportunity. This I consider was partly because they misunderstood the relationship of the Civil Service to the political environment in which it has its being, but equally because their terms of reference precluded them from considering the whole structure of government without which a proper understanding of the Civil Service the country needs is impossible (ibid., c.1165).

Lord Robbins stated that he regarded it as insulting to describe the present race of civil servants as amateurs.

> I must confess . . . to a deep sense of indignation in reading, and re-reading, the first chapter of this Report . . . and I thank Heaven for Lord Simey, one man who had the decency to repudiate the confusion and unfairness of it all. In the end, what matters is not the way some of us feel shame and anger, but how the public interest is affected. And here I am clear that the effect must be almost wholly damaging. The Committee have decked out their indictment with all the cliches of contemporary fashion (ibid., c.1135).

In the absence of Lord Simey through illness, Lord Fulton was left with an unenviable task, given that it was the practice of the House of Lords that on occasions such as this the Chairman of the Committee does not put himself forward as the advocate of the Committee's Report. Fulton pointed out that, for all the criticism of the Report, it (including Chapter 1) was based on evidence, and he drew particular attention to the Management Consultancy Group's work (ibid., c.1165–70), as did Lord Shackleton (ibid., c.1159–60).

The debate in the House of Commons on the Fulton Report took place on 21 November 1968. It was not only less controversial than the House of Lords debate. It was also of a much lower quality. In a rambling speech, which at one stage included consideration of the factors which prevented the size of the Cabinet being reduced (773 HC Deb. 5s. c.1559–61), the Prime Minister inevitably went over much the same ground that he had done on 26 June, especially as regards what had been defined as being the Fulton Committee's main recommendations. The establishment of the CSD was noted (ibid., c.1548), and on the location of the Civil Service College, he was able to say that 'we propose to make an early start by using what so far has been the Civil Defence College at Sunningdale' (ibid., c.1550). As for the introduction of a unified grading structure, the House was told that 'this work is going ahead' (ibid., c.1552). The Prime Minister stated, in response to an intervention from Edward Heath, that the Government was conducting a review examining the possibilities of 'hiving off' some departmental activities, as the Fulton Committee had suggested (ibid., c.1555). He also informed the House that the Government had rejected the majority recommendation of the Committee which had favoured 'preference for relevance' in the direct entry recruitment of administrators, and observed:

> One of the main reasons is that to accept the recommendation would close to the Civil Service a very wide field of possible candidates who have started or who may in future start on their chosen university courses long before they have decided that they wanted to become civil servants, and who had chosen those courses perhaps for other reasons, perhaps non-vocational reasons. Most of us would agree with the Committee, however, in what it was trying to achieve with this recommendation, even if we cannot go all the way with it. This is why we are placing much more emphasis on 'relevant' training after selection,

and the identification of 'relevant' personal qualities during the selection process (ibid., c.1553–4).

Judith Hart, the Paymaster General, told the House that 'preference for relevance' would be 'unworkable in practice' (ibid., c.1677), and when the two MPs from the Fulton Committee, Robert Sheldon (ibid., c.1611–3) and Sir Edward Boyle (ibid., c.1664–5) spoke in favour of the Committee's majority recommendation they did so in vain. The remainder of the debate was only interesting to the extent that it revealed Conservative thinking. Edward Heath seemed to find the Fulton Report to be too narrowly drawn, and thought that more attention needed to be given to the internal organisation of departments (ibid., c.1574). His fellow Conservative, David Howell, thought that Chapter 5 of the Fulton Report really pointed to the 'need for a delegation of budgetary responsibility not only from the Treasury to departments, but to separate divisions, sections and autonomous agencies and units' (ibid., c.1633). Howell's main criticism of the Report was that 'it seems to assume that the State will continue to be, as it has been since the War, the great provider. It seems to assume that the Government will continue to accumulate those tasks of ownership, management, and control that it has accumulated to date at such a fantastic and formidable rate. Looking at the development of pressures on the Government, both in this country and other countries, I question whether this pattern will continue' (ibid., c.1635).

The Fulton Report's reception by the Press was not notably enthusiastic. *The Times* (27.6.68) observed that 'The Northcote-Trevelyan Report of 1853, according to the Fulton Committee, still casts a baleful spell over the Civil Service. It has not been without influence on the Committee itself. To exorcize its predecessor, Fulton has paid it the compliment of adopting its dialectical method'; and went on to express scepticism about some of the Committee's main recommendations. It thought, for instance, that 'the proposal to remove the management of the Civil Service from the Treasury answers well to fashion, which sees the Treasury as the principal source of blight in public affairs, and likes to dream up new Ministries for administrative functions which are held to be neglected.' The newspaper was also doubtful about whether a unified grading structure would work as intended in a Service 'so vast, heterogenous, and scattered.' After recording several doubts, *The Times* concluded that: 'The Report is heavy in the technical appraisal of immediate practical problems, and light in political reflection. It is a thoroughly contemporary essay.'

In an accompanying article, the former Permanent Secretary, Sir Edward Playfair, took a more indulgent view:

> Some years ago the War Office reformed its works service, and turned it over from a sapper-run to a civilian organization. It was a great success. Those who looked back into history found that over the past 150 years the works service had similarly been reformed four or five times: from sapper to civilian, from civilian to sapper and so on. Each

time it was a great success. There is a lot to be said for revolutionary change every so often; not so much for its own sake as to provide the force to break down accumulated adhesions. In that spirit one must welcome the Report of the Fulton Committee.

Playfair wrote accordingly, though he was also to observe with prescience: 'The proposals about training and management education are sensible; but the idea of a csc, though probably necessary, is rather amateurishly set out. As described, it might become a second rate institution. To be of any use it must, at the higher level, be as good as any post-graduate school.'

'The Fulton Committee has done a great deal of good, precise research and has made several good proposals,' *The Guardian* (27.6.68) observed, duly listing them: 'Yet for all its hard work the Committee offers no real solution to a problem which must bedevil a Service which is seen as a complete career – what can be done to see that Buggins the unsuitable does not inevitably get the job for no reason except that Buggins's turn has come?' *The Guardian* did think, though, that 'the management studies conducted by Dr Norman Hunt could well destroy for ever the myth that the Administrative Class is uniquely qualified to take decisions because of its members' broad and humane understanding of the world.' The newspaper's political commentator, Peter Jenkins, condemned what he saw as the Committee's 'utilitarianism' and compared its efforts with those of the Donovan Commission which also reported in June 1968. Jenkins believed that neither the Donovan nor the Fulton Reports were likely to rank with their famous predecessors, the Northcote-Trevelyan Report of 1854 and the 1906 Royal Commission on Trade Unions. 'Both these great studies reached imaginatively, and unfashionably, into the future; their recommendations anticipated the political needs and pressures of British society for a generation ahead. Donovan and Fulton only just manage to keep up with events . . . they visit the present and find that it works; let's do more of what we are doing, they essentially say.' Jenkins added: 'Most of Fulton's actual proposals are sensible enough. They have been knocking around for long enough. They can be found set out in a Fabian pamphlet of 1964 vintage. The final chapter of a contentious book by Mr Peter Shore in 1966 expounds the conventional wisdom now adopted with such bogus radical aplomb' (*The Guardian*, 2.7.68).

'Implement at Once!' ran the heading of Roger Opie's article about the Fulton Report in *The New Statesman* for 28 June 1968, and Thomas Balogh's article in the same journal was entitled 'The End of the Amateur.' For Opie, 'the reforms cannot start too soon'; and the enthusiastic Balogh also counselled against 'a desire to put off the implementation of the Fulton Report . . . since sustained intelligence and professional knowledge in policy making is a pre-condition of success everywhere else, the priority of action in this field is evident if we are to create a better, more balanced, more compassionate, yet more dynamic society.'

The Economist (29.6.68) thought that the Report was 'wide open to criticism as an assault on the whole-time gifted amateurs of Whitehall by a part-time group of gifted amateurs, gathered together in that most nineteenth century of British constitutional mechanisms, an *ad hoc* investigation by a number of uncommitted gentlemen, meeting about once a week for three years, on a Royal Commission or committee.'

The Spectator (28.6.68) was dismissive of 'the astonishing first chapter of the Fulton Report' with its 'grossly exaggerated' criticisms of the Civil Service which were in contrast with 'the Committee's own recommendations, which are worlds away from the root and branch treatment such a diagnosis would suggest.' That journal cited with approval the views of the former Permanent Secretary, F. A. Bishop, who had written in the same issue that

> Lord Fulton and his colleagues ought not to be blamed for failing to prescribe for problems which their terms of reference precluded them from studying. They have concentrated, as they were bound to do, on 'the Home Civil Service,' on a body of men and women, their recruitment, training and organization. The *machinery* of government was deliberately left outside. The Committee recognized that this exclusion imposed many limits on their work and they admit that the problems of machinery 'bear closely' on work and organization. This, it may be thought, is something of an understatement; put more frankly, it could be that the Service organization cannot profitably be studied at all until the machinery has been reformed. Thus, we now have a set of recommendations for improving the recruitment and operation of a work force to man a creaking machine which has outgrown the tasks of yesterday, and which may, as many of us think, be largely irrelevant to the requirements of tomorrow's government.

Bishop thought that the Fulton Committee had been set 'the wrong task' and had been assigned to an activity in which 'the cart is put before the horse' (Bishop, 1968, p.883f). J. H. Robertson, another former official, wrote in similar terms in the same journal six weeks later (Robertson, 1968, p.190f).

Another former civil servant, Maurice Kogan, wrote in *New Society* on 27 June 1968 that the Fulton Report was 'elegantly economic and tightly argued. For its responsible treatment of important issues, it should be compulsory reading for all who care about the future of the country. It raises more issues than it can decide but it is all the better for that' (Kogan, 1968, pp.937ff).

Such indulgence was not present in the articles about the Fulton Report published in *The Listener* for 18 July. The first was a highly critical review of the Fulton Report drawing attention to 'the relative modesty of its proposals' which was written by Lord Helsby (Helsby, 1968, pp.65ff). The second was by the historian Eric Hobsbawm, who condemned the Fulton Report as 'a bad piece of work' characterised by adherence to contemporary fashionable attitudes, and contrasted it with the Donovan Report which was described as 'a first rate piece of analysis' (Hobsbawm, 1968, p.67f). A short unrelated note on Lord Fulton's views (Fulton, 1968, p.68) did not introduce balance into the discussion, and in *The Listener* for 25 July, Norman Hunt published a defence of the Fulton Report (Hunt, 1968, p.100f).

The reaction to the Fulton Report on the part of the Civil Service staff associations tended to be cautious, with the exception of the IPCS. Its General Secretary, William McCall wrote: 'The Report of the Fulton Committee is a welcome confirmation of principles and policies which the Institution has advocated throughout the 50 years of its existence . . . The recommendations . . . deserve a warm welcome. Most of them should be accepted without ado. Only a few give rise to doubt; and there are some detailed suggestions which will need careful examination. But our job now is to ensure that the Report is implemented quickly' (*State Service*, August 1968, p.173). Commenting on the Report, Leslie Williams, the Secretary General of the Staff Side of the National Whitley Council, wrote that

> the staff associations in their evidence criticized various aspects of Civil Service organization. A critical Report was, therefore, expected from the Fulton Committee. The Committee have identified weaknesses which should be removed but also have been deeply impressed by the considerable strengths of the Service and the ability and enthusiasm of its men and women. There are, however, some sweeping and unsupported generalizations about the Civil Service today which will cause resentment among civil servants. Nevertheless, the Staff Side will respond readily to the opportunities which are now opened up (*Whitley Bulletin*, July 1968, p.104).

To judge from its journal, the National Staff Side thought that the Civil Service had come out well from the various discussions that had taken place immediately after the Fulton Report, and it was observed that

> perhaps the most important – and the most revealing – comment was that of the man who will have most to do in sorting out the Fulton Report: the Head of the Civil Service, Sir William Armstrong. Sir William (whose appearance at several Annual Conferences demonstrated his determination to eliminate the Civil Service communications gap) said on television that he regarded the Report as 'an icebreaker.' There could be no more apt description of the real situation which the Fulton Report has created: the opportunity that now arises to carry out necessary reforms which, in normal circumstances, would be virtually impossible to achieve (*Whitley Bulletin*, August 1968, p.117f).

The FDA's view of the Fulton Report was that it turned out to be very much like the curate's egg:

> Upon first reading a lot of the Committee's recommendations seem sensible. However, we must deplore the general criticisms of the administration which they make in their opening Chapter and which seem to us quite unjustified. The Administrative Class has worked wonders with a creaking government machine for years. Understaffed (the Admin-

istrative Class has fallen in numbers by nearly 13 per cent since 1950), overworked, housed in conditions which sometimes border on the squalid, and often lacking essential secretarial services our members have nevertheless managed to provide a service to Ministers and Parliament and equity to the public which, taken altogether, is regarded by our foreign colleagues as the best in the world. It would have been unrealistic to have expected the Report to begin with a song of praise, but we had at least hoped that the Committee would not turn down the once fashionable blind alley of 'specialization'; in fact they have rushed down it headlong. We say it was once fashionable since we know that the leaders of thought on management in the big world outside have now discovered that the alley has a very dead end and have lately been proclaiming the gospel of generalization and the broad approach! (*F. D. A. Monthly Notes*, June 1968; O'Toole, 1989, p.130f).

The journal of the SCS described the Fulton Report as 'the Report of Reports' in its editorial, and noted that 'the Executive Class have come out very well, particularly in the careful detail of Volume 2 of the Report' (*Civil Service Opinion*, July 1968, p.193). The Society's General Secretary, John Dryden, wrote that 'the Report of the Priestley Royal Commission some twelve and a half years earlier was a damp squib by comparison with the display of pyrotechnics which Fulton both produced and provoked.' Dryden, though, criticised the Report for 'criticism based on sweeping generalizations which in many cases do not appear to be supported by positive evidence,' and he was cautious about the implementation of the Report's programme (ibid., pp.195–9).

W. L. Kendall, the General Secretary of the CSCA, wrote that

the Committee's Report is a curious document. Some sensible reforms are proposed but the main recommendations will require the most critical scrutiny . . . It is the absence of a thorough analysis and the proliferation of emotive phrases which is most to be deplored in the Committee's Report. Provided everyone understands this, providing Dr Norman Hunt – who headed the Management Consultancy Group – is not regarded as the Hand of God operating in our midst and, providing there is the most thorough examination of Fulton's recommendations, some good may result. There is something to be said for a periodic shake-up (*Red Tape*, September 1968, p.352).

The contemporary reaction of academics to the Fulton Report was generally less admiring than its subsequent fame might lead one to expect. W. A. Robson, the only one of the long standing Fabian reformers still alive to comment, observed that 'the weaknesses of the Fulton Report is that it contains far too many sweeping generalizations of an unfavourable kind unsupported by any evidence. It gives the impression that the Civil Service is a stuffy collection of Victorian fuddy-duddies who must be swept away and replaced by highly equipped technicians dressed in shining chrome. Little credit is given, and little knowledge shown, of the innovations of recent years; and the appraisal of the achievements and qualities of the British Civil Service is grudging and inadequate' (Robson, 1968, p.403). That said though, Robson believed that 'the recommendations . . . are by no means revolutionary and many of them are sound' (ibid., p.404). D. N. Chester wrote of the Fulton Report that 'it bears the marks of haste, being somewhat repetitive and in parts not wholly clear.' In order to keep it to what the Committee thought to be a reasonable length (and possibly to make a more dramatic impact), 'the Report makes little or no attempt to quote chapter and verse for the problems and shortcomings found by the Committee, nor are the conclusions and recommendations backed up by reference to the evidence or to particular examples. In many ways it is an ungenerous document. It gives little credit to existing civil servants nor to the fact that some of the ideas in the Report are contained in Treasury and other official evidence.' Chester added though that 'nevertheless, even with these defects, the Report is a significant document and will be a major landmark in British public administration' (Chester, 1968, p.297f). Nevil Johnson attributed 'a breezy radicalism' to the Fulton Committee, and wrote that

> it discusses the problems of the Civil Service and advances its proposals for change in the tone of over-confident optimism which one detects so often in popular commentaries on the state of our polity . . . Yet when one has read the Report several times the impression of radicalism begins to fade. One sees that many parts of the diagnosis reflect fashionable criticisms which will one day go out of fashion (e.g. much of the criticism of the generalist and of the Service's alleged neglect of management techniques). Much of the comment and many of the recommendations merely confirm developments which were going ahead in the Civil Service quite independently of this inquiry (e.g. better use of specialist staff, integrated administrative units, quicker recruitment procedures, etc.). The hard core of innovation proposed is really quite small (Johnson, 1968, pp.367f).

The present writer found the Fulton Report to be insufficiently radical, especially as regards provision for post-entry training, and of being deserving of a series of detailed criticisms (Fry, 1969b, pp.484–94) which could be repeated without need for amendment twenty years later (Fry, 1988a, pp.51–5). More importantly, Richard Chapman, already prominent in the mainstream of the academic study of public administration, wrote that 'the Fulton Report was not outstanding either as a document or for its impact on the Service. The Report followed rather than heralded changes, and had many of the defects of the amateurism it criticized' (Chapman, 1970, p.85).

So the Fulton Report's reception in Parliament and among the commentators and the interests involved was mixed, with the House of Lords debate in particular being characterised by adverse criticism. 'Ever since the debate on your Committee's Report, I have meant to tell you that I thought your speech was perfectly suited to the circumstances,' Lord Shackleton wrote to Lord Fulton on 2 August 1968; 'A dignified statement of general approach was just what was needed after the stream of repetitive criticism from the retired mandarins.' Shackleton scrawled at the end of the letter, 'We are getting on with the job' (Fulton Papers). On 2 August too, Richard Wilding, forwarding other material, took the opportunity to congratulate Fulton on his performance in the debate and observed: 'In general, I found the debate rather disturbing. I agree with much that was said about Chapter 1, and the fact that the debate was so largely about that at the expense of the rest of the Report was due to our having written the Chapter in the terms we did. Nevertheless, the cumulative effect of the speeches was to over-do the defence of the Service, and I fear that the impression left upon Ministers, the Commons, and the public may well have been of the mandarins and their friends closing the ranks. If so, it will be counter productive' (Fulton Papers). The support of the Government of the day for the Fulton Report's main recommendations was what really mattered, of course; but before we examine implementation, assessments of the Fulton Report and its more important associated material by members of the Committee and those who worked with it needs to be considered.

Assessments of the Fulton Report and Management Consultancy Group's Report by Those Involved

The divisions on the Fulton Committee naturally persisted when it came to perceptions of the importance of its Report and what then happened when it came to implementation. Norman Hunt never ceased to praise the Fulton Report, and in joint authorship with the political writer Peter Kellner he later produced a book called *The Civil Servants. An Inquiry into Britain's Ruling Class* (London, Macdonald, 1980), which blamed 'the lost reforms' on the obstruction of the Head of the Home Civil Service between 1968 and 1974, Sir William Armstrong. Richard Wilding observed that 'the mythology seemed to be that Sir William Armstrong had blocked the implementation of the Fulton Report, and that his right hand man in sabotaging Fulton had the name of Wilding. What actually happened was that Sir William Armstrong and the Civil Service Department made a perfectly genuine effort to take the Fulton Report and to extract the maximum number of practical proposals that they could. As I was the Assistant Secretary in the Division most concerned, I can testify to the volume of the activity' (Interview, 1988). Whether 'mythology' or not, and rightly or not, the view of the Conservative MP David Howell that 'of course, the Civil Service nobbled the implementation of the Fulton reform programme' (Interview, 1989) came to be widely held. In stark contrast with Hunt, one former member of the Fulton Committee, Walter Anderson, 'never followed up what happened afterwards in any detail.' Anderson added: 'I signed the Fulton Report because I agreed with it. I had no reason to dissent' (Interview, 1988).

'Being on the Fulton Committee was an unrewarding experience and a very odd one too,' Sir James Dunnett observed;

> The Committee was set up in response to a lot of past criticism from *The New Statesman* and Thomas Balogh in particular, but it was essentially criticism of the Treasury and of its handling of economic policy and not of the Civil Service as such. There had been a need for radical change at the time of Northcote-Trevelyan Report, but when the Fulton Committee was appointed nobody seriously believed that the Civil Service generally was incompetent or corrupt. There was no shortage of evidence submitted to the Committee, but none of it made radical proposals. So what was there to say beyond recommending relatively minor changes? The fact was that Harold Wilson was anxious to have a radical Report. The composition of the Fulton Committee reflected this. It was in many ways a political exercise. The Fulton Report was in the event neither a radical nor a revolutionary document.

Dunnett did not agree with the view that the Head of the Home Civil Service had obstructed the implementation of the Fulton Report: 'Sir William Armstrong realized that common grading from the top to the bottom of the Civil Service was an impractical proposal. There was no difficulty about taking common grading down to a certain level, which at that time turned out to be Under Secretary. The one plus that did come from Fulton was that common grading near the top of the Civil Service meant that scientists and engineers were no longer treated as a class apart' (Interview, 1988).

'As a contribution to the debate on the Civil Service, I would not rate the Fulton Committee's Report highly,' Sir Philip Allen observed;

> What the Fulton Report did achieve was the limited objective of stirring the pot and raising the issues. It did not solve any of the problems. One thing that I would credit to the Fulton Report was that its publication meant that for the first time the Civil Service in general thought about the issues, a task that it had previously largely left to the academics. One specific gain from the Fulton Report was that the status of Establishments work was enhanced. There was a time when the job went to the least promising of the Assistant Secretaries. After Fulton, it was recognized that personnel management required expertise, and there was greater interchange between departments of people doing this work, which was all to the good.

As for the 'conspiracy theory' involving Armstrong, Allen said that

> William didn't obstruct the implementation of the Fulton Report. Indeed, for his own reasons, he was only too pleased to take advantage of the Committee's recommendation in favour of the establishment of the CSD. It is absurd to say that William thwarted what the Committee had intended, because this carries the implication that the Committee's recommendations were clear cut, whereas most of them were fudged. The Fulton Report did not amount to a simple programme for reform

and change. What William did was to work on the various issues. The mere fact that Fulton made recommendations that may or may not have been implemented did not mean that they were thwarted. What it meant was that having thought about it, William and others came to a different conclusion, which isn't the same thing at all (Interview, 1988).

'The Fabian report, *The Administrators* was a better argued, clearer, and better written Report than Fulton,' Robert Neild considered;

> but Fulton was a jolly good Report and it's very interesting that a radical Government is now implementing many of the bits of the Fulton Report that were rejected. This shows in a way how un-political the Fulton Report was. Our concern was that a Minister should get alternative streams of advice, and make his will prevail, and that the Civil Service should be expert and that the machinery of government should be efficient. These things are happening. Neild added: The difference seems to me that the Thatcher Government wants change and a machinery to bring it about in contrast with the earlier Governments which were prepared to tolerate a machinery that would resist change and had a high level of inertia.

Neild thought that 'The Fulton Report had two main ingredients – the Fabian conventional wisdom and the management stuff that Hunt and Garrett produced. Many of the recommendations followed on from the Fabian pamphlet, *The Administrators*, which fulfilled the Webbsian ideal of providing either a radical alternative to Royal Commissions or permeating their findings with evidence.' Neild said that

> the Fulton Report was bad on one thing. We did not face adequately the very worrying trend of civil servants leaving for jobs with firms which were within their purview. I regard this as a scandal and it had got going by the time we did the Fulton Report. Now it is almost the universal practice. Higher civil servants get large pensions and titles to set them apart from temptations of this kind. But nowadays they keep their perks and sell themselves for large extra salaries. One solution would be to strip them of their pensions and titles when they take those jobs.

On implementation, Neild commented:

> During the latter part of the Fulton Committee's existence, I was away in Stockholm. I was still in Stockholm when the Fulton Report was supposed to be being implemented, so I did not follow this implementation closely. It seems to me that the Fulton Report was watered down at a good many points and that the new avenues that we opened up were not pursued with much energy. Examples were hiving off and getting rid of the Final Interview Board. The changes in grading structure and the integration of the professionals were not pressed forward hard. The same was true with planning units. I am unsurprised about this because it is too much to expect a bureaucracy to reform itself radically. If you give such a bureaucracy specific instructions to change itself then they may

well be implemented, but suggestions for exploration will run into the mud (Interview, 1988).

'What we were taken by was the Northcote-Trevelyan Report and the prospect of producing something similar,' Robert Sheldon recalled; adding: 'Twenty years later, the Fulton Report stands up. The present Government has introduced unified grading down to Principal, and it is pushing for accountable management.' Sheldon said that 'the Civil Service blocked unified grading immediately after Fulton. They'd have liked to cut the numbers in the lower grades, but they were keen to protect the generalists at the top end. What the Civil Service said was "All you're after is to devise ways of doing generalists out of a job." The higher civil servants didn't like unified grading in principle.' He regretted the eventual demise of the CSD, and blamed its first Principal for wanting 'to make the Civil Service College into a university institution. What was needed was something like the training arrangements that private industry has such as the Administrative Staff College at Henley. Still, the Civil Service College survives and it seems to do useful work' (Interview, 1988).

'The Fulton Report was a better Report than it deserved to be,' Richard Wilding observed; 'Twenty years on and considering how different political realities are compared with the 1960s, the Fulton Report stands up quite well. I make no defence of the first chapter. It was a misconceived hand grenade. The Fulton Committee did identify a number of directions in which the Service ought to develop, even if some of the specifics were not the right ones.' He believed the Committee was right to emphasise accountable management and the need to clarify needs and objectives; to recommend systematic management training; to condemn the excessive frequency of moves among administrators and the need for a greater concentration on subject matter; and to recommend unified grading, though not from top to bottom of the Service. 'Below Principal, the division of labour was most complete. It was at that point meaning Principal and above, at which you need co-ordination, that unified grading has more to offer than separate Classes.' Wilding thought the Committee was wrong to have two armies of administrators whose remit transcended various departments: 'It was unrealistic to treat departmental boundaries in this manner. You can't make water flow uphill. The Committee was wrong about planning units and Senior Policy Advisers. This was unrealistic too.' Wilding believed that 'lots of foundations were laid by the Fulton Committee. Without accountable management, it would not be possible to contemplate the Ibbs changes' (Interview, 1988).

In some contrast with the views of the Committee's Secretary were those of its Assistant Secretary, Michael Simons, who observed that the Report was 'a shoddy piece of work. The Committee did not have the talent in its ranks to do any better than this. The kind of English used gave the game away, with various adjectives and adverbs used to indicate pep. On many matters, such as training, the Committee was kicking at an open door anyway.' He added: 'A remarkable thing about the Fulton Committee is that, after it had sat for nearly two and a half years, had accumulated a mass of written and oral evidence, had commissioned all kinds of investigative projects, nearly all the main conclusions in the Report and its general tone were essentially the same as they would have been had the Committee thrown off a Report after two or three meetings, before it had taken any evidence or had any inquiries carried out' (Interview, 1989).

As John Garrett was to tell a House of Commons committee in 1988 that he was 'an unreconstructed Fultonite' (HC 494-II, 1987–8, Evidence, q.218), it might be expected that this former member of the Fulton Committee's Management Consultancy Group would be uncritical of the Fulton Report. Yet, writing nearer the time, Garrett had observed that 'the imperfections of the Fulton Report obscure the value and significance of the reforms it proposed' (Garrett, 1972, p.52), and had then commented:

> In sum, the Fulton Committee bore out most of the accusations levelled at the Higher Civil Service by its critics in the preceding thirty years. It did, however, present its analysis and its proposals for change in a self defeating way. If implementation was to succeed it had to have some support among the administrators in command at the time, yet its tone and style alienated them from the outset. Rapid and effective implementation also depended on the clear and precise specification of a programme of change, yet the Committee left confusion surrounding most of its proposals. It did, however, spot most of the cracks, pressure points and distortions which had appeared in the management systems of the Civil Service and it gave the initial impetus to a number of overdue reforms which may eventually substantially change the practice of management in British government (ibid., pp.53–4).

Garrett was later to observe that he was 'very proud' of the Report of the Management Consultancy Group and said that 'Volume 2 got across Fulton's central message, which was of the waste of talent and the inefficiency and ineffectiveness that then characterized the organization of the Civil Service. That Volume 2 was published so long after the Fulton Report itself, and with such a small print run, led Norman Hunt to suspect a plot' (Interview, 1989).

Another member of the Group, E. K. Ferguson, considered that Volume 2 was

> a far better piece of work than Volume 1 which in my opinion was wrecked by injudicious phrasing with the use of the term 'amateur' and so on. It is too easy to blame this on Norman Hunt's energetic pressure. There were a lot of sophisticated individuals on the Fulton Committee and they and the Secretary should have stuck to their guns if they objected to the tone of the Report. Perhaps Norman Hunt was always the man with the first draft. Norman Hunt seemed to see me as a cautious businessman, but when it came to writing up the Management Consultancy Group's Report, my line

was that the points that we made ought to depend on the arguments and not on the adjectives' (Interview, 1989).

S. D. Walker, also of the Group, thought the Fulton Report was radical and 'said much the same things' as Volume 2. He added: 'Yet, I have this curious feeling about the two documents. More than one person has said to me that they did not think much of the Fulton Report, but they did consider the second volume to be better . . . Later on, when I was in the CSD, we would not normally cite Volume 2 in aid of implementing the Fulton Report.' Walker did not think that there was any substance to the 'conspiracy' theory about the implementation of the Fulton reforms: 'The Civil Service Department was a creature of the Fulton Report. It was set up in the first instance to implement [it]. I am quite sure that a genuine effort was made to do that. Nobody stopped me from doing so. I was not frustrated. Indeed, consistent with the Fulton Report's emphasis on "accountable management" we carried out what were the first Management Reviews which took a comprehensive look at the way in which the higher management of departments was organized' (Interview, 1989). Under the aegis of the CSD, Walker, together with John Garrett, published a study about the application of management by objectives in the Civil Service (Garrett and Walker, 1969).

So, as might be expected, the various members of the Fulton Committee, and those involved in and associated with its work, had differing views about the value of the Fulton Report. Both that Report and the more generally admired Management Consultancy Group's Report were to have their advocates in the years that followed. There came to be a recognisable 'Fultonite' position in discussion about the Civil Service and its reform. Norman Hunt often led the way, as with his jointly written book in 1980. In the same year, though, John Garrett published a book called *Managing the Civil Service* in which the Fulton themes were prominently displayed, and he had also published an earlier book along similar lines in 1972, and a Fabian pamphlet in 1973, together with, in that instance, Robert Sheldon. Garrett was also one of the signatories of the Minority Report of the English Committee in 1977, the tone of which recalled Chapter 1 of the Fulton Report (HC 535-I, 1976–7, pp.lxxviii–lxxxiii). By the time of that review of the Civil Service conducted by the House of Commons Expenditure Committee, implementing the Fulton Committee's proposals had for some become the test for Civil Service reforming intentions and progress, and the Fulton Report and the Report of the Management Consultancy Group were being treated as if they were the only source of ideas on the subject, which was not realistically the case even before the Thatcher era, let alone during it.

The Fulton Report Twenty Years On

The belief that 'it's all in Fulton' as an explanation of actual and prospective changes in the Civil Service and in the structure of government departments in the twenty years immediately after the publication of the Fulton Report was understandable at least up to a point because that Report, especially when taken together with the Report of the Management Consultancy Group, included not only Fabian ideas but also proposed the adoption within the Civil Service of management practices used in private business organisations, a form of advocacy more commonly associated with economic liberals. At the time of the twentieth anniversary of the Report, John Garrett described the Conservative government of the day as 'promulgating Fulton left, right and centre' (Hennessy et al., 1988, p.45) with political will having overridden Civil Service 'obstruction' of the kind previously experienced particularly in relation to the introduction of unified grading (ibid., p.47f). Earlier, Norman Hunt had attributed Civil Service 'obstruction' of the implementation of the Fulton Report primarily to Sir William Armstrong, the Head of the Home Civil Service between 1968 and 1974, although the account that he and a fellow writer later published of how 'the most important battle of all – for a unified class structure – was lost' in actual fact suggested that in practice Harold Wilson as Prime Minister did not give this reform his full support; and it recognised too that the Civil Service staff association movement was divided on this matter. When the CSD presented a memorandum to the English Committee in 1976 which showed, as Hunt and his fellow critic wrote, that 'the vast majority' of the Fulton Committee's recommendations 'had been or were being implemented,' they observed that: 'Fulton's reforms cannot be reduced to such arithmetical tests. The proposals were . . . constructed round a central criticism of the dominance of the generalists. The 158 recommendations addressed themselves to changing this: they were detailed means to a precisely identified end. For all its detail, the CSD checklist dwelt solely on the means and studiously ignored the end . . . Indeed . . . the word "generalist" does not appear at all' (Kellner and Crowther - Hunt, 1980, pp.59–79).

The term 'generalist' similarly did not appear in the 'List of Recommendations' that the Fulton Report contained (Cmnd. 3638, 1968, pp.194–205) to which, naturally the CSD's check-list was addressed; and its absence was unsurprising because the Fulton Committee was not asked to make recommendations about the current working of the doctrine of ministerial responsibility. Without consideration of the convention of ministerial responsibility, discussion of the 'generalist' becomes unreal, as does that about the machinery of central government, another excluded area.

John Bourn, who helped the Fulton Committee with such historical research as it pursued, later remarked of the Fulton Report that despite giving its main attention to the then Administrative Class at the expense of proper consideration of the Civil Service as a whole, it could be said of the Report that

> it failed to appreciate the role of the general administrator delivers a service for which there is a demand from Ministers. Such an administrator directly helps the Secretary of State in dealing with Parliament,

in preparing legislation, in negotiating the department's PESC allocation, and in assisting in the presentation of departmental policies. And when, under Fulton, scientists and outsiders moved into top jobs (often newly established for them) they found administrators quite willing to put their thoughts on paper for them, to guide them through the committee maze, and to help in lots of other ways. Thus administrators bound the newcomers into the system. Many new ideas got taken in – but on administrators' terms. Another reason why administrators maintained their power and position is that most of them – and certainly those who were going places – were prepared to work every hour God sent, and they were around, year after year. If you work very hard, and are around all the time, you will maintain your position (Interview, 1989).

'The Fulton Report criticized the Administrative Class for its lack of interest in management, and, ironically, Sir William Armstrong, charged with implementing Fulton as Head of the Home Civil Service was not really a managerial type,' John Bourn, who rose to be Comptroller and Auditor General, observed; 'Had he been so, he would simply have got on with implementation, whereas he chose to work through the National Whitley Council Joint Committee, a mechanism which ensured consensus management. Additionally, of course, there was not the financial edge behind the programme to pull the necessary levers' (Interview, 1989). It had been the Prime Minister, Harold Wilson, though, who announced that the Whitley system of joint consultation would be involved in the implementation of the Fulton Report, and this would be expected from a Labour government. Further, having respected convention in the first place by appointing a committee of inquiry of the Fulton type to make proposals for the reform of the Civil Service, that a contemporary equivalent to the National Whitley Council's Reorganization Committee of 1920–21 would be assigned an important role in the implementation process was a predictable corollary. The relevant files of what was then the Staff Side of the National Whitley Council bear out the consensual nature of the discussions (National Staff Side 1968–73: files 349.01, .02, .04, .08–10, .14A, .15, .25A, .25B, .26A).

The implementation of the Fulton Report by the career Civil Service, which, after all, the Committee had wished to retain, was not merely a technical exercise. The various interests within that Service would be bound to assert their positions, and inevitably not all of them were consistent with the Fulton Committee's proposals. Though the Fulton Report seems to have been accorded almost Biblical status by the time of the English Committee in the eyes of a certain sort of outside reformer, what the Report contained was simply a set of recommendations for change. The politically agreed mechanisms for change was the CSD, the establishment of which had been recommended by the Fulton Committee, and the National Whitley Council Joint Committee on the Fulton Report, chaired by Sir William Armstrong. On this latter body, it was agreed by both the Official and Staff Sides at the outset that 'it is wrong to limit our examination of possible changes to those which the Fulton Committee specifically proposed. We believe that our programme should be wide and flexible enough to cover all the major problems that affect the efficiency and well-being of the Service' (C.S. National Whitley Council, 1969a, p.1). In other words, the Fulton Report was like a contribution to a debate, the terms of reference and the outcome of which the Civil Service largely decided. Considerable activity followed down to 1973 even though, as Lord Bancroft, Head of the Home Civil Service between 1978 and 1981, observed, for the Civil Service 'implementing Fulton was just like trying to modify the design of a passenger liner while it was afloat. We couldn't stop working for the Government while we reorganized ourselves. In the end Sir William Armstrong came to believe that there had to be a settlement of the turbulence that Fulton caused. Hence, his famous phrase about the need "to draw a line under Fulton"' (Interview, 1988). If the Government concerned had wanted 'the passenger liner' to proceed at a greater pace in the reform of the Civil Service or to take a different direction, financial pressure might have provided a means, but such pressure was not as readily part of the political armoury in the late 1960s and down to the mid 1970s as it was to be after 1979. Continuing political interest in the reform of the Civil Service was what was crucial and in the immediate post-Fulton period, which is our overriding concern here, such interest was not sustained.

1. The political commitment to the reform of the civil service

'If the post-Fulton reform programme lost momentum this was primarily because of lack of Prime Ministerial and other Ministerial commitment to it rather than any Civil Service obstruction,' John Bourn observed (Interview, 1989); and Marcia Williams, the Prime Minister's Personal and Political Secretary at the time of Fulton, also did not subscribe to the 'conspiracy theory.' She said that Harold Wilson

> wanted an above board inquiry, the opposite of Margaret Thatcher's behind closed doors approach. When the Fulton Report came out, the civil servants may well have muttered in their clubs 'how can we mitigate the effects of this,' but Sir William Armstrong and the others were well aware that we might well win the next General Election in 1970 or 1971, and if they were obstructive before this they might get Fulton plus. Of course, not long after the Fulton Report came out the Labour Government was embroiled in a series of difficulties with major legislation, the House of Lords reform, the Boundary Commission's recommendations, the Redcliffe-Maud Report, the implementation of the Prices and Incomes Policy, and, critically, the *In Place of Strife* legislation, that all took priority over implementing Fulton' (Interview, 1989).

Harold Wilson's opposition to the introduction of 'preference for relevance' in the direct entry recruitment of administrators to the Civil Service proved to be critical, as Lord Shackleton, the Minister directly responsible for the implementation of the Fulton Report between 1968 and 1970, later recalled:

> Everybody knew at whom 'preference for relevance' was aimed. Norman Hunt hated Classicists, and Lord Fulton, though a Greats man himself, seemed to have come to share his outlook, which was that economists and scientists would make the best higher civil servants in the future. That by the time that they had reached the top their knowledge would be out of date never seemed to occur to Norman Hunt. We took a great deal of trouble at the CSD to try to find out which graduates deserved 'preference'. We even found ourselves playing a kind of game. At an early stage we took the view that Greats was relevant with its mixture of philosophy and classics and no authors could be more relevant to anyone aspiring to take part in Government than Thucydides, Plato, Cicero and many other classical authors. We decided that physics was not relevant but that zoology and palaeontology were. We even decided (for fun) that a Cambridge geography degree was relevant but not an Oxford geography degree. Furthermore we were all aware that for good or ill Greats still attracted people of very high ability. We came to the conclusion that it was best to put ability first, and for the Civil Service to look for the relevant man or woman to recruit. We sent our findings to the Prime Minister, and Harold Wilson replied that 'preference for relevance' was a lot of nonsense and that we ought to waste no more of our time trying to implement what always had been a ridiculous proposal (Interview: 29.11.88).

'Harold Wilson was a very effective Prime Minister but he could equally have been a very efficient Secretary of the Cabinet,' Marcia Williams believed;

> In some ways he was a civil servant *manqué*. He was a great admirer of the Civil Service and this made him ambivalent about the reform of the Civil Service. He saw himself as having a great deal in common with the Oxbridge administrators. After all, he had been educated at Oxford himself, and, as a training for the mind, he thought it to be the best in the world. So he would not necessarily align himself with the specialists, and this would explain his attitude to 'preference for relevance' (Interview, 1989).

It will be recalled that Barbara Castle believed that the then Prime Minister had a different outlook. Whether this was so or not, Wilson had been conventional enough in relying on an outside committee of inquiry to review the Civil Service, instead of simply proceeding with familiar Fabian reforms. Further, while the placing of higher civil servants on the Fulton Committee was presumed to be innovative, though the officials concerned could not easily dissent from reformist findings, their inclusion could also be seen as reflecting a wish to make the resulting Report more acceptable to the Service. Then again, in presenting its Report to the House of Commons, Wilson had compared the activities of the Fulton Committee with those of the Donovan Commission, both being engaged in the 'modernization . . . of our great Estates' (767 HC Deb. 5s. c.455). The Civil Service seemed to be being seen on this view as an interest in its own right, and this perception was not only present in the use of the Whitley machinery for implementation, but in the very idea of the CSD.

Edward Heath was later to describe the Fulton Report as not being radical enough for him (letter to author, 1989). 'The Conservatives' preparations for what they planned to do with the machinery of government when they returned to office in 1970 owed nothing to the work of the Fulton Committee,' David Howell, one of the planners, observed;

> We were well down the line before the Fulton Report came out and to us it was a document concerned with the sort of Civil service that was needed to run the machinery of an expanding State . . . What we wanted to do was to cut down the scope of central government – which was far from the intention of the Fulton Committee – and to separate out the functions of policy making and management, hiving off the latter to agencies, ideally as a prelude to privatization. We wanted arrangements which would establish what actually was being done in government departments, which would identify the management objectives, and which would facilitate the presentation to the House of Commons and to the public of details of performance, in other words, accountable management. All this was done independently of the Fulton Committee (Interview, 1989).

John Garrett commented with fairness that the Conservatives were much more structural in their approach than Fulton's Management Consultancy Group.

> They were not really interested in problems of personnel management, and it was clear from his evidence later to the English Committee that Edward Heath himself saw nothing much wrong with the career class system of the Civil Service even then. What had interested the Tories in the 1960s was using conglomerate organization in private business as a model for central government organization, and importing Planning Programming Budgeting as practised in the US Federal administration. In the end, PPB there collapsed under the weight of paper, and over here, when they got into office, the Conservatives only managed to give us Programme Analysis and Review and what studies were done were narrative rather than quantitative . . . Some of the hiving off exercises that the Heath Government did lasted, such as the Defence Procurement Executive, and both Fulton and the Tories left remnants behind to be taken up later (Interview, 1989).

The Conservatives did come into office in 1970, as David Howell said, 'with a Black Book which had a list of candidates for agency treatment that was much the same as the Ibbs programme' (Interview, 1989), and there is no doubting the scale of their preparations in relation to the machinery of government (Conservative Party Archive. Public Sector Research Unit, files 2,3; Boyle Papers: MS 660/23368–23469). The Heath government itself, though, proved to be little interested in the reform of the Civil Service as such. It was the government which introduced the Review Body on Top Salaries and which passed legislation to provide index-linked pensions for civil servants. It was the only government after 1964 to implement in full the Priestley formula on Civil Service pay (Fry, 1985, p.105). Whatever the merits of these actions, they were not those of a government that was antagonistic to the Civil Service as an interest, unlike the Conservative government elected in 1979 which proved to be more challenging in its behaviour (Fry, 1986, pp.533–55) and not content for long to work through organisations like the CSD.

2. *The civil service department*

The establishment of the CSD on 1 November 1968 was not necessarily in itself a reforming act, even if it tended to be widely perceived as such. What mattered was with what success it pursued a programme of reforms in the Civil Service, primarily (though as we have noted not solely along the lines proposed in the Fulton Report. In being charged with both representing the interests of the career Civil Service and yet being required to promote possibly radical change in that Service, the CSD had been assigned a difficult, at times conflicting, role. Sir Laurence Helsby's evidence to the Fulton Committee had indicated its likely long-term fate. Financial power still rested with the Treasury, and there were foreign examples too which made its eventual demise predictable (Fry, 1969a, pp.415–24).

In the immediate post-Fulton period, there were opportunities for the CSD to promote reforms, especially when given political support, and the first Minister for the Civil Service, Lord Shackleton observed twenty years later that

> one thing about the CSD that should be remembered was that, although it started out as being the Treasury Establishments side under a different name, within a year the Department included staff drawn from all over the Civil Service . . . We set out to improve the quality of Establishments work throughout the Civil Service and to make it a job that fliers did and not people doing their last tour of duty. As for the post of Minister for the Civil Service it was admirably suited for occupation with 50 per cent of the time of a Lords' Minister. I believe under Lord Jellicoe (my successor) and myself we were able to achieve real progress but the difficulty was that Ministerial occupation was always too short and it tended to become occupied by Ministers who were much too busy elsewhere and were not all that interested anyway. Lord Jellicoe was certainly extremely keen on reform and indeed sought to take unified grading further than I did (Interview, 1988).

Lord Jellicoe confirmed this, and on the basis of his experience as Minister for the Civil Service between 1970 and 1972 he remained 'an unrepentant defender of the need for a separate CSD with a Cabinet Minister to stand up for the Civil Service' (Interview, 1989).

Though later to be its Permanent Secretary, Lord Bancroft afterwards recalled that 'I was unhappy in 1968 about the establishment of the CSD. I had been Secretary of the Organization Committee which had reconstructed the Treasury in 1962. The remodelled Treasury seemed to be working well to me, and I thought that the CSD would not have enough clout even with Sir William Armstrong moving across to take charge. William though differently.' He added:

> Establishing the CSD worked better than I had anticipated. Previously, in the days of the unified Treasury, people who were posted to the Pay and Management side saw themselves as being assigned to the salt mines. The economic policy side had all the glamour. What the establishment of the CSD achieved was to develop a solid core of people who were dedicated to the management of the Civil Service. The CSD attracted able people who saw their careers as lying within its ranks. The CSD fostered a more coherent approach to every aspect of personnel management. The establishment of the CSD focused attention on personnel management, which was made more effective and became more sophisticated, for example, in succession planning. The CSD also perhaps provided a focal point to which civil servants could look in the belief that it was a department dedicated to making the Service more efficient, and which would help to ensure that the Civil Service collectively and individually was treated in an equitable way (Interview, 1988).

'William Armstrong was a powerful and forbidding Permanent Secretary, with a leonine way of swatting down opposition,' Clive Priestley, another former CSD official recalled; 'He had high intelligence allied to personal modesty, with an almost mystical aloofness. It seemed to me that as long as he was interested in Fulton and Civil Service reform he was a formidable leader of the implementation process, and he did assemble a powerful team to do the work all the way down to Principal level. He seemed to lose interest at about the time that the Heath Government changed course, and he became involved in this Horace Wilson role.' Priestley observed that 'before the Fulton Committee had reported, William Armstrong had already put in place the very able John Hunt as First Civil Service Commissioner, which was a marked and clear signal that he would be taking the outcome of the Fulton Committee seriously.' Then, again, far from conspiring against the Fulton reform programme, Armstrong had been an advocate of the establishment of a CSD because he 'wanted a department of his own to support him in the Head of the Civil Service role, now re-animated by the Fulton Report and given a new *raison d'être*.' The essential political interest and support was not forthcoming, and Priestley believed that 'this lack of Prime Ministerial interest, combined with the low esteem in which the CSD was by then held, meant that by the time that Douglas Allen took over (in 1974) what he thought would still be a position of influence at No. 10, the reform of the Civil Service had long since been downgraded on the political agenda.' Priestley observed that 'there was a continuing link with Fulton in the form of the Machinery of Government Division, the one glamour division of the CSD. . . . They kept the banner of Civil Service reform flying, but without the political support there was little or no progress for a long time' (Interview, 1988).

If a new department had been needed to implement the Fulton Report, as time went by the rationale for its existence was bound to be affected. A departmental history would give a fuller picture, but the time periods covered by the three Reports which the CSD issued (in 1970, 1971 and 1974) indicated a diminution of its role. There were to be no more Reports from the CSD and it was not long before the question of its continuance was raised. It survived two House of Commons inquiries, that of the English Committee, and also by the Treasury and Civil Service Committee in 1980 (HC 54-I, 1980–1). Lord Bancroft observed that 'even though in 1968 I had favoured pressing on with the 1962 model of a unified Treasury, it seemed to me that the CSD had more than justified its existence. After what turned out to be thirteen years and thirteen days, it seemed better to me to let things lie' (Interview, 1988). The Thatcher government took a different line from that of the then Head of the Home Civil Service, and not being given to 'let things lie', it abolished the CSD in 1981 (Fry, 1985, pp.72–95).

3. The civil service college

The first official duty of Edward Heath as Prime Minister was to open the Civil Service College on 26 June 1970. 'The College has never worked as Fulton intended,' Norman Hunt and his fellow author were later to write (Kellner and Crowther-Hunt, 1980, p.89), but in its early years in particular it did function broadly along the lines that the Osmond Working Party had envisaged, and on post-entry training as such the Fulton Committee did not have a fully independent position. The Committee never envisaged anything resembling an anglicised version of the ENA as, for instance, the present writer did (Fry, 1969a, pp.149ff, 325–9). Post-entry training for administrators was subject to what Desmond Keeling of the Working Party once called the 'third year rule,' which on the Civil Service's part reflected as regards careers 'the preference for basing decisions at the end of probation on performance over the full two years in jobs, rather than partly on performance on courses' (Keeling, 1971, p.63). Whatever the virtues of this approach, when applied to the CSC entry, it did raise the question of how seriously courses which mattered little for administrators' careers would be taken.

'The CSC never really recovered from getting off to the start that it did, and the particular appointment of Professor Grebenik as the first Principal had a great deal to do with this,' Lord Shackleton observed:

Denis Healey was particularly critical of the appointee, but no Ministers, even the Prime Minister, had any say about who got this job. I was not in favour of the Principal being a career civil servant, although there were people such as Sir Patrick Nairne who would have been very good. The Civil Service seemed to think that they needed a very strong candidate in order to block Norman Hunt, and Grebenik was considered to be strong enough. The opposition of the Civil Service to Norman Hunt was not altogether unreasonable. Although an able and likeable don he also had strong prejudices and indeed was activated by excessive egalitarian views. Hunt never seemed to appreciate that you got good people trained in any subject, and that the Civil Service had its difficulties in attracting its share of the ablest people without being handicapped in competing for them in the way that Hunt wanted (Interview, 1988).

'It would have been difficult in the late 1960s to have appointed an insider as the first Principal of the CSC, and at that time too the prestige of the social sciences was very high,' John Bourn, who was Assistant Secretary and Director of Programmes at the CSC between 1969 and 1972, later said of the appointment of Eugene Grebenik, who had been Professor of Social Studies at Leeds University since 1954: 'Grebby was both an outsider and as a demographer and statistician he was from the Civil Service's point of view the best sort of social scientist, an overtly politically neutral one.' Bourn thought that 'when he became Principal of the CSC Grebby was put in the position similar to that of having to run a race with a ball and chain on one of his legs. He could not progress as he wanted. He had no interest in subjects like management. What he really wanted to do . . . was to re-create there the BSC (Economics) degree scheme that he had completed with such success at the LSE in 1938. He could not recruit sufficient academic staff of high quality to bring this off.' Bourn added that 'the main difficulty came to be with the Administration Trainees, for whom success at the CSC was not a career requirement. After two years working in the Civil Service, they seemed to see going to the CSC as returning to the cloisters. Given the style of English education, you ended up with courses full of critics. Eventually, I suggested to Grebby that the programme for Administration Trainees should be liquidated or, alternatively, that the Trainees should be made to compete for training, but this did not happen' (Interview, 1989).

'One reason why the Civil Service College had difficulties from the start was that the Fulton Report gave an impossible specification,' Barbara Sloman, Grebenik's eventual successor as Principal of the College, later observed:

> It wanted the College to provide training of very varied types and at all levels of the Service – which was beyond the scope of a single, quite small institution. Mr Grebenik tried without success to get this clarified. His lack of experience of the Civil Service was a handicap in his relationship with the Permanent Secretaries and in the running of the College. And I think that we in the Service did not give him enough help. There were

also difficulties that resulted from the particular way in which the College organized itself. There were Directors of Studies, who were academics, and the Directors of Programmes, who were administrators. The academics were kept one down. Eventually, the structure of the College was sorted out following a Management Review. Clive Priestley did a brilliant job. He proposed getting rid of the divided structure, and, with his help, we drove through this reform.

Mrs Sloman added that, 'The Civil Service College got off to a bad start. The length and intensity of the training given to Administration Trainees were heavily criticised by departments, who were reluctant to spare them for so long and by the ATs themselves. This has now been changed to a menu of short courses spread over a period of two years or so – the sandwich training approach, which I think is good. It was probably a disadvantage that performance on the courses made no difference to the Administration Trainee's career. The College was also compared unfavourably with the ENA, but the elitism of the ENA would not have been easily accepted here' (Interview, 1989).

'What I wanted the CSC to be was an institution of high academic standing comparable with the ENA,' Eugene Grebenik recalled, meaning an institution
which would offer training of the highest quality to both direct entrants to what had been the Administrative Class and members of the Executive Class thought to have the potential to reach the highest ranks of the Civil Service, and which would give serving civil servants that attended it opportunities to develop a wider outlook than departmental work normally seems to allow. In that context, I hoped to develop a Senior Management Course designed for civil servants who were thought to be in line for promotion to Under Secretary posts, so that they could be given a sabbatical term (as their counterparts in the Armed Forces were given a year at the Imperial Defence College) when they could recharge their intellectual batteries and be given an extended period free from their routine duties. This idea was not given an enthusiastic welcome by Establishment Officers, as the Civil Service has no 'training margin.' The view was expressed that it would be difficult to know who the people in line for promotion were. I think that I would add that what I thought that the College would do was in accordance with the views expressed in the Fulton Report, and I was encouraged in this belief by a remark that the late Lord Boyle made, when introducing a public lecture I gave at the University of Leeds. I wanted the Civil Service College to be an outward looking institution, and to be a centre for learning for the study of public administration (Interview, 1988).

'The portrayal of Sir William Armstrong as undermining the Civil Service College that you get in the book by Crowther-Hunt and Kellner seems to me to be wide of the mark,' Grebenik stated; 'It is difficult to say what Sir William Armstrong wanted the CSC to be. He was the type of man who kept his cards close to his chest and I did not know him well, although I had no difficulty of access to him. Sir William Armstrong did disagree with me about one important matter. I put a paper to him asking for security of tenure for academics at the College. He did not agree, and as Permanent Secretary he had, of course, every right to do so.' Grebenik added:

> I would say that Sir Douglas Allen was less enthusiastic about the CSC than Sir William Armstrong seemed to me to have been. Lots of civil servants were unsympathetic to the whole idea of a CSC and their position was strengthened when an outsider was appointed. Even of those who were sympathetic to the College, among whom I would count Sir William Armstrong, they did not seem to be of one mind. The same could not be said of the unions. They were adamant that the CSC was not to be elitist and that everybody from Messenger to Permanent Secretary should have the chance to go there. There had to be universal entry because it was believed that attendance at College courses would lead to improved opportunities for promotion, but as everybody could not be promoted, it followed that the unions' objectives were mutually exclusive (Interview, 1988).

That some of the failures of the CSC were his personal responsibility was recognised by its first Principal. His previous experience of the Civil Service had been in wartime as a relatively junior civil servant, and he had found the transfer from the culture of the university world to that of the Civil Service not altogether easy. 'I found the Administration Trainees to be a difficult lot to deal with,' Grebenik observed;

> The Civil Service Commissioners would not give up their right to allocate the successful candidates from the Administrative competition, which meant that the ATs went to the department before coming to the CSC. They thought that they knew it all by then. In reality, the ATs only had the superficial knowledge that they had obtained in the departments, and they had lost the habit of studying . . . As it was, we were supposed to teach them all together, which meant, for instance, the same economics irrespective of whether they had graduated in economics or in English. Whatever the ATs did, we were not asked to assess them. Coming to the College made no difference to their career at all. This reflected the attitude of most Permanent Secretaries and Establishments people that the best training was to learn on the job. I would have preferred the AT entry to have been sent to the College right away and sorted out there over six months, before going *en stage* and so on as at ENA (Interview, 1988).

'We never got the staffing at the College right,' Grebenik believed, 'Certainly we never got the dual hierarchy of Directors of Programmes and Directors of Studies sorted out properly. Once Sir William Armstrong had ruled out tenure for academics at the College we were forced to rely on people recruited on temporary contracts and people seconded from government departments. Many of the staff that we got from these sources were very good.' Grebenik added that 'I inherited the arrangement whereby the Civil Service College was located at three sites – Sunningdale, London and Edinburgh. If the centres had been organized hierarchically and different categories of civil servant had been allocated to particular places and the specialized teaching staff distributed accordingly, then a proper deployment of such staff would have been possible. This was not the favoured arrangement. The Scots were very keen on their status, and the Head of the College at Edinburgh had a fair degree of independence.' Grebenik emphasised that

> All was not disappointing when it came to the College's work. We had a great deal of success with computing studies when we put our students in for outside examinations. We also established a strong link with the University of Leeds with Professor Philip Thody. When Prime Minister, Edward Heath had said that every civil servant should be able to speak at least one foreign language. The College's response was to ask Philip Thody to lay something on and he ran a highly successful course in administrative and technical French which the civil servants liked. The success of that venture must be credited to Philip Thody. A similar scheme involving German did not work well. Fewer civil servants had a grounding in the language.

Grebenik recalled that Sir John Moore, then a Deputy Secretary at the CSD had told him that 'we recruited you under a false prospectus,' and Grebenik added that he had no inkling of this when he had applied for the post of Principal in 1969 at a time when he had no particular wish to leave the University of Leeds. He had been interviewed by a Board which included the First Civil Service Commissioner and, to his surprise, he had been offered a job which had seemed to be full of possibilities, few of them realisable as it turned out (Interview, 1988).

'The CSC fell between two stools, meaning the deliberately narrow Centre for Administrative Studies on the one hand, and a fully fledged Staff College on the other,' Lord Bancroft observed (Interview, 1988). The College was heavily criticised in an official review of Civil Service training conducted by a former higher civil servant, R. N. Heaton, and Sir Leslie Williams of the National Staff Side, that was published in 1974. The authors attributed some of the College's problems to the 'very widely assorted range of courses' that it had to provide (Heaton and Williams, 1974, para.5.3). In the fifth Annual Report of the College, the Principal literally added 'Amen' to that observation (Civil Service College, 1974–5, p.2). The sixth Annual Report was to be Grebenik's last before premature retirement. He noted the impending closure of the Edinburgh centre as part of expenditure cuts that had fallen disproportionately on the College compared with the rest of the CSD, and he commented adversely on the College having been made subject to the activities of a Management Review Team (ibid., 1975–6, pp.1ff). Following the report of this Team, it was announced in the autumn of 1976 that the College would form part of a new Training Group in the CSD to be led by Barbara

Sloman who would assume the dual role of Principal of the College and Under Secretary in charge of Training Division, combining the responsibilities for both central and departmental training. Grebenik then retired (ibid., 1976–7, p.4). He had been succeeded by his deputy, and Hunt and his fellow critic observed that 'to confirm finally that the College was no longer even expected to fulfil Wilson's and Fulton's ambitions, the post of Principal of the College was downgraded from Deputy Secretary to Under Secretary' (Kellner and Crowther-Hunt, 1980, p.92f). That the College did not do 'the job' that 'Fulton wanted' meant that 'Armstrong won' (ibid., p.94). Armstrong's denial of tenure to academics at the College at a time when it was available to their counterparts elsewhere in other institutions was unhelpful, but the Fulton Committee never recommended tenure for such staff. When the Committee's 'ambitious plans' were referred to (ibid., p.93) it is unclear what these could be, given the reliance on the Osmond Working Party's scheme. Talk of research activity at the College could only be serious if it was a Higher Civil Service College, which was what Grebenik was interested in, but to which, as the Heaton-Williams Report recognised, the staff associations were implacably opposed (Heaton and Williams, 1974, para.5.3). If anybody 'won', their approach did, though, of course, they had no monopoly of influence. The Fulton Committee never recommended an anglicised ENA and, for all the difficulties of importing arrangements from a much different political and administrative culture, the emphasis placed on professionalism in the Fulton Report did point to a CSC of the order of the ENA calibre with a decisive influence in career patterns. Such an institution was not proposed, and of the modest one that eventually developed it could be said by Barbara Sloman twenty years after its inception that 'the CSC has survived and it has done good work' (Interview, 1989).

4. Unified grading and structural change

'Sir William Armstrong . . . was keen on reforming the Civil Service, but among the difficulties he faced was the fact that a number of Permanent Secretaries did not like parts of the Fulton Report,' Lord Shackleton recalled. 'However we were I think making progress but we ran into difficulties over unified grading which though important became almost an article of faith amongst the reformers. I was never quite clear why a reform which was going to take some time to put into effect was regarded with such urgency. There was a genuine belief among senior civil servants that beyond a certain point unified grading would not work' (Interview, 1988). Lord Jellicoe, Shackleton's Conservative successor as Minister for the Civil Service, stated that he found unified grading to be an attractive concept, and so did the Prime Minister. 'Sir William Armstrong advanced fairly strong objections to going anything like the whole hog on unified grading. I recall reading a whole wodge of papers in 1971 which cogently argued against a unified grading structure. When Ted Heath and I discussed the matter with Sir William Armstrong, we were persuaded by the case against going the whole hog with unified grading. Ted Heath was keen on Civil Service reform, but he was perhaps more partial to Civil Service arguments than Mrs Thatcher' (Interview, 1989). An Assistant Secretary at the CSD at the time, Richard Wilding, recalled that on unified grading 'there was a genuine difference of opinion between what Sir William Armstrong thought and what the Fulton Committee had recommended. Sir William was sceptical about the virtues of unified grading below Under Secretary level. I myself was in favour of taking such grading down to Principal level. Sir William was not of this opinion and, as for unified grading from top to bottom of the Service, he thought that it would be expensive and he was sceptical that value for money would result' (Interview, 1988).

Factually, what happened in terms of structural change in the Home Civil Service in the immediate post-Fulton period was clear enough. On 1 January 1972 a system of unified grading was introduced down to and including the Under Secretary grade to form an Open Structure, and below that the Service was divided up into broad categories and occupational groups. On 1 January 1971 the Administrative, Executive and Clerical Classes were merged to form a single Administration Group within the General Category. In September 1971 a Science Group within the Science Category was formed by an amalgamation of the Scientific Officer, Experimental Officer and Scientific Assistant Classes. From 1 January 1972 the Works Group of Professional Classes together with some associated Classes were merged to help to form the Professional and Technology Category (Fry, 1981, p.148f).

'I have serious doubts whether the CSD is any longer actually pursuing the objective of a unified grading structure for the whole of the Service,' Norman Hunt wrote to Michael Halls in December 1969 for the attention of the Prime Minister;

> There is no need at all to give any priority to the abolition of the Class barriers between the Clerical, Executive and Administrative Classes. There is already a great deal of upward movement of individuals between these different Classes . . . If there are to be interim mergers . . . the priority need is in the Scientific Officer and its supporting Classes . . . The priority need of the Service is to make possible more sideways movement from the Scientific and other specialist Classes into adjacent areas of administration/management and to give these specialists some experience of administration/management *at lower levels* of the Service. This means having a real unified grading structure throughout the Service . . . This, however, is now put off to some indeterminate future with vague warnings that it may never be a practical proposition (Fulton Papers).

Norman Hunt's intention must have been to try to encourage Prime Ministerial action to override the politics of the National Whitley Council Joint Committee process. Issuing from that came *Developments on Fulton*, which that Committee later called 'the 1969 Report' (C. S. National Whitley

Council, 1969a), and then *Fulton: A Framework for the Future*, 'the 1970 Report' (ibid., 1970), and *Fulton – The Reshaping of the Civil Service: Developments during 1970*, 'the 1971 Report' (ibid., 1971), and lastly, *The Shape of the Post-Fulton Civil Service* in March 1972 (ibid., 1972). When in July 1969, another document from the Committee called *The Timing of Interim Changes in the Grading Structure of the Civil Service* (ibid., 1969b) set out the strategy of staging, Hunt seemed alerted to the likelihood that the introduction of complete unified grading would be frustrated. Sir William Armstrong was not cited as the source of 'obstruction.' Hunt wrote to Halls in December 1969:

> The Society of Civil Servants will fundamentally oppose the abolition of vertical barriers between Classes. This is because EOs and HEOs etc. will feel their positions threatened by their Experimental Officer counterparts. At the same time the SCS want to abolish the horizontal barrier between Administrative and Executive Classes. To concede the latter demand (as the proposed scheme for interim mergers does) before the Society has been forced to accept the abolition of the vertical barrier is to abandon an important bargaining counter; this could mean that the SCS will be able successfully to resist the further and more vital merger, i.e. the ending of vertical barriers needed to produce a unified grading structure.

After the March 1972 Report ruling out unified grading, Hunt wrote to Lord Fulton saying that 'Eddie Shackleton did not seem particularly put out by the decision, but Robert Sheldon, as you can imagine is "piping mad." ' Hunt added about his analysis of December 1969 that 'it has proved all too accurate' (Fulton Papers).

'An irresponsible extension of unified grading' was how the journal of what was now called the Society of Civil and Public Servants described such grading being taken down to and including the Principal grade from the beginning of 1986 in the same way as it had been extended to Senior Principal level in 1984. Most of the unions in the Council of Civil Service Unions were opposed to the change (*Civil Service Opinion*, September 1985). The IPCS, whose members were expected to benefit, naturally took a different line – 'Career barrier breaks' (IPCS Bulletin, 9/85). In that particular political climate, the opposition of some Civil Service interests to change, or the support of others come to that, was not allowed to matter.

On the role of the Head of the Home Civil Service in the immediate post-Fulton period, the views of a later holder of the post, Lord Armstrong of Ilminster (formerly Sir Robert Armstrong) are worth placing on record:

> My recollection is that William Armstrong concluded that the Fulton proposals for a unified grading structure should be taken by stages; and that they should be applied in the first instance to the Higher Civil Service down to Under Secretary level, where numbers were smaller and complications were less, before going on to tackle the much larger

numbers and greater complications of unified grading at the next levels down. Whether the next stage could have followed earlier it is difficult to say. The time from 1974 to 1979 was a time of digesting and consolidating the changes that had been made after Fulton, and the Government of the day had other and more urgent preoccupations than management reform. When management reform returned to the top of the agenda in 1979, the main preoccupation at first was with the improvement of efficiency, and particularly of financial efficiency, and priority was given to the introduction of management information systems in departments, to the Financial Management Initiative, and of course to Sir Derek Rayner's efficiency scrutinies. But during the period we always had in mind the desirability of taking unified grading down to what is now called Grade 7 (Principal level), and preparatory work was put in hand, so that the change was able to be put into effect in 1986.

Armstrong added that he personally thought that it was unfair of Norman Hunt to accuse William Armstrong of being obstructive.

I am sure that Norman, a naturally impatient man, wanted to see things going faster; I do not think that William Armstrong was out of sympathy with the general principle of unified grading: on the contrary. But I think that he did not want to run the risk of spoiling the effectiveness of the change by pressing it too fast too far. Apart from the practical complexities, I have no doubt that there was some opposition in principle to unified grading, and with the benefit of hindsight I think Sir William Armstrong was wise in deciding to proceed by stages rather than all at once (letter to author, 18.2.92).

A 'Revolutionary' Report?

'The ice was broken' by the Fulton Report, Lord Armstrong of Sanderstead, formerly Sir William Armstrong, told the English Committee in 1977 (HC 535–II, 1976–7, q.1500), but the reality surely was that the development of the Civil Service had not been frozen before 1968. True, the 1950s had been a period of consolidation after the dramatic activities of the 1940s when the Second World War and its aftermath had witnessed substantial changes in the scale and organisation of the Civil Service and in its responsibilities. The Plowden Report on the Control of Public Expenditure of 1961, the reorganisation of the Treasury in 1962, and the establishment of the Centre for Administrative Studies in 1963 marked the beginning of another period of change in the Civil Service which was in progress well before the Fulton Committee was appointed in 1966.

In describing the Fulton Report as 'an ice-breaker,' Lord Armstrong had apparently meant 'that it was a catalyst and enabled all sorts of ideas to come through' (ibid., q.1499). The Fulton Committee, though, was unsuited to the role of 'ice-breaker' because the span of its activity was limited by the exclusion of the machinery of government and the convention of ministerial responsibility from its terms of reference. This meant, for instance, that the Committee was reduced to expressing a preference for less 'secrecy' in the conduct of government, and registering interest in the 'hiving off' of management functions, without being able fully to relate the discussion to the manner in which the existing system of government operated. To have to resort to recommending further inquiries to investigate what it needed to review itself emphasised the restrictions within which the Fulton Committee had to work. The failure to place the Committee's discussion within a political context gave an oddly beheaded appearance to its potentially interesting proposals for introducing a particular form of policy planning unit into government departments. It is not surprising that, in the years immediately following the Report, no planning units of the Fulton type were subsequently established (Fry, 1972, pp.139–55; Macdonald and Fry, 1980, pp.421–37). To have planning units as such was not a new idea even in practice, of course, given that the one in the Board of Customs and Excise dated from 1922, and there was no novelty either in detecting advantages in a Swedish style of central government organisation or in calling for greater openness in public policy making. Giving a seal of approval from an official committee of inquiry did not grant authorship to the Fulton Committee, and this was sometimes forgotten, for example, in later discussion of 'hiving off'. The advocacy of the importing of 'business methods' into government departments by the Fulton Committee, unusual at least from a primarily Fabian source, was not closely related either to the doctrine of ministerial responsibility which determined the existing system of accountability, or to the implications of greater managerialism for a career Civil Service.

Even in that sphere that was its to review, the Fulton Committee risked being overtaken by developments and cast into an endorsing role. As regards post-entry training, there was no need for the Committee largely to accept what the Osmond Working Party proposed, but this it did. In the case of direct entry recruitment, while the Committee divided over the retention of the Method I means of recruiting administrators, the Civil Service Commissioners had made clear their wish to discontinue it, which was done in 1969. The Davies Committee, reporting in 1969, accompanied high praise for Method II with twenty-three recommendations for change (Cmnd. 4156, 1969) which owed little to the Fulton findings.

Even if one recognises the pragmatic arguments against 'preference for relevance' in administrative recruitment (Fry, 1969a, p.402f) the divisions on the Fulton Committee about it robbed the Report of the radical edge many of its members were seeking. There was actually little substance in the supposed difficulty in identifying what was 'relevant,' as Lord Croham (formerly Sir Douglas Allen) later observed:

> I regard as 'relevant' those subjects which form the syllabus of the courses given in the Service to administrative trainees and, of course, include public administration. The optimum way to give a 'preference

for relevance' is to insist that a certain standard is reached in those subjects before confirmation of appointment and a first promotion. That gives those who read 'relevant' subjects the prospect of earlier promotion and that would be enough, in my view. So, in a sense, I agree that the studies can be left to post-entry training, but since we find that trainees tend to have become sick of academic work before they join the Service, they will not take post-entry training seriously unless it counts for promotion, in a way that the post-Fulton CSC courses did not (letter to author, 18.10.88).

Fatally for their ambitions, the radicals on the Fulton Committee had failed to make recommendations which gave the CSC and post-entry training the prominence that their commitment to explicit professionalism required. The recommendations of the divided Fulton Committee made little impact on direct entry recruitment, as we have seen. Those successful in what had been called Method II continued to be drawn from a wide area of the subjects taught in higher education without extensive, compensating 'relevant' post-entry training, arrangements which, ironically, did not command wide support at the time of Fulton. Though the Fulton Committee had little to contribute that was distinctive on recruitment and training, it did produce a formally agreed recommendation favouring the introduction of a unified grading structure. At first sight, if only tactically, it was unhelpful that the Committee's unambitious approach to research allowed scope for a CSD team led by Sir William Armstrong subsequently to conduct its own study of North American Civil Services and their unified grading systems (CSD, 1969); but the reality was that, while it was not made explicit in the Fulton Report, enthusiasm for unified grading was by no means universal on the Committee, and this affected the manner in which the proposal was presented.

To some extent, and inevitably, the Fulton Committee was a creature of its time. 'McNamara is today's hero, not Gladstone,' Robert Neild informed his colleagues on the Committee on 29 March 1967 (PRO: BA1/32). The idea that Robert McNamara's Pentagon was the example to follow in administrative efficiency scarcely survived the 1960s, and, within a decade of the Fulton Report, Gladstone's example in the form of principles of public finance, if less often their observance, was to be restored for a time. 'The Civil Service had to manage itself – to obtain good results with the smallest outlay,' Enoch Powell told the Fulton Committee on 26 July 1966, 'The best method of improvement was to cut expenditure; this was more effective than any amount of O. and M.' (PRO: BA1/4). Though Powell's was a lone voice at the time of the Fulton Committee, the sentiments that he uttered were to become familiar after 1979 when a Conservative government of economic liberal outlook made economies in public spending and cut Civil Service numbers, and in 1982 introduced the Financial Management Initiative into departments, drawing on its own Rayner scrutinies and on the practice of MINIS (Fry, 1988b, pp.1–20).

The influence of the Fulton Report on later developments in the reform of the Civil Service is difficult to trace. The Report did not knowingly influence Michael Heseltine, the author of MINIS, who derived the ideas for it from 'personal experience both in the private sector and in the early days of Ministerial life' (letter to author, 25.7.89). Lord Rayner wrote that

> my work in Government in the periods 1970–74 and 1979–82 was not directly influenced by the Fulton findings. Prior to 1970 and indeed the publication of the Fulton Report, I was working with the Tory Party to develop a fresh approach to Government procurement. The work, together with the work of senior businessmen, owed its inspiration to the wishes of senior members of the Tory Party to use businessmen in Government when they were returned to power . . . My return to Government work on the election of Mrs Thatcher in 1979 arose as a result of investigations carried out prior to 1979. The task I undertook was very much the product of Mrs Thatcher's own thinking, with detailed involvement by Sir Keith Joseph. The way I set about the task was very much my own (letter to author, 5.7.89).

Lord Rayner's Chief of Staff in the Prime Minister's Office between 1979 and 1982, and a CSD official in the immediate post-Fulton period, Clive Priestley, thought that the Fulton Report was seen with 'a new hindsight because of the experience of Thatcherite radicalism.' Priestley considered that 'Fulton was reasonably radical' and said of Mrs Thatcher's approach that the crucial difference between her and her immediate predecessors in respect of the Civil Service was 'that she stuck to the theme of reform, looking to trusted advisers, and not a committee, to put together a programme, and that she had given the programme consistent personal support from the summer of 1979 onwards. Some of the advisers, myself included, drew heavily on post-Fulton work and the thinking of people like Richard Wilding, Brian Pearce, and Johnny Walker in devising the reform programme' (Interview, 1988). The break-up of the career Civil Service, though, was implied by the Financial Management Initiative of 1982 and the Ibbs Report, *Improving Management in Government: The Next Steps* of 1988 (Efficiency Unit, 1988), and notions of a core or central Civil Service and a peripheral Civil Service were alien to Fulton (Fry, 1988c, pp.429–39). How things develop depends on the range of applicability of ministerial responsibility and the extent of the Civil Service and its career patterns; but having traced Civil Service reform we can note with Clive Priestley 'the new irony of *The Next Steps* which may well take us back to the old structure, with a policy cadre in the Ministries and agencies to do the management work' (Interview, 1988).

'The idea of producing a revolutionary Report dominated (Norman) Hunt's thinking. He was obsessed with emulating the Northcote-Trevelyan Report,' Sir James Dunnett later observed (Interview, 1988), and twenty years on opinions still differed about whether or not Hunt and his fellow radicals on the Fulton Committee achieved their 'revolutionary' ambition.

'The main Fulton Report was the last great Fabian document on the Civil Service, assuming a big Service and being concerned to make it more efficient,' John Garrett considered (Interview, 1989). 'The Management Consultancy Group's Report offered the best and most radical re-assessment of the scope and purpose of public administration in central government, and the qualities it requires, since the Northcote-Trevelyan Report,' John Delafons, a higher civil servant, later wrote (Delafons, 1982, p.263). 'My impression is that the Management Consultancy Group's Report itself was shunted, but that the ideas that it promoted such as managerial accountability and unified grading re-emerged later,' E. K. Ferguson, a member of the Group, commented; 'People like Derek Rayner, of course, would not be dependent on the ideas of Fulton's Volume 2 for what they wanted to do, and I do not wish to exaggerate the importance of Management Consultancy Group's Report. The further development of unified grading was pure Fulton, but it was not necessarily generated by Fulton' (Interview, 1989). A measured view of that kind seems a more realistic assessment of the Fulton Committee's influence on the subsequent development of the Civil Service than interpretations of the 'it's all in Fulton' type.

The Fulton Committee was not charged with a 'revolutionary' task but with constructing a programme of reform for a large-scale career Civil Service that was to continue in being. The Fulton Report itself might have been a more impressive document if the Committee had adhered to its original plan and published a brief, pithy statement of reforming intent, accompanied by a substantial supporting volume, in the same way as the Redcliffe-Maud Royal Commission on Local Government of 1966–1969 was to do (Cmnd. 4039, 1969). Again, integrating the Management Consultancy Group's Report into the Fulton Report might also have translated it into a more intellectually formidable piece of work. The Fulton Report that was published, of course, commanded contemporary attention, and was swiftly accorded the status of a State Paper of importance in the development of the British Civil Service.

Bibliography and References

1. The Fulton Committee On the Home Civil Service 1966–1968

(a) The papers of the Fulton Committee

COMMITTEE ON THE CIVIL SERVICE (FULTON COMMITTEE). PRO:
BA1/1-97. Public Record office.

(b) Private Papers

LORD BOYLE OF HANDSWORTH. Brotherton Library, University of Leeds.
LORD CROWTHER-HUNT OF ECCLESHILL. Bodleian Library, University
of Oxford.
LORD FULTON OF FALMER. Privately held.
LORD SIMEY OF TOXTETH. Harold Cohen Library and Sidney Jones
Library, University of Liverpool.

(c) Interviews with members of the Fulton Committee, its Secretariat, and the Man-
agement Consultancy Group

LORD ALLEN OF ABBEYDALE, 17 October 1988.
W. C. ANDERSON, 21 September 1988.
SIR L. J. DUNNETT, 29 November 1988.
E. K. FERGUSON, 21 April 1989.
J. L. GARRETT, 5 April 1989.
R. R. NEILD, 28 October 1988.
R. E. SHELDON, 8 November 1988.
M. A. SIMONS, 30 March 1989.
S. D. WALKER, 1 March 1989.
R. W. L. WILDING, 29 September 1988.

(d) The Fulton Report 1968

FULTON REPORT 1968, *The Civil Service*. Vol. 1, *Report of the Committee
1966–68*, Cmnd. 3638; Vol. 2, *Report of a Management Consultancy Group*; Vol.
3(1), *Surveys and Investigations, Social Survey of the Civil Service*; Vol. 3(2),
Surveys and Investigations; Vol. 4, *Factual, Statistical and Explanatory Papers*;
Vol. 5(1), *Proposals and Opinions*, Parts 1 and 2, *Government Departments and
Staff Associations*; Vol. 5(2), *Proposals and Opinions*, Parts 3 and 4, *Organizations
and Individuals* (London, HMSO).

2. Further Sources

ASSHETON REPORT (1944), *Report of the Committee on Training of Civil Servants*,
Cmd. 6525 (London, HMSO).

ALLEN, SIR C. K. (1931), *Bureaucracy Triumphant*, (London, OUP).

ATTLEE, C. R. (1954), 'Civil Servants, Ministers, Parliament and the Public', *Political Quarterly* 25, pp.308–15.

BALFOUR REPORT (1910), *Report of the Departmental Committee on the Procedure of Royal Commissions*, Cd. 5235 (London, HMSO).

BALOGH, T. (1959), 'The Apotheosis of the Dilettante: The Establishment of Mandarins', in Thomas, H. S. (ed.), *The Establishment* (London, Blond).

BALOGH, T. (1968), 'The End of the Amateur', *New Statesman*, 28 June 1968.

BANCROFT, LORD, Interview, 17 November 1988.

BARLOW REPORT (1945), *The Scientific Civil Service. Reorganization and Recruitment during the Reconstruction Period*, Cmnd. 6679 (London, HMSO).

BATTEN, J. D. (1966), *Beyond Management by Objectives*, (New York, American Management Association).

BEECHING REPORT (1969), *Report of the Royal Commission on Assizes and Quarter Sessions*, Cmnd. 4153 (London, HMSO)

BENN, T. (1987), *Out of the Wilderness. Diaries 1963–67*, (London, Arrow Books).

BENN, T. (1988), *Office Without Power. Diaries 1968–72*, (London, Hutchinson).

BISHOP, F. A. (1968), 'Fulton: The Cart before the Horse', *The Spectator*, 28 June 1968.

BOURN, J. B., Interview, 2 February 1989.

BRADBURY REPORT (1919), *Final Report of the Committee Appointed to Inquire into the Organization and Staffing of Government Offices*, Cmd. 62 (London, HMSO).

BRIDGES, SIR E. E. (1954), 'The Reforms of 1954 in Retrospect', *Political Quarterly* 25, pp.316–23.

BRITISH INSTITUTE OF MANAGEMENT (1967), *Management by Objectives*, Seminar, Manchester, 1 March 1967 (London, British Institute of Management).

BRITTAN, S. (1964), *The Treasury under the Tories 1951–1964*, (Harmondsworth, Penguin Books).

BROWNLOW REPORT (1937), *The President's Committee on Administrative Management. Report of the Committee with Studies of Administrative Management in the Federal Government*, (Washington DC, US Government Printing Office).

BULMER, M. (1980), *Social Research and Royal Commissions*, (London, Allen and Unwin).

BULMER, M., ed. (1983), *Royal Commissions and Departmental Committees of Inquiry. The Lessons of Experience*, (London, Royal Institute of Public Administration).

CAIRNCROSS, SIR A., ed (1989). *The Robert Hall Diaries 1947–53*, (London, Unwin Hyman).

CAIRNCROSS, SIR A., ed (1991), *The Robert Hall Diaries 1954–61*, (London, Unwin Hyman).

CAIRNCROSS, SIR A. and WATTS, N. (1989). *The Economic Section 1939–1961: A Study in Economic Advising*, (London, Routledge).

CARDWELL, D. S. L. (1972), *The Organization of Science in England*, (London, Heinemann).

CARTWRIGHT, T. J. (1975), *Royal Commissions and Departmental Committees in Britain*, (London, Hodder and Stoughton).

CASTLE, B. (1984), *The Castle Diaries 1964–70*, (London, Weidenfeld and Nicolson).

CHAPMAN, B. (1959), *The Profession of Government. The Public Service in Europe*, (London, Allen and Unwin).

CHAPMAN, B. (1963), *British Government Observed. Some European Reflections*, (London, Allen and Unwin).

CHAPMAN, R. A. (1970), *The Higher Civil Service in Britain*, (London, Constable).

CHAPMAN, R. A. (1988), *Ethics in the British Civil Service*, (London, Routledge).

CHESTER, D. N. (1962), 'The Treasury, 1962', *Public Administration* 40, pp.419–26.
CHESTER, D. N. (1963), 'The Plowden Report: Nature and Significance', *Public Administration* 41, pp.3–15.
CHESTER, D. N. (1968), 'The Report of the Fulton Committee on the Civil Service', *Public Administration: The Journal of the Australian Regional Groups of the Royal Institute of Public Administration* XXVII; pp.295–310.
CIVIL SERVICE COLLEGE (1974–5), *Fifth Annual Report by the Principal to the Civil Service College Advisory Council*, (London, HMSO).
CIVIL SERVICE COLLEGE (1975–6), *Sixth Annual Report by the Principal to the Civil Service College Advisory Council*, (London, HMSO).
CIVIL SERVICE COLLEGE (1976–6), *Seventh Annual Report by the Principal to the Civil Service College Advisory Council*. (London, HMSO).
CIVIL SERVICE COMMISSIONERS (1913), *Fifty Seventh Annual Report of* HM Civil Service Commissioners, Cd. 6913 (London, HMSO).
CIVIL SERVICE COMMISSIONERS (1914), *Fifty Eighth Annual Report of* HM Civil Service Commissioners, Cd. 7497 (London, HMSO).
CIVIL SERVICE COMMISSIONERS (1915), *Fifty Ninth Annual Report of* HM Civil Service Commissioners, Cd. 7983 (London, HMSO).
CIVIL SERVICE DEPARTMENT (1969), *The Civil Services of North America*, (London, CSD).
CIVIL SERVICE DEPARTMENT (1970), *First Report of the Civil Service Department 1969*, (London, HMSO).
CIVIL SERVICE DEPARTMENT (1971), *Second Report of the Civil Service Department 1970–71*, (London, HMSO).
CIVIL SERVICE DEPARTMENT (1974), *Third Report of the Civil Service Department 1971–3*, (London, HMSO)
CIVIL SERVICE NATIONAL WHITLEY COUNCIL (1969a), *Developments on Fulton*, (London, Civil Service National Whitley Council).
CIVIL SERVICE NATIONAL WHITLEY COUNCIL (1969b), *The Timing of Interim Changes in the Grading Structure of the Civil Service*, (London, Civil Service National Whitley Council).
CIVIL SERVICE NATIONAL WHITLEY COUNCIL (1970), *Fulton: A Framework for the Future*, (London, Civil Service National Whitley Council).
CIVIL SERVICE NATIONAL WHITLEY COUNCIL (1971), *The Reshaping of the Civil Service: Developments during 1970*, (London, Civil Service National Whitley Council).
CIVIL SERVICE NATIONAL WHITLEY COUNCIL (1972), *The Shape of the Post-Fulton Civil Service*, (London, Civil Service National Whitley Council).
CIVIL SERVICE NATIONAL WHITLEY COUNCIL, Staff Side (1968–73), *Fulton Report Co-ordinating Committee Minutes*.
CLARKE, R. W. B. (1963), 'The Plowden Report: The Formulation of Economic Policy', *Public Administration* 41, pp.17–24.
CLARKE, SIR R. W. B. (1978), *Public Expenditure, Management and Control. The Development of the Public Expenditure Survey Committee*, (London, Macmillan).
CLOKIE, H. M. and ROBINSON, J. W. (1937), *Royal Commissions of Inquiry. The Significance of Investigations in British Politics*, (London, OUP)
COLE, G. D. H. (1942), 'Reconstruction in the Civil and Municipal Services', *Public Administration* 20, pp.1–10.
COLE, G. D. H. (1950), *Essays in Social Theory*, (London, Macmillan).
CONSERVATIVE PARTY ARCHIVE. Bodleian Library, Oxford.
CROOKSHANK REPORT (1943), *Report of the Inquiry into the Post-War Reorganization of the Home Civil Service*, (T162/931/E45491/06/01 and 02; T162/870/E45491/09/01 and 02; Public Record Office).

CROSSMAN, R. H. S. (1974), *The Diaries of a Cabinet Minister*, Vol. 1, *Minister of Housing 1964–1966*, (London, Hamilton, and Cape).

CROSSMAN, R. H. S. (1976), *The Diaries of a Cabinet Minister*, Vol. 2, *Lord President of the Council and Leader of the House of Commons*, (London, Hamilton, and Cape).

CROSSMAN, R. H. S. (1977), *The Diaries of a Cabinet Minister*, Vol. 3, *Secretary of State for the Social Services*, (London, Hamilton, and Cape).

DAVIES REPORT (1969), *Report of the Committee of Inquiry. The Method II System of Selection for the Administrative Class of the Home Civil Service*, Cmnd. 4156 (London, HMSO).

DELAFONS, J. (1982), 'Working in Whitehall: Changes in Public Administration 1952–1982', *Public Administration* 60, pp.253–72.

DIMOCK, M. E. and DIMOCK, G. O. (1953), *Public Administration*, (New York, Rinehart).

DIMOCK, M. E., DIMOCK, G. O. and KOENIG, L. W. (1958), *Public Administration* rev. edn. (New York, Rinehart).

DIMOCK, M. E. and DIMOCK, G. O. (1964). *Public Administration* 3rd edn. (New York, Rinehart and Winston).

DONOUGHMORE-SCOTT REPORT (1932), *Report of the Committee on Ministers' Powers*, Cmd. 4060, (London, HMSO).

DODD, C. H. (1967). 'Recruitment to the Administrative Class', *Public Administration* 45, pp.55–80.

DONOVAN REPORT (1968), *Report of the Royal Commission on Trade Unions and Employers' Associations*, Cmnd. 3623 (London, HMSO).

DRUCKER, P. F. (1955), *The Practice of Management*, (London, Heinemann).

DUNNETT, SIR L. J. (1976), 'The Civil Service: Seven Years After Fulton', *Public Administration* 54, pp.371–78.

EFFICIENCY UNIT (1988), *Improving Management in Government: The Next Steps. Report to the Prime Minister*, (London, HMSO).

FABIAN GROUP (1964), *The Administrators. The Reform of the Civil Service*, (London, Fabian Society).

FABIAN SOCIETY (1947), *The Reform of the Higher Civil Service*, (London, Fabian Society).

FABIAN SOCIETY PAPERS, Nuffield College, Oxford.

FALKENDER, LADY, Interview 2 February 1989.

FOREIGN OFFICE (1943), *Proposals for the Reform of the Foreign Service*, Cmnd. 6420 (London, HMSO)

FORREST, A .(1966), *The Manager's Guide to Setting Targets*, (London, The Industrial Society).

FRY, G. K. (1969a), *Statesmen in Disguise. The Changing Role of the Administrative Class of the British Home Civil Service 1853–1966*, (London, Macmillan).

FRY, G. K. 1969b), 'Some Weaknesses in the Fulton Report on the British Home Civil Service', *Political Studies* XVII, pp. 484–94.

FRY, G. K. (1972), 'Policy Planning Units in British Central Government Departments', *Public Administration* 52, pp. 139–55.

FRY, G. K. (1974), 'Civil Service Salaries in the Post-Priestley Era 1956–1972', *Public Administration* 52, pp. 319–33.

FRY, G. K. (1981), *The Administrative 'Revolution' in Whitehall. A Study of the Politics of Administrative Change in British Central Government since the 1950s*, (London, Croom Helm).

FRY, G. K. (1985), *The Changing Civil Service*, (London, Allen and Unwin).

FRY, G. K. (1986), 'The British Career Civil Service under Challenge', *Political Studies* 34, pp. 533–55.

FRY, G. K. (1988a), 'Fulton Twenty Years On. Dissenting Viewpoint and Bibliography', *Contemporary Record. The Journal of the Institute of Contemporary History* 2, no. 2, 1988, pp. 50–5.

FRY, G. K. (1988b), 'The Thatcher Government, the Financial Management Initiative, and the "New Civil Service"', *Public Administration* 66, pp. 1–20.

FRY, G. K. (1988c), 'Improving Management in Government, Outlining "The Next Steps"', *Public Administration* 66, pp. 429–39.

FULTON, LADY, Interview, 24 June 1989.

FULTON, LORD (1968), 'Lord Fulton on the Findings of the Fulton Report', *The Listener*, 18 July 1968.

GARRETT, J. L. (1972), *The Management of Government*, (Harmondsworth, Penguin Books).

GARRETT, J. L. (1980), *Managing the Civil Service*, (London, Heinemann).

GARRETT, J. L. and WALKER, S. D. (1969), *Management by Objectives in the Civil Service*, Civil Service Department, CAS Occasional Paper, (London: HMSO).

GARRETT, J. L. and SHELDON, R. E. (1973), *Administrative Reform: The Next Step*, Fabian Tract 426, (London, Fabian Society).

GEDDES REPORTS (1922), *First Interim Report on National Expenditure*, Cmd. 1581; *Second Interim Report of the Committee on National Expenditure*, Cmd. 1582; *Third Report of the Committee on National Expenditure*, Cmnd. 1589 (London, HMSO).

GERTH, H. H. and MILLS, C. W., eds (1948), *From Max Weber: Essays in Sociology*, (London, Routledge and Kegan Paul).

GLADDEN, E. N. (1956), *Civil Service or Bureaucracy?* (London, Staples Press).

GLADDEN, E. N. (1958), *The Essentials of Public Administration*, 2nd edn (London, Staples Press).

GLASSCO REPORT (1962, 1963), *Reports of the Royal Commission on Government Organization, 1. Management of the Public Service, 2. Supporting Services for Government, 3. Supporting Services for Government continued, 4. Special Areas of Administration, 5. The Organization of the Government of Canada*, (Ottawa, The Queen's Printer).

GREAVES, H. R. G. (1947). *The Civil Service in the Changing State*. London: Harrap.

GREBENIK, E., Interview, 10 November 1988.

GREENWOOD, M. et al. (1937), 'On the Value of Royal Commissions in Sociological Research', *Journal of the Royal Statistical Society* C, pp. 396–414.

GRIGG, P. J. (1948), *Prejudice and Judgement*, (London, Cape).

GRIMOND, J. et al. (1964), *Whitehall and Beyond*, (London, BBC Publications).

HALDANE REPORT (1918), *Report of the Machinery of Government Committee*, Cd. 9230 (London, HMSO).

HAMILTON REPORT (1909), *Report of the Royal Commission on the Poor Laws and the Relief of Distress*, Cd. 4499 (London, HMSO).

HAMPSHIRE, A. C. (1975), *The Royal Navy since 1945. Its Transition to the Nuclear Age*, (London, Kimber).

HANSER, C. J. (1965), *Guide to Decision: The Royal Commission*, (Totowa NJ, Bedminster Press).

HAWTIN-MOORE REPORT (1980), *The Integration of HM Treasury and the Civil Service Department. Report of a Study Team*, (London, Treasury and Civil Service Department).

HEADLAM, SIR C. et al. (1946), *Some Proposals for Constitutional Reform*, (London, Eyre and Spottiswoode).

HEALEY, D. W. (1989), *The Time of My Life*, (London, Michael Joseph).

HEATH, E. R. G. (1990), 'Sir Edward Charles Gurney Boyle', in Blake, Lord, and Nicolls, C. S. eds, *The Dictionary of National Biography 1981–1985*, (Oxford, OUP).

HEATON-WILLIAMS REPORT (1974), *Civil Service Training. Report by R. N. Heaton and Sir Leslie Williams*, (London, Civil Service Department).

HELSBY, LORD (1968), 'The Fulton Report', *The Listener*, 18 July 1968.

HENNESSY, P. (1989), *Whitehall*, (London, Secker and Warburg).

HENNESSY, P. et al. (1988), 'Fulton Twenty Years On', *Contemporary Record 2*, No. 2, pp. 44–55.

HERBERT, A. P. (1961), 'Anything But Action? A Study of the Uses and Abuses of Committees of Inquiry', in Harris, R., ed., *Radical Reaction*, (London, Hutchinson).

HOBSBAWM, E. (1968), 'The Fulton Report: A Further View', *The Listener*, 18 July 1968.

HOME OFFICE (1947), *Higher Training for the Police Service in England and Wales*, (London, HMSO).

HOME OFFICE (1961), *Police Training in England and Wales*, Cmnd. 1450 (London, HMSO).

HOME OFFICE (1969), *Committee for the Review of Higher Training Courses at the Police College, Bramshill. Report*, (London, Home Office).

HOOVER REPORT (1949), *Report of the Commission on the Organization of the Executive Branch of the Government*, (New York, McGraw-Hill).

HOOVER REPORT (1955), *Final Report of the Commission on the Organization of the Executive Branch of the Government*, (Washington DC, US Government Printing Office).

HOUSE OF COMMONS, SELECT COMMITTEE ON EXPENDITURE 1941–1942, *Sixteenth Report from the Select Committee on National Expenditure. Session 1941–1942. Organizational and Control of the Civil Service*, HC 120 (1941–42), (London, HMSO).

HOUSE OF COMMONS, ESTIMATES COMMITTEE 1957–1958, *Sixth Report from the Select Committee on Estimates. Session 1957–58. Treasury Control of Expenditure*, HC 254-I (1957–58), (London, HMSO).

HOUSE OF COMMONS, ESTIMATES COMMITTEE 1963–64, *Fifth Report from the Select Committee on Estimates. Session 1963–64. Treasury Control of Expenditure*, HC 228 (1963–64), (London, HMSO).

HOUSE OF COMMONS, ESTIMATES COMMITTEE 1964–65, *Sixth Report from the Select Committee on Estimates. Session 1964–65. Treasury Control of Expenditure*, HC 308 (1964–65), London, HMSO).

HOUSE OF COMMONS, ESTIMATES COMMITTEE 1965–1966, *Fifth Special Report from the Estimates Committee. Session 1965–66. Recruitment to the Civil Service Departmental Observations on the Sixth Report from the Estimates Committee 1964–65*, HC 74 (1965–66), (London, HMSO).

HOUSE OF COMMONS, SELECT COMMITTEE ON NATIONALIZED INDUSTRIES 1966–67, *First Report from the Select Committee on Nationalized Industries. The Post Office*, Vol. I *Report and Proceedings of the Committee*, HC 340 (1966–67); Vol. II *Minutes of Evidence, Appendices, and Index*, HC 340-I (1966–67), (London, HMSO).

HOUSE OF COMMONS, EXPENDITURE COMMITTEE 1976–1977 *Eleventh Report from the Expenditure Committee. Session 1976–77. The Civil Service*, Vol. I *Report*, HC 535-I (1976–77); Vol. II *Minutes of Evidence*, HC 535-II (1976–77), Vol. III *Appendices*, HC 535-III (1976–77), (London, HMSO).

HOUSE OF COMMONS, TREASURY AND CIVIL SERVICE COMMITTEE 1980–81, *First Report from the Treasury and Civil Service Committee. Session 1980–81. The Future of the Civil Service Department*, HC 54 (1980–81), (London, HMSO).

HOUSE OF COMMONS, TREASURY AND CIVIL SERVICE COMMITTEE 1987–88, *Eighth Report from the Treasury and Civil Service Committee. Session*

1978–88. *Civil Service Management Reform: The Next Steps*, Vol. I *Report together with the Proceedings of the Committee*, HC 494-I (1987–88); Vol. II *Annexes, Minutes of Evidence and Appendices*, HC 494-ii (1987–88), (London, HMSO).

HOWELL, D., Interview, 22 February 1989.

HUGHES, C. L. (1965), *Goal Setting. Key to Individual and Organizational Effectiveness*, (New York, American Management Association).

HUMBLE, J. W. (1965), *Improving Management Performance*, (London, British Institute of Management).

HUNT, N. C. (1961), *Two Early Political Associations. The Quakers and the Dissenting Deputies in the Age of Sir Robert Walpole*, (Oxford, Clarendon Press).

HUNT, N. C. (1968), 'Norman Hunt of the Fulton Committee replies to last week's criticism of its Report on the Civil Service', *The Listener*, 25 July 1968.

JELLICOE, LORD, Interview, 10 May 1989.

JOHNSON, N. (1968), 'Reforming the Bureaucracy', *Public Administration* 46, pp. 367–74.

KEELING, D. (1971), 'The Development of Central Training in the Civil Service 1963–1970', *Public Administration* 49, pp. 51–71.

KELLNER, P. and CROWTHER-HUNT, LORD (1980), *The Civil Servants. An Inquiry into Britain's Ruling Class*, (London, Macdonald).

KELSALL, R. K. (1955), *Higher Civil Servants in Britain*, (London, Routledge and Kegan Paul).

KIPPING, SIR N. V. (1972), *Summing Up*, (London, Hutchinson).

KNIGHT, M. W. B. (1966), *Management by Objectives*, (London, Smith's Industries).

KOGAN, M. (1968), 'The Fulton Report. A New Civil Service?' *New Society*, 27 June 1968.

LABOUR PARTY NATIONAL EXECUTIVE, *Finance and Economic Policy Sub-Committee. Minutes 1958–1966*, National Museum of Labour History, Manchester.

LASKI, H. J. (1931), 'The Tomlin Report on the Civil Service', *Political Quarterly* 2, 506–19.

LASKI, H. J. (1938), *Parliamentary Government in England*, (London, Allen and Unwin).

LASKI, H. J. (1942), 'Introduction', in Mallalieu, J. P. W., *Passed to You Please*, (London, Gollancz).

LASKI, H. J. (1951), *Reflections on the Constitution*, (Manchester, Manchester University Press).

LEE, J. M. (1977), *Reviewing the Machinery of Government 1942–1952. An Essay on the Anderson Committee and its Successors*, (London, Birkbeck College).

MCGREGOR, D. (1960), *The Human Side of the Enterprise*, (New York, McGraw-Hill).

MACDONALD, J. H. and FRY, G. K. (1980), 'Policy Planning Units – Ten Years On', *Public Administration* 58, pp.421–37.

MACDONNELL REPORT (1914), *Fourth Report of the Royal Commission on the Civil Service*, Cd. 7338 (London, HMSO).

MALLABY REPORT (1967), *Committee on the Staffing of Local Government. Report of the Committee*, (London, HMSO).

MARWICK, A. (1964), 'Middle Opinion in the Thirties: Planning, Progress and Political Argument', *English Historical Review* LXXIX, pp.285–98.

MAY REPORT (1931), *Report of the Committee on National Expenditure*, Cmd. 3920 (London, HMSO).

MENZLER, F. A. A. (1937), 'The Expert in the Civil Service', in Robson, W. A., ed., *The British Civil Servant*, (London, Allen and Unwin).

MILLER, E. C. (1966), *Objectives and Standards. An Approach to Planning and Control*, (New York, American Management Association).

MOE, R. C. (1982), *The Hoover Commissions Revisited*, (Boulder, Colorado, Westview Press).

MONCK, B. (1952), *How the Civil Service Works*, (London, Phoenix House).

MORTON, W. W. (1963), 'The Plowden Report: the Management Functions of the Treasury', *Public Administration* 41, pp.25–35.

NETTL, J. P. (1965), 'Consensus or Elite Domination: The Case of Business', *Political Studies* XXIII, pp.22–44.

NICHOLSON, E. M. (1967), *The System. The Misgovernment of Modern Britain*, (London, Hodder and Stoughton).

NORTHCOTE-TREVELYAN REPORT (1854), *Report on the Organization of the Permanent Civil Service*, C.1713 (London, HMSO).

NOTTAGE, R. and STACK, F. (1972), 'The Royal Institute of Public Administration 1922–1939', *Public Administration* 50, pp.281–304.

ODIORNE, G. S. (1965), *Management by Objectives. A System of Managerial Leadership*, (New York, Pitman Publishing).

O'HALPIN, E. (1989), *Head of the Civil Service. A Study of Sir Warren Fisher*, (London, Routledge).

OPIE, R. (1968), 'Implement at Once!' *New Statesman*, 28 June 1968.

O'TOOLE, B. J. (1989), *Private Gain and Public Service. The Association of First Division Civil Servants*, (London, Routledge).

PARKER, K. A. L. (1980), 'Hendon and After', *Police Journal* 53, pp.219–32.

PARKER, K. A. L. (1990), 'The Police Service after the War', *Public Administration* 68, pp.453–75.

PICKERING, J. F. (1967), 'Recruitment to the Administrative Class 1960–64, Part II', *Public Administration* 45, pp. 169–99.

PIGORS, P., MYERS, C. A. and MALM, F. T., eds. (1964), *Management of Human Resources. Readings in Personnel Administration*, (New York, McGraw-Hill).

PLOWDEN REPORT (1961), *Control of Public Expenditure*, Cmnd. 1432 (London, HMSO).

POLENBERG, R. (1966), *Reorganizing Roosevelt's Government. The Controversy over Executive Reorganization 1936–1939*, (Cambridge, Mass., Harvard University Press).

POLICE COUNCIL (1962), *Report of the Committee on Higher Police Training*, (London, HMSO).

POLICE COUNCIL (1963a), *Second Report of the Committee appointed to Examine and Report upon Proposals for Certain Changes in the Provision for Higher Training at the Police College*, (London, HMSO).

POLICE COUNCIL (1963b), *Supplementary Report of the Committee on Higher Police Training on the Special Course at the Police College*, (London, HMSO).

POLICE COUNCIL (1963c), *Second Supplementary Report of the Committee on Higher Police Training on the Special Course*, (London, Police Council).

POLICE COUNCIL (1963d), *Second Report of the Committee on Higher Police Training* (Senior Staff Course), (London, HMSO).

POLICE COUNCIL (1963e), *Report of the Committee on Higher Police Training on the Senior Staff Course*, (London, HMSO).

POLITICAL AND ECONOMIC PLANNING (1943), 'A Civil General Staff', *Planning* 214, pp.1–20.

PRIESTLEY REPORT (1955), *Report of the Royal Commission on the Civil Service*, Cmd. 9613 (London, HMSO).

PRIESTLEY, C., Interview, 8 December 1988.

REDCLIFFE-MAUD REPORT (1969), *Local Government Reform. Short Version of the Report of the Royal Commission on Local Government in England*, Cmnd. 4039; *Royal Commission on Local Government in England 1966–1969*, Vol. I *Report*,

Cmnd. 4040; Vol. II *Memorandum of Dissent by Mr D. Senior*, Cmnd. 4040-I; Vol. III *Research Appendices*, Cmnd. 4040-II, (London, HMSO).

RHODES, G. (1975), *Committees of Inquiry*, (London, Allen and Unwin).

RIDLEY, F. F., ed. (1968), *Specialists and Generalists. A Comparative Study of the Professional Civil Servant at Home and Abroad*, (London, Allen and Unwin).

ROBERTSON, J. H. (1968), 'HMG Enterprises Ltd. – After Fulton', *The Spectator*, 9 August 1968.

ROBSON, W. A. (1937), 'The Public Service', in Robson, W. A. (ed.) *The British Civil Servant*, (London, Allen and Unwin).

ROBSON, W. A. (1968), 'The Fulton Report on the Civil Service', *Political Quarterly* 39, pp.397–414.

ROBSON BROWN, SIR W. et al. (1963) *Change or Decay*, (London, Conservative Political Centre).

ROSKILL, S. (1968), *Naval Policy Between the Wars*, I. *The Period of Anglo-American Antagonism 1919–1929*, (London, Collins).

ROWAT, D. C. (1963), 'Canada's Royal Commission on Government Organization', *Public Administration* 41, pp.193–205.

SALMON REPORT (1966), *Report of the Royal Commission on Tribunals of Inquiry*, Cmnd. 3121 (London, HMSO).

SCHAFFER, R. H. (1964), *Managing by Total Objectives*, (New York, American Management Association).

SCHLEH, E. C. (1961), *Management by Results. The Dynamics of Profitable Management*, (New York, McGraw-Hill).

SEARLE, G. R. (1971), *The Quest for National Efficiency*, (Oxford, Blackwell).

SEEBOHM REPORT (1968), *Report of the Committee on Local Authority and Allied Personal Social Services*, Cmnd. 3703 (London, HMSO).

SHACKLETON, LORD, Interview, 29 November 1988.

SHARP, DAME E. (1967), 'The British Civil Service: Changes Under Discussion', *Canadian Public Administration* 10, pp.282–97.

SHAW, G. B., ed. (1889), *Fabian Essays in Socialism*, (London, Fabian Society).

SHONFIELD, A. (1959), *British Economic Policy since the War*, 2nd edn. (Harmondsworth, Penguin Books).

SHORE, P. (1966), *Entitled to Know*, (London, MacGibbon and Kee).

SIMEY, T. S. (1937), *Principles of Social Administration*, (London, OUP).

SISSON, C. H. (1959), *The Spirit of British Administration*, (London, Faber and Faber).

SLOMAN, MRS M. B., Interview, 10 June 1989.

STEWART, N. (1967), *Strategies of Managing for Results*, (London, Pitman Publishing).

THOMAS, H. S., ed. (1968), *Crisis in the Civil Service*, (London, Constable).

TOMLIN REPORT (1931), *Report of the Royal Commission on the Civil Service*, Cmd. 3909 (London, HMSO).

TRADES UNION CONGRESS (1964), *Report of the 96th Annual Trades Union Congress*, (London, TUC).

VALENTINE, R. F. (1966), *Performance Objectives for Managers*, (New York, American Management Association).

WALDO, D. (1948), *The Administrative State*, (New York, Ronald).

WALKER, N. (1961), *Morale in the Civil Service. A Study of the Desk Worker*, (Edinburgh, EUP).

WALL, J. E. (1963), 'The Plowden Report: Management Services in Industry', *Public Administration* 41, pp.35–50.

WEBB, S. and WEBB, B. (1920), *A Constitution for the Socialist Commonwealth of Great Britain*, (London, Longmans, Green).

WEBB, S. and WEBB, B. (1932), *Methods of Social Study*, (London, Longmans, Green).
WHEARE REPORT (1950), *Report of the Departmental Committee on Children and the Cinema*, Cmd. 7945 (London, HMSO).
WHEARE, K. C. (1955), *Government by Committee: An Essay on the British Constitution*, (Oxford, Clarendon Press).
WHEATLEY REPORT (1969), *Royal Commission on Local Government in Scotland*, Cmnd. 4150 (London, HMSO).
WHEELER-BENNETT, Sir J. W. (1962), *John Anderson, Lord Waverley*, (London, Macmillan).
WHITEHORN, J. (1986), 'Sir Norman Victor Kipping', in Blake, Lord, and Nicholls, C. S., eds, *The Dictionary of National Biography 1971–1980*, (Oxford, OUP).
WILLINK REPORT (1962), *Royal Commission on the Police. Final Report*, Cmnd. 1728 (London, HMSO).
WILSON, J. H. (1967), 'Where Power Lies', *The Listener*, 9 February 1967.

Index